GENERAL VIEW OF PETRA FROM THE NORTHEAST

Gall sc.

Evidence of the Truth of the Christian Religion
Derived from the Literal Fulfillment of Prophecy
by Rev. Alexander Keith, D.D.
Originally published by Edinburgh: Waugh and Innes, 12th edition, 1834.

Facsimile reproduction copyright © 2011 by Tolle Lege Press

Distributed by:

TOLLE LEGE PRESS
P.O. Box 5069
White Hall, WV 26555

www.TolleLegePress.com
www.1599GenevaBible.com
800-651-0211

Cover design by Luis D. Lovelace

ISBN: 978-0-9831457-3-8

Printed in the United States of America.

EVIDENCE
OF THE
TRUTH
OF THE
CHRISTIAN
RELIGION

ALEXANDER KEITH, D.D.

TOLLE
LEGE
P R E S S

WHITE HALL
WEST VIRGINIA

Publisher's Foreword

Bible prophecy is a favorite topic of many Christians. It seems that everyone wants to know what tomorrow holds. Josh McDowell has capitalized on this public fascination by selling millions of copies of his book, *Evidence That Demands a Verdict*. This book—Alexander Keith's *Evidence of the Truth of the Christian Religion*—is akin to a 19ᵗʰ century version of McDowell's book. Although nowhere near as comprehensive as McDowell's two-volume tome, Keith's book is far more detailed and focused in its approach. McDowell's book is something along the lines of an encyclopedia while Keith's book is a theological treatise.

Predictive prophecy is a major component of the biblical Scriptures. In His infinite wisdom, God has declared that He knows "the end from the beginning" (Isaiah 46:10). In fact, through Moses, God reveals a simple test for those claiming to be prophets: "When a prophet speaks in the name of the Lord, if the thing does not come about or come true, that is the thing which the Lord has not spoken. The prophet has spoken it presumptuously; you shall not be afraid of him" (Deuteronomy 18:22). As the sovereign Creator of all that is, God is not limited by space or time. The future holds less mystery for God than yesterday holds for us. We may not know the future, but we know One who does.

This is why knowing when particular biblical books were written is such a vital issue. Modern liberal scholars have long maintained that many books of the Old Testament were written much later than earlier believed, in effect reducing most of the Bible's pre-dictions to post-dictions. This intellectual sleight of hand not only makes the prophecies meaningless, it turns the

Bible into a work of human imagination rather than a work of divine revelation. Biblical prophecy, however, is not to be taken so lightly.

Alexander Keith was well aware of the importance of predictive prophecy. In a handed-down story surrounding the inspiration for his writing on the subject, Keith witnessed firsthand the power of biblical predictions. It is said that a young agnostic was giving Keith no quarter in his relentless denial of the truth of the Scriptures. Having exhausted many arguments on the young man, Keith finally asked him what he made of all the predicted and fulfilled prophecies of the Old Testament. When the young man said he didn't know, Keith proceeded to give him several examples. Soon after this, the young man converted to Christianity and Keith realized that a book on the topic was sorely needed. The book you now hold in your hands is the fruit of that realization.

A similar story after the publication of the book is told by Edward Giddings in *American Christian Rulers*. Giddings relates how Keith's book was instrumental in persuading Supreme Court chief justice John Marshall of the messianic claims of Jesus Christ in the days before his death on July 6, 1835. Giddings writes:

> [Marshall] believed in the truth of the Christian revelation, but not in the divinity of Christ; therefore he could not commune in the Episcopal Church. But, during the last months of his life, he read Keith on Prophecy, where our Saviour's divinity is incidentally treated, and was convinced by his work, and the fuller investigation to which it led, of the supreme divinity of the Saviour. [1]

Far from taking the liberal approach to prophecy, Keith believed the Bible to be a divinely ordained book of predictions

---

1. Rev. Edward Giddings, *American Christian Rulers, or Religion and Men of Government* (New York: Bromfield and Company, 1889), 332.

and fulfillments. When he opened the Scriptures, he did not see a vast conspiracy of after-the-fact reporting, but the unmistakable fingerprints of the sovereign Author of human history. Keith well understood that Saint Augustine's famous principle of the "new being concealed in the old and the old being revealed in the new" applies to much more than just the two testaments of the Bible. He knew that this principle held true when any prophetic word found its fulfillment, as he writes in his Introduction:

> Prophecy must thus, in many instances, have that darkness which is impenetrable at first, as well as that light which shall be able to dispel every doubt at last; and, as it cannot be an evidence of Christianity until the event demonstrate its own truth, it may remain obscure till history become its interpreter, and not be perfectly obvious till the fulfillment of the whole series with which it is connected. (**p. 7**)

In other words, history is an ally to be welcomed in true Christianity, not an enemy to be fought. History is the evidence of God's declarations and of His covenanting with men. Like the mustard seed spoken of by Jesus (Matthew 13:31–32) and the stone spoken of by Daniel (Dan. 2:31–35), the words of Scripture begin small yet find continual growth and nourishment in the ongoing events of history. Keith knew that far from merely proving the biblical claims to be true, history itself is a necessary aspect of God's divine revelation. Through the fulfillment, we better understand the prophecy; and through the prophecy, we better understand the fulfillment. God's Word and God's world are two parts of a comprehensive whole.

This is what makes *Evidence of the Truth of the Christian Religion* such an important addition to modern books being written about the evidence for the Christian faith. Although it is more than 150 years old, this masterful work is still as relevant as ever because the author doesn't hold a narrow view of biblical prophecy. Most evidence books written during the last 100 years take a "scavenger-hunt" approach that seems to suggest that once the fulfillment of a particular prophecy had been accomplished, it has served all of its primary usefulness. Keith understood, however, that a prophetic statement's fulfillment not only gives greater understanding to the prophecy itself, but to all of the surrounding context as well. Bible prophecy is much more than simply a "this means that" method of connecting the dots. It is, in reality, the strong foundation of a correct interpretation of the biblical text. Indeed, since it has been estimated that the Bible contains somewhere between one-quarter to two-thirds prophetic material, properly understanding prophecy leads to a proper understanding of the complete message of the Bible.

Modern readers may find Keith's book challenging and even tedious in some places, but they certainly will not find it irrelevant. It reveals information that will be new to most, but that will doubtlessly breathe new life into the often cryptic passages of Old Testament prophecy. Much of modern preaching and teaching gives little attention to the Old Testament and therefore most modern Christians are ignorant of the treasures it contains. This reprint of Alexander Keith's classic book will go a long way in reacquainting readers with the eventful and important 2000 years that preceded the birth of Jesus Christ. May a new generation be gripped and inspired by what it finds there.

Eric Rauch
Saint Patrick's Day
2011

EVIDENCE

OF THE

TRUTH OF THE CHRISTIAN RELIGION,

DERIVED FROM THE LITERAL FULFILMENT OF

PROPHECY;

PARTICULARLY AS ILLUSTRATED BY THE HISTORY
OF THE JEWS, AND BY THE DISCOVERIES
OF RECENT TRAVELLERS.

BY

ALEXANDER KEITH, D.D.

MINISTER OF ST. CYRUS, KINCARDINESHIRE,
AUTHOR OF THE SIGNS OF THE TIMES.

TWELFTH EDITION.

Opinionum commenta dies delet, Naturæ judicia confirmat.—*Cic. De. Nat. Deo.*

EDINBURGH: WAUGH AND INNES;

M. OGLE, GLASGOW; J. NICHOL, MONTROSE; R. M. TIMS, AND
W. CURRY, JUN. AND CO. DUBLIN; J. HATCHARD AND SON,
AND WHITTAKER AND CO. LONDON.

MDCCCXXXIV.

TO THE

RIGHT HONOURABLE WILLIAM ADAM,

LORD CHIEF COMMISSIONER, &c.

AS A SMALL MARK

OF THE

MOST SINCERE ESTEEM AND REGARD,

THE FOLLOWING

TREATISE

IS RESPECTFULLY INSCRIBED

BY HIS LORDSHIP'S

MUCH OBLIGED AND VERY FAITHFUL SERVANT,

ALEXANDER KEITH.

CONTENTS.

CHAPTER I.

INTRODUCTION.

CHAPTER II.

PROPHECIES CONCERNING CHRIST AND THE CHRISTIAN RELIGION.

CHAPTER III.

CHAPTER IV.

CHAPTER V.

CONTENTS.

CHAPTER VI.

CHAPTER VII.

CHAPTER VIII.

CHAPTER IX.

EVIDENCE

OF

PROPHECY.

―――――

INTRODUCTION.

No subject can be of greater importance, either to the unbeliever or to the Christian, than an investigation of the evidence of Christianity. The former, if his mind be not fettered by the strongest prejudice, and if he be actuated in the least by a spirit of free and fair inquiry, cannot disavow his obligation to examine its claim to a divine origin. He cannot rest secure in his unbelief, to the satisfaction of his own mind, without manifest danger of the most fatal error, till he has impartially weighed all the reasons that may be urged on its behalf. The proof of a negative is acknowledged and felt to be difficult; and it can never, in any case, be attained till all direct and positive evidence to the contrary be completely destroyed. And this, at least, must be done before it can be proved that Christianity is not true. Without this careful and candid examination, all gratuitous assumptions

B

and fanciful speculations, all hypothetical reasonings or analogical inferences, that seem to militate against the truth of religion, may be totally erroneous ; and though they may tend to excite a transient doubt, they cannot justify a settled unbelief. Being exclusively regarded, or being united to a misapprehension of the real nature of the Christian religion, the understanding may embrace them as convincing ; but such conviction is neither rational nor consistent—it is only a misapplication of the name of freethinking. For, as Christianity appeals to reason and submits its credentials—as it courts and commands the most trying scrutiny—that scrutiny the unbeliever is bound, upon his own principles, to engage in. If he be fearless of wavering in his unbelief, he will not shrink from the inquiry ; or, if truth be his object, he will not resist the only means of its attainment—that he may either disprove what he could only doubt of before, or yield to the conviction of positive evidence and undoubted truth. This unhesitating challenge religion gives, and that man is neither a champion of infidelity, nor a lover of wisdom or of truth, who will disown or decline it.

To the believer such a subject is equally important and interesting. The apathy of nominal Christians, in the present day, is often contrasted with the zeal of those who first became obedient to the faith. The moral influence of the Christian religion is not what it has been, or what it ought to be. The difference in the character of its professors may be greatly attributed to a fainter impression and less confident assurance of its truth. Those early converts who witnessed the miracles of our Lord, and of his apostles, and heard their divine doctrine, and they who received the immediate tradition of those who both saw and heard them, and who could themselves compare the moral darkness from which they had emerged, with the marvellous light of the gospel, founded their faith upon evidence; possessed the firmest conviction of the truth; were distinguished by their virtues, as well as by their profession, according to the testimony even of their enemies;* cherished the consolations, and were inspired by the hopes of religion; and lived and died, actuated by the hope of immortality and the certainty of a future state. The contrast, unhappily, needs no elucidation. The lives of professing Christians, in general, cease to add a confirmation to the truth of Christianity, while they have often been the plea of infidels against it. Yet religion and human nature are still the same as they were when men were first called Christians, and when the believers in Jesus dishonoured not his name. But they sought more than a passive and unexamining belief. They knew in whom they believed; they felt the power of every truth which they professed. And the same cause, in active operation, would be productive of the same effects. The same strong and unwavering faith established on reason and conscious conviction, would be creative of the same peace and joy in believing, and of all their accompanying fruits. And as a mean of destroying the distinction, wherever it exists, between the profession and the reality of faith, it is ever the prescribed duty of all, who profess to believe in the gospel, to search and to try—" to prove all things, and hold fast to that which is good;" and to " be able to give an answer to every one that asketh them a reason of the hope that is in them."

To the sincere Christian, it must ever be an object of the highest interest to search into the reason of his hope. The farther that he searches, the firmer will

* Plinii Epis. 1. 10, ep. 97.

be his belief. Knowledge is the fruit of mental labour—the food and the feast of the mind. In the pursuit of knowledge, the greater the excellence of the subject of inquiry, the deeper ought to be the interest, the more ardent the investigation, and the dearer to the mind the acquisition of the truth. And that knowledge which immediately affects the soul, which tends to exalt the moral nature and enlarge the religious capacities of man, which pertains to eternity, which leads not merely to the contemplation of the works of the great Architect of the universe, but seeks also to discover an accredited revelation of his will and a way to his favour—and which rests not in its progress till it find assurance of faith or complete conviction, a witness without, as well as a witness within, is surely " like unto a treasure which a man found hid in a field, and sold all that he had and bought it." And it is delightful to have every doubt removed by the positive proof of the truth of Christianity—to feel that conviction of its certainty, which infidelity can never impart to her votaries,—and to receive that assurance of the faith, which is as superior in the hope which it communicates, as in the certainty on which it rests, to the cheerless and disquieting doubts of the unbelieving mind. Instead of being a mere prejudice of education, which may be easily shaken, belief thus founded on reason, becomes fixed and immoveable ; and all the scoffings of the scorner, and speculations of the infidel, lie as lightly on the mind, or pass as imperceptibly over it, and make as little impression there, as the spray upon a rock.

In premising a few remarks, introductory to a Sketch of the Prophecies, little can be said on the general and comprehensive evidence of Christianity. The selection of a part implies no disparagement to the whole.

Ample means for the confirmation of our faith are within our reach. Newton, Bacon, and Locke, whose names stand pre-eminent in human science, to which they opened a path not penetrated before, found proof sufficient for the complete satisfaction of *their* minds. The internal evidence could not be stronger than it is. There are manifold instances of undesigned coincidences in the Acts and Epistles of the Apostles, which give intrinsic proof that they are genuine and authentic. No better precepts, no stronger motives, than the gospel contains, have ever been inculcated. No system of religion has ever existed in the world at all to be compared to it; and none can be conceived more completely adapted to the necessities and nature of a sinful being like man, endowed with the faculty of reason and with capacities of religion. And the miracles were of such a nature as excluded the idea of artifice or delusion;—they were wrought openly in the presence of multitudes—they testified the benevolence of a Saviour, as well as the power of the Son of God. The disciples of Christ could not be deceived respecting them; for they were themselves endowed with the gift of tongues, and of prophesying, and with the power of working miracles; they devoted their lives to the propagation of the gospel, in opposition to every human interest, and amidst continual sufferings. The Christian religion was speedily propagated throughout the whole extent of the Roman empire, and even beyond its bounds. The written testimony remains of many who became converts to the truth, and martyrs to its cause; and the most zealous and active enemies of our faith acknowledged the truth of the miracles, and attributed them to the agency of evil spirits. Yet all this accumulation of evidence is disregarded, and every testimony is rejected unheard, because ages have since intervened,

and because it bears witness to works that are miraculous. Though these general objections against the
truth of Christianity have been ably answered and
exposed, yet they may fairly be adduced as confirmatory of the proof which results from the fulfilment of
prophecy, and as binding infidels to its investigation.
For it supplies that evidence which the enemies of
religion, or those who are weak in the faith would require, which applies to the present time, and which
stands not in need of any testimony,—which is always attainable by the researches of the inquisitive,
and often obvious to the notice of all,—and which
past, present, and coming events alike unite in verifying ;—it affords an increasing evidence, and receives
additional attestations in each succeeding age.

But, while some subterfuge has been sought for
evading the force of the internal evidence, and the
conviction which a belief in the miracles would infallibly produce, and while every collateral proof is neglected, the prophecies also are set aside without investigation, as of too vague and indefinite a nature
to be applied, with certainty, to the history either of
past ages or of the present. A very faint view of the
prophecies of the Old and New Testament will suffice to rectify this equally easy and erroneous conclusion. Although some of the prophecies, separately
considered, may appear ambiguous and obscure ; yet
a general view of them all—of the harmony which
prevails throughout the prophecies—and of their
adaptation to the facts they predict, must strike the
mind of the most careless inquirer with an apprehension that they are the dictates of Omniscience. But
many of the prophecies are as explicit and direct as
it is possible that they could have been ; and, as history confirms their truth, so they sometimes tend to
its illustration, of which our future inquiry will fur-

nish us with examples. And if the prophetical part
of Scripture, which refers to the rise and fall of kingdoms, had been more explicit than it is, it would
have appeared to encroach on the free agency of man
—it would have been a communication of the foreknowledge of events which men would have grossly
abused and perverted to other purposes rather than
to the establishment of the truth ; and, instead of
being a stronger evidence of Christianity, it would
have been considered as the cause of the accomplishment of the events predicted, by the unity and combination it would have excited among Christians ;
and thus have afforded to the unbeliever a more reasonable objection against the evidence of prophecy
than any that can be now alleged. It is in cases
wherein they could not be abused, or wherein the
agents instrumental in their fulfilment were utterly
ignorant of their existence, that the prophecies are as
descriptive as history itself. But whenever the knowledge of future events would have proved prejudicial
to the peace and happiness of the world, they are
couched in allegory, which their accomplishment
alone can expound,—and drawn with that degree of
light and shade that the faithfulness of the picture
may best be seen from the proper point of observation,
—the period of their completion. Prophecy must
thus, in many instances, have that darkness which is
impenetrable at first, as well as that light which shall
be able to dispel every doubt at last ; and, as it cannot be an evidence of Christianity until the event
demonstrate its own truth, it may remain obscure till
history become its interpreter, and not be perfectly
obvious till the fulfilment of the whole series with
which it is connected. But the general and often
sole objection against the evidence from the prophecies—that they are all vague and ambiguous—may
best be answered and set aside by a simple exhibition

of those numerous and distinct predictions which have been literally accomplished ; and therefore to this limited view of them the following pages shall chiefly be confined.

Little need be said on the nature of proof from prophecy. That it is the effect of divine interposition cannot be disputed. It is equivalent to any miracle, and is of itself evidently miraculous. The foreknowledge of the actions of free and intelligent agents is one of the most incomprehensible attributes of the Deity, and is exclusively a divine perfection. The past, the present, and the future, are alike open to his view, and to his alone ; and there can be no stronger proof of the interposition of the Most High, than that which prophecy affords. Of all the attributes of the God of the universe, his prescience has bewildered, and baffled the most, all the powers of human conception ; and an evidence of the exercise of this perfection in the revelation of what the infinite mind alone could make known, is the seal of God, which can never be counterfeited, affixed to the truth which it attests. Whether that evidence has been afforded, is a matter of investigation ; but if it has unquestionably been given, the effect of superhuman agency is apparent, and the truth of what it was given to prove, does not admit of a doubt. If the prophecies of the Scriptures can be proved to be genuine—if they be of such a nature as no foresight of man could possibly have predicted—if the events foretold in them were described hundreds or even thousands of years before those events became parts of the history of man—and if the history itself correspond with the prediction, then the evidence which the prophecies impart, is a sign and a wonder to every age : No clearer testimony or greater assurance of the truth can be given, and if men do not believe Moses and the prophets, neither would they

be persuaded though one arose from the dead. Even
if one were to rise from the dead, evidence of the fact
must precede conviction ; and, if the mind be satisfied of the truth of prophecy, the result, in either case,
is the same. The voice of Omnipotence alone could
call the dead from the tomb—the voice of Omniscience alone could tell all that lay hid in dark futurity, which to man is as impenetrable as the man-
sions of the dead—and both are alike the voice of
God.

Of the antiquity of the Scriptures there is the am-
plest proof. The books of the Old Testament were
not, like other writings, detached and unconnected
efforts of genius and research, or mere subjects of
amusement or instruction. They were essential to
the constitution of the Jewish state :—the possession
of them was a great cause of the peculiarities of that
people ;—and they contain their moral and their civil
law, and their history, as well as the prophecies, of which
they were the records and the guardians. They were
received by the Jews as of divine authority ; and as
such they were published and preserved. They were
proved to be ancient, eighteen hundred years ago.*
Instead of being secluded from observation, they were
translated into Greek above two hundred and fifty
years before the Christian era ; and they were read
in the synagogues every Sabbath-day. The most ancient part of them was received, as divinely inspired,
and was preserved in their own language, by the Samaritans, who were at enmity with the Jews. They
have ever been sacredly kept unaltered, in a more remarkable degree, and with more scrupulous care, than
any other compositions whatever.† And the anti-

* Josephus, c. Apion.
† There are not wanting proofs of the most scrupulous
care of the Hebrew text on the part of the Jews : they have

quity and authenticity of them rest so little on Christian testimony alone, that it is from the records of our enemies that they are confirmed, and from which it derived the evidence of our faith. Even the very language in which the Old Testament Scriptures were originally written, had ceased to be spoken before the coming of Christ. No stronger evidence of their antiquity could be alleged, than what is indisputably true ; and if it were to be questioned, every other truth of ancient history must first be set aside.

That the prediction was prior to the event, many facts in the present state of the world abundantly testify ; and many prophecies remain even yet to be fulfilled. But, independently of external testimony, the prophecies themselves bear intrinsic marks of their antiquity, and of their truth. Predictions concerning the same event are sometimes delivered by a succession of prophets. Sometimes the same prophecy concerning any city or nation gradually meets its fulfilment during a long protracted period, where the truth of the prediction must be unfolded by degrees. They are, in general, so interwoven with the history of the Jews—so casually introduced in their application to the surrounding nations—so frequently concealed in their purport, even from the honoured but unconscious organs of their communication, and preserving throughout so entire a consistency—so different in the modes of their narration, and each part preserving its own particular character—so delivered

---

counted the large and small sections, the verses, the words, and even the letters in some of the books. They have likewise reckoned which is the middle letter of the Pentateuch —which is the middle clause of each book—and how many times each letter of the alphabet occurs in all the Hebrew Scriptures. This, at least, shows that the Jews were religiously careful to preserve the literal sense of Scripture.— *Allen's Mod. Judaism. Simon Crit. Hist.* 6, 26.

without form or system—so shadowed under types and symbols—so complete when compared and combined—so apparently unconnected when disjoined, and revealed in such a variety of modes and expressions, that the very manner of their conveyance forbids the idea of artifice ; or if they were false, nothing could admit of more easy detection—if true, nothing could be more impossible to have been conceived by man. And they must either be a number of incoherent and detached pretensions to inspiration, that can bear no scrutiny, and that have no reference to futurity but what deceivers might have devised ; or else, as the only alternative, they give such a comprehensive, yet minute representation of future events—so various, yet so distinct—so distant, yet so true—that none but he who knoweth all things could have revealed them to man, and none but those who have hardened their hearts and closed their eyes, can forbear from feeling and from perceiving them to be credentials of the truth, clear as light from heaven. To justify their pretensions to their cotemporaries, the prophets referred, on particular occasions, to some approaching circumstance as a proof of their prophetic spirit, and as a symbol or representation of a more distant and important event. They could thus be distinguished in their own age from false prophets, if their predictions were then true, and they ventured to raise, from the succeeding ages of the world, that veil which no uninspired mortal could touch. They spoke of a deliverer of the human race—they described the desolation of cities and of nations, whose greatness was then unshaken, and whose splendour has ever since been unrivalled—and their predictions were of such a character, that time would infallibly refute or realize them.

Religion deserves a candid examination, and it demands nothing more. The fulfilment of prophecy

forms part of the evidence of Christianity. And are the
prophecies false, or are they true? Is their fallacy
exposed or their truth ratified by the event? And
whether are they thus proved to be the delusions of
impostors or the dictates of inspiration? To the solution of these questions a patient and impartial inquiry alone is requisite; reason alone is appealed to,
and no other faith is here necessary but that which
arises as the natural and spontaneous fruit of rational
conviction. The man who withholds this inquiry, and
who will not be impartially guided by its result, is
not only reckless of his fate, but devoid of that of
which he prides himself the most—even of all true
liberality of sentiment: He is the bigot of infidelity,
who will not believe the truth because it is the truth.
It is incontestable, that, in a variety of ways, a marvellous change has taken place in the religious and
political state of the world since the prophecies were
delivered. A system of religion, widely different
from any that then existed, has emanated from the
land of Judea, and has spread over the civilized
world. Many remarkable circumstances attended its
origin and its progress. The history of the life and
character of its Founder, as it was written at the
time, and acknowledged as authentic by those who
believed on him, is so completely without a parallel,
that it has often attracted the admiration, and excited
the astonishment of infidels;—and one of them even
asks, if it be possible that the Sacred Personage,
whose history the Scripture contains, should be himself a mere man; and acknowledges that the fiction
of such a character is more inconceivable than the
reality.* He possessed no temporal power,—he inculcated every virtue,—his life was spotless and per-

---

* Rousseau's *Emilius*, vol. ii. p. 215, quoted in *Brewster's
Testimonies*, p. 133.

fect as his doctrine,—he was put to death as a criminal. His religion was rapidly propagated,—his followers were persecuted, but their cause prevailed. The purity of his doctrine was maintained for a time, but it was afterwards corrupted. Yet Christianity has effected a great change. Since its establishment, the worship of heathen deities has ceased :—all sacrifices have been abolished, even where human victims were immolated before ; and slavery, which prevailed in every state, is now unknown in every Christian country throughout Europe ;—knowledge has been increased, and many nations have been civilized. The Christian religion has been extended over a great part of the world, and it is still enlarging its boundary ; and the Jews, though it originated among them, yet continue to reject it. In regard to the political changes or revolutions of states, since the prophecies concerning them were delivered,—Jerusalem was destroyed and laid waste by the Romans—The land of Palestine, and the surrounding countries, are now thinly inhabited, and, in comparison of their former fertility, have been almost converted into deserts—The Jews have been scattered among the nations, and remain to this day a dispersed and yet a distinct people—Egypt, one of the first and most powerful of nations, long ceased to be a kingdom —Nineveh is no more—Babylon is now a ruin— The Persian Empire succeeded to the Babylonian— The Grecian Empire succeeded to the Persian, and the Roman to the Grecian—The old Roman empire has been divided into several kingdoms—Rome itself became the seat of a government of a different nature from any other that ever existed in the world —The doctrine of the gospel was transformed into a system of spiritual tyranny and of temporal power —The authority of the Pope was held supreme in Europe for many ages—The Saracens obtained a

sudden and mighty power; overran great part of
Asia and of Europe ; and many parts of Christendom
suffered much from their incursions—The Arabs
maintain their warlike character, and retain possession
of their own land—The Africans are a humble race,
and are still treated as slaves—Colonies have been
spread from Europe to Asia, and are enlarging there
—The Turkish empire attained to great power ; it
continued to rise for the space of several centuries,
but it paused in its progress, has since decayed, and
now evidently verges to its fall. These form some
of the most prominent and remarkable facts of the
history of the world from the ages of the prophecies
to the present time ; and if, to each and all of them,
from the first to the last, an index is to be found in
the prophecies, we may warrantably conclude that
they could only have been revealed by the Ruler
among the nations, and that they afford more than
human testimony of the truth of Christianity.

In the following treatise an attempt is made to
give a general and concise sketch of such of the prophecies as have been distinctly foretold and clearly
fulfilled, and as may be deemed sufficient to illustrate
the truth of Christianity. And, if one unbeliever be led
the first step to a full and candid investigation of
the truth,—if one doubting mind be convinced,—if
one Christian be confirmed more strongly in his belief,—if one ray of the hope of better things to come
arise from hence, to enliven a single sorrowing heart,
—if one atom be added to the mass of evidence, the
author of this little work will neither have lost his
reward, nor spent his labour in vain.

CHAPTER II.

PROPHECIES CONCERNING CHRIST AND THE CHRISTIAN RELIGION.

IT is one of the remarkable peculiarities of the Jewish religion, that while it claimed superiority over every other, and was distinguished from them all, as alone inculcating the worship of the only living and true God, and while it was perfectly suited to the purpose for which it was designed, it acknowledged that it was itself only preparatory to a future, a better, and perfect revelation.. It was professedly adapted and limited to one particular people ;—it was confined, in many of its institutions, to the land of Judea ;—its morality was incomplete ;—its ritual observances were numerous, oppressive, and devoid of any inherent merit :* and being partial, imperfect and temporary, and full of promises of better things to come, for which it was only the means of preparing the way, it was evidently intended to be the presage of another. It was not even calculated of itself to fulfil the promise which it records as given unto Abraham, that in him all the families of the earth should be blessed : —though its original institution was founded upon this promise, and although the accomplishment of it was the great end to be promoted, by the distinction

* " Because they had not executed my judgments, but had despised my statutes, and had polluted my Sabbaths, and their eyes were after their fathers' idols, wherefore I gave them also statutes that were not good, and judgments whereby they should not live." Ezek. xx. 24, 25. Acts xv. 10.

and separation of his descendants from all the nations
of the earth.   But it was subservient to this end,
though it could not directly accomplish it, for the
coming of a Saviour was the great theme of prophecy,
and the universal belief of the Jews.   From the commencement to the conclusion of the Scriptures of the
Old Testament, it is predicted or prefigured.   They
represent the first act of divine justice, which was
exercised on the primogenitors of the human race,
as mingled with divine mercy.   Before their se-
clusion from paradise, a gleam of hope was seen
to shine around them, in the promise of a suffering but triumphant Deliverer.   To Abraham the
same promise was conveyed in a more definite form.
Jacob spoke distinctly of the coming of a Saviour.
Moses, the legislator and leader of the Hebrews, prophesied of another lawgiver that God was to raise up
in a future age.*   And while these early and general
predictions occur in the historical part of Scripture,
which sufficiently mark the purposed design of the
Mosaic dispensation, the books that are avowedly prophetic are clearly descriptive, as a minuter search
will attest, of the advent of a Saviour, and of every
thing pertaining to the kingdom he was to establish.
Many things, apparently contradictory and irreconcilable, are foretold as referring to a great Deliverer, whose dignity, whose character, and whose office
were altogether peculiar, and in whom the fate of human nature is represented as involved.   Many passages that can bear no other application, clearly testify of him : Thy king cometh—thy salvation cometh
—the Redeemer shall come to Zion—the Lord cometh—the Messenger of the Covenant he shall come
—blessed is he that cometh in the name of the

* Deut. xviii. 15, 18.

Lord,* are expressions that occur throughout the prophecies. These unequivocally speak of the coming of a Saviour. But were every other proof wanting, the prophecy of Daniel is sufficient incontrovertibly to establish the fact, which we affirm in the very words,—that the coming *of the Messiah* is foretold in the Old Testament. The same fact is confirmed by the belief of the Jews in every age. It is so deeply and indelibly impressed on their minds, that notwithstanding the dispersion of their race throughout the world, and the disappointment of their hopes for eighteen hundred years after the prescribed period of his coming, the expectation of the Messiah still forms a bond of union which no distance can dissolve, and which no earthly power can destroy.

As the Old Testament *does* contain prophecies of a Saviour that was to appear in the world ; the only question to be resolved is, whether all that it testifies of him be fulfilled in the person of Jesus Christ ? On a subject so interesting, so extensive and important, which has been so amply discussed by many able divines, the reader is referred to the works of Barrow, of Pearson and of Clarke. A summary view must be very imperfect and incomplete ; but it is here given, as it may serve, to the general reader, to exhibit the connexion between the Old and the New Testament, and as of itself it may be deemed conclusive of the argument in favour of Christianity.

A few of the leading features of the prophecies concerning Christ, and their fulfilment, shall be traced —as they mark the time of his appearance—the place of his birth—and the family out of which he was to arise—his life and character, his miracles, his sufferings, and his death—the nature of his doctrine—the

* Zech. ix. 9; Isa. lix. 20; Isa. lxii. 11; Mal. iii. 1; Isa. xxxv. 4; Psal. cxviii. 26; Dan. ix. 25, 26.

design and the effect of his coming—and the extent of his kingdom.

The time of the Messiah's appearance in the world, as predicted in the Old Testament, is defined by a number of concurring circumstances, that fix it to the very date of the advent of Christ. The last blessing of Jacob to his sons, when he commanded them to gather themselves together that he might tell them what should befall them in the last days, contains this prediction concerning Judah : " The sceptre shall not depart from Judah, nor a lawgiver from between his feet, until Shiloh come ; and unto him shall the gathering of the people be."* The date fixed by this prophecy for the coming of Shiloh, or the Saviour, was not to exceed the time that the descendants of Judah were to continue an united people—that a king should reign among them—that they should be governed by their own laws, and that their judges were to be from among their brethren. The prophecy of Malachi adds another standard for measuring the time ; " Behold I send my messenger, and he shall prepare the way before me, and the Lord, whom ye seek, shall come suddenly to his temple, even the messenger of the covenant, whom ye delight in ; behold he shall come, saith the Lord of Hosts."† No words can be more expressive of the coming of the promised Messiah ; and they as clearly imply his appearance in the temple before it should be destroyed. But it may also be here remarked that Malachi was the last of the prophets : With his predictions the vision and the prophecy were sealed up, or the canon of the Old Testament was completed. Though many prophets immediately preceded him, after his time there was no prophet in Israel ; but all the Jews, whether of ancient or modern times, look for a mes-

* Gen. xlix. 10.   † Mal. iii. 1.

senger to prepare the way of the Lord, immediately before his coming. The long succession of prophets had drawn to a close; and the concluding words of the Old Testament, subjoined to an admonition to remember the law of Moses, import that the next prophet would be the harbinger of the Messiah. Another criterion of the time is thus imparted. In regard to the advent of the Messiah, before the destruction of the second temple, the words of Haggai are remarkably explicit : " The desire of all nations shall come, and I will fill this house with glory, saith the Lord of Hosts. The glory of this latter house shall be greater than of the former, and in this place will I give peace."* The contrast which the prophet had just drawn between the glory of Solomon's temple and that which had been erected in its stead, to which he declares it was, in comparison, as nothing —the solemn manner of its introduction, " Thus saith the Lord of Hosts, yet once it is a little while, and I will shake the heavens and the earth ;" the excellency of the latter house excelling that of gold and silver ; the expression so characteristic of the Messiah, the " desire of all nations ;" and the blessing of peace that was to accompany his coming—all tend to denote that he alone is spoken of, who was the hope of Israel, and of whom all the prophets did testify, and that his presence would give to that temple a greater glory than that of the former. The Saviour was thus to appear, according to the prophecies of the Old Testament, during the time of the continuance of the kingdom of Judah, previous to the demolition of the temple, and immediately subsequent to the next prophet. But the time is rendered yet more definite. In the prophecies of Daniel, the kingdom of the Messiah is not only foretold as commencing in the

* Hag. ii. 7.

time of the fourth monarchy, or Roman empire ; but the express number of years, that were to precede his coming, are plainly intimated : " Seventy weeks are determined upon thy people, and upon thy holy city, to finish the transgression and to make an end of sins, and to make reconciliation for iniquity, and to bring in everlasting righteousness, and to seal up the vision and prophecy, and to anoint the Most Holy.   Know therefore and understand that from the going forth of the commandment to restore and to build Jerusalem, unto Messiah the prince, shall be seven weeks and threescore and two weeks."* Computation by weeks of years was common among the Jews, and every seventh was the Sabbatical year ; seventy weeks thus amounted to four hundred and ninety years.   In these words the prophet marks the very time and uses the very name of Messiah, the prince ; so entirely is all ambiguity done away.

The plainest inference may be drawn from these prophecies. All of them, while, in every respect, they pre-suppose the most perfect knowledge of futurity ; while they were unquestionably delivered and publicly known for ages previous to the time to which they referred ; while there is Jewish testimony of their application to the time of the Messiah,† which was delivered fifty years before Christ ; and while they refer to different contingent and unconnected events, utterly undeterminable and inconceivable by all human sagacity ;—accord in perfect unison to a single precise period where all their different lines terminate at once—the very fulness of time when Jesus appeared. A king then reigned over the Jews in their own land—they were governed

---

* Dan. ix. 24, 25.
† R. Nehumias quoted by Grotius *de Verit.*

by their own laws—and the council of their nation
exercised its authority and power. Before that period,
the other tribes were extinct or dispersed among the
nations. Judah alone remained, and the last sceptre
in Israel had not then departed from it. Every
stone of the temple was then unmoved : it was the
admiration of the Romans, and might have stood for
ages. But in a short space, all these concurring testimonies to the time of the advent of the Messiah,
passed away. During the very year, the twelfth of
his age, in which Christ first publicly appeared in
the temple, Archelaus the king was dethroned and
banished—Coponius was appointed procurator—and
the kingdom of Judea, the last remnant of the greatness of Israel, was debased into a part of the province of Syria.* The sceptre was smitten from the
hands of the tribe of Judah—the crown fell from
their heads—their glory departed—and, soon after
the death of Christ, of their temple one stone was
not left upon another—their commonwealth itself became as complete a ruin, and was broken in pieces—
and they have ever since been scattered throughout
the world, a name but not a nation. After the lapse
of nearly four hundred years posterior to the time of
Malachi, another prophet appeared who was the herald of the Messiah. And the testimony of Josephus
confirms the account given in Scripture of John the
Baptist.† Every mark that denoted the time of
the coming of the Messiah was erased soon after the
crucifixion of Christ, and could never afterwards be
renewed.—And, with respect to the prophecies of
Daniel, it is remarkable, at this remote period, how
little discrepancy of opinion has existed among the
most learned men, as to the space from the time of
the passing out of the edict to rebuild Jerusalem,

---

* Joseph. Ant. 17. c. 13.   † Ib. 18. 5.

after the Babylonish captivity, to the commencement
of the Christian era, and the subsequent events foretold in the prophecy.   Our design precludes detail :
But the minute coincidence of the narrative of the
New Testament and the history of the Jews, with
the subdivisions of time which it enumerates, are
additional attestations of its general accuracy as applicable to Christ.   This coincidence is the more
striking, as it is unnoticed by the relaters of the facts
which establish it, and it has been left, without the
possibility of any adaptation of the events, to the discovery of modern chronologists.   The following observations of Dr. Samuel Clarke, partly communicated to him, as he acknowledges, by Sir Isaac Newton, elucidate this prophecy so clearly that every
reader will forgive their insertion:—" When the angel
says to Daniel, *Seventy weeks are determined upon
thy people, &c.*—Was this written after the event?
Or can it reasonably be ascribed to chance, that from
the seventh year of Artaxerxes the king (when Ezra
went up from Babylon unto Jerusalem, with a commission to restore the government of the Jews,) to
the death of Christ, (from *Ann. Nabon.* 290, to
Ann. Nabon. 780) should be precisely 490 (70
weeks of) years.   When the angel tells Daniel, that
in threescore and two weeks the street (of Jerusalem)
should be built again, and the wall, even in troublous times, (but this, in troublous times, not like
those that should be under Messiah the prince when
he should come to reign :)—Was this written after
the event?   Or can it reasonably be ascribed to
chance, that from the 28th year of Artaxerxes, when
the walls were finished, to the birth of Christ, (from
Ann. Nabon. 311 to 745) should be precisely 434
(62 weeks of) years.   When Daniel farther says,
And he shall confirm (or, nevertheless he shall confirm) the covenant with many for one week.—Was

this written after the event? Or can it reasonably
be ascribed to chance, that from the death of Christ
(Ann. Dom. 33,) to the command given first to
Peter to preach to Cornelius and the Gentiles *(Ann.
Dom.* 40,) should be exactly seven (one week of)
years? When he still adds, *And in the midst of
the week, (and in half a week,) he shall cause the
sacrifice and the oblation to cease, and for the overspreading of abominations he shall make it desolate.*
Was this written after the event? Or, can it with
any reason be ascribed to chance, that from Vespasian's march into Judea in the spring *Ann. Dom.* 67,
to the taking of Jerusalem by Titus in the autumn
Ann. Dom. 70, should be half a septenary of years,
or three years and a half?"*

That the time at which the promised Messiah
was to appear is clearly defined in these prophecies;
that the expectation of the coming of a great king
or deliverer was then prevalent, not only among the
Jews, but among all the eastern nations, in consequence of these prophecies; that it afterwards excited that people to revolt, and proved the cause of
their greater destruction,—the impartial and unsuspected evidence of heathen authors is combined, with
the reluctant and ample testimony of the Jews themselves, to attest.

Tacitus, Suetonius, Josephus, and Philo agree in
testifying the antiquity of the prophecies, and their
acknowledged reference to that period.† Even the

* Clarke's Works, fol. edit. vol. ii. p. 721.

† Pluribus persuasio inerat, *antiquis* sacerdotum libris
contineri—eo ipso tempore fore—ut valesceret Oriens, pro-
fectique *Judæa*, rerum potirentur. Quæ ambages Vespa-
sianum et Titum predixerunt. Sed vulgus (Judæorum)
more humanæ cupidinis, *sibi tantum* fatorum magnitudinem
interpretari, ne adversis, quidem, ad vera mutabantur.—
Tacit. Ann. V. 13. Percrebuerat *Oriente toto constans*

Jews, to this day, own that the time when their Messiah ought to have appeared, according to their prophecies, is long since past, and they attribute the delay of his coming to the sinfulness of their nation. And thus, from the distinct prophecies themselves; from the testimony of profane historians; and from the concessions of the Jews, every requisite proof is afforded that Christ appeared when all the concurring circumstances of the time denoted the prophesied period of his advent.

The predictions contained in the Old Testament respecting both the family out of which the Messiah was to arise, and the place of his birth, are almost as circumstantial, and are equally applicable to Christ, as those which refer to the time of his appearance. He was to be an Israelite, of the tribe of Judah, of the family of David, and of the town of Bethlehem. The two former of these particulars are implied in the promise made to Abraham—in the prediction of Moses—in the prophetic benediction of Jacob to Judah—and in the reason assigned for the superiority of that tribe, because out of it the chief ruler should arise. And the two last, that the Messiah was to be a descendant of David and a native of Bethlehem, are expressly affirmed. *There shall come forth a rod out of the stem of Jesse, and a branch shall grow out of his roots, and the Spirit of the Lord shall rest upon him.** That this prophecy refers to the deliverer of the human race, is evident from the whole of the succeeding chapter, which is

opinio esse in fatis, ut eo tempore Judæa profecti, rerum potirentur. Id de imperio Romano, quantum postea eventu patuit, prædictum Judæi ad se habentes, rebellarunt.—Suet. in Vesp. l. 8. c. 4. Julius Maranathus, quoted by Suetonius, lib. 2, 93—Joseph. de Bello, vii. 31; Philo de Præm. et Pen. p. 923—4.

* Isaiah xi. 1.

descriptive of the kingdom of the Messiah, of the calling of the Gentiles, and of the restoration of Israel. The same fact is predicted in many passages of the prophecies :—" Thine house and thy kingdom shall be established for ever before thee.—I have made a covenant with my chosen. I have sworn to David my servant, thy seed will I establish for ever, and build up thy throne to all generations. Behold the days come, saith the Lord, that I will raise unto David a righteous branch, and a king shall reign and prosper, and shall execute judgment and justice on the earth ; and this is the name whereby he shall be called—the Lord our righteousness."* The place of the birth of the Messiah is thus clearly foretold :— " Thou Bethlehem, Ephratah, in the land of Judah, though thou be little among the thousands of Judah, yet out of thee shall he come forth," or, as the Hebrew word implies,† shall he be born—that is to be ruler in Israel, " whose goings forth have been of old, from everlasting."‡—That all these predictions were fulfilled in Jesus Christ ; that he was of that country, tribe and family, of the house and lineage of David, and born in Bethlehem,—we have the fullest evidence in the testimony of all the evangelists ; in two distinct accounts of the genealogies, (by natural and legal succession), which, according to the custom of the Jews, were carefully preserved ; in the acquiescence of the enemies of Christ to the truth of the fact, against which there is not a single surmise in history ; and in the appeal made by some of the earliest of the Christian writers to the unquestionable testimony of the records of the census, taken at the very time of our Saviour's birth by order of Cæsar.§   Here,

---

* 2 Sam. vii. 16.   Psal. lxxxix. 3, 4.   Jer. xxiii. 5.
† Gen. x. 14 ; xv. 4 ; xvii. 6.   2 Sam. vii. 12, &c.
‡ Mic. v. 2.
§ Justin Mar. ap. 1. p. 55, ed. *Thirl.* Tert. in Mark iv. 19.

indeed, it is impossible not to be struck with the exact
fulfilment of prophecies which are apparently contradictory and irreconcilable, and with the manner in
which they were providentially accomplished.   The
spot of Christ's nativity was distant from the place of
the abode of his parents, and the region in which he
began his ministry was remote from the place of his
birth ; and another prophecy respecting him was in
this manner verified : " In the land of Zebulun and
Naphtali, by the way of the sea beyond Jordan, in
Galilee of the nations, the people that walked in
darkness have seen a great light ; they that dwell in
the land of the shadow of death, upon them hath the
light shined."*   Thus, the time at which the predicted Messiah was to appear, the nation, the tribe,
and the family from which he was to be descended—
and the place of his birth—no populous city—but of
itself an inconsiderable place, were all clearly foretold ; and as clearly refer to Jesus Christ,—and all
meet their completion in him.

But the facts of his life, and the features of his
character, are also drawn with a precision that cannot
be misunderstood.   The obscurity, the meanness, and
poverty of his external condition are thus represented :   " He shall grow up before the Lord like a
tender plant, and as a root out of a dry ground ; he
hath no form or comeliness ; and when we shall see
him, there is no beauty that we should desire him.
Thus saith the Lord, to him whom man despiseth,
to him whom the nation abhorreth, to a servant of
rulers, kings shall see and arise, princes also shall
worship."†   That such was the condition in which
Christ appeared, the whole history of his life abundantly testifies.   And the Jews, looking in the pride
of their hearts for an earthly king, disregarded these

---

* Isaiah ix. 1, 2. Matth. iv. 16.   † Isaiah liii. 2 ; xlix. 7.

prophecies concerning him, were deceived by their traditions, and found only a stone of stumbling, where, if they had searched their Scriptures aright, they would have discovered an evidence of the Messiah. " Is not this the carpenter's son ; is not this the son of Mary ? said they, and they were offended at him." His riding in humble triumph into Jerusalem ; his being betrayed for thirty pieces of silver, and scourged, and buffeted, and spit upon : the piercing of his hands and of his feet ; the last offered draught of vinegar and gall ; the parting of his raiment, and casting lots upon his vesture ; the manner of his death and of his burial, and his rising again without seeing corruption,*—were all expressly predicted, and all these predictions were literally fulfilled. If all these prophecies admit of any application to the events of the life of any individual, it can only be to that of the author of Christianity. And what other religion can produce a single fact which was actually foretold of its founder ?

Though the personal appearance or moral condition of the Messiah was represented by the Jewish prophets, such as to bespeak no grandeur, his personal character is described as of a higher order than that of the sons of men. " Righteousness shall be the girdle of his loins, and faithfulness the girdle of his reins. He hath done no violence, neither was there any deceit in his lips. The Spirit of the Lord shall rest upon him, the spirit of wisdom and understanding, the spirit of counsel and might, the spirit of knowledge and of the fear of the Lord. The Lord God hath given me the tongue of the learned, that I should know how to speak a word in season to him that is weary. He shall feed his flock like a shepherd ; he

* Zech. ix. 9 ; xi. 12. Isa. i. 6. Psa. xxii. 16 ; lxix. 21 ; xxii. 18. Isa. liii. 9. Psa. xvi. 10.

shall gather the lambs with his arm, and carry them in his bosom. A bruised reed shall he not break, and the smoking flax shall he not quench. Behold, thy king cometh unto thee : he is just and having salvation ; lowly and riding upon an ass. He shall not cry, nor lift up, nor cause his voice to be heard in the street. He was oppressed and afflicted, yet he opened not his mouth ; he was brought as a lamb to the slaughter, and as a sheep before her shearers is dumb, so he opened not his mouth. I gave my back to the smiters, and my cheek to them that plucked off the hair ; I did not hide my face from shame and spitting. The Lord God hath opened mine ear that I was not rebellious, neither turned away back. The Lord will help me, therefore shall I not be confounded ; therefore have I set my face like a flint, and I know that I shall not be ashamed."* How many virtues are thus represented in the prophecies, as characteristic of the Messiah ; and how applicable are they all to Christ alone, and how clearly embodied in his character ! His wisdom and knowledge—his speaking as never man spake—the general meekness of his manner and mildness of his conversation—his perfect candour and unsullied purity—his righteousness—his kindness and compassion—his genuine humility—his peaceable disposition—his unrepining patience—his invincible courage—his more than heroic resolution, and more than human forbearance—his unfaultering trust in God, and complete resignation to his will, are all pourtrayed in the liveliest, the most affecting, and expressive terms ; and among all who ever breathed the breath of life, they can be applied to Christ alone.†

* Isa. xi. 2, 5 ; xl. 11 ; l. 4, 6, 7 ; xlii. 2, 3 ; liii. 7, 8, 11 Zech. ix. 9.
† See Barrow on the Creed, p. 19.

Mahomet pretended to receive a divine warrant to sanction his past impurities and to license his future crimes. How different is the appeal of Jesus to earth and to heaven : " If I do not the works of my Father, believe me not.—Search the Scriptures, for these are they which testify of me." They did testify of the coming of a Messiah, and of the superhuman excellence of his moral character. And if the life of Jesus was wonderful and unparalleled of itself, how miraculous does it appear, when all his actions develop the prophetic character of the promised Saviour ! The internal and external evidence are here combined at once ; and while the life of Christ proved that he was a righteous person, it proved also, as testified of by the prophets, that he was the Son of God.

In describing the blessings of the reign of the Messiah, the prophet Isaiah foretold the greatness and the benignity of his miracles :—" The eyes of the blind shall be opened, and the ears of the deaf shall be unstopped : the lame man shall leap as an hart, and the tongue of the dumb shall sing."* The history of Jesus shows how such acts of mercy formed the frequent exercise of his power : at his word the blind received their sight—the lame walked—the deaf heard—and the dumb spake.†

The death of Christ was as unparalleled as his life ; and the prophecies are as minutely descriptive of his sufferings as of his virtues. Not only did the paschal lamb, which was to be killed every year in all the families of Israel—which was to be taken out of the flock, to be without blemish—to be eaten with bitter herbs—to have its blood sprinkled, and to be kept whole that not a bone of it should be broken—not only did the offering up of Isaac, and the lifting up of the brazen serpent in the wilderness, by looking

* Isa. xxxv. 5.   † Matth. xi. 5.

upon which the people were healed,—and many ritual observances of the Jews,—prefigure the manner of Christ's death, and the sacrifice which was to be made for sin :—but many express declarations abound in the prophecies, that Christ was indeed to suffer.   Exclusive of the repeated declarations* in the Psalms, of afflictions which apply literally to him, and are interwoven with allusions to the Messiah's kingdom, the prophet Daniel,† in limiting the time of his coming, directly affirms that the Messiah was to be cut off; and in the same manifest allusion, Zechariah uses these emphatic words : " Awake, O sword, against my Shepherd, and against the man that is my fellow, saith the Lord of Hosts : smite the shepherd, and the sheep shall be scattered.—I will pour upon the house of David, and the inhabitants of Jerusalem, the spirit of grace and of supplications ; and they shall look upon me whom they have pierced, and they shall mourn for him."‡

But Isaiah, who describes with eloquence worthy of a prophet, the glories of the kingdom that was to come, characterises, with the accuracy of a historian, the humiliation, the trials, and the agonies which were to precede the triumphs of the Redeemer of a world ; and the history of Christ forms, to the very letter, the commentary and the completion of his every prediction.   In a single passage,§—the connexion of which is uninterrupted, its antiquity indisputable, and its application obvious,—the sufferings of the servant of God (who under the same denomination, is previously described as he who was to be the light of the Gentiles, the Salvation of God to the ends of the earth, and the Elect of God in whom his soul delighted)‖

---

* Psa. ii. xxii. 1, 6, 7, 16, 18 ; xxxv. 7, 11, 12 ; lxix. 20, 21 ; cix. 2, 3, 5, 25 ; cxviii. 22.

† Dan. ix. 26.　　　　　　　‡ Zech. xiii. 7 ; xii. 10.

§ Isa. lii. 13, &c. and chap. liii.　‖ Isa. xlii. 10 ; xlix. 6.

are so minutely foretold that no illustration is requisite to show that they testify of Jesus. Of the multitude of parallel passages in the New Testament, a few shall be selected and subjoined to the prophecy.

" *He is despised and rejected of men ;* He came unto his own, and his own received him not ; He had not where to lay his head ; they derided him.—*A man of sorrows and acquainted with grief* ; Jesus wept at the grave of Lazarus : He mourned over Jerusalem ; He felt the ingratitude and the cruelty of men ; He bore the contradiction of sinners against himself—and these are expressions of sorrow which were peculiarly his own : ' Father, if it be possible let this cup pass from me ; but for this end came I into the world.—My God ! my God ! why hast thou forsaken me ?' *We hid, as it were, our faces from him ; he was despised, and we esteemed him not.*—All his disciples forsook him, and fled. Not this man, but Barabbas : now Barabbas was a robber. The soldiers mocked him, and bowed the knee before him in derision." The catalogue of his sufferings is continued in the words of the prophecy—" *We did esteem him stricken, smitten of God and afflicted ; He was wounded, he was oppressed, he was afflicted, he was brought as a lamb to the slaughter ; He was taken away by distress and by judgment.*" And to this general description is united the detail of minuter incidents, which fixes the fact of their application to Jesus—" *He was cut off out of the land of the living ;*" He was crucified in the flower of his age. *They* (the people) *made his grave with the wicked, but he was with the rich after his death ;* Joseph of Arimathea, a rich man, went and begged the body of Jesus, and laid it in his own new tomb. *He was numbered with the transgressors ;* He was crucified between two thieves. " *His visage was so marred, more than any*

man's, and his form more than the sons of men,"—
without any direct allusion made to it, but in literal
fulfilment of the prophecy—the bloody sweat, the
traces of the crown of thorns—his having been spitted
on, and smitten on the head—disfigured in the face ;
—while the scourge, the nails in his hands and in
his feet, and the spear that pierced his side, marred
the form of Jesus more than that of the sons of men.

That this circumstantial and continuous description of the Messiah's sufferings might not admit of
any ambiguity—the dignity of his person—the in-
credulity of the Jews—the innocence of the sufferer
—the cause of his sufferings—and his consequent
exaltation, are all particularly marked, and are equally
applicable to the doctrine of the gospel. " *He shall
be exalted and extolled, and be very high ; who hath
believed our report, and to whom is the arm of the
Lord revealed ? For he shall grow up as a tender
plant,*" &c. The mean external condition of Christ is
here assigned as the reason of the unbelief of the
Jews, and it was the very reason which they themselves assigned. The prediction points out the pro-
curing cause of his sufferings.—" *He hath borne our
griefs, he hath carried our sorrows.* Christ was once
offered to bear the sins of many. *He was wounded
for our transgressions, he was bruised for our iniquities, the chastisement of our peace was upon him,
and with his stripes we are healed.* His own self
bare our sins in his body on the tree, that we,
being dead unto sin, should live unto righteousness ;
by whose stripes we are healed. *All we like sheep
have gone astray, and have turned every one to his
own way, and the Lord hath laid on him the iniquity
of us all :* All flesh have sinned ; ye were as sheep
going astray, but ye are now returned unto the Shepherd and Bishop of your souls. *He hath done no*

*violence ; neither was there any deceit in his mouth :
Thou shalt make his soul an offering for sin :* God
made him to be sin for us, who knew no sin."

The whole of this prophecy thus refers to the Messiah. It describes both his debasement and his dignity—his rejection by the Jews—his humility, his
affliction, and his agony—his magnanimity and his
charity—how his words were disbelieved—how his
state was lowly—how his sorrow was severe—how he
opened not his mouth but to make intercession for
the transgressors. In diametrical opposition to every
dispensation of Providence which is registered in the
records of the Jews, it represents spotless innocence
suffering by the appointment of Heaven,—death as
the issue of perfect obedience,—his righteous servant
as forsaken of God,—and one who was perfectly im-
maculate, bearing the chastisement of many guilty,—
sprinkling many nations from their iniquity, by virtue of his sacrifice,—justifying many by his knowledge, and dividing a portion with the great, and the
spoil with the strong, because he hath poured out his
soul in death. This prophecy, therefore, simply as
a prediction prior to the event, renders the very unbelief of the Jews an evidence against them, converts
the scandal of the cross into an argument in favour
of Christianity, and presents us with an epitome of
the truth—a miniature of the gospel in some of its
most striking features. The simple exposition of it
sufficed at once for the conversion of the eunuch of
Ethiopia ; and, without the aid of an apostle, it can
boast, in more modern times, of a nobler trophy of
its truth—in a victory which it was mainly instrumental in obtaining and securing, over the strongly-
rivetted prejudices and long-tried infidelity of a man
of genius and of rank, who was one of the most
abandoned, insidious and successful of the advo-

cates of impurity, and of the enemies of the Christian faith.*

Thus it is written, and thus it behoved Christ to suffer, according to the Scriptures; and thus the apostle testifies—Those things which God had showed by the mouth of all the prophets, that Christ should suffer, he hath so fulfilled.

That the Jews still retain these prophecies, and are the means of preserving them, and communicating them throughout the world, while they bear so strongly against themselves, and testify so clearly of a Saviour that was first to suffer, and then to be exalted,—are facts as indubitable as they are unaccountable, and give a confirmation to the truth of Christianity, than which it is difficult to conceive any stronger. The prophecies, as we have seen, by a simple enumeration of a few of them that testify of the sufferings of the Messiah, need no forced interpretation, but apply, in the plainest, simplest and most literal manner, to the history of the sufferings and of the death of Christ. In the testimony of the Jews to the existence of these prophecies long prior to the Christian era; in their remaining unaltered to this hour; in the accounts given by the evangelists of the life and death of Christ; in the testimony of heathen authors;† and in the arguments of the first opposers of Christianity, from the mean condition of its author, and the manner of his death;—we have now greater evidence of the fulfilment of all these prophecies, than could have been conceived possible at so great a distance of time.

But the prophecies farther present us with the

---

* Burnet's Life of the Earl of Rochester, pp. 70, 71.

† Auctor nominis ejus Christus, Tiberio imperitante, per procuratorem Pontium Pilatum supplicio adfectus erat.— *Tacit. An.* xv. 44.

character of the gospel as well as of its author, and
with a description of the extent of his kingdom as
well as of his sufferings. It was prophesied that the
Messiah was to reveal the will of God to man, and
establish a new and perfect religion :—" I will raise
them up a prophet, and I will put my words in his
mouth, and he shall speak unto them all that I shall
command him ; and it shall come to pass, that who-
soever will not hearken unto my words which he shall
speak in my name, I will require it of him.——Unto
us a child is born, unto us a Son is given, and the
government shall be upon his shoulder, and his name
shall be called Wonderful, Counsellor, the Mighty
God, the Everlasting Father, the Prince of peace.
Of the increase of his government and peace there
shall be no end ; upon the throne of David, and upon
his kingdom to order it, and to establish it with judgment and justice from henceforth, even for ever.   The
zeal of the Lord of Hosts will perform this.——There
shall come forth a rod out of the stem of Jesse ; he
shall not judge after the sight of his eyes, neither reprove after the hearing of his ears ; with righteousness shall he judge the poor, and reprove with equity.
——I, the Lord, have called thee in righteousness, and
will hold thine hand, and will keep thee, and give
thee for a covenant of the people, for a light of the
Gentiles to open the blind eyes.——Incline your ear
and come unto me, hear and your soul shall live ;
and I will make an everlasting covenant with you,
even the sure mercies of David. Behold I have
given him for a witness to the people, for a leader and
a commander to the people. I will set up one shepherd over them, and he shall feed them, and I will
make with them a covenant of peace, and it shall be
an everlasting covenant, and I will set my sanctuary
in the midst of them ; one king shall be king to them
all, neither shall they defile themselves any more with

idols. They shall have one shepherd. They shall also walk in my judgments, and my servant David shall be their prince for ever. Behold the days come, saith the Lord, that I will make a new covenant, and this shall be the covenant that I will make with the house of Israel, after these days : I will put my law in their inward parts, and write it in their hearts, and will be their God, and they shall be my people ; and they shall teach no more every man his neighbour, and every man his brother, saying, Know the Lord ; for they all shall know me, from the least of them unto the greatest of them, saith the Lord, for I will forgive their iniquity, and remember their sins no more."* A future and perfect revelation of the divine will is thus explicitly foretold. That these promised blessings were to extend beyond the confines of Judea, is expressly and frequently predicted :— " It is a light thing that thou shouldst be my servant, to raise up the tribes of Jacob, and to restore the preserved of Israel. I will also give thee for a light to the Gentiles, that thou mayest be my salvation unto the end of the earth."†

While many of the prophecies which are descriptive of the glories of the reign of the Messiah, refer to its universal extension, and to the final restoration of the Jews, they detail and define, at the same time, the nature and the blessings of the gospel ; and no better description or definition could now be given of the doctrine of Christ, and of the conditions which he hath proposed for the acceptance of man, than those very prophecies which were delivered many hundreds of years before he appeared in the world. The gospel, as the name itself signifies, denotes glad tidings.

* Deut. xvii. 18, 19. Isa. ix. 6, 7 ; xlii. 6 ; xi. 1, 6 ; lv. 3, 4. Ezek. xxxiv. 23, 35 ; xxxvii. 26. Jer. xxxi. 31, 33, 34.
† Isa. xlix. 6 ; lvi. 6, &c.

Christ himself invited those who were weary and heavy laden to come unto him that they might find rest unto their souls. He was the messenger of peace. He came, as he professed, to offer a sacrifice for the sins of the world, and to reveal the will of God to man. He published the terms of our acceptance. His word is still that of reconciliation, his law that of love ; and all the duty he has prescribed tends to qualify man for spiritual and eternal felicity, for this is the sum and the object of it all. What more could have been given, and what less could have been required ? In similar terms do the prophecies of old describe the new law that was to be revealed, and the advent of the Saviour that was to come :—" Rejoice greatly, O daughter of Zion ; shout, O daughter of Jerusalem ; behold thy king cometh unto thee.—How beautiful upon the mountains are the feet of him that bringeth good tidings of good, that publisheth salvation. The Spirit of the Lord God is upon me, because the Lord hath anointed me to preach good tidings unto the meek ; he hath sent me to bind up the broken-hearted, to proclaim liberty to the captives, to proclaim the acceptable year of the Lord." Having read these words out of the law, in the synagogue, Jesus said, " this day is the Scripture fulfilled." He was a teacher of righteousness and of peace, and in him alone it could have been fulfilled. The same character of joy, indicative of the kingdom of the Messiah, is also given by different prophets. He was to " finish transgression, to make an end of sins, and to make reconciliation for iniquity ; to sprinkle clean water upon the people of God, to sprinkle many nations, to save them from their uncleanness, and to open a fountain for sin and for uncleanness. Let the wicked forsake his ways, and the unrighteous man his thoughts, and let him return unto the Lord and he will have mercy upon him.

I will forgive their iniquity and remember their sins
no more. The Messiah was to be anointed to con-
fort all that mourn, to appoint unto them that mourn
in Zion, to give unto them beauty for ashes, the oil
of joy for mourning, and the garment of praise for
the spirit of heaviness."* And in the gospel of peace
these promised blessings are realized. We now see
what many prophets and wise men did desire in vain
to see. The Christian religion has indeed been sadly
perverted and corrupted, and its corruptions are the
subjects of prophecy. Bigotry has often tarnished
and obscured all its benignity. Its lovely form has
been shrouded in a mask of superstition, of tyranny
and of murder. But the religion of Jesus, pure from
the lips of its Author, and the pen of his apostles, is
calculated to diffuse universal happiness—tends effectually to promote the moral culture and the civilization of humanity—ameliorates the condition and per-
fects the nature of man. It is a doctrine of righteousness, a perfect rule of duty—It abolishes idolatry,
and teaches all to worship God only—It is full of
promises to all who obey it—It reveals the method
of reconciliation for iniquity, and imparts the means
to obtain it—It is good tidings to the meek—it binds
up the broken-hearted, and presents to us the oil of
joy for mourning, and the garment of praise for the
spirit of heaviness, or the most perfect system of con-
solation, under all the evils of life, that can be conceived by man. For the confirmation of all these
prophecies concerning it, we stand not in need of
Jewish testimony, or that of the primitive Christians,
or of any testimony whatever. It is a matter of experience and of fact. The doctrine of the gospel is in
complete accordance with the predictions respecting it.
When we compare it with any impure, degrading,

* Isa. lii. 7; lxi. 1; xlii. 1, 3. Jer. xxxi. 34. Dan. ix. 24.

vicious, and cruel system of religion that existed in the world when these prophecies were delivered, its superiority must be apparent, and its unrivalled excellence must be acknowledged. Deities were then worshipped whose vices disgraced human nature ; and even impiety could not institute a comparison between them and the God of Christians. Idolatry was universally prevalent, and men knew not a higher honour than the humiliation of bowing down in adoration to stocks and stones, and sometimes even to the beasts. Sacrifices were everywhere offered up, and human victims often bled, when the doctrine of reconciliation for iniquity was unknown. And we have only to look beyond the boundaries of Christianity,— to Ashantee, or to India, or to China,—to behold the most revolting of spectacles in the religious rites and practices of man. Regarding the superiority of the Christian religion only as a subject of prophecy, the assent can hardly be withheld, that the prophecies concerning its excellence, and the blessings which it imparts, have been amply verified by the peace-speaking gospel of Jesus.

But, in ascertaining the accomplishment of ancient predictions, in evidence of the truth, the unbeliever is not solicited to relinquish one iota of his scepticism in any matter that can possibly admit of a reasonable doubt. For there are many prophecies, of the truth of which every Christian is a witness, and to the fulfilment of which the testimony even of infidels must be borne. That the gospel emanated from Jerusalem—that it was rejected by a great proportion of the Jews—that it was opposed at first by human power —that idolatry has been overthrown before it—that kings have become subject to it and supported it— that it has already continued for many ages—and that it has been propagated throughout many countries, are facts clearly foretold and literally fulfilled :

—" Out of Zion shall go forth the law, and the word
of the Lord from Jerusalem, and he shall judge
among the nations.* He shall be for a sanctuary,
but for a stone of stumbling, and for a rock of offence
to both the houses of Israel : for a gin and for a snare
to the inhabitants of Jerusalem.† The kings of the
earth set themselves, and the rulers take counsel together against the Lord, and against his anointed."
In like manner, Christ frequently foretold the persecution that awaited his followers, and the final success of the gospel, in defiance of all opposition.‡
" The Lord alone shall be exalted in that day, and
the idols he shall utterly abolish ;—from all your
idols I will cleanse you ;—I will cut off the name of
idols out of the land, and they shall no more be remembered.§ To a servant of rulers, kings shall see
and arise, princes also shall worship. The Gentiles
shall come to thy light, and kings to the brightness
of thy rising. Kings shall be thy nursing fathers,
and their queens thy nursing mothers.‖ The Gentiles shall see thy righteousness :—a people that
knew me not shall be called after my name. In that
day there shall be a root of Jesse, which shall stand
for an ensign to the people ; to it shall the Gentiles
seek. I will make an everlasting covenant with you.
Behold thou shalt call a nation that thou knowest
not, and nations that knew not thee shall run unto
thee."¶

At the time the prophecies were delivered, there
was not a vestige in the world of that spiritual kingdom and pure religion which they unequivocally represent as extending in succeeding ages, not only
throughout the narrow bounds of the land of Judea,

Isa. ii. 3, 4.   Micah iv. 2.   † Isa. viii. 14.
‡ Psa. ii. 2.   Matt. x. 17; xvi. 18; xxiv. 14; xxviii. 19.
§ Isa. ii. 17.   Ezek. xxxvi. 25.   Zech. xiii. 2.
‖ Isa. xlix. 7—23; lii. 15; lx. 3.   ¶ Isa. xi. 10; lv. 5.

and those countries which alone the prophets knew, but over the Gentile nations also, even to the uttermost ends of the earth. None are now ignorant of the facts that a system of religion which inculcates piety, and purity, and love,—which releases man from every burdensome rite, and every barbarous institution, and proffers the greatest of blessings—arose from the land of Judea, from among a people who are the most selfish and worldly-minded of any nation upon earth ; —that, though persecuted at first, and rejected by the Jews, it has spread throughout many nations, and extended to those who were far distant from the scene of its origin ; and that it freely invites all to partake of its privileges, and makes no distinction between barbarian, Scythian, bond or free. A Latin poet, who lived at the commencement of the Christian era, speaks of the barbarous Britons as almost divided from the whole world ; and yet although far more distant from the land of Judea than from Rome, the law which hath come out from Jerusalem hath taken, by its influence, the name of barbarous from Britain ; and in our " distant isle of the Gentiles" are the prophecies fulfilled, that the kingdom of the Messiah, or knowledge of the gospel, would extend to the uttermost part of the earth. And in the present day, we can look from one distant isle of the Gentiles to another,—from the northern to the southern ocean, or from one extremity of the globe to another,—and behold the extinction of idolatry, and the abolition of every barbarous and cruel rite, by the humanizing influence of the gospel. But it was at a time when no divine light dawned upon the world, save obscurely on the land of Judea alone ; when all the surrounding nations, in respect to religious knowledge, were involved in thick darkness, gross superstition, and blind idolatry : when men made unto themselves gods of corruptible things : when those mortals were

deified, after their death, who had been subject to the
greatest vices, and who had been the oppressors of
their fellow-men ; when the most shocking rites were
practised as acts of religion ; when the most enlightened among the nations of the earth erected an altar
to the " unknown God," and set no limit to the number of their deities ; when one of the greatest of the
heathen philosophers, and the best of their moralists,
despairing of the clear discovery of the truth by human means, could merely express a wish for a divine
revelation, as the only safe and certain guide ;* when
slaves were far more numerous than freemen even
where liberty prevailed the most ; and when there
was no earthly hope of redemption from temporal
bondage or spiritual slavery ;—even at such a time
the voice of prophecy was uplifted in the land of Judea, and it spoke of a brighter day that was to dawn
upon the world.   It was indeed a light shining in a
dark place.   And from whence could that light have
emanated but from heaven ? A Messiah was promised
—a prince of peace was to appear—a stone was to be
cut without hands, that should break in pieces and
consume all other kingdoms.   And the spiritual reign
of a Saviour is foretold in terms that define its duration and extent, as well as describe its nature :—" I
behold him, but not now—I see him, but not nigh.
—His name shall endure for ever,—his name shall
be continued as long as the sun, and men shall be
blessed in him,—all nations shall call him blessed.
He shall have dominion from sea to sea—and from
the river unto the ends of the earth.—Ask of me, and
I shall give thee the heathen for thine inheritance,
and the uttermost part of the earth for thy possession.—All the ends of the earth shall remember
and turn unto the Lord—and all kindreds of the

* Plato in Phædone et in Alcibiade, II.

nations shall worship before thee.*—I will give thee for a light of the Gentiles, that thou mayest be my salvation to the ends of the earth.—The glory of the Lord shall be revealed, and all flesh shall see it together; for the mouth of the Lord hath spoken it.†—The Lord hath made bare his holy arm in the eyes of all the nations. He shall not fail nor be discouraged till he have set judgment in the earth; and the isles shall wait for his law.‡—He will destroy the face of the covering cast over all people, and the veil that is spread over all nations.§—I am sought of them that asked not for me,—I am found of them that sought me not,—I said, Behold me, behold me, unto a nation that was not called by my name.||—It shall come to pass, in the last days, say both Isaiah and Micah in the same words, that the mountain of the Lord's house shall be established on the top of the mountains, and shall be exalted above the hills—and all nations shall flow unto it.¶—In the place where it was said, Ye are not my people, it shall be said, Ye are the sons of the living God.**—The abundance of the sea shall be converted unto Thee—the forces of the Gentiles shall come unto Thee.††—Sing, O barren, thou that didst not bear—break forth into singing and cry aloud—for more are the children of the desolate than the children of the married wife (more Gentiles than Jews.)‡‡—Enlarge the place of thy tent, and let them stretch forth the curtains of thine habitations, —spare not, lengthen thy cords, for thou shalt break forth on the right hand and on the left—and thy seed shall inherit the Gentiles—for thy Maker is thy husband—the Lord of Hosts is his name—the Lord of the whole earth shall he be called—the wilderness and

---

* Psa. lxxii. 8, 17; ii. 8; xxii. 27, 28.   † Isa. xl. 5.
‡ Isa. lii. 10; xliii. 4. § Isa. xxv. 7. || Isa. lxv. 1.
¶ Isa. ii. 2. Micah iv. 1. ** Hosea i. 10.   †† Isa. lx. 5.
‡‡ Isa. liv. 1, 2, 4, 5.

the solitary place shall be glad—the desert shall rejoice and blossom as the rose."*

These prophecies all refer to the extent of the Messiah's kingdom; and clear and copious though they
be, they form but a small number of the predictions
of the same auspicious import;—and we have not
merely to consider what part of them may yet remain
to be fulfilled, but how much has already been accomplished, of which no surmise could have been formed,
and of which all the wisdom of short-sighted mortals
could not have warranted a thought. All of them
were delivered many ages before the existence of that
religion whose progress they minutely describe; and,
when we compare the present state of any country
where the gospel is professed in its purity, with its
state at that period when the Sun of righteousness
began to arise upon it, we see light pervading the region of darkness, and ignorance and barbarism yielding to knowledge and moral cultivation. In opposition to all human probability, and to human wisdom
and power, the gospel of Jesus, propagated at first by
a few fishermen of Galilee, has razed every heathen
temple from its foundation—has overthrown before it
every impure altar—has displaced from every palace
and every cottage which it has reached, the worship
of every false god : the whole civilized world acknowledges its authority—it has prevailed from the first
to the last in defiance of persecution—of opposition
the most powerful and violent—of the direct attacks
of avowed, and the insidious designs of disguised enemies;—and combating, as it ever has been combating, with all the evil passions of men that impel
them to resist or to pervert it, the lapse of eighteen
centuries confirms every ancient prediction, and verifies, to this hour, the declaration of its Author—

* Isa. xxxv. 1.

" the gates of hell shall not prevail against it." How is it possible that it could have been conceived that such a religion would have been characterised in all its parts—would have been instituted—opposed—established—propagated throughout the world—embraced by so many nations—protected at last by princes and kings—and received as the rule of faith and the will of God ? How could all these things, and many more respecting it, have been foretold, as they unquestionably were, many centuries before the Author of Christianity appeared, if these prophecies be not an attestation from on high that every prediction and its completion is the work of God and not of man ? What uninspired mortal could have described the nature, the effect, and the progress of the Christian religion, when none could have entertained an idea of its existence ? For paganism consisted in external rites and cruel sacrifices, and in pretended mysteries. Its toleration, indeed, has been commended, and not undeservedly : For in religion it tolerated whatever was absurd and impious, in morals it tolerated all that was impure and almost all that was vicious. But the Jewish prophets, when the world was in darkness, and could supply no light to lead them to such knowledge, predicted the rise of a religion which could boast of no *such* toleration, but which was to reveal the will and inculcate the worship of the one living and true God—which was to consist in moral obedience—to enjoin reformation of life and purity of heart—to abolish all sacrifice by revealing a better mean of reconciliation for iniquity—to be understood by all from the simplicity of its precepts—and to tolerate no manner of evil ; a religion in every respect the reverse of paganism, and of which they could not have been furnished with any semblance upon earth. They saw nothing among the surrounding nations but the worship of a multiplicity of deities and of idols; if they had traversed the whole world they would have witnessed only the same spiritual degradation, and yet they predicted the final abolition and extinction both of polytheism and of idolatry. The Jewish dispensation was local, and Jews prophesied of a religion beginning from Jerusalem, which was to extend to the uttermost parts of the earth. So utterly unlikely and incredible were the prophecies either to have been foretold by human wisdom, or to have been fulfilled by human power; and when both these wonders are united, they convey an assurance of the truth. As a matter of history, the progress of Christianity is at least astonishing; as the fulfilment of many prophecies, it is evidently miraculous.*

The prophesied success and extension of the gospel is not less obvious in the New Testament than in the Old. A single instance may suffice:—"I saw another angel fly in the midst of heaven, having the everlasting gospel to preach unto them that dwell on the earth, and to every nation, and kindred, and tongue, and people." These are the words of a banished man, secluded in a small island from which he could not remove; a believer in a new religion everywhere spoken against and persecuted. They were uttered at a time when their truth could not possibly have been realized to the degree which it actually is at

---

* Were it even to be conceded—as it never will in reason be—that the causes assigned by Gibbon for the rapid extension of Christianity were *adequate* and true, one difficulty, great as it is, would only be removed for the substitution of a greater. For what human ingenuity, though gifted with the utmost reach of discrimination, can ever attempt the solution of the question—how were all these occult causes, (for hidden they must then have been) which the genius of Gibbon first discovered, foreseen, their combination known, and all their wonderful effects distinctly described for many centuries prior to their existence—or to the commencement of the period of their alleged operation?

present, even if all human power had been combined for extending instead of extinguishing the gospel. The diffusion of knowledge was then extremely difficult—the art of printing was then unknown—and many countries which the gospel has now reached, were then undiscovered. And,—multiplied as books now are, more than at any former period of the history of man—extensive as the range of commerce is, beyond what Tyre, or Carthage, or Rome could have ever boasted,—the dissemination of the Scriptures surpasses both the one and the other :—they have penetrated regions unknown to any work of human genius, and untouched even by the ardour of commercial speculation ; and, with the prescription of more than seventeen centuries in its favour, the prophecy of the poor prisoner of Patmos is now exemplified, and thus proved to be more than a mortal vision, in the unexampled communication of the everlasting gospel unto them that dwell on the earth, to every nation, and kindred, and tongue, and people. Christianity is professed over Europe and America. Christians are settled throughout every part of the earth. The gospel is now translated into one hundred and fifty languages and dialects, which are prevalent in countries from the one extremity of the world to the other : And what other book, since the creation, has ever been read or known in a tenth part of the number ? Whatever may be the secondary causes by which these events have been accomplished, or whatever may be the opinion of men respecting them, the predictions which they amply verify must have originated by inspiration from Him who is the first Great Cause. What divine warrant, equal to this alone, can all the speculations of infidelity supply, or can any freethinker produce, for disbelieving the gospel ?

It is apparent, on a general view of the prophecies

which refer to Christ and to the Christian religion, that they include predictions relative to many of the doctrines of the gospel which are subjects of pure revelation, or which reason of itself could never have discovered; and these very doctrines, to which the self-sufficiency of human wisdom is often averse to yield assent, are thus to be numbered, in this respect, among the criterions of the truth of divine Revelation; for if these doctrines had not been contained in Scripture, the prophecies respecting them could not have been fulfilled. And the more wonderful they appear, they were by so much the more unlikely or inconceivable to have been foretold by man, and to have been afterwards embodied in a system of religion.

It is also evident that there are many prophecies applicable to Jesus, to which no allusion is made in the history of his life. The minds of his disciples were long impressed with the prejudices, arising from the lowliness of his mortal state, which were prevalent among the Jews; and they viewed the prophecies through the mist of those traditions which had magnified the earthly power to which alone they looked, and obscured the divine nature of the expected reign of the Messiah. It was only after the resurrection of Christ, as the Scripture informs us, that their understandings were opened to know the prophecies. But while the accomplishment of many of these predictions is thus unnoticed in the New Testament, the fulfilment of each and all of them is written, as with a pen of iron, in the life and doctrine and death of Jesus;—and the undesigned and unsuspicious proof, thus indirectly but amply given, is now stronger than if an appeal had been made to the prophecies in every instance;—and, freed from the prejudices of the Jews, we may now combine and compare all the antecedent prophecies respecting the Messiah with the narrative of the New Testament, and with the nature and history of Christianity ; and, having seen how the former is a transcript of the latter, we may draw the legitimate conclusion—that the spirit of prophecy is indeed the testimony of Jesus.

And may it not, on a review of the whole, be warrantably asserted, that the time and the place of the birth of Christ—the tribe and the family from which he was descended, the manner of his life, his character, his miracles, his sufferings and his death, the nature of his doctrine ;—and the fate of his religion, that it was to proceed from Jerusalem, that the Jews would reject it, that it would be opposed and persecuted at first, that it would be extended to the Gentiles, that idolatry would give way before it, that kings would submit to its authority, and that it would be spread throughout many nations, even to the most distant parts of the earth—were all of them subjects of ancient prophecy ?

Why, then, were so many prophecies delivered ? Why, from the calling of Abraham to the present time, have the Jews been separated, as a peculiar people, from all the nations of the earth ? Why, from the age of Moses to that of Malachi, during the space of one thousand years, did a succession of prophets arise all testifying of a Saviour that was to come ? Why was the book of prophecy sealed for nearly four hundred years before the coming of Christ ? Why is there still, to this day, undisputed if not miraculous evidence of the antiquity of all these prophecies, by their being sacredly preserved in every age, in the custody and guardianship of the enemies of Christianity ? Why was such a multiplicity of facts predicted that are applicable to Christ and to him alone ? Why, but that all this mighty preparation might usher in the gospel of Righteousness ; and that, like all the works of the Almighty, his

D

word through Jesus Christ might never be left without a witness of his wisdom and his power. And if the prophecies which testify of the gospel and of its Author, display, from the slight glance which has here been given of them, any traces of the finger of God, how strong must be the conviction which a full view of them imparts to the minds of those who diligently search the Scriptures, and see how clearly they testify of Christ.

CHAPTER III.

PROPHECIES CONCERNING THE DESTRUCTION OF JERUSALEM.

THE commonwealth of Israel, from its establishment to its dissolution, subsisted for more than fifteen hundred years. In delivering their law, Moses assumed more than the authority of a human legislator, and asserted that he was invested with a divine commission ; and in enjoining obedience to it, after having conducted them to the borders of Canaan, he promises many blessings to accompany their compliance with the law, and denounces grievous judgments that would overtake them for the breach of it. The history of the Jews, in each succeeding age, attests the truth of the last prophetic warning of the first of their rulers ; but too lengthened a detail would be requisite for its elucidation. Happily, it contains predictions, applicable to more recent events, which admit not of any ambiguous interpretation, and refer to historical facts that admit no cavil. He who founded their government, foretold, notwithstanding the intervention of so many ages, the manner of its overthrow. While they were wandering in the wilderness, without a city, and without a home, he threatened them with the destruction of their cities, and the devastation of their country. While they viewed, for the first time, the land of Palestine, and when victorious and triumphant they were about to possess it, he represented the scene of desolation that it would exhibit to their vanquished and enslaved posterity, on their last departure from it. Ere they themselves had entered it as enemies, he describes those enemies by whom their descendants were to be subjugated and dispossessed, though they were to arise from a very distant region, and although they did not appear till after a millenary and a half of years :—" The Lord shall bring a nation against thee from far—from the end of the earth—as swift as the eagle flieth—a nation whose tongue thou shalt not understand,—a nation of fierce countenance, which shall not regard the person of the old, nor show favour to the young. And he shall eat the fruit of thy cattle, and the fruit of thy land, until thou be destroyed : which also shall not leave thee either corn, wine or oil, or the increase of thy kine or flocks of thy sheep, until he have destroyed thee ; and they shall besiege thee in all thy gates, until thy high fenced walls come down wherein thou trustest, throughout all thy land."* Each particular of this prophecy, though it be only introductory to others, has met its full completion. The remote situation of the Romans—the rapidity of their march—the very emblem of their arms—their unknown language, and warlike appearance—the indiscriminate cruelty, and unsparing pillage which they exercised towards the persons and the property of the Jews, could scarcely have been represented in more descriptive

* Deut. xxviii. 49, &c.

terms. Vespasian, Adrian, and Julius Severus, removed with part of their armies from Britain to Palestine—the extreme points of the Roman world. The
eagle was the standard of their armies—and the utmost activity and expedition were displayed in the
reduction of Judea. They were a nation of fierce
countenance—a race distinct from the effeminate Asiatic troops. At Gadara and Gamala—throughout many
parts of the Roman Empire, and, in repeated instances, at Jerusalem itself—the slaughter of the Jews
was indiscriminate, without distinction of age or sex.
The inhabitants were enslaved and banished,—all
their possessions confiscated—and the kingdom of
Israel, humbled at first into a province of the Roman empire, became at last the private property of
the Emperor. Throughout all the land of Judea every
city was besieged and taken—and their high and fenced
walls were razed from the foundation. But the prophet particularizes incidents the most shocking to humanity, which mark the utmost possible extremity of
want and wretchedness—the last act to which famine
could prompt despair—and the last subject of a prediction, that could have been uttered by man :—"And
thou shalt eat the fruit of thine own body—the flesh of
thy sons and of thy daughters, in the siege and in
the straitness wherewith thine enemies shall distress
thee—so that the man that is tender among you, and
very delicate, his eye shall be evil towards his brother,
and toward the wife of his bosom, and toward the remnant of his children which he shall leave—so that he
will not give to any of them of the flesh of his children,
whom he shall eat, because he hath nothing left him
in the siege and in the straitness wherewith thine enemies shall distress thee in all thy gates. The tender
and delicate woman among you, which would not ad-
venture to set the sole of her foot upon the ground for
delicateness and tenderness, her eye shall be evil to-

wards the husband of her bosom, and towards her son, and towards her daughter, and towards her young one, and towards her children, which she shall bear—for she shall eat them for want of all things, secretly, in the siege and straitness wherewith thine enemy shall distress thee in thy gates."* Six hundred years posterior to this prediction, when Samaria, then the capital of Israel, was besieged by all the host of the king of Syria, the most loathsome substitute for food was of great price,—and an ass's head was sold for eighty pieces of silver.† When Nebuchadnezzar besieged Jerusalem, the famine prevailed in the city, and there was no bread for the people of the land. And Josephus relates the direful calamities of the Jews in their last siege, before they ceased to have a city. The famine was too powerful for all other passions,—for what was otherwise reverenced was in this case despised. Children snatched the food out of the very mouths of their fathers ; and even mothers, overcoming the tenderest feelings of nature, took from their perishing infants the last morsels that could sustain their lives. In every house where there was the least shadow of food, a contest arose ; and the nearest relatives struggled with each other for the miserable means of subsistence.‡ He adds a most revolting detail. While, in all these cases, the eye of man was thus evil towards his brother, in the siege and in the straitness wherewith their enemies distressed them,—the unparalleled inhuman compact between the two women of Samaria ; the bitter lamentation of Jeremiah over the miseries of the siege which he witnessed, " The hands of the pitiful women have sodden their own children—they were their meat in the destruction of the daughter of my people ;" and the harrowing recital, by Josephus, of the noble lady killing,

---

* Deut. xxviii. 53, &c.   † 2 Kings vi. 4.
‡ Joseph de Bello, l. 6, 3, § 4.

with her own hands, and eating, secretly, her own suckling, (the discovery of which struck even the whole suffering city with horror,) which are all recorded as facts, without the least allusion to the prediction,—too faithfully realize, to the very letter, the dread denunciations of the prophet. When any well-authenticated facts, of so singular and appalling a nature, were predicted for ages, they could not possibly have been revealed but by inspiration from that omniscience which alone can foresee the termination of the iniquities of nations.

Moses, and the other prophets, foretold also that the Jews would be left few in number—that they would be slain before their enemies—that the pride of their power would be broken—that their cities would be laid waste—that they would be destroyed and brought to nought—plucked from off the land—sold for slaves —and that none would buy them—that their high places were to be desolate—and their bones to be scattered around their altars—that Jerusalem was to be encamped round about—to be besieged with a mount—to have forts raised against it—to be ploughed over as a field, and to become heaps;—that the end was to come upon it, and that the Lord would judge them according to their ways, and recompense them for all their abominations; the sword without and the pestilence and the famine within;—" he that is in the field shall die with the sword, and he that is in the city, famine and pestilence shall devour him."*

These predictions relative to the siege and destruction of Jerusalem, which are recorded in the Pentateuch, and in the subsequent prophecies, accord with the minute prophetic narrative which Jesus gave of

* Lev. xxvi. 30, &c.   Deut. xxviii. 62, &c.   Isa. xxix. 3. Ezek. vi. 5. Micah iii. 12. Jer. xxvi. 18. Ezek. vii. 7—9—15.

the same sad event.   Any adequate delineation of it alone would far surpass the limits of this treatise. But the subject has been fully and frequently illustrated, and the prediction harmonizes so completely with the unimpeachable testimony of impartial historians, that it is merely necessary, for the elucidation of its truth, to compare the prophetic description with the historical facts.

Besides frequent allusions, in his discourses and parables,* the predictions of Christ, concerning Jerusalem, are recorded at length by three of the Evangelists.   They are omitted by the Apostle John, in whose writings alone, from the age to which he lived, their insertion would have been suspicious.   They were delivered to the disciples of Christ in answer to those direct questions which they put, in their surprise and alarm, at his declaration of the fate of the temple, " When shall these things be ? What shall be the sign of them, and of the end of the world ?" The reply embraces all the subjects of the query, and is equally circumstantial and distinct.   The death of Christ happened thirty-seven years previous to the destruction of Jerusalem.   By the unanimous testimony of antiquity, the three gospels were published, and at least two of the Evangelists were dead, several years before that event.   Copies of the gospels were disseminated so extensively and rapidly, that any deceit must have been instantaneously detected by the powerful and numerous, and watchful enemies of the cross.   And the evidence of the prior publicity of the gospels was so strong, that it remained unchallenged by Julian, by Porphyry, or by Celsus.   The authenticity of the prophecy thus rests on sure grounds, and the facts in which it received its accom-

* Matt. xxi. 18, 19—33; xxii. 1—7; xxv. 14—30. Mark xi. 12, 13—20, &c. Luke xiii. 6—9 ; xiv. 17—24; xx. 9—19; xxiii. 27—31.

plishment are incontestable. Josephus was one of
the most distinguished generals in the commencement
of the Jewish war ; he was an eye-witness of the facts
which he records ; he appeals to Vespasian and to
Titus for the truth of his history ; it received the singular attestation of the subscription of the latter to its
accuracy ; it was published while the facts were recent
and notorious ; and the extreme carefulness with
which he avoids the mention of the name of Christ,
in the history of the Jewish war, is not less remarkable than the great precision with which he describes
the events that verify his predictions.   Not a few of
the transactions are also related by Tacitus, Philostratus, and Dion Cassius.

The different prophecies of Christ respecting Jerusalem may be condensed into a single view.

" And Jesus went out and departed from the temple ; and his disciples came to him for to show him
the buildings of the temple.*   And Jesus said unto
them, See ye not all these things : verily I say unto
you, there shall not be left here one stone upon another
that shall not be thrown down.   And as he sat upon
the Mount of Olives, the disciples came unto him
privately, saying—Tell us when shall these things
be : and what shall be the sign of thy coming, and
of the end of the world ? And Jesus answered and said
unto them, Take heed that no man deceive you ; for
many shall come in my name, saying, I am Christ,
and shall deceive many.   And the time draws near ;
and ye shall hear of wars, and rumours of wars,
—or commotions : these things must first come to
pass, but the end is not yet. Nation shall rise against
nation, and kingdom against kingdom, and great
earthquakes shall be in divers places, and famines
and pestilences, and fearful sights, and great signs

* Matt. xxiv.   Mark xiii.   Luke xxi.

shall there be from heaven. All these things are the beginning of sorrows. But, before all these things, shall they lay their hands upon you, and persecute you, delivering you up to the synagogues and into prisons, being brought before kings and rulers for my name's sake. And many shall be offended. Ye shall be betrayed both by parents and brethren, and kinsfolk and friends; and some of you shall they cause to be put to death, and ye shall be hated of all men for my name's sake. But there shall not a hair of your head perish. And many false prophets will arise and will deceive many; and, because iniquity shall abound, the love of many shall wax cold. And the gospel must first be published among all nations, and then shall the end come. When ye, therefore, shall see Jerusalem encompassed with armies, and the abomination of desolation stand in the holy place, and where it ought not, then let them which are in Judea flee to the mountains, and let him which is in the midst of it depart out. Let him which is on the house-top not go down into the house, neither enter therein to take any thing out of his house. Neither let him that is in the field turn back again for to take up his garment, for these are the days of vengeance. But woe unto them that are with child, and to them that give suck in those days; for there will be great distress in the land, and wrath upon this people—and they shall fall by the edge of the sword, and shall be led captive into all nations. There shall be great tribulation, such as was not from the beginning of the world to this time—no, nor ever shall be—and Jerusalem shall be trodden down of the Gentiles, until the time of the Gentiles be fulfilled. This generation shall not pass away till all these things be done.

"Woe unto you, scribes and Pharisees—fill ye up the measure of your fathers. Behold I send unto you prophets, and wise men, and scribes, and some of them ye will scourge in your synagogues, and persecute from city to city. All these things shall be done in this generation. O Jerusalem, Jerusalem, thou that killest the prophets, and stonest them that are sent unto thee, how often would I have gathered thy children together, even as a hen gathereth her chickens under her wings, and ye would not. Behold your house is left unto you desolate; for I say unto you, Ye shall not see me henceforth till ye shall say, Blessed is he that cometh in the name of the Lord.*

"When he came near, he beheld the city, and wept over it, saying, If thou hadst known, even thou, at least in this thy day, the things which belong to thy peace; but now they are hid from thine eyes.† For the days shall come upon thee, that thine enemies shall cast a trench about thee, and compass thee round, and keep thee in on every side, and shall lay thee even with the ground, and thy children within thee; and they shall not leave in thee one stone upon another, because thou knewest not the time of thy visitation."

These prophecies from the Old Testament and from the New, repel the charge of ambiguity. They are equally copious and clear. History attests the truth of each and all of them; and a recapitulation of them forms an enumeration of the facts. *False Christs appeared.* Simon Magus boasted that he was some great one.—Dositheus, the Samaritan, pretended that he was the lawgiver prophesied of by Moses.—Theudas, promising the performance of a miracle, persuaded a great multitude to follow him to Jordan, and deceived many.‡ The country was filled with impostors and deceivers, who induced the people to fol-

---

* Matt. xxiii. 34.   † Luke xix. 41.
‡ Joseph. Ant. xx. 5, 1; Jos. xx. 7, 5.

low them into the wilderness ;—their credulity became the punishment of their previous scepticism, and, in one instance, the tumult was so great that the soldiers took two hundred prisoners, and slew twice that number. *There were wars and rumours of wars ; nation rose against nation, and kingdom against kingdom.* The Jews resisted the erection of the statue of Caligula in the temple ; and, such was the dread of Roman resentment, that the fields remained uncultivated.* At Cæsarea, the Jews and the Syrians contended for the mastery of the city. Twenty thousand of the former were put to death, and the rest were expelled. Every city in Syria was then divided into two armies, and multitudes were slaughtered. Alexandria and Damascus presented a similar scene of bloodshed. About fifty thousand of the Jews fell in the former, and ten thousand in the latter.† The Jewish nation rebelled against the Romans ; Italy was convulsed with contentions for the empire ; and, as a proof of the troubles and warlike character of the period, within the brief space of two years, four emperors, Nero, Galba, Otho, and Vitellius, suffered death. *There were famines, pestilences, and earthquakes in divers places.* In the reign of Claudius Cæsar there were different famines. They continued to be severe for several years throughout the land of Judea. Pestilence succeeded them. In the same reign there were earthquakes at Rome, at Apamea, and at Crete. In that of Nero there was an earthquake in Campania, and another in which Laodicea, Hierapolis, and Colosse were overthrown, and others are recorded to have happened in various places, before the destruction of the city of Jerusalem.‡   " The

* Joseph. *de Bell.* l. ii. 18. 1, 2.
† Joseph. ib. ii. c. 13 ; c. 18. 1, 2, 7, 8.
‡ Suet. *Vit. Clau.* 18. Tac. Ann. l. 12, c. 43, l. 14, c. 27. Jos. iv. 6.   Tac. l. xiv. 27 ; xii. 43, 58.

constitution of nature," says the Jewish historian,* " was confounded for the destruction of men, and one might easily conjecture that no common calamities were portended." *And there were fearful sights and signs from heaven.* Tacitus and Josephus agree in relating and in describing events so surprising and supernatural, that their narrative perfectly accords with the previous prediction.† And the fact cannot be disputed, that, whatever these sights were, the minds of men were impressed with the idea that they were indeed signs from heaven : And even this could never have been foreseen by man. There is surely something at least unaccountable in their prediction and in their relation by historians, unprejudiced and unfriendly to the cause which their testimony supports. *The disciples of Jesus were persecuted, imprisoned, afflicted, and hated of all nations, for his name's sake, and many of them were put to death.* Peter, Simeon, and Jude were crucified.‡ Paul was beheaded; Matthew, Thomas, James, Matthias, Mark, and Luke were put to death in different countries, and in various manners. There was a war against the very name. They were accused of hatred to the human race. The prejudices and the interest of the supporters of paganism were everywhere against them ; and, in one memorable instance, Nero, to screen himself from the guilt of being the incendiary of his capital, accused the innocent but hated Christians of that atrocious deed, and inflicted upon them the most ex-

---

* Jos. iv. 4.

† Evenerant prodigia, quæ neque hostiis, neque votis piare fas habet gens superstitioni obnoxia religionibus adversa. Visæ per cœlum concurrere acies, rutilantia arma, et subito nubium igne collucere templum. Expassæ repente delubri fores et audita major humana vox *excedere deos;* simul ingens motus excedentium. Tacit. Hist. l. 5, c. 13.

‡ Cave's *Lives of the Ap.* Dupin.

cruciating tortures.* He made their sufferings a spectacle and a sport to the Romans. To compensate for
his disappointment in not trampling on the ashes of
Rome, as well as to cloak his iniquity, the monster
(for the man and the monarch were both laid aside,)
gratified his savage lust of cruelty, by the substitution
of one feast for another; he selected the Christians for
his victims, from the general odium under which they
lay—and their very name became the warrant for
that selection, and sufficed to sanction the infliction,
of unheard of barbarities. *Many shall be offended,
and shall betray one another; and the love of many
shall wax cold.* The apostle of the Gentiles often
complained of false brethren, that many turned away
from him, and that he stood alone, forsaken by all,
when he first appeared before Nero. And Tacitus
testifies that very many were convicted, on the evidence of others who had previously been accused.
But the gospel was published throughout the world, in
defiance of all peril and persecution. In the age of the
apostles, epistles were addressed to Christians at Rome,
Corinth, Ephesus, Philippi, Colosse, Thessalonica, and
in Pontus, Galatia, Cappadocia, Asia, and Bithynia.
After Christ delivered this prophecy, he was in a little
time forsaken by all his disciples, and put to death as
a criminal. At their first assembly, they were a little
flock, the number of the names together were about a
hundred and twenty. And, unpromising as the
prospect was, a few fishermen of Galilee, aided afterwards by a tent-maker of Tarsus, circumscribed not
their labours, in the preaching of the gospel, by the
boundaries of the Roman empire. Could the reception or the fate of Christ himself have warranted such
a conclusion? Did ever any cause triumph by such
means? or was ever any cause opposed like his?

* Tac. Ann. l. xv. c. 44.

And could any thing be more unlikely to have been clearly foreseen and positively affirmed? All these events preceded the destruction of Jerusalem, and then the end of that city was at hand. The signs of its approaching ruin are given as a warning to depart from it. *Jerusalem was encompassed with armies.* The Roman armies, with their idolatrous ensigns, which were an abomination to the Jews, surrounded it —but instead of being a signal for flight, this would naturally have implied the impossibility of escape, and the warning would have been in vain. Yet the words of Jesus did not deceive his disciples. Cestius Gallus, the Roman general, besieged Jerusalem; but, immediately after, contrary to all human probability, an interval was given for escape. He suddenly and causelessly retreated, though some of the chief men of the city had offered to open to him the gates. Josephus acknowledges that the utmost consternation prevailed among the besieged, and that the city would infallibly have been taken.* And he attributes it to the just vengeance of God, that the city and the sanctuary were not then taken, and the war terminated at once. He relates also, how many of the most illustrious inhabitants departed from the city, as from a sinking vessel; and how, upon the approach of Vespasian afterwards, multitudes fled from Jericho into the mountainous country. Thither, and to the city of Pella, fled all the disciples of Jesus, as credible historians assert.† And, amidst all the succeeding calamities, *not a hair of their heads did perish.*

There shall be great tribulation, such as was not from the beginning of the world to this time—no, nor ever shall be. There shall be great distress in the

---

* Joseph, l. 2, c. 19, 20.
† *Epiphanius in Heres. Nazar.* c. 7. *Eusebii Ec. His.* lib. iii. c. 5.

land, and wrath upon this people. These are the days of vengeance. Such are some of the words of Jesus, relative to the destruction of Jerusalem; and all the previous prophecies regarding it were of the same sad import. The particulars of the siege are all related by Josephus, and form a detail of miseries that admit not of exaggeration; and which he repeatedly declares, in terms that entirely accord with the language of prophecy, are altogether unequalled in the history of the world.—No general description can give a just idea of calamities the most terrible that ever nation suffered. The Jews had assembled in their city from all the surrounding country, to keep the feast of unleavened bread. It was crowded with inhabitants when they were all imprisoned within its walls. The passover, which was commemorative of their first great deliverance, had collected them for their last signal destruction. Before any external enemy appeared, the fiercest dissensions prevailed—the blood of thousands was shed by their brethren; they destroyed and burned in their frenzy their common provisions for the siege; they were destitute of any regular government, and divided into three factions. On the extirpation of one of these, each of the others contended for the mastery. The most ferocious and frantic,—the robbers or zealots, as they are indiscriminately called, prevailed at last. They entered the temple, under the pretence of offering sacrifices, and carried concealed weapons for the purpose of assassination. They slew the priests at the very altar; and their blood, instead of that of the victims for sacrifice, flowed around it. They afterwards rejected all terms of peace with the enemy: None were suffered to escape from the city—every house was entered—every article of subsistence was pillaged—and the most wanton barbarities were committed. Nothing could restrain their fury; wherever there was the ap-

pearance or scent of food, the human bloodhounds
tracked it out ; and, though a general famine raged
around ; though they were ever trampling on the
dead ; and though the habitations for the living were
converted into charnel-houses, nothing could intimi-
date, or appal, or satisfy, or shock them, till Mary,
the daughter of Eleazar, a lady once rich and noble,
displayed to them and offered them all her remaining
food, the scent of which had attracted them in their
search—the bitterest morsel that ever mother or mortal tasted—the remnant of her half-eaten suckling.
Sixty thousand Roman soldiers unremittingly besieged them ; they encompassed Jerusalem with a
wall, and hemmed them in on every side ; they
brought down their high and fenced walls to the
ground ; they slaughtered the slaughterers, they
spared not the people ; they burned the temple in defiance of the commands, the threats and the resistance
of their general. With it the last hope of all the
Jews was extinguished. They raised, at the sight, an
universal, but an expiring cry of sorrow and despair.
Ten thousand were there slain, and six thousand victims were enveloped in its blaze. The whole city,
full of the famished dying, and of the murdered dead,
presented no picture but that of despair—no scene
but of horror. The aqueducts and the city sewers
were crowded as the last refuge of the hopeless. Two
thousand were found dead there, and many were
dragged from thence and slain. The Roman soldiers
put all indiscriminately to death, and ceased not till
they became faint and weary and overpowered with
the work of destruction. But they only sheathed the
sword to light the torch. They set fire to the city in
various places. The flames spread everywhere, and
were checked but for a moment by the red streamlets
in every street. Jerusalem became heaps, and the
Mountain of the house as the high places of the

forest. Within the circuit of eight miles, in the space of five months—foes and famine, pillage and pestilence, within—a triple wall around, and besieged every moment from without—eleven hundred thousand human beings perished—though the tale of each of them was a tragedy. Was there ever so concentrated a mass of misery? Could any prophecy be more faithfully and awfully fulfilled? The prospect of his own crucifixion, when Jesus was on his way to Calvary, was not more clearly before him, and seemed to affect him less, than the fate of Jerusalem. How full of tenderness, and fraught with truth, was the sympathetic response of the condoling sufferer, to the wailings and lamentations of the women who followed him, when he turned unto them, and beheld the city, which some of them might yet see wrapt in flames and drenched in blood, and said : "Daughters of Jerusalem, weep not for me, but weep for yourselves and for your children. For behold, the days are coming, in the which they will say—Blessed are the barren, and the womb that never bare, and the paps which never gave suck. Then shall they begin to say to the mountains, fall on us ; and to the hills, cover us. For if they do these things in the green tree, what shall be done in the dry?" No impostor ever betrayed such feelings as a man, nor predicted events so unlikely, astonishing, and true, as an attestation of a divine commission. Jesus revealed the very judgments of God ; for such the instrument, by whom it was accomplished, interpreted the capture and destruction of Jerusalem, acknowledging that his own power would otherwise have been ineffectual. When eulogized for the victory, Titus disclaimed the praise, affirming that he was only the instrument of executing the sentence of the divine justice. And their own historian asserts, in conformity with every declaration of Scripture upon the subject, that the iniquities of the Jews were as unparalleled as their punishment.

All these prophecies, of which we have been reviewing the accomplishment, were delivered in a time of perfect peace, when the Jews retained their own laws, and enjoyed the protection, as they were subject to the authority, of the Roman empire, then in the zenith of its power. The wonder excited in the minds of his disciples at the strength and stability of the temple, drew forth from Jesus the announcement of its speedy and utter ruin. He foretold the appearance of false Christs and pretended prophets ; the wars and rumours of wars ; the famines and pestilences and earthquakes and fearful sights that were to ensue ; the persecution of his disciples ; the apostacy of many ; the propagation of the gospel ; the sign that should warn his disciples to fly from approaching ruin ; the encompassing and enclosing of Jerusalem ; the grievous affliction of the tender sex ; the unequalled miseries of all ; the entire destruction of the city ; the shortening of their sufferings, that still some might be saved ; and that all this dread crowd of events, which might well have occupied the progress of ages, was to pass away within the limits of a single generation. None but He who discerns futurity could have foretold and described all these things : and their complete and literal fulfilment shows them to be indubitably the revelation of God.

But the prophecies also mark minuter facts, if possible more unlikely to have happened. Jerusalem was to be ploughed over as a field ; to be laid even with the ground ; of the temple one stone was not to be left upon another ; the Jews were to be few in number ; to be led captive into all nations ; to be sold for slaves and none would buy them. And each of these predictions was strictly verified. Titus commanded the whole city and temple to be razed from the foundation. The soldiers were not then disobedient to their general. Avarice combined with duty and with resentment : The altar, the temple, the walls, and the city, were overthrown from the base, in search of the treasures which the Jews, beset on every hand by plunderers, had concealed and buried during the siege. Three towers and the remnant of a wall alone stood ; the monument and memorial of Jerusalem ; and the city was afterwards ploughed over by Terentius Rufus. In the siege, and in the previous and subsequent destruction of the cities and villages of Judea, according to the specified enumeration of Josephus, about one million three hundred thousand suffered death. Ninety-seven thousand were led into captivity. They were sold for slaves, and were so despised and disesteemed, that many remained unpurchased. And their conquerors were so prodigal of their lives, that, in honour of the birthday of Domitian, two thousand five hundred of them were placed, in savage sport, to contend with wild beasts, and otherwise to be put to death.*

* Tacitus, who flourished about thirty years after the destruction of Jerusalem, speaks of the strength of the fortifications of that city, the immense riches and strength of the emple, the factions that raged during the siege, as well as of he prodigies that preceded its fall. And he particularly mentions the large army brought by Vespasian to subdue Judea, " a fact which shows the magnitude and importance of the expedition." Philostratus particularly relates that Titus declared, after the capture of Jerusalem, that he was not worthy of the crown of victory, as he had only lent his hand to the execution of a work in which God was pleased to manifest his anger. Dion Cassius records the conquest of Judea by Titus and Vespasian, the obstinate and bloody resistance of the Jews during the siege, the destruction of the temple by fire. It is recorded by Maimonides, and in the Jewish Talmud, (as cited by Basnage and Lardner,) that Terentius Rufus, an officer in the Roman army, tore up with a ploughshare the foundations of the temple. The

But the miseries of their race were not then at a close. There was a curse on the land, that hath scathed it, a judgment on the people that hath scattered them throughout the world. Many prophecies respecting them yet remain to be considered, and much of their history is yet untold. The prophecies are as clear as the facts are visible.

CHAPTER IV.

PROPHECIES CONCERNING THE JEWS.

WHILE Moses, as a divine legislator, promised to the Israelites that their prosperity, and happiness, and peace, would all keep pace with their obedience, he threatened them with a gradation of punishments, rising in proportion to their impenitence and iniquity; and neither in blessings nor in chastisements hath the Ruler among the Nations dealt in like manner with any people. But their wickedness, and consequent calamities, greatly preponderated, and are yet prolonged. The retrospect of the history of the Jews, since their dispersion, could not, at the present day, be drawn in truer terms, than in the unpropitious auguries of their prophet above three thousand two hundred years ago. In the most an-

triumphal arch of Titus, commemorative of the destruction of Jerusalem, and with figures of Roman soldiers, bearing on their shoulders the holy vessels of the temple, is still to be seen at Rome.

cient of all records, we read the lively representation
of the present condition of the most singular people
upon earth. Moses professed to look through the
glass of ages : The revolution of many centuries has
brought the object immediately before us—we may
scrutinize the features of futurity as they then appeared to his prophetic gaze,—and we may determine
between the probabilities whether they were conjectures of a mortal, who " knows not what a day may
bring forth," or the revelation of that Being, " in
whose sight a thousand years are but as yesterday."

" I will scatter you among the heathen, and draw
out a sword after you,—and your land shall be desolate, and your cities waste ; and upon them that are
left of you I will send a faintness into their hearts, in
the land of their enemies ; and the sound of a shaken
leaf shall chase them—and they shall flee as fleeing
from a sword—and they shall fall when none pursueth
—and ye shall have no power to stand before your
enemies—and ye shall perish among the heathen ;—
and the land of your enemies shall eat you up—and
they that are left of you shall pine away in their iniquity in your enemies' land ; and also in the iniquities of their fathers, shall they pine away with them,
—and yet for all that, when they be in the land of
their enemies, I will not cast them away, neither will
I abhor them to destroy them utterly.* And the
Lord shall scatter you among the nations, and ye
shall be left few in number among the heathen whither the Lord will lead you.† The Lord shall cause
thee to be smitten before thine enemies—thou shalt
go out one way against them, and flee seven ways before them—and shalt be removed into all the kingdoms of the earth.‡ The Lord shall smite thee with

---

* Lev. xxvi. 33, 36, 37, 38, 39, 44.   † Deut. v. 27.
‡ Deut. xxviii. 25, 28, 29, 32, 33, 34, 37—45, 46.

madness, and blindness, and astonishment of heart,—
and thou shalt grope at noon-day as the blind gropeth
in darkness, and thou shalt not prosper in thy ways,
and thou shalt be only oppressed and spoiled evermore, and no man shall save thee. Thy sons and
thy daughters shall be given to another people.
There shall be no might in thine hand. The fruit of
thy land and all thy labour shall a nation, which thou
knowest not, eat up, and thou shalt be only oppressed
and crushed alway—so that thou shalt be mad for the
sight of thine eyes which thou shalt see. The Lord
shall bring thee unto a nation which neither thou nor
thy fathers have known,—and thou shalt become an
astonishment, a proverb, and a by-word among all
the nations whither the Lord shall lead thee. Because thou servedst not the Lord thy God with joy-
fulness and with gladness of heart for the abundance
of all things, therefore shalt thou serve thine enemies
which the Lord shall send against thee, in hunger
and in thirst—and in nakedness, and in want of all
things—and he shall put a yoke of iron upon thy
neck, until he have destroyed thee.—And the Lord
will make thy plagues wonderful, and the plague of
thy seed, even great plagues and of long continuance.*
All these curses shall come upon thee, and shall pur-
sue thee, and overtake thee, and they shall be upon
thee for a sign and for a wonder, and upon thy seed
for ever—and it shall come to pass, that as the Lord
rejoiced over you to do you good, and to multiply you
—so the Lord will rejoice over you to destroy, and to
bring you to nought, and ye shall be plucked from off
the land whither thou goest to possess it, and the
Lord will scatter thee among all people, from the one
end of the earth even unto the other—and among
these nations shalt thou find no ease, neither shall the

* Deut. xxviii. 47, 48, 59.

sole of thy foot have rest ; but the Lord shall give thee there a trembling heart, and failing of eyes, and sorrow of mind—and thy life shall hang in doubt before thee, and thou shalt fear day and night, and shalt have none assurance of thy life. In the morning, thou shalt say, would God it were even ! and at even thou shalt say, would God it were morning, for the fear of thine heart wherewith thou shalt fear, and for the sight of thine eyes which thou shalt see.*

The writings of all the succeeding prophets abound with similar predictions. " I will cause them to be removed into all nations of the earth. I will cast them out into a land that they know not, where I will show them no favour. I will feed them with wormwood, and give them water of gall to drink.† I will scatter them also among the heathen—whom neither they nor their fathers have known. I will deliver them to be removed into all the kingdoms of the earth for their hurt, to be a reproach, a proverb, a taunt, and a curse in all places whither I shall drive them : and I will send the sword, the famine, and the pestilence among them, till they be consumed from off the land that I gave unto them and to their fathers.‡ I will bereave them of children. I will deliver them to be removed into all the kingdoms of the earth, to be a curse, and an astonishment, and a hissing, and a reproach, even among all the nations whither I have driven them.§ I will execute judgment in thee—and the whole remnant of thee will I scatter into all the winds.|| I will scatter them among the nations, among the heathen, and disperse them in the countries.¶ They shall cast their silver in the streets, and their gold shall be removed—their silver

---

* Deut. xxviii. 63—67.　　† Jer. ix. 16.
‡ Jer. xxiv. 9, 10 ; xv. 7.　　§ Jer. xxix. 18.
|| Ezek. v. 10.　　¶ Ezek. xii. 15.

and their gold shall not be able to deliver them in the day of the wrath of the Lord,—they shall not satisfy their souls, neither fill their bowels, because it is the stumbling-block of their iniquity.* I will sift the house of Israel among the nations, like as corn is sifted in a sieve, yet shall not the least grain fall upon the earth. Death shall be chosen rather than life by all the residue of them that remain of this evil family, which remain in all the places whither I have driven them, saith the Lord of hosts. They shall be wanderers among the nations.† Make the heart of this people fat, and make their ears heavy, and shut their eyes, lest they see with their eyes, and hear with their ears, and convert and be healed. Then said I, Lord, how long? and he answered, until the cities be wasted without inhabitants, and the houses without man, and the land be utterly desolate—and the Lord have removed men far away—and there be a great forsaking in the midst of the land.‡ Though they go into captivity before their enemies, thence will I command the sword, and it shall slay them,—and I will set mine eyes upon them for evil, and not for good. But he that scattereth Israel will gather him and keep him.§ And fear not thou, my servant Jacob, and be not dismayed, O Israel; for behold I will save thee from afar off, and thy seed from the land of their captivity. I will make a full end of all the nations whither I have driven thee; but I will not make a full end of thee, but correct thee in measure; yet will I not utterly cut thee off, or leave thee wholly unpunished.‖ The children of Israel shall abide many days without a king and without a prince, and without a sacrifice, and without an image, and without an ephod, and without

* Ezek. vii. 19.   † Amos ix. 9. Jer. viii. 3. Hos. ix. 17.
‡ Is. vi. 10, 11, 12.   § Jer. xxxi. 16.
‖ Jer. xlvi. 27, 28.

teraphim. Afterward shall the children of Israel return, and seek the Lord their God, and David their king, and shall fear the Lord, and his goodness, in the latter days."*

All these predictions respecting the Jews are delivered with the clearness of history and the confidence of truth. They represent the manner—the extent—the nature—and the continuance of their dispersion—their persecutions—their blindness—their sufferings—their feebleness—their fearfulness—their pusillanimity,—their ceaseless wanderings—their hardened impenitence—their insatiable avarice,—and the grievous oppression—the continued spoliation—the marked distinction—the universal mockery—the unextinguishable existence, and unlimited diffusion of their race. *They were to be plucked from off their own land—smitten before their enemies—consumed from off their own land, and left few in number.* The Romans destroyed their cities and ravaged their country, and the inhabitants who escaped from the famine, the pestilence, the sword, and the captivity, were forcibly expelled from Judea, and fled as houseless wanderers into all the surrounding regions. But they clung, for a time, around the land which their fathers had possessed for so many ages, and on which they looked as an inheritance allotted by heaven to their race; and they would not relinquish their claim to the possession of it by any single overthrow, however great. Unparalleled as were the miseries which they had suffered in the slaughter of their kindred, the loss of their property and their homes, the annihilation of their power, the destruction of their capital city, and in the devastation of their country by Titus —yet the fugitive and exiled Jews soon resorted again to their native soil; and sixty years had scarcely

* Hos. iii. 4, 5.
E

elapsed, when, deceived by an impostor, allured by
the hope of a triumphant Messiah, and excited to
revolt by intolerable oppression, they strove, by a
vigorous and united, but frantic effort, to reconquer
Judea—to cast off the power of the Romans, which
had everywhere crushed them, and to rescue themselves and their country from ruin.   A war,—which
their enthusiasm and desperation alike protracted for
two years, and in which, exclusive of a vast number
that perished by famine and sickness and fire, five
hundred and eighty thousand Jews are said to have
been slain,—terminated in their entire discomfiture
and final banishment.   They were so beset on every
side, and cut down in detached portions by the Roman soldiers, that, in the words of a heathen historian, very few of them escaped.   Fifty of their strongholds were razed from the ground, and their cities
sacked and consumed by fire ; Judea was laid waste
and left as a desert.*   Though a similar fate never
befell any other people without proving the extirpation
of their race or the last of their miseries, that awful
prediction, in its reference to the Jews, met its full
completion—which yet they survive to await, in every
country when exiles from their own, an accumulation
of almost unceasing calamities, protracted throughout many succeeding ages.   *The cities shall be wasted
without inhabitant.   Every city shall be forsaken, and
not a man dwell therein.   They were rooted out of
their land in anger, and in wrath, and in great indignation.*†   A public edict of the emperor Adrian
rendered it a capital crime for a Jew‡ to set a foot in
Jerusalem ; and prohibited them from viewing it even

* Dion. lib. lxix.
† Isaiah vi. 11.   Jer. iv. 29.   Deut. xxix. 28.
‡ Tert. Ap. c. 21, Basnage's *Continuation of Josephus,*
b. vi. § 1.

at a distance. Heathens, Christians, and Mahometans have alternately possessed Judea : It has been
the prey of the Saracens : —the descendants of Ishmael
have often overrun it : The children of Israel have
alone been denied the possession of it, though thither
they ever wish to return—and though it forms the
only spot on earth where the ordinances of their religion can be observed. And, amidst all the revolutions
of states, and the extinction of many nations, in so
long a period, the Jews alone have not only ever been
aliens in the land of their fathers, but whenever any
of them have been permitted, at any period since the
time of their dispersion to sojourn there, they have
experienced even more contumelious treatment than
elsewhere. Benjamin of Tudela, who travelled in
the twelfth century through great part of Europe and
of Asia, found the Jews everywhere oppressed, *particularly in the Holy Land.* And to this day, (while
the Jews who reside in Palestine, or who resort thither
in old age, that their bones may not be laid in a
foreign land, are alike ill treated and abused by
Greeks, Armenians, and Europeans,[*]) the haughty
deportment of the despotic Turkish soldier, and the
abject state of the poor and helpless Jews, are painted
to the life by the prophet. *The stranger that is
within thee shall get up above thee very high, and thou
shalt come down very low.*[†]

But the extent is still more remarkable than the
manner of their dispersion. Many prophecies describe
it, and foretold, thousands of years ago, what we now
behold. *They have been scattered among the nations,
—among the heathen—among the people, even from
one end of the earth unto the other : They have been
removed into all the kingdoms of the earth ; the whole
remnant of them have been scattered into all the winds ;*

---

[*] General Straton's MS. Travels. [†] Deut. xxviii. 43.

they have been dispersed throughout all countries, and sifted among the nations like as corn is sifted in a sieve, and yet not the least grain has fallen upon the earth—though dispersed throughout all nations, they have remained distinct from them all. And there is not a country on the face of the earth where the Jews are unknown. They are found alike in Europe, Asia, America, and Africa. They are citizens of the world without a country. Neither mountains, nor rivers, nor deserts, nor oceans—which are the boundaries of other nations,—have terminated their wanderings. They abound in Poland, in Holland, in Russia and in Turkey. In Germany, Spain, Italy, France, and Britain, they are more thinly scattered. In Persia, China, and India—on the east and on the west of the Ganges,—they are *few in number among the heathen.* They have trode the snows of Siberia, and the sands of the burning desert ;—and the European traveller hears of their existence in regions which he cannot reach—even in the very interior of Africa, south of Timbuctoo.* From Moscow to Lisbon—from Japan to Britain—from Borneo to Archangel—from Hindostan to Honduras, no inhabitant of any nation upon the earth would be known in all the intervening regions but a Jew alone.

But the history of the Jews throughout the whole world, and in every age since their dispersion, verifies the most minute predictions concerning them,—and to a recital of facts too well authenticated to admit of dispute, or too notorious for contradiction, may be added a description of them all in the very terms of the prophecy. In the words of Basnage, the elaborate historian of the Jews—" Kings have often employed the severity of their edicts, and the hands of the executioner, to destroy them—the seditious mul-

* Lyon's Travels in Africa, p. 146.

titude has performed massacres and executions infinitely more tragical than the princes. Both kings
and people, heathens, Christians, and Mahometans,
who are opposite in so many things, have united in
the design of ruining this nation, and have not been
able to effect it. The Bush of Moses, surrounded with
flames, has always burnt without consuming. The
Jews have been driven from all places of the world,
which has only served to disperse them in all parts
of the universe. They have, from age to age, run
through misery and persecution, and torrents of their
own blood."* Their banishment from Judea was
only the prelude to their expulsion from city to city,
and from kingdom to kingdom. Their dispersion
over the globe is an irrefragable evidence of this,
and many records remain that amply corroborate the
fact. Not only did the first and second centuries of
the Christian era see them twice rooted out of their
own land, but each succeeding century has teemed
with new calamities to that once chosen but now long
rejected race. The history of their sufferings is a
continued tale of horror. Revolt is natural to the
oppressed; and their frequent seditions were productive
of renewed privations and distresses. Emperors,
kings, and caliphs all united in subjecting them to
the same " iron yoke." Constantine, after having
suppressed a revolt which they raised, and having
commanded their ears to be cut off, dispersed them
as fugitives and vagabonds into different countries,
whither they carried, in terror to their kindred, the
mark of their suffering and infamy. In the fifth
century they were expelled from Alexandria, which
had long been one of their safest places of resort. Jus-
tinian, from whose principles of legislation a wiser
and more humane policy ought to have emanated,

* Basnage, b. vi. c. 1.

yielded to none of his predecessors in hostility and
severity against them.   He abolished their synagogues—prohibited them even from entering into
caves for the exercise of their worship—rendered their
testimony inadmissible, and deprived them of the
natural right of bequeathing their property : and when
such oppressive enactments led to insurrectionary
movements among the Jews, their property was confiscated, many of them were beheaded, and so bloody
an execution of them prevailed, that, as is expressly
related, " all the Jews of that country trembled ;"*
a trembling heart was given them.   In the reign of
the tyrant Phocas, a general sedition broke out among
the Jews in Syria.   They and their enemies fought
with equal desperation.   They obtained the mastery
in Antioch ; but a momentary victory only led to a
deeper humiliation, and to the infliction of more ag-
gravated cruelties than before.   They were soon subdued and taken captive ; many of them were maimed,
others executed, and all the survivors were banished
from the city.   Gregory the Great afforded them a
temporary respite from oppression, which only rendered their spoliation more complete, and their suffering more acute, under the cruel persecutions of Heraclius.   That emperor, unable to satiate his hatred
against them by inflicting a variety of punishments
on those who resided within his own dominions, and
by finally expelling them from the empire, exerted
so effectually against them his influence in other
countries, that they suffered under a general and sim-
ultaneous persecution from Asia to the farthest extremities of Europe.†   In Spain, conversion, im-
prisonment, or banishment, were their only alterna-
tives.   In France a similar fate awaited them.   They

---

* Basnage's Hist. b. vi. c. 21, sect. 9.
† Ibid. b. vi. c. 21, sect. 17.

fled from country to country, seeking in vain any
rest for the sole of their foot. Even the wide-extend-
ed plains of Asia afforded them no resting-place, but
have often been spotted with their blood, as well as
the hills and vallies of Europe. Mahomet, whose
imposture has been the law and the faith of such
countless millions, has, from the precepts of the Koran, infused into the minds of his followers a spirit of
rancour and enmity towards the despised and misbe-
lieving Jews. He set an early example of persecution against them, which the Mahometans have not
yet ceased to imitate. In the third year of the He-
gira, he besieged the castles which they possessed in
the Hegiasa, compelled those who had fled to them
for refuge and defence to an unconditional surrender,
banished them the country, and parted their property
among his mussulmen. He dissipated a second time
their re-combined strength, massacred many of them,
and imposed upon the remnant a permanent tribute.
The church of Rome ever ranked and treated them
as heretics. The canons of different councils pronounced excommunication against those who should
favour or uphold the Jews against Christians—enjoined all Christians neither to eat nor to hold any
commerce with them—prohibited them from bearing
public offices or having Christian slaves—appointed
them to be distinguished by a mark—decreed that
their children should be taken from them, and brought
up in monasteries ; and what is equally descriptive of
the low estimation in which they were held, and of
the miseries to which they were subjected, there was
often a necessity, even for those who otherwise oppressed them, to ordain that it was not lawful to take
the life of a Jew without any cause.* Hallam's account of the Jews, during the middle ages, is short,

---

* Dupin's Ecc. Hist. Canons of different councils.

but significant. " They were everywhere the objects of popular insult and oppression, frequently of a general massacre. A time of festivity to others was often the season of mockery and persecution to them. It was the custom at Thoulouse to smite them on the face every Easter. At Beziers they were attacked with stones from Palm Sunday to Easter, an anniversary of insult and cruelty generally productive of bloodshed, and to which the populace were regularly instigated by a sermon from the bishop.* It was the policy of the kings of France to employ them as a sponge to suck their subjects' money, which they might afterwards express with less odium than direct taxation would incur. It is almost incredible to what a length extortion of money from the Jews was carried. A series of alternate persecution and tolerance was borne by this extraordinary people with an invincible perseverance and a talent of accumulating riches which kept pace with the exactions of their plunderers. Philip Augustus released all Christians in his dominions from their debts to the Jews, reserving a fifth part to himself. He afterwards expelled the whole nation from France." St. Louis twice banished, and twice recalled them ; and Charles VI. finally expelled them from France. From that country, according to Mezeray, they were seven times banished. They were expelled from Spain ; and, by the lowest computation, one hundred and seventy thousand families departed from that kingdom.† " At Verdun, Treves, Mentz, Spires, Worms, many thousands of them were pillaged and massacred. A remnant was saved by a feigned and transient conversion ; but the greater part of them barricadoed their houses, and precipitated themselves,

* Hallam, v. i. 2, 33, c. ii. p. 2.
† Basnage, b. vii. c. 21.

their families, and their wealth into the rivers or the flames. These massacres and depredations on the Jews were renewed at each crusade."* In England, also, they suffered great cruelty and oppression at the same period. During the crusades, the whole nation united in the persecution of them. In a single instance, at York, fifteen hundred Jews, including women and children, were refused all quarter—could not purchase their lives at any price—and, frantic with despair, perished by a mutual slaughter. Each master was the murderer of his family, when death became their only deliverance. The scene of the castle of Massada, which was their last fortress in Palestine, and when nearly one thousand perished in a similar manner,† was renewed in the castle of York. So despised and hated were they, that the barons, when contending with Henry III., to ingratiate themselves with the populace, ordered seven hundred Jews to be slaughtered at once, their houses to be plundered, and their synagogue to be burned. Richard, John,‡ and Henry III. often extorted money

* Gibbon's Hist. v. vi. p. 17.

† Basnage, b. vii. c. 10, sect. 20; Rapin's Hist. of England, vol. iii. p. 97; Joseph. b. vii. ch. 8.

‡ The persecutions to which the Jews were subjected at that period, are described with strict truth in the historical romance of Ivanhoe. They are characterised as " a race which, during these dark ages, was alike detested by the credulous and prejudiced vulgar, and persecuted by the greedy and rapacious nobility."—(v. i. p. 83.)—" Except perhaps the flying fish, there was no race existing on the earth, in the air, or the waters, who were the objects of such an unremitting, general, and relentless persecution as the Jews of this period. Upon the slightest and most unreasonable pretences, as well as upon accusations the most absurd and groundless, their persons and property were exposed to every turn of popular fury; for Norman, Saxon, Dane, and Briton, however adverse the races were to each other, contended which would look with greatest detestation upon a people whom it was accounted a point of religion to hate, to

from them ; and the last, by the most unscrupulous
and unsparing measures, usually defrayed his extraordinary expenses with their spoils, and impoverished
some of the richest among them.   His extortions at
last became so enormous, and his oppression so grievous, that, in the words of the historian, he reduced
the miserable wretches to desire leave to depart the
kingdom ;* but even self-banishment was denied them.
Edward I. completed their misery, seized on all their
property, and banished them the kingdom.   Above
fifteen thousand Jews were rendered destitute of any
residence, were despoiled to the utmost, and reduced
to ruin.   Nearly four centuries elapsed before the
return to Britain of this abused race.

revile, to despise, to plunder and to persecute.   The kings
of the Norman race, and the independent nobles, who followed their example in all acts of tyranny, maintained against
this devoted people a persecution of a more regular, calculated, and self-interested kind.   It is a well known story of
King John, that he confined a wealthy Jew in one of the
royal castles, and daily caused one of his teeth to be torn
out, until, when the jaw of the unhappy Israelite was half
disfurnished, he consented to pay a large sum, which it was
the tyrant's object to extort from him.   The little ready
money that was in the country was chiefly in the possession
of this persecuted people, and the nobility hesitated not to
follow the example of their sovereign in wringing it from
them by every species of oppression, and even personal tor-
ture." (Pp. 120, 121.)   The fictitious history of Isaac of
York is delineated in a manner equally descriptive of the
facts, and confirmatory of the prophecies respecting the
Jewish people; and there exists not the history of any individual of any other nation, whether drawn from fancy or
from fact, which combines so many of the prophetic characteristics of the fate of a Jew, as that which has thus been
delineated, by a master's hand, as a representation of their
condition, at a period about twenty-six centuries posterior to
the prediction, and in a country two thousand miles remote
from the place where it was first uttered, and from the only
land ever possessed by the Jews.

* Rapin's *Hist. of Eng.* b. viii. vol. iii. p. 405.

Some remarkable circumstances attest, without a prolonged detail of their miseries, that they have been a people everywhere peculiarly oppressed. The first unequivocal attempt at legislation in France was an ordinance against the Jews. And towards them alone one of the noblest charters of liberty on earth—Magna Charta, the Briton's boast—legalized an act of injustice.* For many ages after their dispersion, they found no resting-place in Europe, Africa, or Asia, but penetrated in search of one to the extremities of the world. In Mahometan countries they have ever been subject to persecution, contempt, and every abuse. They are in general confined to one particular quarter of every city (as they formerly were to old Jewry in London;) they are restricted to a peculiar dress; and in many places shut up at stated hours. In Hamadan, as in all parts of Persia, " they are an abject race, and support themselves by driving a peddling trade;—they live in a state of great misery—pay a monthly tax to the government—and are not permitted to cultivate the ground, or to have landed possessions."† They cannot appear in public, much less perform their religious ceremonies, without being treated with scorn and contempt.‡ The revenues of the prince of Bohara are derived from a tribute paid by five hundred families of Jews, who are assessed according to the means of each. In Zante they exist in miserable indigence, and are exposed to considerable oppression.§ At Tripoli, when any criminal is condemned to death, the first Jew who happens to be at hand is compelled to become the executioner,—a degradation to the children of Israel to which no Moor is ever subjected.‖ In Egypt they are despised and

---

* Articles XII. XIII.
† Morier's Travels, p. 379.
‡ Sir J. Malcolm's Hist. of Persia, vol. ii. p. 425.
§ Hugh's Travels, vol. i. p. 150. ‖ Lyon's Travels, p. 16.

persecuted incessantly.* In Arabia they are treated
with more contempt than in Turkey.† The remark
is common to the most recent travellers both in Asia
and Africa,‡ that the Jews themselves are astonished, and the natives indignant, at any act of kindness,
or even of justice, that is performed towards any
of this " despised nation" and persecuted people. In
Southey's Letters from Spain and Portugal, this remarkable testimony is borne respecting them : " Till
within the last fifty years the burning of a Jew formed the highest delight of the Portuguese ; they
thronged to behold this triumph of the faith, and the
very women shouted with transport as they saw the
agonized martyr writhe at the stake. Neither sex
nor age could save this persecuted race ; and Antonio
Joseph de Silvia, the best of their dramatic writers,
was burned alive because he was a Jew."—Few years
have elapsed since there was a severe persecution
against them in Prussia and in Germany, and in several of the smaller states of the latter country they
are not permitted to sell any goods even in the common markets. The Pope has lately re-enacted some
severe edicts against them : and ukases have recently
been issued in quick succession§ restraining the Jews
from all traffic throughout the interior government of
Russia. They are absolutely prohibited, (on pain of
immediate banishment,) from " offering any article
to sale,"‖ whether in public or private, either by
themselves or by others. They are not allowed to

---

* Denon's Travels in Egypt, vol. i. p. 213.
† Niebhur's Travels, vol. i. p. 408.
‡ Morier's Travels in Persia, p. 266. Lyon's Travels in
Africa, p. 32.
§ 15th November 1797. 25th February 1823. 8th June
1826. (August or November) 1827.
‖ Ukase, quoted from " the World," of date 31st October
1827. Ib. Article VIII.

reside, even for a limited period in any of the cities
of Russia, without an express permission from government, which is granted only in cases where
their services are necessary, or directly beneficial to
the state. A refusal to depart when they become
obnoxious to so rigid a law, subjects them to be
treated as vagrants ; and none are suffered to protect or to shelter them. Though the observance of
such edicts must, in numerous instances, leave them
destitute of any means of support, yet their breach or
neglect exposes them to oppression under the sanction
of the law, and to every privation and insult, without
remedy or appeal. And though they may thus become the greatest objects of pity, all laws of humanity
are reversed, by imperial decrees towards them. For
those who harbour Jews that are condemned to banishment for having done what all others may innocently do, are, as the last Russian ukase respecting
them bears, " amenable to the laws as the abettors of
vagrants,"* *and*, as in numberless instances besides,
no man shall save them.

* *Note.*—While the prophecies described the past and existing miseries of the Jews, they refer with no less precision
to the time yet to come, when the children of Israel shall
have returned to the loved land of their fathers, and their
rebuke shall have ceased from off the face of the earth, and
when they shall prize their blessings the more highly, as
contrasted with the former sufferings of their race. And
the Word of God, confirmed as its prophetic truth is by the
workings of the wrath of man, and by the policy of earthly
monarchs, will doubtless triumph over the highest mandates
of mortals, and receive new illustrations of its truth, when
these shall have passed away. And the eleventh article of
the ukase, now in force, merits, in reference to a special prediction, particular notice, and may here be subjoined, together with its corresponding text, premising merely that it
is to a specific district of dismembered Poland that the Rab-
bis are sent away, " Rabins, or other religious functionaries,
are to be sent away by the police officer, immediately on the

These facts, though they form but a brief and most imperfect record, and therefore but a very faint image of all their sufferings, show that the Jews *have been removed into all kingdoms for their hurt*—*that a sword has been drawn after them*—*that they have found no rest for the sole of their foot*—*that they have not been able to stand before their enemies ;*—*there has been no might in their hands*—*their very avarice has proved their misery*—*they have been spoiled evermore*—*they have been oppressed and crushed alway*—*they have been mad for the sight of their eyes that they did see*, as the tragical scenes at Massada, and York, and many others testify—*they have often been left in hunger, and thirst, and nakedness, and in want of all things ;*—*a trembling heart and sorrow of mind have been their portion :*—*they have often had none assurance of their life,*—*their plagues have been wonderful and great, and of long continuance,*—*and that they have been for a sign and for a wonder during many generations.*

But the predictions rest not even here. It was distinctly prophesied that the Jews would reject the gospel ; that, from the meanness of his mortal appearance, and the hardness of their hearts, they would not believe in a suffering Messiah,—*that they*

discovery that they are such." "Thy teachers shall not be removed into a corner any more, but thine eyes shall see thy teachers." Isaiah xxx. 20.

Lord Byron's brief and emphatic description of the Jews is equally characteristic of the fact, and illustrative of the predictions.

Tribes of the *wandering foot* and *weary breast,*
When shall we flee away and be at rest ?

"They shall find no rest for the sole of their foot—I will send a faintness into their heart,—a trembling heart and sorrow of mind."

*would be smitten with blindness and astonishment of
heart—that they would continue long, having their
ears deaf, their eyes closed, and their hearts hardened
—and that they would grope at noon-day as the blind
gropeth in darkness.** And the great body of the
Jewish nation has continued long to reject Christianity. They retain the prophecies, but discern not their
light, having obscured them by their traditions.
Many of their received opinions are so absurd and
impious, their rites are so unmeaning and frivolous,
their ceremonies are so minute, frivolous, and con-
temptible,—that the account of them would surpass
credulity, were it not a transcript of their customs
and of their manners, and drawn from their own authorities.† No words can more strikingly or justly
represent the contrast between their irrational tenets
—their degraded religion—their superstitious observances, and the dictates of enlightened reason, and of
the gospel which they vilify, than the emphatic description,—" They grope at noon-day, as the blind
gropeth in darkness." And if any other instances be
wanting of the prediction of events infinitely exceeding human foresight, the dispositions of all nations
respecting them are revealed as explicitly as their
own. That the Jews have been a proverb, an astonishment, a by-word, a taunt, and a hissing among
all nations,—though one of the most wonderful of
facts, unparalleled in the whole history of mankind,
and as inconceivable in its prediction as miraculous
in its accomplishment,—is a truth that stands not
in need of any illustration or proof—and of which
witnesses could be found in every country under
heaven. Many prophecies concerning the Jews, of

* Deut. xxviii. 29.
† See Allen's Modern Judaism. Brewster's Encyclopædia,
Art. Jews.

more propitious import, that yet remain to be accomplished, are reserved for testimonies to future generations, *if not to the present.* But it is worthy of remark, as prophesied concerning them, that they have not been utterly destroyed, though a full end has been made of their enemies,—that the Egyptians, the Assyrians, the Babylonians, the Romans—though some of the mightiest monarchies that ever existed,— have not a single representative on earth ; while the Jews, oppressed and vanquished—banished and enslaved—and spoiled evermore, have survived them all —and to this hour overspread the world. Of all the nations around Judea, the Persians alone, who restored them from the Babylonish captivity, yet remain a kingdom.

The Scriptures also declare that the covenant with Abraham,—that God would give the land of Canaan to his seed for an everlasting possession—would never be broken ; but that the children of Israel shall be taken from among the heathen,—gathered on every side, and brought into their own land, to dwell for ever where their fathers dwelt. Three thousand seven hundred years have elapsed since the promise was given to Abraham : And is it less than a miracle, that, if this promise had been made to the descendants of any but of Abraham alone, it could not now possibly have been realized, as there exists not on earth the known and acknowledged posterity of any other individual, or almost of any nation, contemporary with him ?

That the people of a single state (which was of very limited extent and power in comparison of some of the monarchies which surrounded it) should first have been rooted up out of their own land in anger, wrath, and great indignation, the like of which was never experienced by the mightiest among the ancient empires, which all fell imperceptibly away at a lighter

stroke,—and that afterwards, though scattered among
all nations, and finding no ease among them all, they
should have withstood eighteen centuries of almost
unremitted persecution, and that after so many generations have elapsed, they should still retain their distinctive form, or, as it may be called, their individu-
ality of character, is assuredly the most marvellous
event that is recorded in the history of nations ; and
if it be not acknowledged as a " sign," it is in reality
as well as in appearance, " a wonder," the most inexplicable within the province of the philosophy of
history.   But that, after the endurance of such manifold woes, such perpetual spoliation, and so many
ages of unmitigated suffering, during which their life
was to hang in doubt within them, they should still
be, as actually they are, the possessors of great
wealth ; and that this fact should so strictly accord
with the prophecy, which describes them on their final
restoration to Judea, as taking their silver and their
gold with them ;* and also that, though captives or
fugitives " few in number," and the miserable remnant of an extinguished kingdom at the time they
were " scattered abroad,"—they should be to this hour
a numerous people,—and that this should have been
expressly implied in the prophetic declaration descriptive of their condition on their restoration to Judea,
after all their wanderings—that the land shall be too
narrow by reason of the inhabitants—and that place
shall not be found for them,† are facts which as clearly show, to those who consider them at all, the operation of an overruling providence, as the revelation of
such an inscrutable destiny is the manifest dictate of
inspiration.

Such are the *prophecies*, and such are the *facts* respecting the Jews ;—and from premises like these the

* Isa. lx. 9.   † Isa. lxix. 19.   Zech. x. 10.

feeblest logician may draw a moral demonstration. If they had been utterly destroyed—if they had mingled among the nations,—if, in the space of nearly eighteen centuries after their dispersion, they had become extinct as a people, even if they had been secluded in a single region, and had remained united—if their history had been analogous to that of any nation upon the earth, an attempt might, with some plausibility or reason, have been made, to show cause why the prediction of their fate, however true to the fact, ought not in such a case to be sustained as evidence of the truth of inspiration. Or if the past history and present state of the Jews were not of a nature so singular and peculiar, as to bear out to the very letter the truth of the prophecies concerning them, with what triumph would the infidel have produced those very prophecies, as fatal to the idea of the inspiration of the Scriptures? And when the Jews had been scattered throughout the whole earth—when they have remained everywhere a distinct race—when they have been despoiled evermore, and yet never destroyed—when the most wonderful and amazing facts, such as never occurred among any people—form the ordinary narrative of their history, and fulfil literally the prophecies concerning them,—may not the believer challenge his adversary to the production of such credentials of the faith that is in *him?* They present an unbroken chain of evidence, each link a prophecy and a fact, extending throughout a multitude of generations, and not yet terminated. Though the events, various and singular as they are, have been brought about by the instrumentality of human means, and the agency of secondary causes, yet they are equally prophetic and miraculous ; for the means were as impossible to be foreseen, as the end and the causes were as inscrutable as the event ; and they have been, and still in numberless instances are, accomplished by the instrumentality of the enemies of Christianity. Whoever seeks a miracle, may here behold a sign and a wonder, than which there cannot be a greater. And the Christian may bid defiance to all the assaults of his enemies from this stronghold of Christianity, impenetrable and impregnable on every side.

These prophecies concerning the Jews are as clear as a narrative of the events. They are ancient as the oldest records in existence; and it has never been denied that they were all delivered before the accomplishment of one of them. They were so unimaginable by human wisdom, that the whole compass of nature has never exhibited a parallel to the events. And the facts are visible, and present, and applicable even to a hair's breadth. Could Moses, as an uninspired mortal, have described the history, the fate, the dispersion, the treatment, the dispositions of the Israelites to the present day, or for three thousand two hundred years, seeing that he was astonished and amazed, on his descent from Sinai, at the change in their sentiments, and in their conduct, in the space of forty days? Could various persons have testified, in different ages, of the self-same and of similar facts, as wonderful as they have proved to be true? Could they have divulged so many secrets of futurity, when of necessity they were utterly ignorant of them all? The probabilities were infinite against them. For the mind of man often fluctuates in uncertainty over the nearest events, and the most probable results; but in regard to remote ages, when thousands of years shall have elapsed —and to facts respecting them, contrary to all previous knowledge, experience, analogy, or conception,—it feels that they are dark as death to mortal ken. And, viewing only the dispersion of the Jews, and some of its attendant circumstances—how their city was laid desolate,—their temple, which formed the constant place of their resort before, levelled with the ground, and ploughed over like a field—their country ravaged, and themselves murdered in mass—falling before the sword, the famine and the pestilence—how a remnant was left, but despoiled, persecuted, enslaved, and led into captivity—driven from their own land, not to a mountainous retreat, where they might subsist with safety, but dispersed among all nations, and left to the mercy of a world that everywhere hated and oppressed them—shattered in pieces like the wreck of a vessel in a mighty storm—scattered over the earth, like fragments on the waters,—and, instead of disappearing, or mingling with the nations, remaining a perfectly distinct people, in every kingdom the same, retaining similar habits and customs, and creeds, and manners, in every part of the globe, though without ephod, teraphim, or sacrifice—meeting everywhere the same insult, and mockery, and oppression —finding no resting-place without an enemy soon to dispossess them—multiplying amidst all their miseries—surviving their enemies—beholding, unchanged, the extinction of many nations, and the convulsions of all—robbed of their silver and of their gold, though cleaving to the love of them still, as the stumbling-block of their iniquity—often bereaved of their very children—disjoined and disorganized, but uniform and unaltered—ever bruised, but never broken— weak, fearful, sorrowful and afflicted—often driven to madness at the spectacle of their own misery—taken up in the lips of talkers—the taunt, and hissing, and infamy of all people, and continuing ever, what they are to this day, the sole proverb common to the whole world ; how did every fact, from its very nature, defy all conjecture, and how could mortal man, overlooking a hundred successive generations, have foretold any one of these wonders that are now conspicuous in these latter times ? Who but the Father of Spirits, possessed of perfect prescience, even of the knowledge, of the will and of the actions of free, intelligent and moral agents, could have revealed their unbounded and yet unceasing wanderings—unveiled all their destiny—and unmasked the minds of the Jews, and of their enemies, in every age and in every clime? The creation of a world might as well be the work of chance as the revelation of these things. It is a visible display of the power and of the prescience of God, an accumulation of many miracles. And although it forms but a part of a small portion of the Christian evidence, it lays not only a stone of stumbling—such as infidels would try to cast in a Christian's path,—but it fixes an insurmountable barrier at the very threshold of infidelity, immoveable by all human device, and impervious to every attack.

CHAPTER V.

PROPHECIES CONCERNING THE LAND OF JUDEA AND CIRCUMJACENT COUNTRIES.

THE writings of the Jewish prophets not only described the fate of that people for many generations, subsequent to the latest period to which the most unyielding scepticism can pretend to affix the date of these predictions, but while the cities were teeming with inhabitants, and the land flowing with abundance, for centuries before Judea ceased to count its millions, they foretold the long reign of desolation that would ensue. The land is a witness as well as the people. Its aspect in the present day, and for many a past age, is the precise likeness delineated by the pencil of prophecy, when every feature that could admit of change was the reverse of what it now is:

And it is necessary only to compare the predictions themselves with that proof of their fulfilment, which, were all other testimony to be excluded, heathens and infidels supply.

The calamities of the Jews were to arise progressively with their iniquities. They were to be punished again and again, "yet seven times, for their sins."* And in the greatest of the denunciations which were to fill up the measure of their punishments, the long-continued desolation of their country is ranked among the worst and latest of their woes : and the prophecies respecting it, which admit of a *literal* interpretation, and which have been literally fulfilled, are abundantly clear and expressive.

" I will make your cities waste, and bring your sanctuaries into desolation. And I will bring the land into desolation ; and your enemies which dwell therein shall be astonished at it. And I will scatter you among the heathen, and draw out a sword after you ; and your land shall be desolate and your cities waste. Then shall the land enjoy her sabbaths, as long as it lieth desolate, and ye be in your enemies' land ; even then shall the land rest and enjoy her sabbaths. The land also shall be left of them, and shall enjoy her sabbaths while she lieth desolate without them.† So that the generation to come of your children that shall rise up after you, and the stranger that shall come from a far land, shall say, when they see the plagues of that land, and the sickness which the Lord hath laid upon it :—Wherefore hath the Lord done this unto the land, what meaneth the heat of this great anger ? The anger of the Lord was kindled against this land, to bring upon it all the curses that are written in this book.‡ Your country is de-

---

* Levit. xxvi. 18, 21, 24.　　† Levit. xxvi. 31, 45, 53.
‡ Deut. xxix. 22, 24, 27.

solate, your cities burned with fire ; your land, strangers devour it in your presence, and it is desolate as overthrown by strangers. And the daughter of Zion is left as a cottage in a vineyard, as a lodge in a garden of cucumbers, as a besieged city. Except the Lord of Hosts had left a very small remnant, we should have been as Sodom, and we should have been like unto Gomorrah.* Ye shall be as an oak whose leaf fadeth, and as a garden that hath no water.† I will lay my vineyard waste. Of a truth many houses shall be desolate, even great and fair, without inhabitant. Yea, ten acres of vineyard shall yield one bath, and the seed of an homer shall yield an ephah. There shall the lambs feed after their manner, and the waste places of the fat ones shall strangers eat.‡ Then said I, Lord, how long? and he answered, Until the cities be wasted without inhabitant, and the houses without man, and the land be utterly desolate ; and the Lord have-removed men far away, and there be a great forsaking in the midst of the land. But yet in it shall be a tenth ; and it shall return and shall be eaten ; as a teil-tree, and as an oak, whose substance is in them when they cast their leaves.§ The Lord of Hosts shall make a consumption, even determined, in the midst of all the land.‖ The glory of Jacob shall be made thin, and the fatness of his flesh shall wax lean ; and it shall be as when the harvest-man gathereth the corn, and reapeth the ears with his arm ; and it shall be as he that gathereth ears in the valley of Rephaim. Yet gleaning grapes shall be left in it, as the shaking of an olive tree, two or three berries in the top of the uppermost bough, four or five in the outmost fruitful branches thereof, saith the Lord God of Israel.¶ Behold the Lord maketh the

* Isa. i. 7, 8, 9. † Isa. i. 30. ‡ Isa. v. 6, 9, 10, 17.
§ Isa. vi. 11, 12, 13. ‖ Isa. x. 23. ¶ Isa. xvii. 4, 5, 6.

earth* (the land) empty, and maketh it waste, and turneth it upside down, and scattereth abroad the inhabitants thereof. The land shall be utterly emptied and utterly spoiled : for the Lord hath spoken this word. The earth (land) mourneth and fadeth away : it is defiled under the inhabitants thereof ; because they have transgressed the laws, changed the ordinance, broken the everlasting covenant. Therefore hath the curse devoured the land, and they that dwell therein are desolate, and few men left. The new wine mourneth, the vine languisheth, all the merry-hearted do sigh. The mirth of tabrets ceaseth, the noise of them that rejoice endeth, the joy of the harp ceaseth. They shall not drink wine with a song, strong drink shall be bitter to them that drink it. The city of confusion is broken down ; every house is shut up that no man may come in. There is a crying for wine in the streets, all joy is darkened, the mirth of the land is gone. When thus it shall be in the midst of the land among the people, there shall be as the shaking of an olive-tree, and as the gleaning grapes when the vintage is done.† Yet the defenced city shall be desolate, and the habitation forsaken, and left like a wilderness : there shall the calf feed, and there shall he lie down and consume the branches thereof. When the boughs thereof are

---

* The twenty-fourth chapter of Isaiah contains a continuous prophetic description (exactly analogous to other predictions) of the desolation of Judea, during the time that the "inhabitants thereof" were to be "scattered abroad ;" and it is only necessary, in order to prevent any appearance of ambiguity, to remark, that the *very same word* in the original, which, in the English translation, is here rendered *earth*,—is, in subsequent verses of the same chapter, also translated *land*—evidently implying the land of Israel, the inhabitants of which were to be "scattered abroad,"—and so obviously is this the meaning of the word, that the chapter is properly entitled " the deplorable judgments of God upon the land."

† Isa. xxix. 12, 13.

withered they shall be broken off: the women come
and set them on fire; for it is a people of no understanding.* Many days and years shall ye be troubled,
ye careless women; for the vintage shall fail, the gathering shall not come.   Tremble, ye women that are
at ease; be troubled ye careless ones; strip you and
make you bare, and gird sackcloth upon your loins.
They shall lament for the teats, for the pleasant fields,
for the fruitful vine.   Upon the land of my people shall
come up thorns and briars; yea upon all the houses of
joy in the joyous city; because the palaces shall be forsaken, the multitude of the city shall be left; the forts
and towers shall be for dens for ever, a joy of wild
asses, a pasture of flocks; until the Spirit be poured
upon us from on high, and the wilderness be a fruitful
field, and the fruitful field be counted for a forest.†—
The highways lie waste, the wayfaring man ceaseth;
he hath broken the covenant, he hath despised the
cities, he regardeth no man.   The earth mourneth and
languisheth; Lebanon is ashamed and hewn down;
Sharon is like a wilderness; and Bashan and Carmel
shake off their fruits.‡   Destruction upon destruction
is cried; for the whole land is spoiled.   I beheld,
and lo the fruitful place was a wilderness, and all the
cities thereof were broken down at the presence of the
Lord; for thus hath the Lord said, the whole land
shall be desolate, yet will I not make a full end.   For
this shall the earth mourn, because I have spoken it.
I have purposed it, and will not repent, neither will
I turn back from it.§   How long shall the land
mourn and the herbs of every field wither, for the
wickedness of them that dwelt therein?—I have forsaken mine house, I have left mine heritage.—Many
pastors have destroyed my vineyard, they have trod-

* Isa. xxvii. 10, 11.   † Isa. xxxiv. 10—15.
‡ Isa. xxxiii. 8, 9.   § Jer. iv. 20, 26—28.

den my portion under foot, they have made my pleasant portion a desolate wilderness. They have made
it desolate, and being desolate it mourneth unto me;
the whole land is made desolate, because no man
layeth it to heart. The spoilers are come upon all
high places through the wilderness;—no flesh shall
have peace. They have sown wheat, but shall reap
thorns; they have put themselves to pain, but shall
not profit; and they shall be ashamed of your revenues because of the fierce anger of the Lord.* Thus
saith the Lord God to the mountains of Israel, and
to the hills, and to the rivers, and to the vallies; behold I, even I, will bring a sword upon you, I will
destroy your high places. In all your dwelling-places
the cities shall be laid waste, and the high places
shall be desolate, and your altars shall be laid waste
and made desolate; I will stretch out my hand upon
them, and make the land more desolate than the
wilderness towards Diblath, in all their habitations.†
I will bring the worst of the heathen, and they shall
possess their houses; I will also make the pomp of
the strong to cease; and their holy places shall be
defiled. Say unto the people of the land, thus saith
the Lord God of the inhabitants of Jerusalem and
of the land of Israel, they shall eat their bread with
carefulness, and drink their water with astonishment,
that her land may be desolate from all that is therein, because of the violence of all them that dwell
therein.‡ Every one that passeth thereby shall be
astonished.—Hear this, all ye inhabitants of the land.
Hath this been in your days, or even in the days of
your fathers? Tell ye your children of it, and let
your children tell their children, and their children
another generation. That which the palmer-worm

---

* Jer. xii. 4, 7, 10—13.   † Ezek. vi. 2, 3, 6, 14.
‡ Ezek. xii. 19.

hath left hath the locust eaten ; and that which the locust hath left hath the canker-worm eaten ; and that which the canker-worm hath left hath the caterpillar eaten.—The field is wasted, the land mourneth, and joy is withered from the sons of men.—And I will restore unto you the years that the locust hath eaten, and the canker-worm, and the caterpillar, and the palmer-worm. And my people shall never be ashamed.*—The city that went out by a thousand shall leave a hundred, and that which went out by a hundred shall leave ten, to the house of Israel.—Seek not Bethel. Bethel shall come to nought.†—Behold I will set a plumb-line in the midst of my people Israel. I will not pass by them any more. And the high places of Isaac shall be desolate, and the sanctuaries of Israel shall be laid waste.‡ I will make Samaria as an heap of the field, and as plantings of a vineyard ; and I will pour down the stones thereof into the valley, and I will discover the foundations thereof."§

Numerous and clear as these denunciations are, yet such was the long-suffering patience of God, and such the rebellious spirit of the Israelites of old, that it had become a proverb in the land, " the days are prolonged, and every vision faileth." But though that proverb ceased, when great calamities did overtake them, and a temporary desolation came over their land, yet the curses denounced against it were not obliterated by a partial and transient fulfilment, but, on the renewed and unrepented wickedness of the people, fell upon them and their land with stricter truth, and, as foretold, with sevenfold severity.

Moses and all the prophets set blessings and curses before the Israelites, with the avowed purpose that

* Joel i. 2, 4, 10, 12 ; ii. 25, 26.   † Amos v. 2, 5.
‡ Amos vii. 8, 9.   § Micah i. 6.

they might choose between them. But while the prophetical writings abound with warnings, the Scriptural records of Israelitish history show how greatly these warnings were disregarded. The word of God, which is perfect work, abideth for ever:—and it returns not to him void, but fulfils the purpose for which he sent it. And after the statutes and judgments of the Lord had been set before the Israelites for the space of a thousand years from the time that they were first declared, the " burden of the word of the Lord to Israel by Malachi," instead of speaking, even then, of repealed judgments, closes the Jewish Scriptures with this last command, " Remember ye the law of Moses my servant, which I commanded unto him in Horeb for all Israel, with the statutes and judgments;"* and, affixed to the command to remember these, the very last words of the Old Testament, which seal up the vision and the prophecies, plainly indicate that however long the God of Israel might bear with the Jews for transgressing the law, while the law only was given them, yet on their refusal to repent when the prophet, who was to be " the messenger of the Lord," would be sent unto *them*, the Lord would come and " smite the earth, or the land, with a curse."

The term of the continuance of these judgments and of their full completion, is distinctly marked, as commensurate with the dispersion of the Jews, and terminating with their *final* restoration. So long as they be in their enemies' land, their own land lieth desolate. The judgments were not to be removed from it " until the Spirit be poured (upon the Jews) from on high, and the wilderness be a fruitful field."†
And the prophecies not only pourtray Judea while forsaken of the Lord, his heritage left, and given into

---

* Malachi iv. 4.   † Isa. xxxii. 15.

the hands of its enemies, but they also delineate the character and condition of the dwellers therein, while its ancient inhabitants were to be scattered abroad, and ere the time come when he shall reign in Jerusalem before his ancients gloriously.* Annunciations of a future and final restoration, almost uniformly accompany the curses denounced against the land. And frequent, and express as words can be, are the references throughout the prophecies to the period yet to come, when the children of Israel shall be gathered out of all nations, and when the land then, at last and for ever, brought back from desolation, and the cities, repaired after the *desolations of many generations*, and the mountains of Israel, which have been *always waste*, shall be no more desolate, nor the people termed forsaken any more.† After the Messiah was to be cut off, and the sacrifice and oblation to cease, the ensuing *desolations* were to reach *even to the consummation*, and till that determined shall be poured upon the desolate.‡ And Jerusalem, as Jesus hath declared, shall be trodden down of the Gentiles, till the times of the Gentiles be fulfilled.§

Neither the dispersion of the Jews nor the desolation of Judea are to cease, according to the prophecies, till other evidence shall thereby be given of prophetic inspiration. The application to the present period, or to modern times, of the prophecies relative to the desolation of Judea, is thus abundantly manifest. And the more numerous they are, so much the more severe is the test which they abide. And while the Jews are not yet gathered from all the nations, nor planted in their own land to be no more pulled out of it,‖—nor its destroyers and they that

---

* Isa. xxiv. 1, 23.

† Isa. lxi. 4. Ezek. xxvi. 8, 10; xxxvii. 21; xxxviii. 8. Isa. lxii. 4.

‡ Dan. ix. 27. § Luke xxi. 24. ‖ Amos ix. 14, 15.

laid it waste, gone forth from it ; * nor the *old waste places* built, nor the *foundations of many generations* raised up—nor the land brought back from desolation ; †—the effect of every vision is still to be seen, and even now, at this late period of the times of the Gentiles, though the blessed consummation may not be very distant, there is abundant evidence to complete the proof that that which was determined has been poured upon the desolate, and that ALL the curses that are written in the book of the Lord have been brought upon the land.‡

The devastation of Judea is so " astonishing," and its poverty as a country so remarkable, that, forgetful of the prophecies respecting it, and in the rashness of their zeal, infidels once attempted to draw an argument from thence against the truth of Christianity, by denying the possibility of the existence of so numerous a population as can accord with scriptural history, and by representing it as a region singularly unproductive and irreclaimable.§ But though they have, in some

---

* Isa. xlix. 17. † Ib. lviii. 12. ‡ Deut. xxix. 27.

§ Voltaire, without adducing any authority whatever in support of his assertion, and without expressly declaring that, in lieu of such evidence, he was gifted with an intuitive knowledge of the historical and geographical fact,—speaks of the ancient state of Palestine with derision, describes it as one of the worst countries of Asia ; likens it to Switzerland, and says that it can only be esteemed fertile when compared with the desert. (La Palestine n'était que ce qu'elle est aujourd'hui, un des plus mauvais pays de l'Asie. Cette petite province, &c. *Oeuvres de Voltaire. Ed. A. Gotha, Tom.* xxvii. p. 107.) Without citing, on the other hand, the ample evidence of Josephus and of Jerome, both of whom were inhabitants of Judea, and more adequate judges of the fact, the following testimony to the great fertility of that country, not being chargeable with the partiality which might be attached to the opinion either of a Christian or of a Jew, may be given in answer to the groundless assertion of Voltaire— testimony which ought to have been better known and appreciated even by that high priest of modern infidelity, if the

instances at least, voluntarily abandoned this indefen-
sible assumption, they have left to the believer the
fruits of their concession ; they have given the most
unsuspicious testimony to the confirmation of the prophecies, and have served to establish the cause which
they sought to ruin. The evidence of ancient authors
—the fertility of the soil wherever a single spot can
be cultivated—the remains of vegetable mould piled
by artificial means, upon the sides of the mountains,
which may have clothed them with a richer and more
frequent harvest than the most fertile vale ; and the
multitude of the ruins of cities that now cover the extensive but uncultivated and desert plains, bear witness that there was a numerous and condensed population in a country flowing with food ; and that, if
any history recorded its greatness, or any prophecies
revealed its desolation, they have both been amply
verified.

The acknowledgments of Volney, and the description which he gives from personal observation, are
sufficient to confute entirely the gratuitous assumptions and insidious sarcasms of Voltaire ; and, wonderful as it may appear, copious extracts may be drawn

---

sacrifice of truth on the altar of wit had not been too common an act of his devotion to the chief god of his idolatry.
Corpora hominum salubria et ferentia laborem; rari imbres,
*uber solum, fruges nostrum ad morem ; præterque eas balsa-
mum et palmæ.* Magna pars Judeæ vicis dispergitur, habent
et oppida. Hierosolyma genti caput. Illic immensæ opu-
lentiæ templum et primis munimentis urbs.—*Taciti Hist.*
lib. v. c. 6, 8. Ultima Syriarum est Palestina, per intervalla
magna protenta, cultis abundans terris et nitidis, et civitates
habens quasdam egregias, nullam sibi cedentem sed sibi vicis-
sim velut ad perpendiculum æmulas.—*Ammiani Marcell.* lib.
xiv. cap. 8, sect. 11. Ed. Lips. 1808. Nec sane viris, opi-
bus, armis quicquam copiosius Syria.—*Flori Hist.* lib. ii. cap.
8, sect. 4. Syria in hortis operosissima est. Inde quoque
est proverbium Græcis. Multa Syrorum olera.—*Plinii
Hist. Nat.* lib. xx. cap. 5.

from that writer, whose unwitting or unwilling testimony is as powerful an attestation of the completion
of many prophecies, when he relates facts of which he
was an eye-witness, as his untried theories, his ideal
perfectibility of human nature, if released from the
restraints of religion, and his perverted views both of
the nature and effects of Christianity, have proved
greatly instrumental in subverting the faith of many,
who, unguarded by any positive evidence, gave heed
to such seductive doctrines. There needs not to be
any better witness of facts confirmatory of the prophecies, and in so far conclusive against all his speculations, than Volney himself. Of the natural fertility
of the country, and of its abounding population in ancient times, he gives the most decisive evidence.
" Syria unites different climates under the same sky,
and collects within a small compass pleasures and productions which nature has elsewhere dispersed at great
distances of time and places. To this advantage,
which perpetuates enjoyments by their succession, it
adds another, that of multiplying them by the variety
of its productions." " With its numerous advantages
of climate and soil, it is not astonishing that Syria
should always have been esteemed a most delicious
country, and that the Greeks and Romans ranked it
among the most beautiful of their provinces, and even
thought it not inferior to Egypt.* After having
assigned several just and sufficient reasons to account
for the large population of Judea in ancient times, in
contradiction to those who were sceptical of the fact,
he adds—" Admitting only what is conformable to
experience and nature, there is nothing to contradict
the great population of high antiquity. Without appealing to the positive testimony of history, there are

* Volney's Travels in Egypt and Syria. Eng. Trans.
Lond. 1787, vol. i. pp. 316, 321.

innumerable monuments which depose in favour of the fact. Such are the prodigious quantity of ruins dispersed over the plains, and even in the mountains, at this day deserted. On the remote parts of Carmel are found wild vines and olive trees, which must have been conveyed thither by the hand of man: and in the Lebanon of the Druses and Maronites, the rocks, now abandoned to fir-trees and brambles, present us in a thousand places with terraces, which prove that they were anciently better cultivated, and consequently much more populous than in our days."*

" Syria," says Gibbon, " one of the countries that have been improved by the most early cultivation, is not unworthy of the preference. The heat of the climate is tempered by the vicinity of the sea and mountains, by the plenty of wood and water; and the produce of a fertile soil affords the subsistence and encourages the propagation of men and animals. From the age of David to that of Heraclius the country was overspread with ancient and flourishing cities; the inhabitants were numerous and wealthy." Such evidence has merely been selected as the most unsuspicious, though that of many others might also be adduced. The country in the *immediate* vicinity of Jerusalem is indeed rocky, as Strabo represents it, and apparently sterile, and is now, in general, perfectly barren : " but even the sides of the most barren mountains in the neighbourhood of Jerusalem had been rendered fertile, by being divided into terraces, like steps rising one above another, where soil has been accumulated with astonishing labour."† " In any

* Volney's Travels in Egypt and Syria, vol. ii. p. 368.
† Clarke's Travels, vol. ii. p. 520. General Straton describes these terraces as resembling the *gradus* of a theatre, and particularly marked them as vestiges of ancient " luxuriance."

part of Judea," Dr. Clarke adds, " the effects of a beneficial change of government are soon witnessed, in the conversion of desolated plains into fertile fields.—Under a wise and beneficent government the produce of the Holy Land would exceed all calculation. Its perennial harvest, the salubrity of its air, its limpid springs, its rivers, lakes, and matchless plains, its hills and vales, all these, added to the serenity of the climate, prove this to be indeed a field which the Lord hath blessed."* But the facts of the former fertility, as well as of the present desolation of Judea, are established beyond contradiction ; and, in attempting in this respect to invalidate the truth of sacred history, infidels have either been driven, or have reluctantly retired, from the defenceless ground which they themselves had once assumed, and have given room whereon to rest an argument against their want of faith as well as of veracity. For, in conclusion of this matter, it surely may, without any infringement of truth or of justice, be remarked, that the extent of the present and long-fixed desolation, the very allegation on which they would discredit the scriptural narrative of the ancient glory of Judea, being itself a clearly predicted truth, then the greater the difficulty of reconciling the knowledge of what it was to the fact of what it is, and the greater the difficulty of believing the possibility of so " astonishing " a contrast, the more wonderful are the prophecies which revealed it all, the more completely are they accredited as a voice from heaven, and the argument of the infidel leads the more directly to proof against himself. Such is " the positive testimony of history," and such the subsisting proofs of the former grandeur and fertility of Palestine, that we are now left, without a cavil, to the calm investigation of the change in that country from one

---

* Clarke's Travels, v. ii. p. 521.

extreme to another, and of the consonance of that change with the dictates of prophecy.

Under any regular and permanent government, a region so favoured by climate, so diversified in surface, so rich in soil, and which had been so luxuriant for ages, would naturally have resumed its opulence and power; and its permanent desolation, alike contradictory to every suggestion of experience and of reason, must have been altogether inconceivable by man. But *the land was to be overthrown by strangers, to be trodden down; mischief was to come upon mischief, and destruction upon destruction, and the land was to be desolate.* The Chaldeans devastated Judea, and led the inhabitants into temporary captivity. The kings of Syria and Egypt, by their extortions and oppression, impoverished the country. The Romans held it long in subjection to their iron yoke. And the Persians contended for the possession of it. But in succeeding ages, still greater destroyers than any of the former appeared upon the scene to perfect the work of devastation. " In the year 622 (636) the Arabian tribes collected under the banners of Mahomet, seized, or rather laid it waste. Since that period, torn to pieces by the civil wars of the Fatimites and the Ommiades; wrested from the califs by their rebellious governors; taken from them by the Turkmen soldiery; invaded by the European crusaders; retaken by the Mamelouks of Egypt, and ravaged by Tamerlane and his Tartars—it has at length fallen into the hands of the Ottoman Turks."* *It has been overthrown by strangers—trodden under foot,—destruction has come upon destruction.*

The cities were to be laid waste. By the concurring testimony of all travellers, Judea may now be called a field of ruins. Columns, the memorials of

---

* Volney's Travels, v. i. p. 357.

ancient magnificence, now covered with rubbish, and
buried under ruins, may be found in all Syria.[*] From
Mount Tabor is beheld an immensity of plains, interspersed with hamlets, fortresses, and heaps of ruins.
The buildings on that mountain were destroyed and
laid waste by the Sultan of Egypt in 1290, and the
accumulated vestiges of successive forts and ruins are
now mingled in one common and extensive desolation.[†] Of the celebrated cities Capernaum, Bethsaida, Gadara, Tarichea, and Chorazin, nothing remains but shapeless ruins.[‡] Some vestiges of Em-
maus may still be seen. Cana is a very paltry village. The ruins of Tekoa present only the foundations of some considerable buildings."[§] The city of
Nain is now a hamlet. The ruins of the ancient
Sapphura announce the previous existence of a large
city ; and its name is still preserved in the appellation
of a miserable village called Sephoury.[||] Loudd, the
ancient Lydda and Diospolis, appear like a place
lately ravaged by fire and sword, and is one continued
heap of rubbish and ruins.[¶] Ramla, the ancient
Arimathea, is in almost as ruinous a state. Nothing
but rubbish is to be found within its boundaries. In
the adjacent country there are found at every step dry
wells, cisterns fallen in, and vast vaulted reservoirs,
which prove that in ancient times this town must have
been upwards of a league and a half in circumference.[**]
Cæsarea can no longer excite the envy of a conqueror,
and has long been abandoned to silent desolation.[††]

[*] Mariti's Travels, v. ii. p. 141.
[†] Buckingham's Travels in Palestine, p. 107. Mariti's
Travels, v. ii. p. 177.
[‡] Ib. Wilson's Travels, p. 227.
[§] Macmichael's Journey to Constantinople, p. 196.
[||] Clarke's Travels, v. ii. p. 401.
[¶] Volney's Travels, v. ii. pp. 332—334.
[**] Ibid. v. ii. p. 334.
[††] Captain Light's Travels, p. 204. Buckingham's Tra-
vels, 126.

The city of Tiberias is now almost abandoned, and its subsistence precarious ; of the towns that bordered on its lake there are no traces left.* Zabulon, once the rival of Tyre and Sidon, is a heap of ruins. A few shapeless stones, unworthy the attention of the travel-ler, mark the sight of the Saffre.† The ruins of Je-richo, covering no less than a square mile, are sur-rounded with complete desolation ; and there is not a tree of any description, either of palm or balsam, and scarcely any verdure or bushes to be seen about the site of this abandoned city.‡ Bethel is not to be found. The ruins of Sarepta, and of several large cities in its vicinity, are now " mere rubbish, and are only distinguishable as the sites of towns by heaps of dilapidated stones and fragments of columns."§ But at Djerash (supposed to be the ruins of Gerasa) are the magnificent remains of a splendid city. The form of streets, once lined with a double row of columns, and covered with pavement still nearly entire, in which are the marks of the chariot wheels, and on each side of which is an elevated path-way—two theatres, and two grand temples, built of marble, and others of in-ferior note—baths—bridge—a cemetery, with many sarcophagi, which surrounded the city—a triumphal arch—a large cistern—a picturesque tomb, fronted with columns, and an aqueduct, overgrown with wood —and upwards of two hundred and thirty columns still standing amidst deserted ruins without a city to adorn—all combine in presenting to the view of the traveller, in the estimation of those who were succes-sively eye-witnesses of them both, " a much finer

* Captain Light's Travels, p. 204.
† Mariti's Travels, v. ii. pp. 158—169.
‡ Buckingham's Travels, p. 300.
§ Captains Irby and Mangles' Travels, p. 199.

mass of ruins" than even that of the boasted Palmyra.*
But how marvellously are the predictions of their desolation verified, when, in general, nothing but ruined
ruins form the most distinguished remnants of the cities of Israel; and when the multitude of its towns
are almost all left, with many a vestige to testify of
their number, but without a mark to tell their name.

*And your land shall be desolate, and your cities waste.
Then shall the land enjoy her sabbaths as long as it
lieth desolate, and ye be in your enemies land: even then
shall the land rest and enjoy her sabbaths, &c.* A
single reference to the Mosaic law respecting the sabbatical year, renders the full purport of this prediction perfectly intelligible and obvious. " But in the
seventh year shall be a sabbath of rest unto the land,
thou shalt neither sow thy field nor prune thy vineyard." And the land of Judea hath even thus enjoyed its sabbaths so long as it hath lain desolate. In
that country, where every spot was cultivated like a
garden by its patrimonial possessor, where every little
hill rejoiced in its abundance—where every steep ac-
clivity was terraced by the labour of man, and where
the very rocks were covered thick with mould, and
rendered fertile; even in that self-same land, with a
climate the same,† and with a soil unchanged, save
only by neglect, a dire contrast is now, and has, for a
lengthened period of time, been displayed by fields
untilled and unsown, and by waste and desolated

---

* Irby and Mangles' Travels, pp. 317, 318.
   The ruins of Djerash were first discovered by Seetzen, in
1806. They have since been visited by Sheikh Ibrahim,
(Burckhardt) Sir William Chatterton, Mr. Bankes, the Hon.
Captain Irby, Captain Mangles, Mr. Leigh, Mr. Leslie, and
Mr. Buckingham. Both Burckhardt and Mr. Buckingham
have also given a description of them. Many of the edifices
were built long after the period of the prediction; yet they
are not excluded from the sentence of desolation.
   † See Brewster's Philosophical Journal, No. xvi. p. 227.

plains. Never since the expatriated descendants of
Abraham were driven from its borders, has the land
of Canaan been so " plenteous in goods," or so abundant in population as once it was ; never, as it did
for ages unto them, has it vindicated to any other
people a right to its possession or its own title of the
land of promise—it has rested from century to century ;
and while that marked, and stricken, and scattered
race, who possess the recorded promise of the God of
Israel as their charter to its final and everlasting possession, still " *be in the land of their enemies, so long
their land lieth desolate.*" There may thus almost be
said to be the semblance of a sympathetic feeling between this bereaved country and banished people, as if
the land of Israel felt the miseries of its absent children,
awaited their return, and responded to the undying
love they bear it, by the refusal to yield to other
possessors the rich harvest of those fruits, with which,
in the days of their allegiance to the Most High, it
abundantly blessed *them*. And striking and peculiar,
without the shadow of even a semblance upon earth,
as is this accordance between the fate of Judea and of
the Jews, it assimilates as closely, and may we not
add, as miraculously, to those predictions respecting
both, which Moses uttered and recorded ere the tribes
of Israel had ever set a foot in Canaan. *The land
shall be left of them, and shall enjoy her rest while
she lieth desolate without them.*

To the desolate state of Judea every traveller bears
witness. The prophetic malediction was addressed to
the mountains and to the hills, to the rivers and to the
vallies ; and the beauty of them all has been blighted.
Where the inhabitants once dwelt in peace, each under
his own vine, and under his own fig-tree, the tyranny
of the Turks, and the perpetual incursions of the
Arabs, the last of a long list of oppressors, have spread
one wide field of almost unmingled desolation.   The

1

plain of Esdraelon, naturally most fertile, its soil consisting of " fine rich black mould," level like a lake, except where Mount Ephraim rises in its centre, bounded by Mount Hermon, Carmel, and Mount Tabor,[*] and so extensive as to cover about three hundred square miles, is a solitude,[†] " almost entirely deserted : the country is a complete desert."[‡] Even the vale of Sharon is a waste. In the valley of Canaan, formerly a beautiful, delicious, and fertile valley, there is not a mark or vestige of cultivation.[§] The country is continually overrun with rebel tribes ; the Arabs pasture their cattle upon the spontaneous produce of the rich plains with which it abounds.[||] Every ancient landmark is removed. Law there is none. Lives and property are alike unprotected. The vallies are untilled, the mountains have lost their verdure, the rivers flow through a desert and cheerless land. All the beauty of Tabor that man could disfigure is defaced ; immense ruins on the top of it, are now the only remains of a once magnificent city ; and Carmel is the habitation of wild beasts.[¶] " The art of cultivation," says Volney, " is in the most deplorable state, and the countryman must sow with the musket in his hand ; and no more is sown than is necessary for subsistence." " Every day I found fields abandoned by the plough."[**] In describing his journey through Galilee, Dr. Clarke remarks, that the earth was covered with such a variety of thistles, that a complete collection of them would be a valua-

[*] General Straton's MS. Travels.
[†] Clarke's Travels, vol. ii. p. 497. Maundrell's Travels, p. 95.
[‡] Burckhardt's Travels in Syria, pp. 334, 342.
[§] General Straton's MS.
[||] Clarke's Travels, vol. ii. pp. 484, 491.
[¶] Mariti, vol. ii. p. 140.
[**] Volney's Travels, vol. ii. p. 413. Volney's Ruins, c. 11, p. 7.

ble acquisition to botany.* Six new species of that plant, so significant of wildness, were discovered by himself in a scanty selection. " From Kane-Leban to Beer, amidst the ruins of cities, the country, as far as the eye of the traveller can reach, presents nothing to his view but naked rocks, mountains and precipices, at the sight of which pilgrims are astonished, balked in their expectations, and almost startled in their faith."† " From the centre of the neighbouring elevations (around Jerusalem) is seen a wild, rugged, and mountainous desert ; no herds depasturing on the summit, no forests clothing the acclivities, no waters flowing through the vallies ; but one rude scene of savage melancholy waste, in the midst of which the ancient glory of Judea bows her head in widowed desolation."‡ It is needless to multiply quotations to prove the desolation of a country which the Turks have possessed, and which the Arabs have plundered for ages. Enough has been said to prove that *the land mourns and is laid waste, and has become as a desolate wilderness.*

But yet in it shall be a tenth, and it shall return and shall be eaten : as a teil-tree and an oak whose substance is in them when they cast their leaves. Though the cities be waste, and the land be desolate, it is not from the poverty of the soil that the fields are abandoned by the plough, nor from any diminution of its ancient and natural fertility that the land has rested for so many generations. Judea was not forced only by artificial means, or from local and temporary causes, into a luxuriant cultivation, such as a barren country might have been, concerning which it would not have needed a prophet to tell, that if once devastated and

* Clarke's Travels, vol. ii. p. 451.
† Maundrell's Travels, p. 168.
‡ Joliffe's Letters from Palestine, vol. i. p. 104.

abandoned it would ultimately and permanently revert
into its original sterility.   Phenicia at all times held
a far different rank among the richest countries of the
world ; and it was not a bleak and sterile portion of
the earth, nor a land which even many ages of desolation and neglect could impoverish, that God gave, in
possession and by covenant, to the seed of Abraham.
No longer cultivated as a garden, but left like a wilderness, Judea is indeed greatly changed from what it
was ; all that human ingenuity and labour did devise,
erect, or cultivate, men have laid waste and desolate ;
all the " plentous goods," with which it was enriched,
adorned, and blessed, have fallen like seared and withered leaves, when their greenness is gone ; and stripped of its " ancient splendour," it is left as *an oak whose
leaf fadeth :*—but its inherent sources of fertility are
not dried up ; the natural richness of the soil is un-
blighted ; *the substance is in it*, strong as that of the
teil-tree or the solid oak, which retain their substance
when they cast their leaves.—And as the leafless oak
waits throughout winter for the genial warmth of
returning spring, to be clothed with renewed foliage,
so the once glorious land of Judea is yet full of latent
vigour, or of vegetative power strong as ever, ready
to shoot forth, even " better than at the beginning,"
whenever the sun of heaven shall shine on it again,
and the " holy seed" be prepared for being finally
" the substance thereof." The *substance that is in it*
—which alone has here to be proved—is, in few words,
thus described by an enemy :   " The land in the
plains is *fat and loamy*, and exhibits every sign of the
greatest fecundity."—" Were nature assisted by art,
the fruits of the most distant countries might be produced within the distance of twenty leagues."* " Galilee," says Malte-Brun, " would be a paradise, were

* Volney's Travels, i. pp. 308, 317.

it inhabited by an industrious people, under an enlightened government. Vine-stocks are to be seen here a foot and a half in diameter."*

I will give it into the hands of STRANGERS *for a prey, and unto the wicked of the earth for a* SPOIL. *The* ROBBERS *shall enter into it and defile it.* Instead of abiding under a settled and enlightened government, Judea has been the scene of frequent invasions, " which have introduced a succession of foreign nations (des peuples *etrangers*.")† " When the Ottomans took Syria from the Mamelouks, they considered it as the *spoil* of a vanquished enemy. According to this law, the life and *property* of the vanquished belong to the conqueror. The government is far from disapproving of a system of *robbery* and plunder which it finds so profitable."‡

Many PASTORS *have destroyed my vineyard, they have* TRODDEN *my portion under foot.* The ravages committed even by hosts of enemies are in general only temporary : or if an invader settle in a conquered country, on becoming the possessor, he cultivates and defends it. And it is the proper office of government to render life and property secure. In neither case has it fared thus with Judea. But besides successive invasions by foreign nations, and the systematic spoliation exercised by a despotic government, other causes have conspired to perpetuate its desolation, and to render abortive the substance that is in it. Among these has chiefly to be numbered, its being literally *trodden under foot by many pastors.* Volney devotes a chapter, fifty pages in length, to a description, as he entitles it, " Of the *pastoral or wandering* tribes of Syria," chiefly of the Bedouin Arabs, by whom, espe-

---

* Schulze, in Pallas, cited by Malte-Brun, Geogr. v. ii. p. 148.
† Volney's Travels, i. p. 356.   ‡ Ib. v. ii. pp. 370, 381.

cially, Judea is incessantly traversed. " The pachalics
of Aleppo and Damascus may be computed to contain
about thirty thousand wandering Turkmen (Turkomans). All their property consists in cattle." In the
same pachalics, the number of the Curds " exceed
twenty thousand tents and huts," or an equal number
of armed men. " The Curds are almost everywhere
looked upon as robbers. Like the Turkmen, these
Curds are *pastors* and *wanderers*.* A third wandering
people in Syria are the Bedouin Arabs."† " It often
happens that even individuals turned *robbers*, in order
to withdraw themselves from the laws, or from tyranny,
unite and form a little camp, which maintain themselves by arms, and increasing, become new hordes
and new tribes. We may pronounce that in culti-
vable countries, the wandering life originates in the
injustice or want of policy of the government ; and
that the sedentary and the cultivating state is that to
which mankind is most naturally inclined."‡ " It is
evident that agriculture must be very precarious in
such a country, and that, under a government like that
of the Turks, it is safer to lead a wandering life, than
to choose a settled habitation, and rely for subsistence
on agriculture.§ " The Turkmen, the Curds, and
the Bedouins, have *no fixed habitations*, but keep *perpetually wandering* with their tents and *herds*, in
limited districts, of which they look upon themselves
as the proprietors. The Arabs spread over the whole
frontier of Syria, and even the plains of Palestine."‖
—Thus, contrary to their natural inclination, the
peasants, often forced to abandon a settled life, and
pastoral tribes in great numbers, or *many*, and without fixed habitations, divide the country, as it were
by mutual consent, and apportion it in limited districts

* Volney's Travels, ii. 370, i. 4, 5.   † Ibid. i. p. 377.
‡ Ibid. p. 363.   § Ibid. p. 357.   ‖ Ibid. pp. 367, 368.

among themselves by an assumed right of property, and the Arabs, subdivided also into different tribes, spread over the plains of Palestine, " wandering perpetually," as if on very purpose to *tread it down.*— What could be more unlikely or unnatural in such a land ! yet what more strikingly and strictly true ! or how else could the effect of the vision have been seen ! Many *pastors* have destroyed my vineyard ; they have *trodden* my portion *under foot.*

Ye shall be as a garden that hath no water. How long shall the land mourn and the herbs of every FIELD *wither, for the wickedness of them that dwell therein.* —" In all hot countries, wherever there is water, vegetation may be perpetually maintained and made to produce an uninterrupted succession of fruits to flowers, and flowers to fruits."* " The remains of cisterns are to be found (throughout Judea,) in which they collected the rain-water ; and *traces* of the canals by which those waters were distributed on the *fields.*— These labours necessarily created a prodigious fertility under an ardent sun, where a little water was the only requisite to revive the vegetable world."† Such labours, with very slight exceptions, are now unknown. Judea is as a garden that hath no water, and the herbs of every field wither. " We see there *none* of that gay carpeting of *grass and flowers* which decorate the meadows of Normandy and Flanders, nor those clumps of beautiful trees which give such richness and animation to the landscapes of Burgundy and Brittany.—The land of Syria has almost always *a dusty appearance.*‡ Had not these countries been *ravaged by the hand of man,* they might perhaps at this day have been shaded with forests. That its productions do not correspond with its natural advantages is less owing to its physi-

---

* Volney's Travels, ii. 359.
† Malte-Brun's Geo. ii. 150, 151.
‡ Volney's Travels, ii. p. 359.

cal than political state."*   " The whole of the mountain (near Tiberias) is covered with *dry* grass."†

The forts and TOWERS *shall be for* DENS *for ever.*
" At every step we meet with ruins of *towers*, dun-
geons, and castles with fosses—frequently *inhabited
by jackals, owls, and scorpions*."‡

*The multitude of the city shall be left. The defenced
city shall be desolate, and the habitation* FORSAKEN.
There are a " prodigious quantity of ruins dispersed
over the plains, and even in the mountains, at this
day *deserted*."§

*There shall the calf feed, and there shall he lie down
and consume the branches thereof. A* PASTURE *of
flocks. There shall the* LAMBS *feed after their manner, and the waste places of the fat ones shall strangers
eat.* Josephus describes Galilee, of which he was the
governor, as " full of plantations of trees of all sorts,
the soil universally rich and fruitful, and all, without
the exception of a single part, cultivated by the inhabitants. Moreover," he adds, " the cities lie here
very thick, and there are very many villages, which
are so full of people by the richness of their soil, that
the very least of them contained above fifteen thousand inhabitants."‖   Such was Galilee, at the commencement of the Christian era, several centuries after the prophecy was delivered ; but now, " the plain
of Esdraelon, and all the other parts of Galilee which
afford *pasture*, are occupied by Arab tribes, around
whose brown tents the sheep and *lambs* gambol to
the sound of the reed, which at night-fall calls them
home."¶   The calf feeds and lies down amidst the
ruins of the cities, and consumes, without hinderance,

---

* Volney's Travels, ii. pp. 359, 360.
† Burckhardt's Travels, p. 331.
‡ Volney's Travels, ii. p. 336.   § Ibid. p. 368.
‖ Josephus' Wars, book iii. chap. 3, sect. 2.
¶ Schulze, quoted by Malte-Brun, vol. ii. p. 148.

the branches of the trees; and however changed
may be the condition of the inhabitants, the *lambs
feed after their manner*, and, while the land mourns,
and the merry-hearted sigh, they gambol to the sound
of the reed.

The precise and complete contrast between the
ancient and existing state of Palestine, as separately
described by Jewish and Roman historians and by
modern travellers, is so strikingly exemplified in their
opposite descriptions, that, in reference to whatever
constituted the beauty and the glory of the country,
or the happiness of the people, an entire change is
manifest, even in minute circumstances. The universal richness and fruitfulness of the soil of Galilee,
together with its being " full of plantations of all
sorts of trees," are represented by Josephus as " invit-
ing the most slothful to take pains in its cultivation."
And the other provinces of the Holy Land are also
described by him as " having abundance of trees, full
of autumnal fruit, both that which grows wild and
that which is the effect of cultivation."* Tacitus
relates, that, besides all the fruits of Italy, the palm
and balsam-tree flourished in the fertile soil of Judea.
And he records the great carefulness with which,
when the circulation of the juices seemed to call for
it, they gently made an incision in the branches of
the balsam, with a shell, or pointed stone, not ventur-
ing to apply a knife. No sign of such art or care is
now to be seen throughout the land. The balm-tree
has disappeared where it long flourished : and hardier
plants have perished from other causes than the want
of due care in their cultivation. And instead of relating how the growth of a delicate tree is promoted,
and the medicinal liquor, at the same time, extracted
from its branches, by a nicety or perfectibility of art

---

* Josephus' Wars, book iii. chap 3, sect. 2.

worthy of the notice of a Tacitus, a different task has
fallen to the lot of the traveller from a far land, who
describes the customs of those who now dwell where
such arts were practised. " The olive trees (near
Arimathea) are daily perishing through age, the
ravages of contending factions, and even *from secret
mischief.* The Mamelouks, having cut down all the
olive trees, for the pleasure they take in destroying,
or to make *fires*, Yafa has lost its greatest conveni-
ence."*   Instead of " abundance of trees being still
the effect of cultivation," such, on the other hand,
has been the effect of these ravages, that many places
in Palestine are now " absolutely destitute of fuel."
Yet in this devastation, and in all its progress, may
be read the literal fulfilment of the prophecy, which
not only described the desolate cities of Judea as a
pasture of flocks, and as places for the calf to feed
and lie down, and consume the branches thereof;
but which, with equal truth, also declared, *when the
boughs thereof are withered, they shall be broken off;
the women come and set them on fire.*

For it is a people of NO *understanding.* " The
most simple arts are in a state of barbarism. The
sciences are *totally* unknown."†

*Upon the land of my people shall come up thorns
and briars.* " The earth produces (only) *briars* and
wormwood."‡   A thorny shrub, (Merar) and others
of a similar kind, abound throughout the desolated
plains and hills of Palestine. Some of the latter are
so closely beset, in many places, with thorns, that
they can be ascended only with great difficulty : and
" the whole district of Tiberias is covered with a
thorny shrub."§

* Volney's Travels, vol. ii. pp. 332, 333.
† Ibid. p. 442.   ‡ Volney's Ruins, p. 9.
§ Burckhardt's Travels in Syria, p. 333.

Your highways shall be desolate. * *The highways lie waste ; the way-faring man ceaseth.* So great must have been the intercourse, in ancient times, between the populous and numerous cities of Judea, and so much must that intercourse have been increased by the frequent and regular journeyings, from every quarter, of multitudes going up to Jerusalem to worship, in observance of the rites, and in obedience to the precepts of their law, that scarcely any country ever possessed such means of crowded highways, or any similar reason for abounding so much in wayfaring men. In the days of Isaiah, who uttered the latest of these predictions, " the land was full of horses, neither was there any end of their chariots."† And there not only subsist to this day in the land of Judea, numerous remains of paved ways formed by the Romans at a much later period, and " others evidently *not* Roman ;"‡ but among the precious literary remains of antiquity which have come down to our times, three Roman itineraries are to be numbered, that can here be confidently appealed to. From these, and from the testimony of Arrian and Diodorus Siculus, as well as of Josephus and Eusebius, it appears, as Reland has clearly shown, that in Palestine, long after it came under the power of the Romans, and after it was greatly debased from its ancient glory, there were forty-two different highways, (viæ publicæ) all being distinctly specified, which intersected it in various directions ; and the number of miles exceeding eight hundred and eighty.§ Yet the prophecy is literally true. " In the interior part of the country, there are neither great roads, nor canals,

* Levit. xxvi. 22.   † Isaiah xxxiii. 8.
‡ General Straton's MS.
§ Relandi Palestina ex monumentis veteribus illustrata. Tom. i. lib. ii. cap. 3, 4, 5, pp. 405, 425.

G

nor even bridges over the greatest part of the rivers
and torrents, however necessary they may be in winter. Between town and town there are neither post
nor public conveyances. Nobody travels alone, from
the insecurity of the roads. One must wait for several travellers who are going to the same place, or take
advantage of the passage of some great man who
assumes the office of protector, but is more frequently
the oppressor of the caravan. The roads in mountains are extremely bad ; and the inhabitants are so
far from levelling them, that they endeavour to make
them more rugged, in order, as they say, to cure the
Turks of their desire to introduce their cavalry. It
is remarkable that there is not a waggon nor a cart
in all Syria."* " There are," continues Volney,
" no inns anywhere. The lodgings in the khans (or
places of reception for travellers) are cells where you
find nothing but bare walls, dust, and sometimes scorpions. The keeper of the khan gives the traveller
the key and the mat, and he provides himself the
rest. He must therefore carry with him his bed, his
kitchen utensils, and even his provisions ; for frequently not even bread is to be found in the villages."†
" There are no carriages in the country," says another
traveller, " under any denomination." " Among the
hills of Palestine,"‡ according to a third witness,
" the road is impassable ; and the traveller finds himself among a set of infamous and ignorant thieves,
who would cut his throat for a farthing, and rob him
of his money for the mere pleasure of doing it."§ In
a country where there is a total want of wheel carriages of every description, *the highways*, however
excellent and numerous they once might have been,

* Volney's Travels, vol. ii. pp. 417, 419.
† Ibid. pp. 417, 418, 419.
‡ Wilson's Travels, p. 100.
§ Richardson's Travels, vol. ii. 225.

must *lie waste;* and where such dangers have to be encountered at every step, and such privations at every stage, it is not now to be wondered that the *wayfaring man ceaseth.* But let the disciples of Volney tell by what dictates of human wisdom the whole of his description of these existing facts was summed up, in a brief sentence, by Moses and Isaiah ; by the former, thirty-three, and, by the latter, twenty-five centuries past.

The spoilers shall come upon all high places through the wilderness. "These precautions are above all necessary in the countries exposed to the Arabs, such as Palestine, and the whole frontier of the desert."*

The inhabitants of Jerusalem and of the land of Israel, shall eat their bread with carefulness, and drink their water with astonishment, that her land may be desolate from all that is therein, because of the violence of all them that dwell therein. " In the great cities" (in Syria, none of which are in the Holy Land) " the people have much of that dissipated and *careless* air which they usually have with us, because there, as well as here," says Volney, alluding to France, " inured to suffering from habit, and devoid of reflection from ignorance, they enjoy a kind of security. Having nothing to lose, they are in no dread of being plundered. The merchant, *on the contrary,* lives in a state of perpetual alarm, under the double apprehension of acquiring no more, and losing what he possesses. He trembles lest he should attract the attention of rapacious authority, which would consider an air of satisfaction as a proof of opulence and the signal for extortion. The *same dread* prevails throughout the villages, where *every peasant is afraid* of exciting the envy of his equals, and the avarice of the Aga and his soldiers. In such a country, where

* Volney's Travels, vol. ii. p. 417.

the subject is perpetually watched by a despoiling government, he must assume a serious countenance for the same reason that he wears ragged clothes;"* or, as the description might appropriately have been concluded, in the very words of the prophet, because of the violence of them that dwell therein.

They shall be ashamed of your revenues. "From the state of the contributions of each pachalic, it appears that the annual sum paid by Syria into the Kasna, or treasury of the Sultan, amounts to 2345 purses, viz.

For Aleppo,	.	.	800 purses.
Tripoli,	.	.	750
Damascus,	.	.	45
Acre,	.	.	750
Palestine,	.	.	—
			2345 purses :

Which are equal to 2,931,250 livres, or £122,135 sterling." After the specification of some identical sources of revenue, it is added; " we cannot be far from the truth, if we compute the total of the Sultan's revenue from Syria to be 7,500,000 livres," (£312,500 sterling,)† or less than the third part of one million sterling, and less than a seventh part of what it yielded, in tribute, unto Egypt, long after the prophecies were sealed. This is the whole amount that a government which has reached the acme of despotism, and which accounts pillage a right, and all property its own, can extort from impoverished Syria. But, insignificant as this sum is as the revenues of those extensive territories, which included in ancient times several opulent and powerful states, the greater part must be deducted from it, before estimating the pitiful pittance, which, under the name

* Volney's Travels, v. ii. pp. 477, 478.   † Ibid. p. 360.

of revenue, its oppressive masters can now drain from the land of Israel. A single glance at the preceding statement, affords the obvious means of distinguishing the comparative desolation and poverty of the different provinces of Syria. And the least unproductive of these in revenue,—the pachalics of Aleppo and Tripoli, and a considerable portion of what now forms the pachalic of Acre, were not included within the boundaries of ancient Judea. Palestine,—containing the ancient territory of Philistia and part of Judea—was then gifted in whole, by the Sultan, to two individuals. The very extensive pachalic of Damascus, so unproductive of revenue, includes Jerusalem and a great proportion of ancient Judea, so that of it, even with greater propriety than of the rest, it may be said,—*they shall be ashamed of your revenues.*

Instead of viewing separately each special prediction, the prophecies respecting the desolation of the land of Judea are so abundant, that several may be grouped together ; and their meaning is so clear that any explanatory remarks would be superfluous. Nor is the evidence of their complete fulfilment indistinct or difficult to be found ; for Volney illustrates six predictions in a single sentence, to which he subjoins a reflection, not less confirmatory than them all, of prophetic inspiration.

I will destroy your high places, and bring your SANCTUARIES *into desolation.—The* PALACES *shall be forsaken.—I will destroy the remnant of the seacoast.—I will make your cities waste.—The multitude of the city shall be left, the habitation forsaken, &c. The land shall he utterly spoiled.—I will make the land more desolate than the wilderness.* "The *temples* are thrown down—the *palaces* demolished—the *ports* filled up—the *towns* destroyed—and the earth, *stripped of inhabitants,* seems a *dreary burying-place.*"*

* Volney's Ruins, c. 11, p. 8.

" Good God !" exclaims Volney, " from whence proceed such melancholy revolutions ? For what cause is the fortune of these countries so *strikingly changed?* Why are so many cities destroyed ? Why is not that ancient population reproduced and perpetuated ?" " I wandered over the country—I traversed the provinces—I enumerated the kingdoms of Damascus and Idumea ; of Jerusalem and Samaria. This Syria, SAID *I to myself,* now almost depopulated, then contained a hundred flourishing cities. and abounded with towns, villages, and hamlets. What are become of so many productions of the hands of man ? What are become of those ages of abundance and of life ?" &c. Seeking to be wise, men become fools, when they trust to their own vain imaginations, and will not look to that word of God, which is as able to confound the wise, as to give understanding to the simple. These words, from the lips of a great advocate of infidelity, proclaim the certainty of the truth which he was too blind or bigotted to see. For not more unintentionally or unconsciously do *many* illiterate Arab *pastors,* or herdsmen, verify one prediction, while they literally *tread* Palestine *under foot,* than Volney, the academician, himself verifies another, while, speaking in his own name, and the spokesman also of others, he thus confirms the unerring truth of God's holy word, by what he *said,*—as well as by describing what he saw. " *The generation to come of your children that shall rise up after you, and* THE STRANGER THAT SHALL COME FROM A FAR LAND *shall* SAY, *when they see the plagues of that land and the sickness which the Lord hath laid upon it, Wherefore hath the Lord done this unto the land? what meaneth the heat of his great anger ?*"

It is no " secret malediction," spoken of by Volney, which God has pronounced against Judea. It is the curse of a broken covenant that rests upon the land—the consequences of the iniquities of the people, not of those only who have been plucked from off it and scattered throughout the world, but of those also that dwell therein. The ruins of empires originated not from the regard which mortals paid to revealed religion, but from causes diametrically the reverse. Neither Jews nor Christians who possessed a revelation, were the desolators: Under them Judea flourished. The destruction of Jerusalem, and of the cities of Palestine, was the work of the Romans, who were pagan idolaters; and the devastation in more recent ages, was perpetuated by the Saracens and Turks, believers in the impostor Mahomet, and the desolations were wrought by the enemies of the Mosaic and Christian dispensations. The desolations are not of divine appointment, but only as they have followed the violations of the laws of God, or have arisen from thence. The virtual renunciation of a holy faith brought on destruction. And none other curses have come upon the land than those that are written in the book. The character and condition of the people are not less definitely marked, than the features of the land, that has been smitten with a curse because of their iniquities. And when the unbeliever asks, wherefore hath the Lord done this unto the land, the same word which foretold that the question would be put, supplies an answer and assigns the cause. *Then shall men say, because they have forsaken the covenant of the Lord God of their fathers, &c.*

The land is defiled under the inhabitants thereof, because they have transgressed the laws, changed the ordinances, broken the everlasting covenant. Therefore hath the curse devoured the earth, &c. These expressive words, while they declare the cause of the judgments and desolation, denote also the great depravity of those who were to inhabit the land of Judea during the time of its desolation, and while its ancient inhabitants were to be " scattered abroad." And although the ignorance of those who dwell therein may be pitied, their degeneracy will not be denied. The ferocity of the Turks, the predatory habits of the Arabs, the abject state of the few poor Jews who are suffered to dwell in the land of their fathers, the base superstitions of the different Christian sects,— the frequent contentions that subsist among such a mingled and diversified people, and the gross ignorance and great depravity that prevail throughout the whole, have all sadly changed and stained the moral aspect of that country, which, from sacred remembrances, is denominated the Holy Land,—have converted that region, where alone in all the world, and during many ages, the only living and true God was worshipped, and where alone the pattern of perfect virtue was ever exhibited to human view, or in the human form—into one of the most degraded countries of the globe, and in appropriate terms, may well be said to have *defiled the land*. And it has been defiled throughout many an age. The Father of mercies afflicteth not willingly, nor grieves the children of men. Sin is ever the precursor of the actual judgments of heaven. It was on account of their idolatry and wickedness that the ten tribes were earliest plucked from off the land of Israel. The blood of Jesus, according to their prayer, and the full measure of their iniquity, according to their doings, was upon the Jews and upon their children. Before they were extirpated from that land which their iniquities had defiled—it was drenched with the blood of more than a million of their race. Judea afterwards had a partial and temporary respite from desolation, when Christian churches were established there. But in that land, the nursery of Christianity, the seeds of its corruption, or perversion, began soon to appear. The moral power of religion decayed, the worship of images prevailed, and the nominal disciples of a pure faith "broke the everlasting covenant."* The doctrine of Mahomet,—the Koran or the sword,—was the scourge and the cure of idolatry; but all the native impurities of the Mahometan creed succeeded to a grossly corrupted form of Christianity. Since that period, hordes of Saracens, Egyptians, Fatimites, Tartars, Mamelukes, Turks, (a combination of names of unmatched barbarism, at least in modern times,) have, for the space of twelve hundred years, *defiled the land* of the children of Israel with iniquity and with blood. And in very truth the prophecy savours not in the least of hyperbole,—*the worst of the heathen shall possess their houses. And the holy places shall be defiled.* Omar, on the first conquest of Jerusalem by the Mahometans, erected a mosque on the site of the temple of Solomon; and, jealous as the God of Israel is that his glory be not given to another, the unseemly and violent and bloody contentions among Christian sects around the very sepulchre of the author of the faith which they dishonour—bear not a feebler testimony in the present day, than the preceding fact bore, at so remote a period, to the truth of this prediction. The frenzied zeal of crusading Christians could not expel the heathen from Judea, though Europe then poured like a torrent upon Asia. But the defilement of the land, no less than that of the holy places, is not yet cleansed away. And Judea is still defiled to this hour, not only by oppressive rulers, but by an unprincipled and a lawless people. "The barbarism of Syria," says Volney, "is complete."† "I have often reflected," says Burck-

* Isa. xxiv. 5.
† Volney's Travels, vol. ii. p. 442.

hardt, in describing the dishonest conduct of a Greek priest in the Hauran, (but in words that admit of too general an application,) " that if the English penal laws were suddenly promulgated in this country, there is scarcely any man in business, or who has money dealings with others, who would not be liable to transportation before the end of the first six months."*
" Under the name of Christianity, every degrading superstition and profane rite, equally remote from the enlightened tenets of the gospel and the dignity of human nature, are professed and tolerated. The pure gospel of Christ, everywhere the herald of civilization and of science, is almost as little known in the Holy Land as in California or New Holland. A series of legendary traditions, mingled with remains of Judaism, and the wretched phantasies of illiterate ascetics, may now and then exhibit a glimmering of heavenly light; but if we seek for the effects of Christianity in the land of Canaan, we must look for that period, when the desert shall blossom as the rose, and the wilderness become a fruitful field."† *The land is defiled under the inhabitants thereof: because they have transgressed the laws, changed the ordinances, broken the everlasting covenant.—Therefore hath the curse devoured the land, and*

They that dwell therein are desolate. " The government of the Turks in Syria is a pure military despotism, that is, the bulk of the inhabitants are subject to the caprices of a faction of armed men, who dispose of every thing according to their interest and fancy."
" In each government the pasha is an absolute despot. In the villages, the inhabitants, limited to the mere necessaries of life, have no arts but those without which they cannot subsist." " There is no safety

* Burckhardt's Travels in Syria, p. 89.
† Clarke's Travels, vol. ii. p. 405.

without the towns, nor security within their pre-
cincts;"* and

Few men left. While their character is thus depraved and their condition miserable, their number is
also small indeed, as the inhabitants of so extensive
and fertile a region. After estimating the number of
inhabitants in Syria, in general, Volney remarks—
" So feeble a population in so excellent a country,
may well excite our *astonishment;* but this will be increased, if we compare the present number of inhabitants with that of ancient times. We are informed
by the philosophical geographer, Strabo, that the territories of Yanmia and Yoppa, in Palestine alone,
were formerly so populous as to bring forty thousand
armed men into the field. At present they could
scarcely furnish three thousand. From the accounts
we have of Judea, in the time of Titus, which are to
be esteemed tolerably accurate, that country must
have contained four millions of inhabitants. If we
go still farther back into antiquity, we shall find the
same populousness among the Philistines, the Phœni-
cians, and in the kingdoms of Samaria and Damascus."† Though the ancient population of the land
of Israel be estimated at the lowest computation, and
the existing population be rated at the highest, yet
that country does not now contain a tenth part of the
number of inhabitants, which it plentifully supported exclusively from the industry and from the rich
resources of its own luxuriant soil, for many successive centuries; and how could it possibly have been
imagined that this identical land would ever yield so
scanty a subsistance to the desolate dwellers therein,
and that there would be so *few men left?*

Yet in it shall be a tenth. The city that went out

---

* Volney's Travels, vol. ii. pp. 370, 376, 380.
† Ibid. p. 366.

by a thousand shall leave an hundred, and that which went out by an hundred shall leave ten. The present population of Judea has been estimated, without reference to any prediction, at a *tenth* of the number by which it was peopled previous to the dispersion of the Jews. Volney, on a comparative estimate, reduces it even to less. It is impossible to ascertain the precise proportion. The words of Pierre Bello, quoted by Malte-Brun, though the same in substance with the testimony of others, here afford the closest commentary. " A tract from which a *hundred* individuals draw a scanty subsistence, formerly maintained *thousands*."*

The mirth of the tabret ceaseth, the noise of them that rejoice endeth, the joy of the harp ceaseth. Instrumental music was common among the Jews. The tabret and the harp, the cymbal, the psaltery, and the viol, and other instruments of music, are often mentioned as in familiar use among the Israelites, and regularly formed a great part of the service of the temple. At the period when the prediction was delivered, the harp, the viol, and the tabret, and pipe, and wine were in their feasts; and even though the Jews have long ceased to be a nation, the use of these instruments has not wholly ceased from among them. But in the once happy land of Judea, the voice of mirthful music is at rest. In a general description of the state of the arts and sciences in Syria (including the whole of the Holy Land,) Volney remarks, that adepts in music are very rarely to be met with. " They have no music but vocal; for they neither know nor esteem *instrumental ;* and they are in the right, for such instruments as they have, not excepting their flutes, are detestable."† *The mirth of the harp ceaseth, the joy of the tabret ceaseth.*

* Malte-Brun's Geography, vol. ii. p. 151.
† Volney's Travels, vol. ii. p. 439.

But this is not the sole instance in which the melancholy features of that desolate country seem to be transferred to the minds of its inhabitants.   And the plaintive language of the prophet (the significancy of which might well have admitted of some slight modification, if one jot or tittle could pass away till all be fulfilled,) is true to the very letter, when set side by side, unaided by one syllable of comment, with the words of a bold and avowed unbeliever.

All the merry-hearted do SIGH ; *they shall not drink wine with a song ; all joy is darkened, the mirth of the land is gone.   Their shouting shall be no shouting.* " Their performance," (singing) " is accompanied with sighs and gestures.   They may be said to excel most in the *melancholy* strain.   To behold an Arab with his head inclined, his hand applied to his ear, his eyebrows knit, his eyes languishing ; to hear his plaintive tones, his *sighs* and sobs, it is almost impossible to refrain from tears."[*]   If any further illustration of the prediction be requisite, the same ill-fated narrator of facts exhibits anew the visions of the prophet.   From his description (chap. xl.) of the manners and character of the inhabitants of Syria, it is obvious that melancholy is a predominating feature. " Instead of that open and cheerful countenance, which we either naturally possess or assume, their behaviour is serious, austere, and melancholy.   They rarely laugh ; and the gaiety of the French appears to them a fit of delirium.   When they speak, it is with deliberation, without gesture, and without passion ; they listen without interrupting you ; they are silent for whole days together ; and by no means pique themselves on supporting conversation.   Continually seated, they pass whole days musing, with their legs crossed, their pipes in their mouths, and almost with-

* Volney's Travels, pp. 439, 440.

out changing their attitude.   The orientals, in general, have a grave and phlegmatic exterior ; a stayed
and almost listless deportment ; and a serious, nay,
even sad and melancholy countenance."*   Having
thus explicitly stated the fact, Volney, by many arguments, equally judicious and just, most successfully
combats the idea that the climate and soil are the
radical cause of so striking a phenomenon : and after
assigning a multiplicity of facts from ancient history,
which completely disprove the efficacy of such causes,
he instances that of the Jews, " who, limited to a
little state, never ceased to struggle for a thousand
years against the most powerful empires.†   If the
men of these nations were inert," he adds, " what is
activity ?   If they were active, where then is the influence of climate ?   Why, in the same countries,
where so much energy was displayed in former times,
do we at present find such profound indolence ?"   And
having thus relieved the advocate for the inspiration
of the Scriptures from the necessity of proving that
the contrast in the manner and character of the present and of the ancient inhabitants of Syria is (even
now, when the change has become matter of history
and observation, and when the circumstances respecting it are known,) incapable of solution from any
natural causes, such as by some conceivable possibility
might have been foreseen, he proceeds to point out
those real, efficacious, and efficient causes, viz. the
mode of government and the state of religion and of
the laws—the nature of which no human sagacity
could possibly have descried, and which came not
into existence or operation in the manner in which
they have so long continued, for many ages subsequent to the period when their full and permanent
effect was laid open to the full view of the prophets·

* Volney's Travels, pp. 461, 476.   † Ibid. p. 464.

of Israel. The fact, thus clearly predicted and proved, is not only astonishing as referable to the inhabitants of Judea, and as exhibiting a contrast, than which nothing, of a similar kind, can be more complete; but it is so very contradictory to the habits of men and customs of nations, that it is totally inexplicable, how, by any human means, such a fact, even singly, could ever have been foretold. From the congregated groups of savages, cheered by their simple instruments of music, exulting in their war-songs, and revelling in their mirth, to the more elegant assemblages of polished society, listening with delight to the triumphs of music : from the huts of the wilderness to the courts of Asia and of Europe, and from the wilds of America, the jungles of India, and even the deserts of central Africa, to the meadows of England, the plains of France, or the valleys of Italy ; the experience of mankind in every clime, —except partially where the blasting influence of the crescent is felt,—proclaims as untrue to nature the predicted fact, which actually has been permanently characteristic of the inhabitants of the once happy land of Israel. The fact perhaps would have been but slowly credited ; and the synonymous terms of the ample description, and of the repeated prophecies, might have been reckoned the fiction of a biassed judgment, had a Christian, instead of Volney, been the witness.

They shall not drink wine with a song. Strong drink shall be BITTER *unto them that drink it.* The more closely that the author of the *Ruins of Empires* traces the causes in which the desolation of these regions, and the calamities of the inhabitants originate, he supplies more abundant data for a demonstration that the prophecies respecting them cannot but be divine. " One of the chief sources," continues Volney, " of gaiety with us is the social intercourse of the table, and the use of wine. The orientals (Syrians) are almost strangers to this double enjoyment. Good cheer would infallibly expose them to extortion, and wine to corporal punishment, from the zeal of the police in enforcing the precepts of the Koran. It is with great reluctance the Mahometans tolerate the Christians the use of the liquor they envy them."[*] To this statement may be subjoined the more direct, but equally unapplied, testimony of recent travellers. "The wines of Jerusalem," says Mr. Joliffe, "are most execrable. In a country where every species of vinous liquor is strictly prohibited by the concurrent authorities of law and gospel, a single fountain may be considered of infinitely greater value than many wine-presses."[†] Mr. Wilson relates that "the wine drank in Jerusalem is probably the very worst to be met with in any country."[‡] While the intolerance and despotism of the Turks, and the rapacity and wildness of the Arabs, have blighted the produce of Judea, and render abortive all the influence of climate, and all the fertility of that land of vines, the unnatural prohibition of the use of wine, and the rigour with which that prohibition is enforced, have peculiarly operated against the cultivation of the vine, and turned the treading of the wine-press into an odious and unprofitable task. Yet in a country where the vine grows spontaneously, and which was celebrated for the excellence of its wines,[§] nothing less than the operation of causes unnatural and extreme as these, could have verified the language of prophecy. But in this instance, as truly as in every other, a recapitulation of the prophecies is the best summary of the facts. And, by only changing the future into the

* Volney's Travels, v. ii. p. 480.
† Joliffe's Letters from Palestine, v. i. p. 184.
‡ Wilson's Travels, p. 130.
§ Reland. Palest. pp. 381, 792.

present and the past, after an interval of two thousand
five hundred years, no eye-witness, writing on the spot,
could delineate a more accurate representation of the
existing state of Judea, than in the very words of Isaiah, in which, as in those of other prophets, the various and desultory observations of travellers are concentrated into a description equally perspicuous and
true.

" Many days and years shall ye be troubled, for the
vintage shall fail, the gathering shall not come. They
shall lament for the teats, for the pleasant fields, for
the fruitful vine. Upon the land of my people shall
come up thorns and briars; yea, upon all the houses of
joy in the joyous city. Because the palaces shall be
forsaken—the multitude of the city shall be left—the
forts and towns shall be for dens—a joy of wild asses
—a pasture of flocks.* The highways lie waste—the
wayfaring man ceaseth—the earth mourneth and languisheth. Lebanon is ashamed, or hewn down, or
withered away—Sharon is like a wilderness—and Bashan and Carmel shake off their fruits.† The land
shall be utterly emptied and utterly despoiled. The
earth mourneth and fadeth away—it is defiled under
the inhabitants thereof. Because they have transgressed the laws, therefore hath the curse devoured
the earth, and they that dwell therein are desolate, and
few men left: the vine languisheth, all the merry-
hearted do sigh. The mirth of tabrets ceaseth—the
noise of them that rejoice endeth—the joy of the harp
ceaseth. They shall not drink wine with a song—
strong drink shall be bitter to them that drink it—the
city of confusion is broken down—all joy is darkened
—the mirth of the land is gone."‡

To this picture of common and general devastation,

---

* Isaiah xxxii. 10—14.   † Isaiah xxxiii. 8, 9.
‡ Isaiah xxiv. 3, &c.

that no distinguishing feature might be left untouched
or untraced by his pencil, the prophet adds :—" When
thus it shall be in the midst of the land, there shall be
as the shaking of an olive tree, and as the gleaning
of grapes when the vintage is done.* The glory of
Jacob shall be made thin ; and it shall be, as when
the harvestman gathereth the corn and reapeth the
ears with his arm—yet gleaning grapes shall be left
in it, as the shaking of an olive tree, two or three
berries in the top of the uppermost bough, four or
five in the outmost fruitful branches thereof."† These
words imply, as is otherwise declared without a metaphor, that a small remnant would be left—that though
Judea should become poor like a field that has been
reaped, or like a vine stripped of its fruits, its desolation
would not be so complete but that some vestige of its
former abundance would be still visible, like the few
grains that are left by the reaper when the harvest
is past, or the little remaining fruit that hangs on the
uppermost branch, or on a neglected bough, after the
full crop has been gathered, and the vine and the
olive have been shaken.   And is there yet a gleaning left of all the glory of Israel ?   There is ; and
there could not be any simile more natural or more
expressive of the fact.   Napolose (the ancient Sychar or Sichem) is luxuriantly embosomed in the
most delightful and fragrant bowers, half concealed
by rich gardens and by stately trees, collected into
groves all around the beautiful valley in which it
stands.‡—The garden of Geddin, situated on the

_____

* Isaiah xxiv. 13.   † Isaiah xvii. 5, 6.
   ‡ Clarke, vol. ii. 506.   The remark may be interesting to
the Christian reader, that,—while Capernaum, the capital of
Galilee, which was " exalted unto heaven," or the highest
prosperity, when Jesus and his apostles preached there in
vain, is brought down to hell, (to hades) to death, or entire
destruction, being nothing now but shapeless ruins, as Chorazin and Bethsaida also are,—and while Samaria, the capital

borders of Mount Sharon, and protected by its chief,
extends several miles in a spacious valley, abounding with excellent fruits, such as olives, almonds,
peaches, apricots and figs. A number of streams
that fall from the mountains, traverse it, and water
the cotton plants that thrive well in this fertile
soil.* The scenery in the plain of Zabulon is, to
the full, as delightful as in the rich vale upon the
south of the Crimea;—it reminds the traveller of
the finest part of Kent and Surrey.† The soil, although stony, is exceedingly rich, but now entirely neglected. But the delightful vale of Zabulon
appears everywhere covered with spontaneous vegetation, flourishing in the wildest exuberance. Even
along the mountains of Gilead, the land possessing
extraordinary riches, abounds with the most beautiful prospects, is clothed with rich forests, varied with
verdant slopes ; and extensive plains of a fine red soil,
are now covered with thistles as the best proof of its
fertility.‡ The valley of St. John's, in the vicinity of
Jerusalem, is crowned to the top with olives and vines,
while the lower part of the valley bears the milder fig
and almond.§ Whenever any spot is fixed on as the
residence, and seized as the property, either of a Turkish Aga or of an Arab Sheikh, it enjoys his protection,
is made to administer to his wants, or to his luxury,
and the exuberance and beauty of the land of Canaan

of the country which bore its name, is cast down into the valley,—Sychar, then one of its inferior cities, from which the
inhabitants came forth to meet Jesus, and in which many
believed in him as the Saviour when they heard his word—
is ranked by every traveller, who describes it, among the
most striking exceptions to the general desolation, which has
otherwise left but a remembrance of the *cities* of Judah, of
Samaria and Galilee.

* Mariti's Travels, ii. 151.   † Clarke, ii. 400.
‡ Buckingham's Travels, p. 322.
§ General Straton's MS. Travels.

soon appear. But such spots are, in the words of an
eye-witness, only " mere sprinklings" in the midst of
extensive desolation. And how could it ever have been
foreseen, that the same cause, viz. the residence of despotic spoliators, was to operate in so strange a manner
as to spread a wide wasting desolation over the face
of the country, and to be, at the same time, the very
means of preserving the thin gleanings of its ancient
glory ; or that a few berries on the outmost bough
would be saved by the same hand that was to shake
the olive ?

Among such a multiplicity of prophecies, where the
prediction and the fulfilment of each is a miracle, it is
almost impossible to select any as more amazing than
the rest. But that concerning Samaria is not the
least remarkable. That city was, for a long period,
the capital of the ten tribes of Israel. Herod the
Great enlarged and adorned it, and, in honour of
Augustus Cæsar, gave it the name of Sebaste. There
are many ancient medals which were struck there.*
It was the seat of a bishopric, as the subscription of
some of its bishops to the acts of ancient councils attest. Its history is thus brought down to a period
unquestionably far remote from the time of the prediction ; and the narrative of a traveller, which alludes not to the prophecy, and which has even been
unnoticed by commentators, shows its complete fulfilment. Besides other passages which speak of its
extinction as a city, the word of the Lord which Micah saw concerning Samaria, is—" I will make Samaria as a heap of the field, and as plantings of a
vineyard : and I will pour down the stones thereof
into the valley ; and I will discover the foundations
thereof." And this great city is now wholly converted into gardens ; and all the tokens that remain to
testify that there has ever been such a place, are only

* Calmet's Dictionary. Relandi Palest. p. 981.

on the north side—a large square piazza, encompassed with pillars,—and on the east some poor remains
of a great church.   Such was the first notice of that
ancient capital given by Maundrell in 1696, and it is
confirmed by Mr. Buckingham in 1816.   The relative distance, local position, and unaltered name of
Sebaste, leave no doubt as to the identity of its site;
and he adds, its local features are equally seen in the
threat of Micah.*

But the predicted fate of Jerusalem has been more
conspicuously displayed and more fully illustrated
than that of the capital of the ten tribes of Israel.   It
formed the theme of prophecy from the deathbed of
Jacob,—and, as the seat of the government of the
children of Judah, the sceptre departed not from it
till the Messiah appeared, on the expiration of seventeen hundred years after the death of the Patriarch,
and till the period of its desolation, prophesied of by
Daniel, had arrived.   A destiny diametrically opposite
to the former, then awaited it, even for a longer duration ; and, ere its greatness was gone, even at the
very time when it was crowded with Jews, from all quarters, resorting to the feast, and when it was inhabited by
a numerous population dwelling in security and peace,
its doom was denounced—that it was to be trodden
down of the Gentiles, till the time of the Gentiles should
be fulfilled.   The time of the Gentiles is not yet fulfilled, and Jerusalem is still trodden down of the Gentiles.   The Jews have often attempted to recover it :
No distance of space or of time can separate it from
their affections—they perform their devotions with
their faces towards it, as if it were the object of their

* Buckingham's Travels, pp. 511, 512.   It has also been described in similar terms by other travellers.   The stones are
poured down into the valley, the foundations discovered, and
there is now only to be seen " the hill where once stood Samaria."   Napolose has been mistaken by one traveller for the
ancient Samaria.

worship as well as of their love ; and although their
desire to return be so strong, indelible, and innate,
that every Jew, in every generation, counts himself an exile—yet they have never been able to
rebuild their temple, nor to recover Jerusalem
from the hands of the Gentiles.   But greater power
than that of a proscribed and exiled race has been
added to their own, in attempting to frustrate the counsel that professed to be of God.   Julian, the emperor
of the Romans, not only permitted but invited the Jews
to rebuild Jerusalem and their temple ; and promised
to re-establish them in their paternal city.   By that
single act, more than by all his writings, he might have
destroyed the credibility of the gospel, and restored
his beloved but deserted paganism.   The zeal of the
Jews was equal to his own—and the work was begun
by laying again the foundations of the temple.   In the
space of three days, Titus had formerly encompassed
that city with a wall when it was crowded with his enemies; and, instead of being obstructed, that great work,
when it was confirmatory of an express prediction of
Jesus, was completed with an astonishing celerity ;—
and what could hinder the emperor of Rome from building a temple at Jerusalem, when every Jew was zealous for the work ?   Nothing appeared against it but a
single sentence uttered, some centuries before, by one
who had been crucified.   If that word had been of
man, would all the power of the monarch of the world
have been thwarted in opposing it ?   And why did not
Julian, with all his inveterate enmity and laborious
opposition to Christianity, execute a work so easy and
desirable ?   A heathen historian relates—that fearful
balls of fire, bursting from the earth, sometimes burned
the workmen, rendered the place inaccessible, and
caused them to desist from the undertaking.*   The

* Imperii sui memoriam magnitudine operum gestiens pro-
pagare, ambitosum quondam apud Hierosolymam templum,

same narrative is attested by others. Chrysostom, who was a living witness, appealed to the existing state of the foundations, and to the universal testimony which was given of the fact. And an eminent modern traveller, who visited, and who minutely examined the spot, testifies that " there seems every reason for believing, that, in the reticulated remains still visible on the site of the temple, is seen a standing memorial of Julian's discomfiture."* While destitute of this additional confirmation of its truth, the historical evidence was too strong even for the scepticism of Gibbon altogether to gainsay; and brought him to the acknowledgment that such authority must astonish an incredulous mind. Even independent of the miraculous interposition, the fulfilment is the same. The attempt was made avowedly, and it was abandoned without any apparent cause. It was never accomplished—and the prophecy stands fulfilled. But, even if the attempt of Julian had never been made, the truth of the prophecy itself is unassailable. The Jews have never been reinstated in Judea. Jerusalem has ever been trodden down of the Gentiles. The edict of Adrian

---

quod, post multa et interneciva certamina obsidente Vespasiano, posteaque Tito, ægre est expugnatum, instaurare sumptibus cogitabat immodicis; negotiumque maturandum Alypio dederat Antiochensi, qui olim Britannias curaverat pro præfectis. Cum itaque rei eidem instaret Alypius, juvaretque provinciæ rector, metuendi globi flammarum, prope fundamenta, crebris assultibus erumpentes, fecere locum exustis aliquoties operantibus inaccessum; hocque modo, elemento destinatius repellente, cessavit inceptum—Ammian. Marcell. lib. xxiii. cap. 1. § 2, 3. Rufini Hist. Eccles. lib. i. c. 37. Socrat. lib. ii. c. 17. Theodorit. l. iii. c. 17. Sozomin, l. v. c. 21. Cassiod. Hist. Tripart. l. vi. c. 43. Nicephor. Callis. lib. x. 32. Greg. Naziaz. in Julian. Orat. 2. Chrysos. de lau. Bab. Mart. et contra Judeos, iii. p. 491. Lind.—Vide Am. Mar. tom. iii. p. 2.

* Clarke's Travels, vol. ii. note 1, at the end of the volume.

was renewed by the successors of Julian—and no
Jews could approach unto Jerusalem but by bribery
or by stealth. It was a spot unlawful for them to
touch. In the crusades, all the power of Europe
was employed to rescue Jerusalem from the heathens,
but equally in vain. It has been trodden down for
nearly eighteen centuries by its successive masters—
by Romans, Grecians, Persians, Saracens, Mamelukes, Turks, Christians—and again by the worst of
rulers, the Arabs and the Turks. And could any
thing be more improbable to have happened, or more
impossible to have been foreseen by man, than that
any people should be banished from their own capital and country, and remain expelled and expatriated
for nearly eighteen hundred years? Did the same
fate ever befall any nation, though no prophecy existed respecting it? Is there any doctrine in Scripture so hard to be believed as was this single fact at
the period of its prediction? And even with the example of the Jews before us, is it likely, or is it credible, or who can foretell—that the present inhabitants of any country upon earth shall be banished into all nations—retain their distinctive character—
meet with an unparalleled fate—continue a people—
without a government and without a country—and
remain for an indefinite period, exceeding seventeen
hundred years, till the fulfilment of a prescribed
event which has yet to be accomplished? Must not
the knowledge of such truths be derived from that
prescience alone which scans alike the will and the
ways of mortals, the actions of future nations, and
the history of the latest generations?

But the prophecies are not confined to the land of
Judea; they are equally unlimited in their range over
space as over time. After a lapse of many ages, the
countries around Judea are now beginning to be
known. And each succeeding traveller, in the com-

munication of new discoveries concerning them, is gradually unfolding the very description which the prophets gave of their poverty and desolation, at the time of their great prosperity and luxuriance. The countries of the Ammonites—of the Moabites—of the Edomites, or inhabitants of Idumea, and of the Philistines, all bordered with Judea, and each is the theme of prophecy. The relative positions of them all are distinctly defined in Scripture, and have been clearly ascertained.* And the territories of the ancient enemies of the Jews, long overrun by the enemies of Christianity, present many a proof of the inspiration of the Jewish Scriptures, and of the truth of the Christian religion.

AMMON.

The country anciently peopled by the Ammonites, is situated to the east of Palestine, and is now possessed partly by the Arabs and by the Turks. It is naturally one of the most fertile provinces of Syria, and it was for many ages one of the most populous. The Ammonites often invaded the land of Israel; and at one period, united with the Moabites, they retained possession of a great part of it, and grievously oppressed the Israelites for the space of eighteen years. Jephthah repulsed them, and took twenty of their cities; but they continued afterwards to harass the borders of Israel—and their capital was besieged by the forces of David, and their country rendered tributary. They regained and long maintained their

* Relandi *Palestina Illustrata;* D'Anville's Map ; Maps in Volney's, Burckhardt's, and Buckingham's Travels; Well's Scripture Geography; Gibbon's History; Shaw's Travels, &c.

independence, till Jotham, the king of Judah, subdued them, and exacted from them an annual tribute
of an hundred talents, and thirty thousand quarters
of wheat and barley; yet they soon contested again
with their ancient enemies, and exulted in the miseries that befell them, when Nebuchadnezzar took
Jerusalem, and carried its inhabitants into captivity.
In after times, though successively oppressed by the
Chaldeans, (when some of the earliest prophecies respecting it were fulfilled) and by the Egyptians and
Syrians, Ammon was a highly productive and populous country, when the Romans became masters of
all the provinces of Syria; and several of the ten al-
lied cities, which gave name to the celebrated Deca-
polis, were included within its boundaries. Even
" when first invaded by the Saracens, this country
(including Moab) was enriched by the various benefits of trade, was covered with a line of forts, and
possessed some strong and populous cities."* Volney bears witness, " that, in the immense plains of
the Hauran, ruins are continually to be met with, and
that what is said of its actual fertility perfectly corresponds with the idea given of it in the Hebrew writings."† The fact of its natural fertility is corroborated
by every traveller who has visited it. And " it is evident," says Burckhardt, " that the whole country
must have been extremely well cultivated, in order to
have afforded subsistence to the inhabitants of so
many towns,"‡ as are now visible only in their ruins.

* Gibbon's Hist. vol. v. p. 240, c. 51.
† Volney's Travels, vol. ii. p. 299.
‡ Burckhardt's Travels in Syria, p. 357.
Having frequent occasion, in the subsequent pages, to refer to the authority of the celebrated and lamented traveller,
J. Lewis Burckhardt, the following ample testimonies to his
talents, perseverance, and veracity, will show with what perfect confidence his statements may be relied on, especially as
the subject of the fulfilment of prophecy, being never once

While the fruitfulness of the land of Ammon, and the high degree of prosperity and power in which it subsisted, long prior and long subsequent to the date of the predictions, are thus indisputably established by historical evidence, and by existing proofs, the researches of recent travellers (who were actuated by the mere desire of exploring these regions and obtaining geographical information,) have made known its present aspect; and testimony the most clear, unexceptionable, and conclusive, has been borne to the state of dire desolation to which it is, and has long been reduced.

It was prophesied concerning AMMON—" Son of man, set thy face against the Ammonites, and prophesy against them. I will make Rabbah of the

---

alluded to in all his writings, seems to have been wholly foreign to his view.—" He was a traveller of no ordinary description, a gentleman by birth, and a scholar by education; he added to the ordinary acquirements of a traveller, accomplishments which fitted him for any society. His description of the countries through which he passed, his narrative of incidents, his transactions with the natives, are all placed before us with equal clearness and simplicity. In every page they will find that ardour of research—that patience of investigation—that passionate pursuit after truth, for which he was eminently distinguished."— *Quarterly Review*, Vol. xxii. p. 437. " He appears, from his books and letters, to have been a modest, laborious, learned, and sensible man; exempt from prejudice, *unattached to systems ;* detailing what he saw plainly and correctly, and of very prudent and discreet conduct."—*Edinburgh Review*, No. lxvii. p. 109. The following extract from General Straton's manuscript travels, was written at Cairo, and is the more valuable, as containing the result of personal knowledge and observation.—" Burckhardt speaks Arabic perfectly, has adopted the costume, and goes to the religious places of worship, has been at Mecca; in short, follows in every thing the Turkish manners and customs, and he is not to be distinguished from a Mussulman. With what advantage must he travel! He is by birth a Swiss, but having been educated in England, speaks our language perfectly."

Ammonites a stable for camels and a couching-place
for flocks. Behold I will stretch out my hand upon
thee, and deliver thee for a spoil to the heathen ; I
will cut thee off from the people, and cause thee to
perish out of the countries ; I will destroy thee. The
Ammonites shall not be remembered among the nations. Rabbah (the chief city) of the Ammonites
shall be a desolate heap. Ammon shall be a perpetual desolation."*

*Ammon was to be delivered to be a spoil to the hea-
then—to be destroyed, and to be a perpetual desolation.*
" All this country, formerly so populous and flourishing, is now changed into a vast desert."† Ruins
are seen in every direction. The country is divided
between the Turks and the Arabs, but chiefly possessed by the latter. The extortions of the one and
the depredations of the other, keep it in *perpetual desolation* and make it *a spoil to the heathen.* " The
far greater part of the country is uninhabited, being
abandoned to the wandering Arabs, and the towns
and villages are in a state of total ruin."‡ " At every
step are to be found the vestiges of ancient cities, the
remains of many temples, public edifices, and Greek
churches."§ The cities are desolate. " Many of
the ruins present no objects of any interest. They
consist of a few walls of dwelling-houses, heaps of
stones, the foundations of some public edifices, and a
few cisterns filled up ; there is nothing entire, but it
appears that the mode of building was very solid, all
the remains being formed of large stones.—In the
vicinity of Ammon there is a fertile plain interspersed
with low hills, which for the greater part are covered
with ruins."‖

---

* Ezek. xxv. 2, 5, 7, 10; xxi. 32. Jerem. xlix. 2. Zeph. ii. 9.
† Seetzen's Travels, p. 34.   ‡ Ibid. p. 37.
§ Burckhardt's Travels in Nubia, introd. pp. 37, 38, 44.
‖ Burckhardt's Travels in Syria, pp. 355, 357, 364.

While the country is thus despoiled and desolate, there are vallies and tracts throughout it, which " are covered with a fine coat of verdant pasture, and are places of resort to the Bedouins, where they pasture their camels and their sheep."* " The whole way we traversed," says Seetzen, " we saw villages in ruins, and met numbers of Arabs with their *camels*," &c. Mr. Buckingham describes a building among the ruins of Ammon, " the masonry of which was evidently constructed of materials gathered from the ruins of other and older buildings on the spot. On entering it at the south end," he adds, " we came to an open square court, with arched recesses on each side, the sides nearly facing the cardinal points. The recesses in the northern and southern wall were originally open passages, and had arched door-ways facing each other—but the first of these was found wholly closed up, and the last was partially filled up, leaving only a narrow passage, just sufficient for the entrance of one man and of the goats, which the Arab keepers drive in here occasionally for shelter during the night." He relates that he lay down among " flocks of sheep and goats," close beside the ruins of Ammon ;—and particularly remarks that, during the night, he was almost entirely prevented from sleeping by the bleating of flocks."† So literally true is it, although Seetzen, and Burckhardt, and Buckingham, who relate the facts, make no reference or allusion whatever to any of the prophecies, and travelled for a different object than the elucidation of the Scriptures—that *the chief city of the Ammonites is a stable for camels, and a couching-place for flocks.*

The Ammonites shall not be remembered among the nations. While the Jews, who were long their here-

* Buckingham's Travels in Palestine, &c. p. 329.
† Buckingham's Travels among the Arab Tribes, under the title of Ruins of Ammon, pp. 72, 73, &c.

ditary enemies, continue as distinct a people as ever,
though dispersed among all nations, no trace of the
Ammonites remain—none are now designated by
their name, nor do any claim descent from them.
They did exist, however, long after the time when
the eventual annihilation of their race was foretold, for
they retained their name, and continued a great multitude until the second century of the Christian era.*
*Yet they are cut off from the people. Ammon has per-
ished out of the countries ; it is destroyed.* No people
is attached to its soil—none regard it as their country
and adopt its name : *And the Ammonites are not remembered among the nations.*

Rabbah—(Rabbah Ammon, the chief city of Ammon,) *shall be a desolate heap.* Situated as it was, on
each side of the borders of a plentiful stream—encircled by a fruitful region—strong by nature and fortified by art, nothing could have justified the suspicion,
or warranted the conjecture in the mind of an uninspired mortal, that the royal city of Ammon, whatever
disasters might possibly befall it in the fate of war or
change of masters, would ever undergo so total a trans-
mutation as to become a desolate heap. But although,
in addition to such tokens of its continuance as a city,
more than a thousand years had given uninterrupted
experience of its stability, ere the prophets of Israel
denounced its fate—yet a period of equal length has
now marked it out,—as it exists to this day,—a desolate heap ; a perpetual or permanent desolation. Its
ancient name is still preserved by the Arabs, and its
site is now " covered with the ruins of private buildings—nothing of them remaining except the foundations and some of the door-posts. The buildings, exposed to the atmosphere, are all in decay,"† so that

---

* Justin Martyr, p. 392.   Ed. Thirlb.
† Burckhardt's Travels in Syria, p. 359.

they may be said literally to form a desolate heap.
The public edifices, which once strengthened or adorned the city, after a long resistance to decay, are now
also desolate; and the remains of the most entire
among them, subjected as they are to the abuse and
spoliation of the wild Arabs, can be adapted to no
better object than *a stable for camels.* Yet these broken walls and ruined palaces, which attest the ancient
splendour of Ammon, can now be made subservient,
by means of a single act of reflection, or simple process of reason, to a far nobler purpose than the most
magnificent edifices on earth can be, when they are
contemplated as monuments on which the historic and
prophetic truth of Scripture is blended in one bright
inscription. A minute detail of them may not therefore be uninteresting.

Seetzen, (whose indefatigable ardour led him, in
defiance of danger, the first to explore the countries
which lie east of the Jordan, and east and south of the
Dead Sea, or the territories of Ammon, Moab, and
Edom,) justly characterises Ammon as " once the residence of many kings—an ancient town which flourished long before the Greeks and Romans, and even
before the Hebrews ;"* and he briefly enumerates
those remains of ancient greatness and splendour
which are most distinguishable amidst its ruins. " Although this town has been destroyed and deserted for
many ages, I still found there some remarkable ruins,
which attest its ancient splendour. Such as, 1st, a
square building, very highly ornamented, which has
been perhaps a mausoleum. 2dly, The ruins of a
large palace. 3dly, A magnificent amphitheatre of
immense size, and well preserved, with a peristyle of

* A brief account of the countries adjoining the Lake of
Tiberias, the Jordan, and the Dead Sea, by M. Seetzen,
Conseiller d'Ambassade de S. M. l'Empereur de Russe,
pp. 35, 36.

Corinthian pillars without pedestals. 4th, A temple with a great number of columns. 5th, The ruins of a large church, perhaps the see of a bishop in the time of the Greek Emperors. 6th, The remains of a temple with columns set in a circular form, and which are of an extraordinary size. 7th, The remains of the ancient wall, with many other edifices."[*] Burckhardt, who afterwards visited the spot, describes it with greater minuteness. He gives a plan of the ruins; and particularly noted the ruins of many temples, of a spacious church, a curved wall, a high arched bridge, the banks and bed of the river still partially paved; a large theatre, with successive tiers of apartments excavated in the rocky side of a hill; Corinthian columns, fifteen feet high; the castle, a very extensive building, the walls of which are thick, and denote a remote antiquity; many cisterns and vaults; and a plain covered with the decayed ruins of private buildings:[†]—monuments of ancient splendour standing amidst a *desolate heap.*

MOAB.

The prophecies concerning Moab are more numerous and not less remarkable. Those of them which met their completion in ancient time, and which related to particular events in the history of the Moabites, and to the result of their conflicts with the Jews or any of the neighbouring states, however necessary they may have been at the time for strengthening the faith or supporting the courage of the children of Israel, need not now be adduced in evidence of inspiration; for there are abundant predictions which refer

[*] Seetzen's Travels, pp. 35, 36.
[†] Burckhardt's Travels in Syria, p. 358, &c.

so clearly to decisive and unquestionable facts, that
there is scarcely a single feature peculiar to the land
of Moab, as it now exists, which was not marked by
the prophets in their delineation of the low estate to
which, from the height of its wickedness and haughtiness, it was finally to be brought down.

" Against Moab, thus saith the Lord of Hosts, the
God of Israel, Woe unto Nebo! for it is spoiled;
Kiriathaim is confounded and taken: Misgab is confounded and dismayed. There shall be no more
praise of Moab.—And the spoiler shall come upon
every city, and no city shall escape ; the valley also
shall perish, and the plain shall be destroyed, as the
Lord hath spoken. Give wings unto Moab, that it
may flee and get away ; for the cities thereof shall be
desolate, without any to dwell therein.—Moab hath
been at ease from his youth, and he hath settled on
his lees ; and hath not been emptied from vessel to
vessel, neither hath he gone into captivity. Behold
the days come, saith the Lord, that I will send unto
him wanderers, that shall cause him to wander.—How
is the strong staff broken, and the beautiful rod ?—
Thou daughter that dost inhabit Dibon, come down
from thy glory and sit in thirst ; for the spoiler of
Moab shall come upon thee, and he shall destroy
thy strongholds. Moab is confounded, for it is broken
down. Moab is spoiled. And judgment is come
upon the plain country : upon Holon, and upon Ja-
hazah, and upon Mephaath, and upon Dibon, and
upon Nebo, and upon Beth-diblathaim ; upon Kiriathaim, Bethgamul, Bethmeon, and upon Kerioth,
and upon Bozrah, and upon all the cities of the land
of Moab, far and near. The horn of Moab is cut
off, and his arm is broken, saith the Lord. O ye that
dwell in Moab, leave the cities and dwell in the rock ;
and be like the dove that maketh her nest in the sides
of the hole's mouth. We have heard of the pride

of Moab, (he is exceeding proud) his loftiness, and his arrogancy, and his pride, and the haughtiness of his heart.—And joy and gladness is taken from the plentiful field, and from the land of Moab. I have caused wine to fail from the wine-presses. None shall tread with shouting; their shouting shall be no shouting. From the city of Heshbon even unto Elealeh; and even unto Jahaz, have they uttered their voice from Zoar even unto Horonaim; the waters also of Nimrim shall be desolate. I have broken Moab like a vessel wherein is no pleasure. They shall cry, how is it broken down! And Moab shall be destroyed from being a people, because he hath magnified himself against the Lord. The cities of Aroer are forsaken; they shall be for flocks, which shall lie down, and none shall make them afraid. Moab shall be a perpetual desolation."*

The land of Moab lay to the east and south-east of Judea, and bordered on the east, north-east, and partly on the south of the Dead Sea. Its early history is nearly analogous to that of Ammon; and the soil, though perhaps more diversified, is, in many places where the desert and plains of salt have not encroached on its borders, of equal fertility. There are manifest and abundant vestiges of its ancient greatness. "The whole of the plains are covered with the sites of towns, on every eminence or spot convenient for the construction of one. And as the land is capable of rich cultivation, there can be no doubt that the country, now so deserted, once presented a continued picture of plenty and fertility."† The form of fields is still visible; and there are the remains of Roman highways, which in some places are completely paved, and on which

---

* Jerem. xlviii. 1, 2, 8, 9, 11, 12, 18—28, 29—12. Isaiah xvii. 2. Zeph. ii. 9.

† Captains Irby and Mangles' Travels, p. 370.

there are milestones of the times of Trajan, Marcus
Aurelius, and Severus, with the number of the miles
legible upon them. Wherever any spot is cultivated
the corn is luxuriant ; and the riches of the soil cannot
perhaps be more clearly illustrated than by the fact,
that one grain of Heshbon wheat exceeds in dimensions
two of the ordinary sort, and more than double the
number of grains grow on the stalk. The frequency,
and almost, in many instances, the close vicinity of
the sites of the ancient towns, " prove that the population of the country was formerly proportioned to its
natural fertility."* Such evidence may surely suffice to prove, that the country was well cultivated and
peopled at a period so long posterior to the date of
the predictions, that no cause less than supernatural
could have existed at the time when they were delivered, which could have authorized the assertion, with
the least probability or apparent possibility of its
truth, that Moab would ever have been reduced to
that state of great and permanent desolation in which
it has continued for so many ages, and which vindi-
cates and ratifies to this hour the truth of the Scriptural prophecies.

*The cities of Moab were to be desolate without any
to dwell therein ; no city was to escape. Moab was to
flee away.* And the cities of Moab have all disappeared. Their place, together with the adjoining
part of Idumea, is characterised, in the map of Volney's Travels, by the *ruins of towns.* His information respecting these ruins was derived from some of
the wandering Arabs ; and its accuracy has been fully
corroborated by the testimony of different European
travellers of high respectability and undoubted veracity, who have since visited this devastated region. The

---

* Captains Irby and Mangles' Travels, pp. 377, 378, 456,
460.

whole country abounds with ruins. And Burckhardt, who encountered many difficulties in so desolate and dangerous a land, thus records the brief history of a few of them ; " The ruins of Eleale, Heshbon, Meon, Medaba, Dibon, Aroer, still subsist to illustrate the history of the Beni Israel."* And it might, with equal truth, have been added, that they still subsist to confirm the inspiration of the Jewish Scripture, or to prove that the seers of Israel were the prophets of God, for the desolation of each of these very cities was the theme of a prediction. Every thing worthy of observation respecting them has been detailed, not only in Burckhardt's Travels in Syria, but also by Seetzen, and, more recently, by Captains Irby and Mangles, who, along with Mr. Bankes and Mr. Legh, visited this deserted district. The predicted judgment has fallen with such truth upon these cities, and upon all the cities of the land of Moab far and near, and they are so utterly *broken down*, that even the prying curiosity of such indefatigable travellers could discover among a multiplicity of ruins, only a few remains so entire as to be worthy of particular notice. The subjoined description is drawn from their united testimony.—Among the ruins of El Aal (Eleale) are a number of large cisterns, fragments of buildings, and foundations of houses.† At Heshban (Heshbon) are the ruins of a large ancient town, together with the remains of a temple, and some edifices. A few broken shafts of columns are still standing ; and there are a number of deep wells cut in the rock.‡ The ruins of *Medaba* are about two miles in circumference. There are many remains of the walls of private houses constructed with blocks of silex, but not a single edifice is standing. The chief object of

---

* Burckhardt's Travels in Nubia, Introduction, p. 38.
† Burck. Travels in Syria, p. 365.   ‡ Ibid.

interest is an immense tank or cistern of hewn stones, "which, as there is no stream at Medaba," Burckhardt remarks, "might still be of use to the Bedouins, were the surrounding ground cleared of the rubbish to allow the water to flow into it ; *but such an undertaking is far beyond the views of the wandering Arabs.*" There is also the foundation of a temple built with large stones, and apparently of great antiquity, with two columns near it.* The ruins of *Diban* (Dibon) situated in the midst of a fine plain, are of considerable extent, but present nothing of interest.† The neighbouring hot wells, and the similarity of the name, identify the ruins of Myoun with *Meon*, or Beth Meon of Scripture.‡ Of this ancient city, as well as of Araayr, (Aroer) nothing is now remarkable but what is common to them with all the cities of Moab—their entire desolation. The extent of the ruins of *Rabba* (Rabbath Moab,) formerly the residence of the kings of Moab, sufficiently proves its ancient importance, though no other object can be particularized among the ruins, except the remains of a palace or temple, some of the walls of which are still standing ; a gate belonging to another building ; and an insulated altar. There are many remains of private buildings, but none entire. There being no springs on the spot, the town had two birkets, the largest of which is cut entirely out of the rocky ground, together with many cisterns.§

Mount *Nebo* was completely barren when Burck-

* Burck. p. 366. Seetzen's Travels, p. 37. Captains Irby and Mangles' Travels, p. 471.

† Captains Irby and Mangles' Travels, p. 462. Seetzen's Travels, p. 38.

‡ Burckhardt's Travels, p. 365. Irby and Mangles' Travels, p. 464.

§ Seetzen's Travels, p. 39. Burckhardt's Travels, p. 377.

hardt passed over it, and the site of the ancient city had not been ascertained.* *Nebo is spoiled.*

While the ruins of all these cities still retain their ancient names, and are the most conspicuous amidst the wide scene of general desolation, and while each of them was in like manner particularized in the visions of the prophet, they yet formed but a small number of the cities of Moab ; and the rest are also in similar verification of the prophecies, *desolate, without any to dwell therein.*　None of the ancient cities of Moab now exist, as tenanted by men.　Kerek, which neither bears any resemblance in name to any of the cities of Moab which are mentioned as existing in the time of the Israelites, nor possesses any monuments which denote a very remote antiquity, is the only nominal town in the whole country ; and, in the words of Seetzen, who visited it, " in its present ruined state it can only be called a hamlet ;" "and the houses have only one floor."† But the most populous and fertile province in Europe (especially any situated in the interior of a country like Moab) is not covered so thickly with towns as Moab is plentiful in ruins, deserted and desolate though now it be.　Burckhardt enumerates about *fifty* ruined sites within its boundaries, many of them extensive.　In general they are a *broken down* and undistinguishable mass of ruins ; and many of them have not been closely inspected.　But, in some instances, there are the remains of temples, sepulchral monuments, the ruins of edifices constructed of very large stones, in one of which buildings " some of the stones are twenty feet in length, and so broad, that one constitutes the thickness of the wall ;" traces of hanging

---

* Burckhardt's Travels, p. 370.
† Burckhardt's Travels, p. 338.　Seetzen's Travels, p. 39.

gardens; entire columns lying on the ground, three feet in diameter, and fragments of smaller columns; and many cisterns cut out of the rock.—When the towns of Moab existed in their prime, and were at ease,—when arrogance, and haughtiness and pride prevailed amongst them—the desolation, and total desertion and abandonment of them all, must have utterly surpassed all human conception. And that such numerous cities,—which subsisted for many ages— which were diversified in their sites, some of them being built on eminences, and naturally strong; others on plains, and surrounded by the richest soil; some situated in vallies by the side of a plentiful stream; and others where art supplied the deficiencies of nature, and where immense cisterns were excavated out of the rock—and which exhibit in their ruins many monuments of ancient prosperity, and many remains easily convertible into present utility—should have all fled away—all met the same indiscriminate fate—and be all *desolate without any to dwell therein*, notwithstanding all these ancient assurances of their permanent durability, and their existing facilities and inducements for being the habitations of men—is a matter of just wonder in the present day,—and had any other people been the possessors of Moab, the fact would either have been totally impossible, or unaccountable. Trying as this test of the truth of prophecy is—*that* is the word of God, and not of erring man, which can so well and so triumphantly abide it. *They shall cry of Moab, how is it broken down!*

The valley also shall perish, and the plain shall be destroyed. Moab has often been a field of contest between the Arabs and the Turks; and although the former have retained possession of it, both have mutually reduced it to desolation. The different tribes of Arabs who traverse it, not only bear a permanent and habitual hostility to Christians and to Turks,

but one tribe is often at variance and at war with
another ; and the regular cultivation of the soil, or
the improvement of those natural advantages, of which
the country is so full, is a matter either never thought
of, or that cannot be realized.   Property is there the
creature of power and not of law ; and possession
forms no security when plunder is the preferable right.
Hence the extensive plains, where they are not partially covered with wood, present a barren aspect,
which is only relieved at intervals by a few clusters
of wild fig-trees, that show how the richest gifts of
nature degenerate when unaided by the industry of
man.   And instead of the profusion which the plains
must have exhibited in every quarter, nothing but
"patches of the best soil in the territory are now
cultivated by the Arabs ;" and these only " whenever
they have the prospect of being able to secure the
harvest against the incursions of enemies."*   The
Arab herds now roam at freedom over the vallies and
the plains ; and " the many vestiges of field en-
closures"† form not any obstruction ; they wander
undisturbed around the tents of their masters, over
the face of the country ; and while *the valley is perished, and the plain destroyed, the cities also of Aroer
are forsaken ; they are for flocks which lie down, and
none make them afraid.*

The strong contrast between the ancient and the
actual state of Moab is exemplified in the condition of
the inhabitants as well as of the land ; and the coincidence between the prediction and the fact is as striking in the one case as in the other.

*The days come, saith the Lord, that I will send unto
him (Moab) wanderers that shall cause him to wander,
and shall empty his vessels.*   The Bedouin (wander-

* Burckhardt's Travels in Syria, p. 369.
† Ibid, p. 365.

ing) Arabs are now the chief and almost the only inhabitants of a country once studded with cities. Traversing the country, and fixing their tents for a short time in one place, and then decamping to another, depasturing every part successively, and despoiling the whole land of its natural produce, they *are wanderers who have come up against it, and who keep it in a state of perpetual desolation.* They lead a wandering life; and the only regularity they know or practise, is to act upon a systematic scheme of spoliation. They prevent any from forming a fixed settlement who are inclined to attempt it; for although the fruitfulness of the soil would abundantly repay the labour of settlers, and render migration wholly unnecessary, even if the population were increased more than tenfold; yet the Bedouins forcibly deprive them of the means of subsistence, compel them to search for it elsewhere, and, in the words of the prediction, literally *cause them to wander.* " It may be remarked generally of the Bedouins," says Burckhardt, in describing their extortions in this very country, " that wherever they are the masters of the cultivators, the latter are soon reduced to beggary by their unceasing demands."*

O ye that dwell in Moab, leave the cities and dwell in the rock, and be like the dove that maketh her nest in the sides of the hole's mouth. In a general description of the condition of the inhabitants of that extensive desert which now occupies the place of these ancient flourishing states, Volney, in plain but unmeant illustration of this prediction, remarks, that the " wretched peasants live in perpetual dread of losing the fruit of their labours; and no sooner have they gathered in their harvest, than they hasten to secrete it in private places, and retire among the rocks

* Burckhardt's Travels in Syria, p. 381.

which border on the Dead Sea."* Towards the opposite extremity of the land of Moab, and at a little distance from its borders, Seetzen relates, that " there are many families living in caverns ;" and he actually designates them " the inhabitants of the rocks."† And at the distance of a few miles from the ruined site of Heshbon, " there are many artificial caves in a large range of perpendicular cliffs—in some of which are chambers and small sleeping apartments."‡ While the cities are desolate without any to dwell therein, the rocks are tenanted. But whether flocks lie down in the former, without any to make them afraid, or whether men are to be found dwelling in the latter, and are like the dove that maketh her nest in the sides of the hole's mouth—the wonderful transition, in either case, and the close accordance, in both, of the fact to the prediction, assuredly mark it in characters that may be visible to the purblind mind, as the word of that God before whom the darkness of futurity is as light, and without whom a sparrow cannot fall unto the ground.§

* Volney's Travels, vol. ii. p. 344.

† Seetzen's Travels, p. 26.   See Monthly Review, vol. lxxi. p. 405.

‡ Captains Irby and Mangles' Travels, p. 473.

§ Another prediction respecting the dwellers in Moab ought not perhaps to be passed over in silence, although the terms in which it is expressed are not so clear and unambiguous as those to which the observations in the text are confined, and although it may have met its primary fulfilment in a much earlier age.   Yet it is so intelligible, that the fact, to which it bears an unrestrained application, may be left as its sole and adequate exposition ; and the continued truth of the prophecy greatly strengthens, instead of weakening the evidence of its inspiration.   And how is Moab broken down and spoiled, when, in lieu of the arrogancy and exceeding pride and haughtiness of its ancient inhabitants, the following description is characteristic of the wanderers who now possess it. " In the valley of Wale," which is situated in the immediate vicinity of the river *Arnon*, into which the Wale flows,

And although chargeable with the impropriety of being somewhat out of place, it may not be here altogether improper to remark, that, demonstrative as all these clear predictions and coincident facts are of the inspiration of the Scriptures, it cannot but be gratifying to every lover of his kind, when he contemplates that desolation, caused by many sins, and fraught with many miseries, which the wickedness of man has wrought, and which the prescience of God revealed, to know that all these prophecies, while they mingle the voice of wailing with that of denunciation, are the word of that God, who, although he suffers not iniquity to pass unpunished, overrules evil for good, and makes the wrath of man to praise him, and who in the midst of judgment can remember mercy. And reasoning merely from the " uniform experience" (to borrow a term, and draw an argument from Hume) of the truth of the prophecies already fulfilled, the unprejudiced mind will at once perceive the full force of the truth derived from experience,* and acknowledge that it would be a rejection of the authority of reason as well as of revelation, to mistrust the truth of that

Burckhardt observed "a large party of Arabs Shererat encamped—Bedouins of the Arabian desert, who resort hither in summer for pasturage." Being oppressed and hemmed in by other Arab tribes, " they *wander about in misery,* have very few horses, and are not able to feed any flocks of sheep or goats." "Their tents are very miserable ; both men and women go almost naked, the former being only covered round the waist, and the women wearing nothing but a loose shirt hanging in rags about them." *Moab shall be a derision. As the wandering bird cast out of the nest, so the daughters of Moab shall be at the ford of* ARNON. Burckhardt's Travels, pp. 370, 371. Isaiah xvi. 2.

* "Being determined by custom to transfer the past to the future, in all our inferences ; where the past has been entirely regular and uniform, we expect the event with the greatest assurance, and leave no room for any contrary supposition." Hume's Essays of Probability, vol. ii. p. 61. Edin. 1800.

prophetic affirmation of resuscitating and redeeming import, respecting Ammon and Moab, which is the last of the series, and which alone now awaits futurity to stamp it with the brilliant and crowning seal of its testimony. I will bring again the captivity of Moab in the latter days, saith the Lord.* I will bring again the captivity of the children of Ammon, saith the Lord.† The remnant of my people shall possess them.‡ They shall build the old wastes, they shall raise up the former desolations, and they shall repair the waste cities, the desolations of many generations.§

IDUMEA.

But a heavier and irreversible doom was denounced against the land of Edom or Idumea ; and the testimony of an infidel was the first to show how it has been realized : That testimony, as forming an exposition of itself, may, in a primary view of them, be subjoined to the prophecies, and must have its due influence on every unbiassed mind. There are numerous prophecies respecting Idumea, that bear a literal interpretation, however hyperbolical they may appear. " (My sword shall come down upon Idumea, and upon the people of my curse to judgment.) —From generation to generation it shall lie waste, none shall pass through it for ever and ever. But the cormorant and the bittern shall possess it ; the owl also and the raven shall dwell in it ; and he shall stretch out upon it the line of confusion, and the stones of emptiness. They shall call the nobles thereof to the kingdom, but none shall be there, and all her princes shall be nothing. And thorns shall

---

* Jerem. xlviii. 47.   † Ib. xlix. 6.   ‡ Zeph. ii. 9.
§ Isa. lxi. 4 ; lviii. 11.   Ezek. xxxvi. 33, 36.

come up in her palaces, nettles and brambles in the
fortresses thereof ; and it shall be a habitation of dragons, and a court for owls. The wild beasts of the
desert shall also meet wtih the wild beasts of the island, and the satyr (or hairy creature) shall cry to
his fellow ; the screech-owl also shall rest there, and
find for herself a place of rest. There shall the great
owl make her nest, and lay, and hatch, and gather
under her shadow; there shall the vultures also be
gathered every one with her mate. Seek ye out of
the book of the Lord and read ; no one of these shall
fail, none shall want her mate ; for my mouth it hath
commanded, and his spirit it hath gathered them.
And he hath cast the lot for them, and his hand
hath divided it unto them by line ; they shall possess
it for ever, from generation to generation shall they
dwell therein."* " Concerning Edom, thus saith the
Lord of Hosts : Is wisdom no more in Teman ? Is
counsel perished from the prudent ? I will bring the
calamity of Esau upon him the time that I will visit
him. If grape-gatherers come to thee, would they
not leave some gleaning grapes ? If thieves by night,
they will destroy till they have enough. But I have
made Esau bare, I have uncovered his secret places,
and he shall not be able to hide himself. Behold
they whose judgment was not to drink of the cup
have assuredly drunken ; and art thou he that shalt
altogether go unpunished ? Thou shalt not go unpunished, but thou shalt surely drink of it.—I have
sworn by myself, saith the Lord, that Bozrah (the
strong or fortified city) shall become a desolation, a
reproach, a waste, and a curse ; and all the cities
thereof shall be perpetual wastes. Lo, I will make
thee small among the heathen, and despised among
men. Thy terribleness hath deceived thee, and the

---

* Isaiah xxxiv. 5, 10—17.

pride of thine heart, O thou that dwellest in the
clefts of the rock, that holdest the height of the hill :
Though thou shouldst make thy nest as high as the
eagle, I will bring thee down from thence, saith the
Lord.   Also Edom shall be a desolation ; every
one that goeth by shall be astonished, and shall
hiss at all the plagues thereof.   As in the overthrow of Sodom and Gomorrah, and the neighbour
cities thereof, saith the Lord, no man shall abide
there, neither shall a son of man dwell in it."*
" Thus saith the Lord God, I will stretch out mine
hand upon Edom, and will cut off man and beast
from it, and I will make it desolate from Teman."†
" The word of the Lord came unto me, saying, Son
of man, set thy face against Mount Seir, and prophesy against it, and say unto it, Thus saith the Lord
God, I will stretch out my hand against thee, and I
will make thee most desolate.   I will lay thy cities
waste, and thou shalt be desolate."‡   Thus will I
make Mount Seir most desolate, and cut off from it
him that passeth out, and him that returneth.§   I
will make thee perpetual desolations, and thy cities
shall not return.|| When the whole earth rejoiceth,
I will make thee desolate.   Thou shalt be desolate,
O Mount Seir, and all Idumea, even all of it ; and
they shall know that I am the Lord.¶   Edom shall
be a desolate wilderness.**   " For three transgressions
of Edom, and for four I will not turn away the punishment thereof."††   " Thus saith the Lord concerning Edom, I have made thee small among the heathen, thou art greatly despised.   The pride of thine
heart hath deceived thee, thou that dwellest in the
clefts of the rock, whose habitation is high.   Shall

---

* Jerem. xlix 7—10, 12—18.   † Ezek. xxv. 13.
‡ Ezek. xxxv. 1, 2, 3, 4.   § Ib. 7. || Ib. 9.
¶ Ib. 14, 15.   ** Joel iii. 19.   †† Amos i. 11.

I not destroy the wise men out of Edom, and understanding out of the Mount of Esau? The house of Jacob shall possess their possessions, but there shall not be any remaining of the house of Esau.* I laid the mountains of Esau and his heritage waste for the dragons of the wilderness. Whereas Edom saith we are impoverished, but we will return and build the desolate places; thus saith the Lord of Hosts, they shall build, but I will throw down; and they shall call them the border of wickedness."† Is there any country once inhabited and opulent, so utterly desolate? There is, and that land is Idumea. The territory of the descendants of Esau affords as miraculous a demonstration of the inspiration of the Scriptures, as the fate of the children of Israel.

Idumea was situated to the south of Judea and of Moab; it bordered on the east with Arabia Petrea, under which name it was included in the latter part of its history, and it extended southward to the eastern Gulph of the Red Sea. A single extract from the Travels of Volney will be found to be equally illustrative of the prophecy and of the fact. " This country *has not been visited by any traveller*, but it well merits such an attention; for from the report of the Arabs of Bakir, and the inhabitants of Gaza, who frequently go to Maan and Karak, on the road of the pilgrims, there are to the south-east of the lake Asphaltites (Dead Sea,) *within three days' journey*, upwards of thirty ruined towns *absolutely deserted*. Several of them have large edifices, with columns that may have belonged to the ancient temples, or at least to Greek churches. The Arabs sometimes make use of them to fold their cattle in; but in general avoid them on account of the enormous scorpions with which they swarm. We cannot be surprised at these traces of ancient population, when

---

* Obad. v. 2, 3, 8, 17, 18.   † Malachi i. 3, 4.

we recollect that this was the country of the Nabatheans, the most powerful of the Arabs, and of the
Idumeans, who, at the *time of the destruction of Jerusalem*, were almost as numerous as the Jews, as appears from Josephus, who informs us, that on the first
rumour of the march of Titus against Jerusalem, thirty
thousand Idumeans instantly assembled, and threw
themselves into that city for its defence. It appears
that besides the advantages of being under a tolerably
good government, these districts enjoyed a considerable
share of the commerce of Arabia and India, which increased their industry and population.   We know that
as far back as the time of Solomon, the cities of Asti-
oum Gaber (Esion Gaber,) and Ailah (Eloth) were
highly frequented marts.   These towns were situated
on the adjacent Gulph of the Red Sea, where we still
find the latter yet retaining its name, and perhaps the
former in that of El Akaba, or the end (of the sea.)
These two places are in the hands of the Bedouins,
who, being destitute of a navy and commerce, do not
inhabit them.   But the pilgrims report that there is
at El Akaba a wretched fort.*   The Idumeans, from
whom the Jews only took their ports at intervals, must
have found in them a great source of wealth and population.   It even appears that the Idumeans rival-
led the Tyrians, who also possessed a town, the name
of which is unknown, on the coast of Hedjaz, in the
desert of Tih, and the city of Faran, and without
doubt, El-Tor, which served it by way of port.   From
this place, the caravans might reach Palestine and Judea," (through Idumea,) " in eight or ten days.
This route, which is no longer than that from Suez to
Cairo, is infinitely shorter than that from Aleppo to
Bassorah."†   Evidence which must have been unde-

* This fort is at present in the possession of the Pasha of
Egypt.
† Volney's Travels, vol. ii. pp. 344—6.

signed, which cannot be suspected of partiality, and which no illustration can strengthen, and no ingenuity pervert, is thus borne to the truth of the most wonderful prophecies. That the Idumeans were a populous and powerful nation long posterior to the delivery of the prophecies ; that they possessed a tolerably good government, (even in the estimation of Volney,) —that Idumea contained many cities—that these cities are now absolutely deserted, and that their ruins swarm with enormous scorpions—that it was a commercial nation, and possessed highly frequented marts —that it forms a shorter route than an ordinary one to India, and yet that it had not been visited by any traveller, are facts all recorded, or proved to a wish, by this able but unconscious commentator.

A greater contrast cannot be imagined than the ancient and present state of Idumea. It was a kingdom previous to Israel, having been governed first by dukes or princes, afterwards by eight successive kings, and again by dukes, before there reigned any king over the children of Israel.* Its fertility and early cultivation are implied not only in the blessings of Esau, whose dwelling was to be the fatness of the earth, and of the dew of heaven from above ; but also in the condition proposed by Moses to the Edomites, when he solicited a passage for the Israelites through their borders, " that they would not pass through the fields nor through the vineyards ;" and also in the great wealth, especially in the multitudes of flocks and herds, recorded as possessed by an individual inhabitant of that country, at a period, in all probability, even more remote.† The Idumeans were, without doubt, both an opulent and a powerful people. They often contended with the Israelites,

---

* Genesis xxxvi. 31, &c.
† Genesis xxvii. 39.   Numbers xx. 17.   Job xlii. 12.

I

and entered into a league with their other enemies against them. In the reign of David they were indeed subdued and greatly oppressed, and many of them even dispersed throughout the neighbouring countries, particularly Phœnicia and Egypt. But during the decline of the kingdom of Judah, and for many years previous to its extinction, they encroached upon the territories of the Jews, and extended their dominion over the south-western part of Judea. Though no excellence whatever be now attached to its name, which exists only in past history, Idumea, including perhaps Judea, was then not without the praise of the first of Roman poets.

> Primus Idumeas referam tibi, Mantua, palmas.
> *Virg. Georg.* lib. iii. l. 12.

And of Lucan, (Phars. lib. iii.)

> Arbustis palmarum dives Idume.

But Idumea, as a kingdom, can lay claim to a higher renown than either the abundance of its flocks, or the excellence of its palm trees. The celebrated city of Petra, (so named by the Greeks, and so worthy of the name, on account both of its rocky vicinity and its numerous dwellings excavated from the rocks,) was situated within the patrimonial territory of the Edomites. There is distinct and positive evidence that it was a city of Edom,* and the metropolis of

---

* Petra being afterwards more particularly noticed, some quotations from ancient authors respecting it may here be subjoined.

> Πέτρα πόλις ἐν γῆ Εδώμ της Ἀραβίας.
> *Eusebii Onomast.*

Petra, civitas Arabiæ in terra Edom.—*Hieron.*
Vide Relandi Palestina, tom. i. p. 70.

5

the Nabatheans,* whom Strabo expressly identifies
with the Idumeans—possessors of the same country,
and subject to the same laws.† "Petra," to use
the words of Dr. Vincent, by whom the state of its
ancient commerce was described before its ruins were
discovered, "is the capital of Edom or Seir, the Idumea or Arabia Petræa of the Greeks, the Nabatea,
considered both by geographers, historians, and poets
as the source of all the precious commodities of the
east."‡ "The caravans, in all ages, from Minea, in
the interior of Arabia, and from Gerrha on the Gulf
of Persia, from Hadramaut on the ocean, and some
even from Sabea or Yemen, appear to have pointed
to Petra as a common centre ; and from Petra the
trade seems again to have branched out into every
direction, to Egypt, Palestine, and Syria, through
Arsinoe, Gaza, Tyre, Jerusalem, Damascus, and a
variety of subordinate routes that all terminated on
the Mediterranean. There is every proof that is requisite to show that the Tyrians and Sidonians were
the first merchants who introduced the produce of India to all the nations which encircled the Mediterranean, so is there the strongest evidence to prove
that the Tyrians obtained all their commodities from
Arabia. But if Arabia was the centre of this commerce, Petra § was the point to which all the Arabians
tended from the three sides of their vast peninsula."‖
At a period subsequent to the commencement of the
Christian era, there always reigned at Petra, according

---

* Μητροπολις δε των Ναβαταιων εσιν ή Πετρα καλουμενη.
    Strabo, lib. xvi. p. 779. Ed. Paris, 1620.
† Ναβαταιοι δε εισιν οι Ιδυμαιοι.
    Strabo, lib. xvi. p. 760. Ed. Paris, 1620.
‡ Vincent's Commerce of the Ancients, vol. xi. p. 263.
§ Agatharchides Huds. p. 57. Pliny, lib. vi. c. 28, quoted
by Vincent. Ibid. p. 262.
‖ Ibid. 260, 261, 262.

to Strabo, a king of the royal lineage, with whom a prince was associated in the government.* It was a place of great strength in the time of the Romans. Pompey marched against it, but desisted from the attack ; and Trajan afterwards besieged it. It was a metropolitan see, to which several bishoprics were attached in the time of the Greek emperors, and Idumea was included in the third Palestine—*Palestina tertia sive salutaris.* But the ancient state of Idumea cannot in the present day be so clearly ascertained from the records respecting it which can be gleaned from history, whether sacred or profane, as by the wonderful and imperishable remains of its capital city, and by "the traces of many towns and villages," which indisputably show that "it must once have been thickly inhabited."† It not only can admit of no dispute, that the countries and cities of Idumea subsisted in a very different state from that absolute desolation in which, long prior to the period of its reality, it was represented in the prophetic vision ; but there are prophecies regarding it, especially those in the thirty-fourth chapter of Isaiah, that have yet a prospective view, and which refer to the time when "the children of Israel shall possess their possessions, or to "the year of recompenses for the controversy of Zion." But, dangerous as it is to explore the land of Idumea, and difficult to ascertain those existing facts, and precise circumstances, which form the strongest features of its desolate aspect, (and that ought to be the subject of scientific as well as of religious inquiry,) enough has been discovered to show that the sentence against it, though fulfilled by the agency of nature and of man, is precisely such as was first recorded in the annals of inspiration.

---

* Strabo, p. 779.
† Burckhardt's Travels in Syria, p. 436.

There is a prediction which, being peculiarly remarkable as applicable to Idumea, and bearing reference to a circumstance explanatory of the difficulty of access to any knowledge respecting it, is entitled in the first instance to notice. *None shall pass through it for ever and ever.—I will cut off from Mount Seir him that passeth out and him that returneth.** The ancient greatness of Idumea must, in no small degree, have resulted from its commerce. Bordering with Arabia on the east, and Egypt on the south-west, and forming from north to south the most direct and most commodious channel of communication between Jerusalem and her dependencies on the Red Sea, as well as between Syria and India, through the continuous vallies of El Ghor and El Araba, which terminated on the one extremity at the borders of Judea, and on the other at Elath and Esiongaber, on the Elanitic gulph of the Red Sea, Idumea may be said to have formed the emporium of the commerce of the east. A Roman road passed directly through Idumea, from Jerusalem to Akaba, and another from Akaba to Moab ;† and when these roads were made, at a time long posterior to the date of the predictions, the conception could not have been formed, or held credible by man,—that the period would ever arrive when none would pass through it. Above seven hundred years after the date of the prophecy, Strabo relates, that " many Romans and other foreigners" were found at Petra by his friend Athenodorus, the philosopher, who visited it.‡ The predic-

---

* Isaiah xxxiv. 10. Ezek. xxxv. 7. The first of these predictions is conjoined with others, the period of whose full completion—the year of recompenses for the controversy of Zion—is yet to come.

† Map in Burckhardt's Travels.

‡ πολλαις μεν Ρωμαιων, πολλοις δε και των αλλων ξενων. Strabo, p. 779.

tion is yet more surprising, when viewed in conjunction with another, which implies that travellers would *pass by* Idumea,—every one that goeth by shall be astonished. And the Hadj routes (routes of the Pilgrims) from Damascus and from Cairo to Mecca, the one on the east and the other towards the south of Idumea, along the whole of its extent, go by it, or touch partially on its borders without passing through it. The truth of the prophecy (though hemmed in thus by apparent impossibilities and contradictions, and with extreme probability of its fallacy, in every view that could have been visible to man,) may yet be tried.

The words of the prediction might well be understood as merely implying that Idumea would cease to be a thoroughfare for the commerce of the nations which adjoined it, and that its " highly frequented marts" would be forsaken as centres of intercourse and traffic ; and easy would have been the task of demonstrating its truth in this limited sense, which scepticism itself ought not to be unwilling to authorize. But the fact to which it refers, forbids that the prophecy should be limited to a general interpretation, and demands that it be literally understood and applied. The fact itself being of a negative nature, requires a more minute investigation and detail than any matter of observation or discovery that is proveable at once by a simple description. And instead of merely citing authorities in affirmation of it, evidence, as remarkable as the prediction, or at once the most undesigned and conclusive, shall be largely adduced to establish its truth.

The remark of Volney, who passed at a distance to tke *west* of Idumea, and who received his information from the Arabs in that quarter, " that it had not been visited by any traveller," will not be unobserved by the attentive reader. Soon after Burckhardt had entered, on the *north-east*, the territories of the Edomites, the boundary of which he distinctly marks, he says, that " he was without protection in the midst of a desert, where no traveller had ever before been seen."* It was then, " that for the first time he had ever felt fear during his travels in the desert, and his route thither was the most dangerous he had ever travelled."† Mr. Joliffe, who visited the northern shore of the Dead Sea, in alluding to the country south of its opposite extremity, describes it as " one of the wildest and most dangerous divisions of Arabia," and says that any research in that quarter was impracticable.‡ Sir Frederick Henniker, in his Notes, dated from Mount Sinai, on the *south* of Idumea, unconsciously concentrates striking evidence in verification of the prediction, while he states a fact that would seem, at first sight, to militate against it. " Seetzen, on a vessel of paper pasted against the wall, notifies his having penetrated the country in a direct line between the Dead Sea and Mount Sinai," (through Idumea), " *a route never before accomplished*.§ This was the more interesting to me, as I had previously determined to attempt the same, it being the *shortest* way to Jerusalem. The Cavaliere Frediani, whom I met in Egypt, would have persuaded me that it was impracticable, and that he having had the same intention himself, after having been detained in hope five weeks, was compelled to relinquish his design. While I was yet ruminating over this scrap of paper, the Superior paid me a morning visit; he also said it was *impossible;* but at length promised to search for guides. I had already endeavoured to persuade those who had

* Burckhardt's Syria, p. 421.   † Ibid. p. 400.
‡ Letters from Palestine, vol. i. p. 129.
§ The words upon the paper itself are, entre la ville d'Hebron et entre le Mont Sinai, par un chemin jusqu'à ce tems là *inconnu.* Burck. Syr. p. 553.

accompanied me from Tor, but they also talked of
dangers, and declined."* Guides were found, who,
after resisting for a while his entreaties and bribes,
agreed to conduct him by the desired route; but,
unable to overcome their fears, deceived him, and led
him towards the Mediterranean coast, through the
desert to Gaza.

There yet remains a detail of the complication of
difficulties, which, in another direction still, the nearest to Judea, and apparently the most accessible, the
traveller has to encounter in reaching that desolate
region, which once formed the kingdom of Idumea,
difficulties that it may safely be said are scarcely to be
met with in any other part of Asia, or even in any
other quarter of the world, where no natural obstruc-
tions intervene. "To give an idea," says Captains
Irby and Mangles, "of the difficulties which the
Turkish government supposed there would be for an
Englishman to go to Kerek and Wady Mousa, it
is necessary to say, that when Mr. Bankes applied
at Constantinople to have these places inserted in his
firman, they returned for answer, ' that they knew of
none such within the Grand Seignor's dominions;'†
but as he and Mr. Frere, the British Minister, pressed the affair very much, they at length referred him
to the Pasha of Damascus, who, (equally averse to
have any thing to do with the business) passed him
on to the Governor of Jerusalem."‡ The Governor
of Jerusalem, "having tried all he could to dissuade
them from the undertaking," referred them in like
manner to the Governor of Jaffa, who not only "evad-
ed the affair altogether," but endeavoured to put a
stop to their journey. Though frustrated in every
attempt to obtain any protection or assistance from

* Sir Frederick Henniker's Travels, pp. 223, 224.
† Captains Irby and Mangles' Travels, p. 336. ‡ Ib. 337

the public authorities, and also warned of the danger
that awaited them from " Arabs of a most savage
and treacherous race," these adventurous travellers,
intent on visiting the ruins of Petra, having provided
themselves with horses and arms, and Arab dresses,
and being eleven in number, including servants and
two guides, " determined to proceed to try their fortune with the Sheikh of Hebron." He at first expressed compliance with their wishes, but being soon
" alarmed at his own determination," refused them the
least aid or protection. Repeated offers of money to
guides, met a decided refusal ; and they procured no
means of facilitating their journey.* The peculiar
difficulty not only of *passing through* Idumea, (which
they never attempted,) but even of entering within its
borders, and the greater hazard of travelling thither,
than in any other direction, are still further illustrated
by the acquiescence of an Arab tribe afterwards to accompany and protect them to Kerek, at a reasonable
rate, and by their positive refusal, upon any terms or
stipulation whatever, to conduct them to a spot that
lay within the boundaries of Edom. " We offered
five hundred piastres if they would conduct us to
Wady Mousa, but nothing could induce them to consent. They said they would not go if we would give
them five thousand piastres," (forty times the sum
for which they had agreed to accompany them to
Kerek, although the distance was not nearly double)
" observing that money was of no use to a man if he
lost his life."† Having afterwards obtained the protection of an intrepid Arab chief, with his followers,
and having advanced to the borders of Edom, their
further progress was suddenly opposed in the most

* Macmichael's Journey to Constantinople in 1818. Ap-
pend. p. 199.
† Captains Irby and Mangles' Travels, p. 349.

threatening and determined manner. And in the whole course of their travels, which extended to about three thousand miles, in Thrace, Asia Minor, Cyprus, the Desert, Egypt, and in Syria in different longitudinal and lateral directions, from one extremity to the other, they found nowhere such a barrier to their progress except in a previous abortive attempt to reach Petra from another quarter; and though they were never better prepared for encountering it, they never elsewhere experienced so formidable an opposition. The Sheikh of Wady Mousa and his people swore that they would not suffer them to go forward, and, " that they should neither drink of their water, *nor pass into their territory.*" The Arab chief who had espoused their cause, also took an oath, " by the faith of a true Mussulman," that they should drink of the water of Wady Mousa, and go whithersoever he pleased to carry them. " Thus," it is remarked, " were both the rival chiefs oppositely pledged in their resolutions respecting us."

Several days were passed in entreaties, artifices, and mutual menaces, which were all equally unavailing. The determination and perseverance of the one party of Arabs was equalled by the resistance and obstinacy of the other. Both were constantly acquiring an accession of strength and actively preparing for combat. The travellers, thus finding all the dangers and difficulties of which they had been forwarned fully realized, " could not but compare their case to that of the Israelites under Moses, *when Edom refused to give them a passage through his country.*"[*] " They offered even to abandon their object rather than proceed to extremities," and endanger the lives of many others, as well as their own; and they were told that they were fortunate in the protection of the chief who

---

[*] Captains Irby and Mangles' Travels, p. 392.

accompanied them, otherwise they never would have returned. The hostile Arabs, who defied them and their protectors to approach, having abandoned their camps, and having concentrated their forces, and possessed themselves of the passes and heights, sent messengers with a renewal of oaths and protestations *against entering their territory :* announced that they were fully prepared to maintain their purpose—that war " was positively determined on as the only alternative of the travellers not being permitted to see what they desired ;"* and their Sheikh vowed that " if they *passed through* his lands, they should be shot like so many dogs."† Abou Raschid, the firm and fearless chief who had pledged his honour and his oath in guarantee for the advance of the travellers, and whose obstinate resolution nothing could exceed, his arguments, artifices, and falsehoods having all failed, despatched messengers to the camps under his influence, rejected alike all compromise with the opposing Arabs, and all remonstrances on the part of his adherents and dependants (who thought that the travellers were doomed to destruction by their rashness,) and resolved to achieve by force what he had sworn to accomplish. " The camp assumed a very warlike appearance ; the spears stuck in the sand : the saddled horses before the tents with the arms hanging up within, altogether had an imposing effect." The travellers, however, were at last permitted to proceed in peace : but a brief space was allowed them for inspecting the ruins, and they could plainly distinguish the opposing party of Arabs, in great numbers, watching them from the heights. Abou Raschid was then dismayed, " he was never at his ease, and constantly urged them to depart." Nothing

* Captains Irby and Mangles' Travels, p. 392.
† Macmichael's Journey to Constantinople, p. 218.

could obtain an extension of the time allotted them, and they returned, leaving much unexplored, and even unable by any means or possibility to penetrate a little farther, in order to visit a large temple which they could clearly discern. Through Idumea they did not pass.

Thus Volney, Burckhardt, Joliffe, Henniker, and Captains Irby and Mangles, not only give their personal testimony to the truth of the fact which corroborates the prediction, but also adduce a variety of circumstances, which all conspire in giving superfluity of proof that Idumea, which was long resorted to from every quarter, is so beset on every side with dangers to the traveller, that *none pass through it*. Even the Arabs of the neighbouring regions, whose home is the desert, and whose occupation is wandering, are afraid to enter it, or to conduct any within its borders. Yet amidst all this manifold testimony to its truth, there is not in any single instance the most distant allusion to the prediction ; and the evidence is as unsuspicious and undesigned, as it is copious and complete.*

* Not even the cases of two individuals, Seetzen and Burckhardt, can be stated as at all opposed to the literal interpretation of the prophecies. Seetzen did indeed pass through Idumea, and Burckhardt traversed a considerable part of it. But the former met his death not long after the completion of his journey through Idumea, the latter never recovered from the effects of the hardships and privations which he suffered there, and without even commencing the exclusive design which he had in view (viz. to explore the interior of Africa), to which all his journeyings in Asia were merely intended as preparatory, he died at Cairo. Neither of them lived to return to Europe. *I will cut off from Mount Seir him that passeth out, and him that returneth.* Strabo mentions that there was a direct road from Petra to Jericho, of three or four days' journey. Captains Irby and Mangles were eighteen days in reaching it from Jerusalem. They did not *pass through* Idumea, and they did return. Seetzen

Edom shall be a desolation. From generation to generation it shall lie waste, &c. Judea, Ammon, and Moab, exhibit so abundantly the remains and the means of an exuberant fertility, that the wonder arises in the reflecting mind, how the barbarity of man could have so effectually counteracted, for so " many generations," the prodigality of nature. But such is Edom's desolation, that the first sentiment of *astonishment* on the contemplation of it is, how a wide extended region, now diversified by the strongest features of desert wildness, could ever have been adorned with cities, or tenanted for ages, by a powerful and opulent people. Its present aspect would belie its ancient history, were not that history corroborated by " the many vestiges of former cultivation," by the remains of walls and paved roads, and by the ruins of cities still existing in this ruined country.

The total cessation of its commerce—the artificial irrigation of its vallies wholly neglected—the destruction of all the cities, and the continued spoliation of the country by the Arabs, while aught remained that they could destroy—the permanent exposure, for ages, of the soil unsheltered by its ancient groves, and unprotected by any covering from the scorching rays of the sun—the unobstructed encroachments of the desert, and of the drifted sands from *the borders of the Red Sea,* the consequent absorption of the water of the springs and streamlets during summer, are causes which have all combined their baneful operation in rendering Edom *most desolate, the desolation of desolations.* Volney's account is sufficiently descriptive of the desolation which now reigns over Idumea : and the information which Seetzen derived at

and Burckhardt did pass through it, and they did not return. The period, however, to which the prediction, that *none* shall pass through it, expressly refers, is still future.

Jerusalem respecting it is of similar import.* He was told " that at the distance of two days' journey and a half from Hebron, he would find considerable ruins of the ancient city of Abde, and that for all the rest of the journey he would see *no place of habitation;* he would meet only with a few tribes of wandering Arabs." From the borders of Edom, Captains Irby and Mangles beheld a boundless extent of desert view, which they had hardly ever seen equalled for singularity and grandeur. And the following extract, descriptive of what Burckhardt actually witnessed in the different parts of Edom, cannot be more graphically abbreviated than in the words of the Prophet. Of its eastern boundary, and of the adjoining part of Arabia Petræa, strictly so called, Burckhardt writes —" It might with truth be called Petræa, not only on account of its rocky mountains, but also of the elevated plain already described,† which is so much covered with stones, especially flints, that it may with great propriety be called a stony desert, although susceptible of culture ; in many places it is overgrown with wild herbs, and must once have been thickly inhabited ; for the traces of many towns and villages are met with on both sides of the Hadj road, between Maan and Akaba, as well as between Maan and the plains of the Hauran, in which direction are also many springs. At present all this country is a desert, and Maan, (Teman)‡ is the only inhabited place in it.§ *I will stretch out my hand against thee, O Mount Seir, and will make thee most desolate. I will stretch out my hand upon Edom, and will make it desolate from Teman.*"

In the interior of Idumea, where the ruins of some

* Seetzen's Travels, p. 46.
† Sheera (Seir) the territory of the Edomites, pp. 410, 435.
‡ See map prefixed to Burckhardt's Travels.
§ Burckhardt's Travels, p. 436.

of its ancient cities are still visible, and in the extensive valley which reaches from the Red to the Dead Sea —the appearance of which must now be totally and sadly changed from what it was—" the whole plain presented to the view an expanse of shifting sands, whose surface was broken by innumerable undulations and low hills. The same appears to have been brought from *the shores of the Red Sea*, by the southern winds; and the Arabs told me that the vallies continue to present the same appearance beyond the latitude of Wady Mousa. In some parts of the valley the sand is very deep, and there is not the slightest appearance of a road, or of any work of human art. A few trees grow among the sand hills, but the depth of sand precludes *all vegetation* of herbage."* *If grape gatherers come to thee, would they not leave some gleaning grapes? if thieves by night, they will destroy till they have enough; but I have made Esau* BARE. *Edom shall be a desolate wilderness.* " On ascending the western plain on a higher level than that of Arabia, we had before us an immense expanse of dreary country, entirely covered with black flints, and here and there some hilly chain rising from the plain."† *I will stretch out upon Idumea the line of confusion, and the stones of emptiness.*

Of the remains of ancient cities still exposed to view in different places throughout Idumea, Burckhardt describes " the ruins of a large town of which nothing remains but broken walls and heaps of stones, the ruins of several villages in its vicinity;‡ the ruins of an ancient city consisting of large heaps of hewn blocks of silicious stone; the extensive ruins of Gherandel Arindela, an ancient town of Palestina Tertia."§ " The following ruined places are situated in *Djebal Shera*

* Burckhardt's Travels, p. 442.   † Ib. p. 444.
‡ Ib. p. 418.   § Ib. p. 441.

(Mount Seir) to the S. and S. W. of Wady Mousa,
Kalaat, Djerba, Basta, Eyl, Ferdakh, Anyk, Bir el
Beytar, Shemakh, and Syk. Of the towns* laid down
in D'Anville's map, Thona excepted, no *traces* remain."† *I will lay thy cities waste, and thou shalt
be desolate. O Mount Seir, I will make thee perpetual desolations ; and thy cities shall not return.*

While the cities of Idumea, in general, are thus
most desolate ; and while the ruins themselves are as
indiscriminate, as they are undefined in the prediction, (there being nothing discoverable, as there was
nothing foretold, but their excessive desolation, and
that they shall not return,) there is one striking exception to this promiscuous desolation, which is alike
singled out by the inspired prophet and by the scientific traveller.

Burckhardt gives a description of no ordinary interest, of the site of an ancient city which he visited, the
ruins of which not only attest its ancient splendour,
but they " are entitled to rank among the most curious
remains of ancient art." Though the city be desolate,
the monuments of its opulence and power are durable.
These are—a channel on each side of the river for conveying the water to the city—numerous tombs—above
two hundred and fifty sepulchres, or excavations—
many mausoleums, one, in particular, of colossal dimensions in perfect preservation, and a work of immense
labour, containing a chamber, sixteen paces square, and
above twenty-five feet in height, with a colonnade in
front thirty-five feet high, crowned with a pediment
highly ornamented, &c.; two large truncated pyramids,
and a theatre with all its benches, capable of contain-

---

* The names of these towns, in the map referred to, are
Elusa, Tamara, Zoara, Thoana, Necta, Phenon, Suzuma,
Carcaria, Oboda, Berzumma, Lysa, Gypsaria, Zodocata, Gerasa, Havara, Presidium ad Dianam, Œlana, Asion Gaber.

† Burckhardt's Travels, pp. 443, 444.

ing about three thousand spectators, ALL *cut out of the rock*. In some places these sepulchres are excavated one over the other, and the side of the mountain is so perpendicular, that *it seems impossible to approach the uppermost*, no path whatever being visible. " The ground is covered with heaps of hewn stones, foundations of buildings, fragments of columns, and vestiges of paved streets, all clearly indicating that a large city once existed here. On the left bank of the river is a rising ground, extending westwards for nearly three quarters of a mile, entirely covered with similar remains. On the right bank, where the ground is more elevated, ruins of the same description are to be seen. There are also the remains of a palace and of several temples. In the eastern *cliff* there are upwards of fifty separate sepulchres close to each other."* These are not the symbols of a feeble race, nor of a people that were to perish utterly. But a judgment was denounced against the strongholds of Edom. The prophetic threatening has not proved an empty boast, and it could not have been the word of an uninspired mortal. *I will make thee small among the heathen; thy terribleness hath deceived thee, and the pride of thine heart, O thou that dwellest in the clefts of the rock, that holdest the height of the hill; though thou shouldest make thy nest as high as the eagle, I will bring thee down from thence, saith the Lord: also Edom shall be a desolation.*

These descriptions given by the prophet and by the observer are so analogous, and the precise locality of the scene, from its peculiar and characteristic features, so identified—and yet the application of the prophecy to the fact so remote from the thoughts or view of Burckhardt, as to be altogether overlooked—that his single delineation of the ruins of the chief (and assur-

---

* Burckhardt's Travels in Syria, pp. 422—432.

edly the strongest and best fortified) city of Edom was
deemed in the first edition of this treatise, and in the
terms of the preceding paragraph, an illustration of
the prophecy, alike adequate and legitimate. And
though deprecating any allusion whatever of a personal nature, and earnest only for the elucidation of
the truth, the author yet trusts that he may here be
permitted to disclaim the credit of having been the
first to assign to the prediction its wonderful and appropriate fulfilment ; and it is with no slight gratification that he is now enabled to adduce higher evidence than any opinion of his own, and to state, that
the self-same prophecy has been applied by others—
with the Bible in their hands, and with the very
scene before them—to the self-same spot. Yet it
may be added, that this coincident application of the
prophecy, without any collusion, and without the possibility at the time of any interchange of sentiment,
affords, at least, a strong presumptive evidence of the
accuracy of the application, and of the truth of the
prophecy, and it may well lead to some reflection in
the mind of any reader, if scepticism has not barred
every avenue against conviction.

On entering the pass which conducts to the theatre
of Petra, Captains Irby and Mangles remark ;—" The
ruins of the city here burst on the view, in their full
grandeur, shut in on the opposite side by barren
craggy precipices from which numerous ravines and
vallies branch out in all directions ; the sides of the
mountains covered with an endless variety of excavated tombs and private dwellings, (*O thou that dwellest
in the clefts of* THE ROCK, &c.—Jer. xlix. 16,) presented altogether the most singular scene we ever beheld."

In still farther confirmation of the identity of the
site, and the accuracy of the application, it may be
added, in the words of Dr. Vincent, that " the name

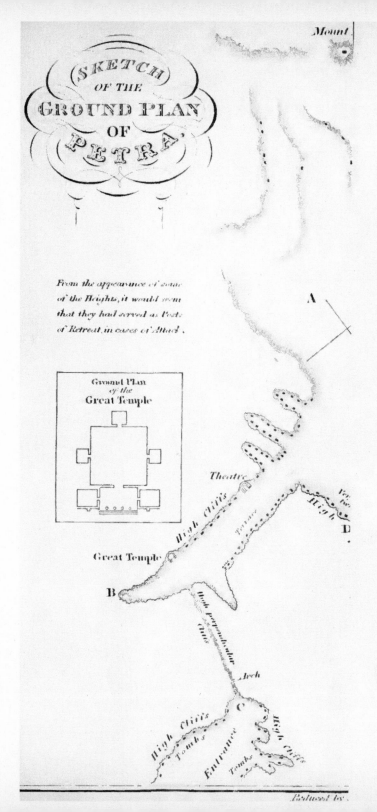

Mount

SKETCH
OF THE
GROUND PLAN
OF
PETRA

A

From the appearance of some
of the Heights, it would seem
that they had served as Posts
of Retreat, in cases of Attack.

Ground Plan
of the
Great Temple

Theatre

High Cliffs

Terrace

High

D

Great Temple

B

High Perpendicular
Cliffs

Arch

C

High Cliffs

Tombs

Entrance

Tombs

High Cliffs

Reduced by

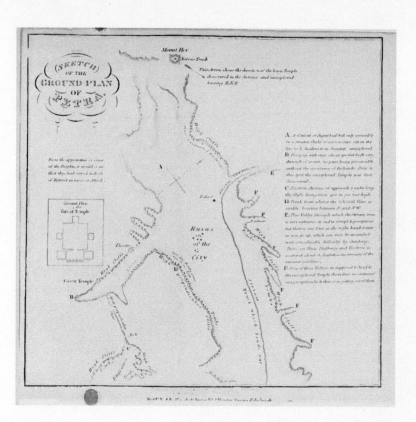

Gaß sc.

VIEW TAKEN FROM ENTRANCE OF THE VALLEY.

of this capital, in all the various languages in which
it occurs, implies a rock, and as such it is described
in the Scriptures, in Strabo, and Al Edrissi."* And
in a note he enumerates among the various names
having all the same signification—Sela, a rock, (the
very word here used in the original), Petra, a rock,
the Greek name, (which has precisely the same signification) and The Rock, pre-eminently—expressly
referring to this passage of Scripture.†

Captains Irby and Mangles, having, together with
Mr. Bankes and Mr. Legh, spent two days in diligently examining them, give a more particular detail
of the ruins of Petra than Burckhardt's account supplied ; and the more full the description, the more
precise and wonderful does the prophecy appear.
Near the spot where they awaited the decision of the
Arabs, " the high land was covered upon both its
sides, and on its summits, with lines and solid masses
of dry wall. The former appeared to be traces of ancient cultivation, the solid ruins seemed to be only
the remains of towers for watching in harvest and
vintage time. The whole neighbourhood of the spot
bears similar traces of former industry ; all which
seem to indicate the vicinity of a great metropolis."‡
A narrow and circuitous defile, surrounded on each
side by precipitous or perpendicular rocks, varying
from four hundred to seven hundred feet in altitude,
and forming, for two miles, " a sort of subterranean
passage," opens on the east the way to the ruins of
Petra. The rocks, or rather hills, then diverge on
either side, and leave an oblong space, where once
stood the metropolis of Edom, deceived by its terribleness, where now lies a waste of ruins, encircled on

---

* Commerce of the Ancients, vol. ii. p. 264.
† See Blaney, *in loco.*
‡ Captains Irby and Mangles' Travels, p. 402.

every side, save on the north-east alone, by stupendous cliffs, which still show how the pride and labour of art tried there to vie with the sublimity of nature. Along the borders of these cliffs, detached masses of rock, numerous and lofty, have been wrought into sepulchres, the interior of which is excavated into chambers, while the exterior has been cut from the live rock into the forms of towers, with pilastres, and successive bands of frieze and entablature, wings, recesses, figures of animals, and columns.* The subjoined cut may convey an idea of some of these singular excavations :

Yet, numerous as these are, they form but a part of " the vast necropolis of Petra." " Tombs present themselves, not only in every avenue to the city, and upon every precipice that surrounds it, but even intermixed almost promiscuously with its public and domestic edifices ; the natural features of the defile grew more and more imposing at every step, and the excavations and sculpture more frequent on both sides, till it presented at last a continued street of tombs."

* Captains Irby and Mangles' Travels, p. 407.

The base of the cliffs wrought out in all the symmetry and regularity of art, with colonnades, and pedestals, and ranges of corridors adhering to the perpendicular surface ; flights of steps chiselled out of the rock ; grottos in great numbers, " which are certainly not sepulchral ;" some excavated residences of large dimensions, (in one of which is a single chamber, sixty feet in length, and of a breadth proportioned ;) many other dwellings of inferior note, particularly abundant in one defile leading to the city, the steep sides of which contain a sort of excavated suburb, accessible by flights of steps ; niches, sometimes thirty feet in excavated height, with altars for votive offerings, or with pyramids, columns or obelisks ; a bridge across a chasm now apparently inaccessible ; some small pyramids hewn out of the rock on the summit of the heights ; horizontal grooves, for the conveyance of water, cut in the face of the rock, and even across the architectural fronts of some of the excavations ; and, in short, " the rocks hollowed out into innumerable chambers of different dimensions, whose entrances are variously, richly, and often fantastically decorated with every imaginable order of architecture"*—all united, not only form one of the most singular scenes that the eye of man ever looked upon, or the imagination painted—a group of wonders perhaps unparalleled in their kind—but also give indubitable proof, both that in the land of Edom there was a city where human ingenuity, and energy, and power, must have been exerted for many ages, and to so great a degree, as to have well entitled it to be noted for its strength or *terribleness*, and that the description given of it by the prophets of Israel was as strictly literal as the prediction respecting it is true. " The barren state

---

* Captains Irby and Mangles' Travels, pp. 407—437. Macmichael's Journey, pp. 228, 229.

of the country, together with the desolate condition of
the city, without a single human being living near it,
seem," in the words of those who were spectators of
the scene, " strongly to verify the judgment denounced against it."*   *O thou that dwellest in the
clefts of the rock, &c.—also Edom shall be a desolation, &c.*

Of all the ruins of Petra, the mausoleums and sepulchres are among the most remarkable, and they
give the clearest indication of ancient and long continued royalty, and of courtly grandeur.   Their immense number corroborates the accounts given of
their successive kings and princes, by Moses and Strabo ; though a period of eighteen hundred years intervened between the dates of their respective records
concerning them.   The structure of the sepulchres
also shows that many of them are of a more recent
date.   " Great," says Burckhardt, " must have been
the opulence of a city which could dedicate such monuments to the memory of its rulers."†   But the
long line of the kings, and of the nobles of Idumea,
has for ages been cut off; they are without any representative now, without any memorial but the multitude and the magnificence of their unvisited sepulchres.   *They shall call the nobles thereof to the kingdom,* (or rather, they shall call, or summon, the nobles thereof,) *but there shall be no kingdom there, and
all her princes shall be nothing.*

Amidst the mausoleums and sepulchres, the remains
of temples or palaces, and the multiplicity of tombs,
which all form, as it were, the grave of Idumea, where
its ancient splendour is interred, there are edifices, the
Roman and Grecian architecture of which decides that
they were *built* long posterior to the era of the pro-

* Irby and Mangles' Travels, p. 439.
† Burckhardt's Travels, p. 425.

phets.* *They shall build, but I will throw down.*
The description given by Volney, and depending for
its accuracy on the authority of Arabs, formed till
very recently the only account of the modern state of
Idumea; and though the testimony was recorded in
a manner and came through a channel the most unsuspected possible, yet the evidence was not sufficiently direct or discriminating to mark, as Volney had
otherwise done, the exact, prophetic, and characteristic features of the scene. The interesting details,
from personal observation, communicated by Burckhardt, and subsequently by Captains Irby and Mangles, rescued the subject from obscurity, and brought
to light the remarkable fact of the ruins of a city, so
to speak, cut out of the rock, in the midst of a desert.

When, in the streets of Jerusalem, the people shouted hosannahs to the Son of David, and while some of
the Pharisees among the people said unto him, Master, rebuke thy disciples, he answered and said unto
them, I tell you that if these should hold their peace,
the stones would immediately cry out. And in an infidel age, while many modern cities and nations dis-
owned the authority of the God of Israel, and disbelieved his word, those of ancient times stood forth
anew before the world, like witnesses arisen from the
dead, to show the authority, the power, and the truth
of his word over them, and to raise a warning and in-
structive voice to the *cities of the nations*, lest they
too should become the monuments of the wrath which
they have defied. And when men would not hear of
hosannahs to the Son of David, or of divine honours to
the name of Christ, deserts immediately spake and
rocks cried out, and, responding to the voice of the
prophets, testified of them who testified of Jesus. The
capital of Edom, as well as those of other ancient

* Burckhardt's Travels, p. 425.

kingdoms, was heard of again ; and its rocks now
send forth a voice that may well reach unto the ends
of the earth.

It entered not into the thoughts of the writer, and
far surpassed his hopes, when first led to look into the
prophecies concerning Edom, from the statement of
an Arab report, recorded by Volney, that in so short
a time, the fulfilment of these prophecies might be
set before the eyes of men, even without their having
to " come and see." And after having adduced new
evidence in successive editions from striking facts,
clearly illustrative of the predictions relative to Edom,
and to its once terrible metropolis, an appeal may
now be made to the sight as well as to the understanding of men. For just as these pages are passing through the press, the author has timely received
from Paris, (and would that that city would give
heed to the truth, which it thus farther affords the
means of confirming,) the first six livraisons of a
work entitled, *Voyage de L'Arabie Pétrée par Mess.
Leon de Laborde et Linant,* now in the course of publication, which contains, in the numbers already published, seventeen splendid engravings of the Ruins of
Petra alone, in which, by merely affixing a text, the
beauties of art become immediately subservient to the
interests of religion. Where, very recently, it was
difficult, if not impossible, to ascertain a single fact,
and where only indirect evidence could be obtained,
men may now, as it were, look upon Idumea, and
see how the lines of confusion and the stones of
emptiness have been stretched over it. And we may
now, in like manner, look upon the ruins of the chief
city of Edom, of which the very existence was, till
lately, altogether unknown. All the plates attest its
vast magnificence, and the almost incredible and inconceivable labour, continued as it must have been
from age to age, prior to the days of Moses and later

2

than the Christian era—by which so great a multiplicity of dwellings, tombs, and temples were excavated from the rock. And Truth speaks out, not from the lips of a lying spirit evoked by the fancy of a sceptical philosopher, but from the face of the live rock, which exhibits the dwellings in the clefts, singularly characteristic of the scene, and declares by the order of architecture, as if still told by every stroke of the chisel, that the citizens of Petra did *build*, after the era of the prophets, while the fragments of ruins, of Grecian and Roman architecture, as well as of more ancient date, which are strewed over the ground, and cover the valley which was the site of the city, and which is surrounded by precipitous hills and excavated rocks, shows that those buildings whose doom was pronounced before their erection, have, according to the same sure word, been *thrown down*.

The topographical view of the land of Idumea, taken from d'El Nakb, gives us to see that Edom is *most desolate, the desolation of desolations*. That the country which was given unto Esau, as the *fatness of the earth*, and in which many cities were built, has been *made bare, and that the lines of confusion and the stones of emptiness have been stretched over it*. In the brief explanatory note which accompanies the plate, it is stated that " no map, however well executed, can represent the aspect of a country so well as views taken from *an elevated point, and comprehending a great extent*. It is from such *demi-panoramas* alone that a correct idea can be formed. Such has been the object proposed in drawing these two views." (The other view, of a similar character, represents the southern coast of Edom, on the borders of the Red Sea. The accompanying view has been selected, as comprehending the greatest extent, and showing the aspect of the country.)

" The view is taken from d'El Nakb, a precipitous

K

ascent, six miles south of Mount Hor, and consequently of Petra.   It comprehends to the left, or the west,
Ouadi Araba, (or the valley of Araba) a long and
straight plain of sand, which, commencing at the Red
Sea, extends to the north, in a direct line, to the Jordan, and was, without doubt, the ancient bed of that
river before the volcanic eruption which formed the
actual basin of the Dead Sea, and of which the Bible
has given so faithful a recital.   On the right bank,
towards the west, lies the adjoining valley of *Ouadi*
Gebb, through which the Fellahs of Petra repair to
Gaza.   Towards the east, (on the right of the view)
there is seen, in the middle of a small plain, an insulated rock called *El Aase*, on which is a tomb of the
same form of construction as those of Petra.   Farther
to the right is a high rock, which forms, as it were,
the first rampart in the environs of Petra, elevated in
the form of a cone, with a tree on the summit.   Following the same direction, we meet with Mount Hor,
the highest rock in the country, on the summit of
which is seen the *Tomb of Aaron*, held in great veneration in that region.   To the east of that mountain, in a small plain of unequal surface enclosed in
the midst of rocks, of which the masses seem to be
accumulated and pressed together, is built the city of
Petra, the capital of the Nabatheans.   The picture
is terminated by the grand chain of mountains, which
separates Arabia Deserta from Arabia Petrea, properly
so called "

One engraving is peculiarly striking, as indirectly
exemplifying the *unique* character of the scenery, by
which, at a glance, Petra is identified, and distinguished from any other city that ever existed.   The
design of the picture is to represent an isolated column.   But the back-ground exhibits to view " a
part of the valley of Moses" (Ouadi Mousa) with the
high rocks in the more distant perspective " pierced

WADI MOUSA
PETRA

Eng.d by Ya Lieu.

A TRIUMPHAL ARCH IN RUINS
PETRA

with thousands of excavations, (percés de milliers excavations.") The reader will be aware that the minute appearance of the excavations is occasioned by the distance of the view, and consequent diminution of the apparent height of the rocks ; and in the multiplicity of excavations, perceptible even in the rocks which border the elongated valley, he will not fail to observe the dwellings in the clefts of the rocks, and to see how the inhabitants of the capital of Edom made their *nest as high as the eagle's.* This perfect coincidence both with the description, as identifying the spot, and with the prediction of the prophet, as now abandoned and desolate, is the more remarkable as it is incidentally and indirectly placed in view, the title of the print being, A View of an Isolated or Deserted Column, (Vue d'une Colonne Isolée.)

In the notes connected with the *ruins of a temple,* of which two views are given, it is stated that—" besides the gigantic and singular tombs cut out of the rock, Petra contains a great number of monuments, of which the ruins attest the beautiful style and the magnificence ; *but of all these buildings,* the only one which has resisted the ravages of time is that which is here represented. Situated to the west of the city, on the bank of the river, it towers over the innumerable wreck of buildings, (debris) which cover the soil, and yet present, though in ruins, a beautiful mass, and beautiful details of architecture. The cornice which surmounts the temple is in a pure and elegant style. In the back-ground is seen the antique pavement, as it still exists."

In explanation of the plate which represents the ruins of a triumphal arch, it is stated, " The passage under the triumphal arch leads to a public place, a species of forum, paved with large flag-stones, which reach to the temple that is seen in the back-ground. The monument represented in this view formed three arcades, of which one, that in the middle, is by far the largest, and served for carriages, and the two others for foot-passengers. There is observable in the construction some analogy to the triumphal arch which terminates the colonnade of Palmyra, towards the east. The pilaster, which still remains, is that which separates the middle arch from that of one of the corners." " This view is taken from the west, and represents the same monument described (as above) in the preceding livraison. In the back-ground is seen one part of the grand funereal monuments."

Other plates present to view the vast magnificence of the tombs of Petra—the effect of which, it is apprehended, would in a great measure be lost, in etchings on so small a scale as the size of this volume could conveniently admit. There is one tomb, of which a view is given, which is peculiarly deserving of notice, there being engraven on it a Latin inscription, with the name of a magistrate, Quintus Pretextus Florentinus, who died in that city, being governor of that part of Arabia Petrea. " It behoved to be," it is said, " about the time of Adrian or Antoninus Pius," or at a period unquestionably several centuries posterior to the predictions.

They shall be called the border of wickedness. Strabo contrasts the quiet disposition of the citizens of Petra with the contentious spirit of the foreigners who resided there ; and the uninterrupted tranquillity which the townsmen mutually maintained together, excited the admiration of Athenodorus.* The fine gold is changed: no such people are there now to be found. Though Burckhardt travelled as an Arab, associated with them, submitted to all their privations, and was so completely master of their language and of their manners, as to escape detection, he was

* Strabo, p. 779.

yet reduced to that state, within the boundaries of
Edom, which can alone secure tranquillity to the traveller in the desert; " he had nothing with him that
could attract the notice, or excite the cupidity of the
Bedouins," and was even stripped of some rags that
covered his wounded ankles.* The Arabs in that
quarter, he observes, " have the reputation of being
very daring thieves." In like manner, a Motselim,
who had been twenty years in office, pledged himself
to Captains Irby and Mangles, and the travellers who
accompanied them, (in presence of the Governor of
Jerusalem,) that the Arabs of Wady Mousa are " a
most savage and treacherous race," and added, that
they would make use of their Franks' blood for a
medicine. That this character of wickedness and
cruelty was not misapplied, they had too ample proof,
not only in the dangers with which they were threatened, but by the fact which they learned on the spot,
that upwards of thirty pilgrims from Barbary had
been murdered at Petra the preceding year, by the
men of Wady Mousa.† Even the Arabs of the surrounding deserts, as already stated, dread to approach
it; and towards the borders of Edom on the south,
" the Arabs about Akaba," as described by Pococke,
and as experienced by Burckhardt, " are a very bad
people, and notorious robbers, and are at war with
all others."‡ Such evidence, all undesignedly given,
clearly shows that in truth Edom is called *the border
of wickedness.*

*Thorns shall come in her palaces, nettles and bram-
bles in the fortresses thereof.* In lieu of any direct
and explicit statement in corroboration of the literal

---

* Burckhardt's Travels, p. 438.
 † Irby and Mangles' Travels, p. 417. Macmichael's Jour-
ney, pp. 202, 234.
 ‡ Pococke's Description of the East, vol. i. p. 136.

fulfilment of this prediction, it may be worthy of observation that the camels of the Bedouins feed upon the thorny branches of the Talh (gum arabic) tree, of which they are extremely fond; that the large thorns of these trees are a great annoyance to them, and to their cattle; and that they are so abundant in different parts of Idumea, that each Bedouin carries in his girdle a pair of small pincers to extract the thorns from his feet.*

I will make thee small among the nations; thou art greatly despised. Though the border of wickedness, and the retreat of a horde of thieves, who are distinguished as peculiarly savage even among the wild Arabs, and thus an object of dread, as well as of astonishment to those who pass thereby, yet contrasted with what it was, or reckoned among the nations, Edom is small indeed. Within almost all its boundary, it may be said, that none *abide*, or have any fixed or permanent residence; and instead of the superb structures, the works of various ages, which long adorned its cities, the huts of the Arabs, where even huts they have, are mere mud hovels of " mean and ragged appearance," which, in general, are deserted on the least alarm. But, miserable habitations as these are, they scarcely seem to exist anywhere throughout Edom, but on a single point on its borders; and wherever the Arabs otherwise wander in search of spots for pasturage for their cattle, (found in hollows, or near to springs after the winter rains,) tents are their only covering. Those which pertain to the more powerful tribes, are sometimes both numerous and large; yet, though they form at best but a frail dwelling, many of them are " very low and small." Near to the ruins of Petra, Burckhardt passed an encampment of Bedouin tents, most of which

* Burckhardt's Travels in Syria, p. 446.

were " the smallest he had ever seen, about four feet
high, and ten in length ;" and towards the south-
west border of Edom, he met with a few wanderers
who had no tents with them, and whose only shelter
from the burning rays of the sun, and the *heavy
dews of night*, was the scanty branches of the Talh
trees. The subsistence of the Bedouins is often as
precarious as their habitations are mean ; the flocks
they tend, or which they pillage from more fertile
regions, are their only possessions ; and in that land
where commerce long concentrated its wealth, and
through which the treasures of Ophir passed, the
picking of gum arabic from thorny branches is now
the poor occupation, the only semblance of industry,
practised by the wild and wandering tenants of a
desert. Edom is *small among the nations ;* and how
greatly is it despised, when the public authorities at
Constantinople deny any knowledge of it, or of the
ruins of its capital, which once defied the power of
Rome—when the city of Petra is thus forgotten and
unknown among the representatives of the villagers
of Byzantium !

*Concerning Edom, thus saith the Lord, Is wisdom
no more in Teman? Is understanding perished from
the prudent? Shall I not destroy the wise men out of
Edom, and understanding out of the Mount of Esau?*
Fallen and despised as it now is, Edom, did not the
prescription of many ages abrogate its right, might
lay claim to the title of having been the first seat of
learning, as well as the centre of commerce. Sir Isaac
Newton, who was no mean master in chronology, and
no incompetent judge to give a decision in regard to
the rise and first progress of literature, considers Edom
as the nursery of the arts and sciences, and adduces
evidence to that effect from profane as well as from
sacred history. " The Egyptians," he remarks, " *having learned the skill of the Edomites*, began now to

observe the position of the stars, and the length of the
solar year, for enabling them to know the position of
the stars at any time, and to sail by them at all times
without sight of the shore, and this gave a beginning
to astronomy and navigation."*   " It seems that
letters, and astronomy, and the trade of carpenters,
were invented by the merchants of the Red Sea, and
that they were propagated from Arabia Petræa, into
Egypt, Chaldea, Syria, Asia Minor, and Europe."†
While the philosopher may thus think of Edom with
respect, neither the admirer of genius, the man of
feeling, nor the child of devotion will, even to this
day, seek from any land a richer treasure of plaintive
poetry, of impassioned eloquence, and of fervid piety,
than Edom has bequeathed to the world in the book
of Job.   It exhibits to us, in language the most pa-
thetic and sublime, all that a man could feel, in the
outward pangs of his body and the inner writhings of
his mind, of the frailties of his frame, and of the dissolution of his earthly comforts and endearments; all
that mortal can discern, by meditating on the ways,
and contemplating the works of God, of the omniscience and omnipotence of the Most High, and of the
inscrutable dispensations of his providence; all *that*
knowledge which could first tell, in written word, of
Arcturus, and Orion, and Pleiades; and all that
devotedness of soul, and immortality of hope, which—
with patience that faultered not even when the heart
was bruised, and almost broken, and the body covered over with distress—could say, " Though he slay
me, yet will I trust in him."

But if the question now be asked, *is* understanding perished out of Edom? the answer, like every
response of the prophetic word, may be briefly given:

* Sir Isaac Newton's Chronology of Ancient Kingdoms,
p. 208.   † Ibid. p. 212.

it is. The minds of the Bedouins are as uncultivated as the deserts they traverse. Practical wisdom is, in general, the first that man learns and the last that he retains. And the simple but significant fact, already alluded to, that the clearing away of a little rubbish, merely " to allow the water to flow " into an ancient cistern, in order to render it useful to themselves, " is an undertaking far beyond the views of the wandering Arabs," shows that *understanding is* indeed *perished from among them.* They view the indestructible works of former ages, not only with wonder, but with superstitious regard, and consider them as the work of genii. They look upon a European as a magician, and believe that, having seen any spot where they imagine that treasures are deposited, he can afterwards command the guardian of the treasure to set the whole before him."* In Teman, which yet maintains a precarious existence, the inhabitants possess the desire without the means of knowledge. The Koran is their only study, and contains the sum of their wisdom.—And although he was but a " miserable comforter," and was overmastered in argument by a kinsman stricken with affliction, yet no *Temanite* can now discourse with either the wisdom or the pathos of *Eliphaz* of old. *Wisdom is no more in Teman, and understanding has perished out of the Mount of Esau.*

While there is thus subsisting evidence and proof that the ancient inhabitants of Edom were renowned for wisdom, as well as for power, and while desolation has spread so widely over it, that it can scarcely be said to be inhabited by man ; there still are tenants who hold possession of it, to whom it is abandoned by man, and to whom it was decreed by a voice more than mortal. And insignificant and minute as it

* Burckhardt's Travels, p. 429.

may possibly appear to those who reject the light of
revelation, or to the unreflecting mind, (that will
use no measuring line of truth, which stretches beyond that which inches out its own shallow thoughts,
and wherewith rejecting all other aid, it tries, by the
superficial touch of ridicule alone, to sound the un-
fathomable depths of infinite wisdom) yet the following scripture, mingled with other words already
verified as the voice of inspiration, and voluntarily in-
volving its title to credibility in the appended appeal
to fact and challenge to investigation, may, in conjunction with kindred proofs, yet tell to man—if
hearing he will hear, and show him, if seeing he will
see—the verity of the divine word, and the infallibility of the divine judgments ; and not without the
aid of the rightful and unbiassed exercise of reason,
may give understanding to the sceptic, that he may
be converted, and that he may be healed by him
whose word is ever truth.

" But the cormorant and the bittern shall possess
it (Idumea) ; the owl also, and the raven shall dwell
in it. It shall be a habitation for dragons and a
court for owls ; the wild beasts of the desert shall also
meet with the wild beasts of the island, and the satyr
(the hairy or rough creature) shall cry to his fellow ;
the screech owl also shall rest there, and find for herself a place of rest ; there shall the great owl make
her nest, and lay, and hatch, and gather under her
shadow ; there shall the vultures also be gathered every
one with her mate. Seek ye out of the book of the
Lord and read ; no one of these shall fail, none shall
want her mate ; for my mouth it hath commanded,
and his Spirit it hath gathered them. And he hath
cast the lot for them, and his hand hath divided it
unto them by line : they shall possess it for ever ;
from generation to generation shall they dwell there-

in."* " I laid the mountains of Esau, and his heritage waste, for the dragons of the wilderness."†

Such is the precision of the prophecies, so remote are they from all ambiguity of meaning, and so distinct are the events which they detail, that it is almost unnecessary to remark, that the different animals here enumerated were not all in the same manner, or in the same degree, to be possessors of Edom. Some of them were to rest, to meet, to be gathered there; the owl and the raven were to dwell in it, and it was to be a habitation for dragons; while of the cormorant and bittern, it is emphatically said, that they were to possess it. And is it not somewhat beyond a mere fortuitous coincidence, imperfect as the information is respecting Edom, that, in " seeking out" proof concerning these animals, and whether none of them do fail, the most decisive evidence should, in the first instance, be unconsciously communicated from the boundaries of Edom, of the one which is first noted in the prediction, and which was to possess the land? It will at once be conceded, that in whatever country any particular animal is unknown, no proper translation of its name can there be given; and that for the purpose of designating or identifying it, reference must be had to the original name, and to the natural history of the country in which it is known. And, without any ambiguity or perplexity arising from the translation of the word, or any need of tracing it through any other languages to ascertain its import, the identical word of the original, with scarcely the slightest variation (and that only the want of the final vowel in the Hebrew word; vowels in that language being often supplied in the enunciation, or by points) is, from the affinity of the Hebrew and Arabic, used on the very spot by the Arabs, to

* Isa. xxxiv. 11, 13—17. † Mal. i. 3.

denote the very bird, which may literally be said to possess the land. While in the last inhabited village of Moab, and close upon the borders of Edom, Burckhardt noted the animals which frequented the neighbouring territory, in which he distinctly specifies Shera, the land of the Edomites ; and he relates that " the bird katta* is met with in immense numbers. They fly in such large flocks that the Arab boys often kill two or three of them at a time, merely by throwing a stick among them."† If any objector be here inclined to say, that it is not to be wondered at, that any particular bird should be found in any given country, that it might continue to remain for a term of ages, and that such a surmise would not exceed the natural probabilities of the case, the fact may be freely admitted as applicable, perhaps, to most countries of the globe. But who ever, elsewhere, saw any wild bird in any country, in flocks so immensely numerous that two or three of them could be killed by the single throw of a stick from the hand of a boy ; and that this could be stated, not as a forcible, and perhaps false, illustration, to denote their number, nor as a wonderful chance, or unusual incident, but as a fact of frequent occurrence ? Who ever, elsewhere, heard of such a fact, not as happening merely on a sea-rock, the resort of myriads of birds, or their temporary resting-place when exhausted in their flight, but in an extensive country, their permanent abode ? Or if, among the manifold discoveries of travellers in modern times, it were really related that such occupants of a country are to be found, or that a corresponding fact exists in any other region of the earth which was once

---

* קאת kat, a species of partridge. It is sometimes written, in the original, kata. Onkel. קטא vide Simonis Lexicon. p. 1393.

† Burckhardt's Travels in Syria, p. 406.

tenanted by man, who can also "find" in the records of a high antiquity, the prediction that declared it? Of what country now inhabited could the same fact be now with certainty foretold; and where is the seer who can discern the vision, fix on the spot over the world's surface, and select, from the whole winged tribe, the name of the first in order, and the greatest in number, of the future and chief possessors of the land?

Of the bittern (kephud) as a joint possessor with the katta of Idumea, evidence has not been given or ascertained;—but numerous as the facts have been which modern discoveries have consigned over to the service of revelation, that word of truth which fears no investigation can appeal to other facts, unknown to history, and still undiscovered—but registered in prophecy, and there long since revealed.

The owl also, and the raven (or crow) shall dwell in it.—The owl and raven do dwell in it. Captain Mangles relates, that while he and his fellow-travellers were examining the ruins, and contemplating the sublime scenery of Petra,—" the screaming of the eagles, hawks, and owls, who were soaring above their heads in considerable numbers, seemingly annoyed at any one approaching their lonely habitation, added much to the singularity of the scene." "The fields of Tafyle," situated in the immediate vicinity of Edom, are, according to the observation of Burckhardt, "frequented by an immense number of crows."[*] "I expected," says Seetzen, (alluding to his purposed tour through Idumea, and to the information he had received from the Arabs,) "to make several discoveries in mineralogy, as well as in the animals and vegetables of the country, on the manna of the desert, the ravens,"[†] &c.

* Burckhardt's Travels, p. 405.
† Seetzen's Travels, p. 46.

*It shall be a habitation for dragons (serpents.)   I
laid his heritage waste for the dragons of the wilderness.*—The evidence, though derived from testimony,
and not from personal observation, of two travellers of
so contrary characters and views as Shaw and Volney,
is so accordant and apposite, that it may well be sustained in lieu of more direct proof. The former
represents the land of Edom, and the wilderness of
which it now forms part, as abounding with a variety
of lizards and vipers, which are very dangerous and
troublesome.*   And the narrative given by Volney,
already quoted, is equally decisive as to the fact. The
Arabs, in general, avoid the ruins of the cities of
Idumea, " on account of *the enormous scorpions with
which they swarm.*" Its cities thus deserted by man,
and abandoned to their undisturbed and hereditary
possession, Edom may be justly called *the inheritance
of dragons.*

*The wild beasts of the desert shall also meet with
the wild beasts of the island,* (or of the borders of the
sea.) Instead of these words of the English version,
Parkhurst renders the former the *ravenous birds inha-
biting the wilderness.* The interpretation was given
long before the fact to which it refers was made
known. But it has now been ascertained, (and without any allusion, on the other hand, to the prediction,) that eagles,† hawks, and ravens, all ravenous
birds, are common in Edom, and *do not fail* to illustrate the prediction as thus translated. But when
animals from different regions are said to meet, the
prophecy thus implying that some of them at least
did not properly pertain to the country, would seem
to require some farther verification. And of all the
wonderful circumstances attached to the history, or

---

* Shaw's Travels, vol. ii. pp. 105, 338.
† Burckhardt's Travels, p. 405.

pertaining to the fate of Edom, there is one which is
not to be ranked among the least in singularity, that
bears no remote application to the prefixed prophecy,
and that ought not, perhaps, to pass here unnoted.
It is recorded in an ancient Chronicle, that the emperor Decius caused fierce lions and lionesses to be
transported from (the deserts of) Africa to the borders
of Palestine and Arabia, in order that propagating
there they might act as an annoyance and a barrier
to the barbarous Saracens :*   Between Arabia and
Palestine lies the doomed and execrated land of Edom.
And may it not thus be added, that a cause so unnatural and unforeseen would greatly tend to the destruction of the flocks, and to the desolation of all the adjoining territory,—and seem to be as if the king of
the forest was to take possession of it for his subjects?
And may it not be even literally said *that the wild
beasts of the desert meet there with the wild beasts of
the borders of the sea!*

The Satyr shall dwell there.—The satyr is entirely a
fabulous animal.   The word (soir) literally means *a
rough hairy one*: and, like a synonymous word in both
the Greek and Latin languages which has the same
signification, has been translated both by lexicogra-
phers and commentators, *the goat.*†   Parkhurst says,
that, in this sense, he would understand this very passage : and Lowth distinctly asserts, without assigning
to it any other meaning, that " the word originally sig-

---

* Ὁ αὑτος Δεχιος βασιλευς ἡγαγεν απο της Αφριχης λεον-
τας φοβερχς και λεαινας και απελυσιν εις το λιμιτον ανατολης
απο Αραβιας και Παλαιστινης εως τ̃ Κεγισιχ Κασχ προς το
ποιησαι γενεαν δια τχς βαρχαρχς Σαραχηνχς.   *Chronicon Alex-
andrinum, ad ann. C. 358. Relan. Palest. p. 97.*

† " So the Greek τραγος a he-goat, is from τραχυς rough,
on account of the *roughness* of his hair, and the Latin hir-
cus, a he-goat, from hirtus, rough." Parkhurst's Lexicon.

nifies *goat*."* Such respectable and well known authorities have been cited, because their decision must have rested on criticism alone, as it was impossible that their minds could have been biassed by any knowledge of the fact in reference to Edom. It was their province, and that of others, to illustrate its meaning—it was Burckhardt's, however unconsciously, to bear, from ocular observation, witness to its truth. " In all the Wadys south of the Modjel and El Asha," (pointing to Edom,) " large herds of mountain-goats are met with. They pasture in flocks of forty and fifty together."†—*They dwell there.*

But the evidence respecting all the animals specified in the prophecy, as the future possessors of Edom. is not yet complete, and is difficult to be ascertained. And, in words that seem to indicate this very difficulty, it is still reserved for future travellers,—perhaps some unconscious Volney—to disclose the facts ; and for future inquirers, whether Christian or infidel, to seek out of the book of the Lord and read : and to " find that no one of these do fail." Yet recent as the disclosure of any information respecting them has been ; and offered, as it now for the first time is, for the consideration of every candid mind, the positive terms and singleness of object of the prophecies themselves, and the undesigned and decisive evidence, are surely enough to show how greatly these several specific predictions and their respective facts exceed all possibility of their being the word or the work of man, and how clearly there may be discovered in them all, if sight itself be conviction, the credentials of inspiration, and the operation of His hands, to whose pre-

---

* Lowth assigns the reason why the word is translated *satyr*—it is supposed, that evil spirits of old time appeared in the shape of goats, as the learned Bochart hath proved. Isa. xiii. 21.

† Burckhardt's Travels in Syria.

science futurity is open,—to whose power all nature is subservient,—and " whose mouth it hath commanded, and whose spirit it hath gathered them."

Noted as Edom was for its terribleness, and possessed of a capital city, from which even a feeble people could not easily have been dislodged, there scarcely could have been a question, even among its enemies, to what *people* that country would eventually belong. And it never could have been thought of by any native of another land, as the Jewish prophets were, nor by any uninspired mortal whatever, that a kingdom, which had previously subsisted so long, (and in which princes ceased not to reign, commerce to flourish, and " a people of great opulence" to dwell for more than six hundred years thereafter,) would be finally extinct, that all its cities would be for ever desolate, and though it could have boasted, more than any other land, of indestructible habitations for men, that their *habitations* would be *desolate;* and that certain *wild animals*, mentioned by name, would, in different manners and degrees, possess the country from generation to generation.

There shall not be any remaining of the house of Esau. Edom shall be cut off for ever. The aliens of Judah ever look with wistful eyes to the land of their fathers; but no Edomite is now to be found to dispute the right of any animal to the possession of it, or to banish the owl from the temples and palaces of Edom. But the House of Esau did remain, and existed in great power, till after the commencement of the Christian era, a period far too remote from the date of the prediction for their subsequent history to have been foreseen by man. The Idumeans were soon after mingled with the Nabatheans. And in the third century, their language was disused, and their very name, as designating any people, had utterly perished;* and their country itself having become an outcast from Syria, among whose kingdoms it had long been numbered, was united to Arabia Petræa. Though the descendants of the twin-born Esau and Jacob have met a diametrically opposite fate, the fact is no less marvellous and undisputed, than the prediction in each case is alike obvious and true. While the posterity of Jacob have been " dispersed in every country under heaven," and are " scattered among all nations," and have ever remained distinct from them all, and while it is also declared that " a full end will never be made of them ;" the Edomites, though they existed as a nation for more than seventeen hundred years, *have*, as a period of nearly equal duration has proved, *been cut off for ever ;* and while Jews are in every land, *there is not any remaining* on any spot of earth, *of the house of Esau.*

Idumea, in aid of a neighbouring state, did send forth, on a sudden, an army of twenty thousand armed men,—it contained at least eighteen towns, for centuries after the Christian era—successive kings and princes reigned in Petra,—and magnificent palaces and temples, whose empty chambers and naked walls of wonderful architecture still strike the traveller with amazement, were constructed there, at a period unquestionably far remote from the time when it was given to the prophets of Israel to tell, that the house of Esau was to be cut off for ever, that there would be no kingdom there, and that wild animals would possess Edom for a heritage. And so despised is Edom, and the memory of its greatness lost, that there is no record of antiquity that can so clearly show us what once it was, in the days of its power, as we can now read, in the page of prophecy, its existing deso-

* Origen. lib. iii. in Job.

lation. But in that place where kings kept their court, and where nobles assembled, where manifest proofs of ancient opulence are concentrated, where princely habitations, retaining their external grandeur, but bereft of all their splendour, still look as if " fresh from the chisel,"—even there no man dwells, it is given by lot to birds, and beasts, and reptiles ; it is a " court for owls," and scarcely are they ever frayed from their " lonely habitation," by the tread of a solitary traveller from a far distant land, among deserted dwellings and desolated ruins.

Hidden as the history and state of Edom has been for ages, every recent disclosure, being an echo of the prophecies, amply corroborates the truth, that the word of the Lord does not return unto him void, but ever fulfils the purpose for which he hath sent it. But the whole of its work is not yet wrought in Edom, which has farther testimony in store : and while the evidence is not yet complete, so neither is the time of the final judgments on the land yet fully come. Judea, Ammon, and Moab, according to the word of prophecy, shall revive from their desolation, and the wild animals who have conjoined their depredations with those of barbarous men, in perpetuating the desolation of these countries, shall find a refuge and undisturbed possession in Edom, when, the year of recompenses for the controversy of Zion being past, it shall be divided unto them by line, when they shall possess it for ever, and from generation to generation shall dwell therein. But without looking into futurity, a retrospect may here warrant, before leaving the subject, a concluding clause.

That man is a bold *believer*, and must with whatever reluctance forego the name of *sceptic*, who possesses such redundant credulity as to think, that all the predictions respecting Edom, and all others recorded in Scripture, and realized by facts, were the

mere hap-hazard results of fortuitous conjectures.
And he who thus, without reflecting how incongruous
it is to " strain at a gnat and swallow a camel," can
deliberately, and with an unruffled mind, place such
an opinion among the articles of his faith, may indeed
be pitied by those who know in whom they have believed, but, if he forfeit not thereby all right of ever
appealing to reason, must at least renounce all title
to stigmatize, in others, even the most preposterous
belief. Or if such, after all, must needs be his philosophical creed, and his rational conviction! what
can hinder him from believing also that other chance
words—such as truly marked the fate of Edom, but
more numerous and clear, and which, were he to
" seek out and read," he would find in the self-same
" book of the Lord,"—may also prove equally true
to the spirit, if not to the letter, against all the enemies of the gospel, whether hypocrites or unbelievers?
May not his belief in the latter instance be strengthened by the experience that many averments of Scripture, in respect to times then future, and to facts
then unknown, have already proved true? And may
he not here find some analogy, at least, on which to
rest his faith, whereas the conviction, which, in the
former case, he so readily cherishes, is totally destitute
of any semblance whatever to warrant the possibility
of its truth? Or is this indeed the sum of his boasted wisdom, to hold to the conviction of the fallacy of
all the coming judgments denounced in Scripture till
" experience," personal though it should be, prove
them to be as true as the past, and a compulsory and
unchangeable but unredeeming faith be grafted on
despair? Or if less proof can possibly suffice, let him
timely read and examine, and disprove also, all the
credentials of revelation, before he account the believer credulous, or the unbeliever wise; or else let
him abandon the thought that the unrepentant ini-

quity and wilful perversity of man, and an evil heart
of unbelief (all proof derided, all offered mercy rejected, all meetness for an inheritance among them that
are sanctified unattained, and all warning lost,) shall
not finally forbid that Edom stand alone—the seared
and blasted monument of the judgments of heaven.

A word may here be spoken even to the wise.
Were any of the sons of men to be uninstructed
in the fear of the Lord, which is the beginning of
wisdom, and in the knowledge of his word, which
maketh wise unto salvation, and to be thus ignorant
of the truths and precepts of the gospel, which
should all tell upon every deed done in the body;
what in such a case—if all their superior knowledge
were unaccompanied by religious principles—would
all mechanical and physical science eventually prove
but the same, in kind, as the wisdom of the wise men
of Edom ?   And were they to perfect in astronomy,
navigation and mechanics, what, according to Sir
Isaac Newton, the Edomites began, what would the
moulding of matter to their will avail them, as moral and accountable beings, if their own hearts were
not conformed to the divine will ; and what would all
their labour be at last, but strength spent for nought ?
For were they to raise column above column, and
again to hew a city out of the cliffs of the rock, let
but such another word of that God, whom they seek
not to know, go forth against it, and all their mechanical ingenuity and labour would just end in forming—
that which Petra is, and which Rome itself is destined to be—" a cage of every unclean and hateful bird."
The experiment has already been made ; it may well
and wisely be trusted to, as much as those which mortals make ; and it is set before us that, instead of pro-
voking the Lord to far worse than its repetition in
personal judgments against ourselves, we may be
warned by the spirit of prophecy, which is the testi-

mony of Jesus, to hear and obey the words of Him—
" even of Jesus, who delivereth from the wrath to
come." For how much greater than any degradation
to which hewn but unfeeling rocks can be reduced, is
that of a soul, which while in the body might have
been formed anew after the image of an all-holy God,
and made meet for beholding his face in glory,—
passing from spiritual darkness into a spiritual state
where all knowledge of earthly things shall cease to
be power,—where all the riches of this world shall
cease to be gain—where the want of religious principles and of Christian virtues shall leave the soul naked, as the bare and empty dwellings in the clefts of
the rocks,—where the thoughts of worldly wisdom, to
which it was inured before, shall haunt it still, and be
more unworthy and hateful occupants of the immortal
spirit than are the owls amid the palaces of Edom—
and where all those sinful passions, which rested on
the things which were seen, shall be like unto the
scorpions which hold Edom as their heritage for ever,
and which none can now scare away from among the
wild vines that are there entwined around the broken
altars, where false gods were worshipped.

PHILISTIA.

The land of the Philistines bordered on the west
and south-west of Judea, and lies on the south-east
point of the Mediterranean sea. The country to the
north of Gaza is very fertile, and long after the Christian era, it possessed a very numerous population,
and strongly fortified cities. No human probability
could possibly have existed, in the time of the prophets, or at a much more recent date, of its eventual
desolation. But it has belied, for many ages, everl-
promise which the fertility of its soil, and the excey

lence both of its climate and situation, gave for many
preceding centuries, of its permanency as a rich and
well cultivated region. And the voice of prophecy,
which was not silent respecting it, proclaimed the fate
that awaited it, in terms as contradictory, at the time,
to every natural suggestion, as they are descriptive of
what Philistia now actually is.

" I will stretch out my hand upon the Philistines
and destroy the remnant of the sea-coasts."* " Baldness is come upon Gaza ; Ashkelon is cut off with the
remnant of their valley."† " Thus saith the Lord,
for three transgressions of Gaza, and for four, I will
not turn away the punishment thereof. I will send a
fire upon the wall of Gaza which shall devour the
palaces thereof. And I will cut off the inhabitant
from Ashdod, and him that holdeth the sceptre from
Ashkelon ; and I will turn my hand against Ekron ;
and the remnant of the Philistines shall perish, saith
the Lord God."‡ " For Ashkelon shall be a desolation ; it shall be cut off with the remnant of the valley ; and Ekron shall be rooted up—O Canaan, the
land of the Philistines, I will even destroy you, that
there shall be no inhabitant ; and the sea-coast shall
be dwellings and cottages for shepherds, and folds for
flocks."§ " The king shall perish from Gaza, and
Ashkelon shall not be inhabited."‖

The land of the Philistines was to be destroyed. It
partakes of the general desolation common to it with
Judea and other neighbouring states. While ruins
are to be found in all Syria, they are particularly
abundant along the sea-coast, which formed, on the
south, the realm of the Philistines. But its aspect
presents some existing peculiarities, which travellers

* Ezekiel xxv. 16.   † Jeremiah xlvii. 5.
‡ Amos i. 6, 7, 8.   § Zephaniah ii. 4, 5, 6.
‖ Zechariah ix. 5.

fail not to particularize, and which, in reference, both
to the state of the country, and the fate of its different
cities, the prophets failed not to discriminate as justly,
as if their description had been drawn both with all
the accuracy which ocular observation, and all the
certainty which authenticated history could give.
And the authority, so often quoted, may here again
be appealed to.   Volney, (though, like one who in
ancient times was instrumental to the fulfilment of a
special prediction, " he meant not so, neither did his
heart think so,") from the manner in which he gene-
ralizes his observations, and marks the peculiar features of the different districts of Syria, with greater
acuteness and perspicuity than any other traveller
whatever, is the ever ready purveyor of evidence in all
the cases which came within the range of his topographical description of the wide field of prophecy—
while, at the same time, from his known, open, and
zealous hostility to the Christian cause, his testimony
is alike decisive and unquestionable ; and the vindication of the truth of the following predictions may
safely be committed to this redoubted champion of
infidelity.

*The sea-coasts shall be dwellings and cottages for
shepherds, and folds for flocks.   The remnant of the
Philistines shall perish.   Baldness is come upon Gaza ;
it shall be forsaken.   The king shall perish from Gaza.
I will cut off the inhabitants from Ashdod.   Ashkelon
shall be a desolation, it shall be cut off with the remnant
of the valley ; it shall not be inhabited.*   " In the
plain between Ramla and Gaza," (the very plain of the
Philistines along the sea-coast) " we met with a
number of villages badly built of dried mud, and
which, like the inhabitants, exhibit every mark of
poverty and wretchedness.   The houses, on a nearer
view, are only so many huts (cottages), sometimes
detached, at others ranged in the form of cells, around

a court-yard, enclosed by a mud wall. In winter,
they and their cattle may be said to live together, the
part of the dwelling allotted to themselves being only
raised two feet above that in which they lodge their
beasts—*(dwellings and cottages for shepherds, and
folds for flocks.)* Except the environs of these villages all the rest of the country is a *desert*, and abandoned to the Bedouin Arabs, who feed their flocks
on it.* *The remnant* shall perish: the land of the
Philistines shall be destroyed that there shall be no
inhabitant, and the *sea-coasts* shall be dwellings, and
cottages for shepherds, and folds for flocks.

  "The ruins of white marble sometimes found at
Gaza, prove that it was formerly the abode of luxury
and opulence. It has shared in the general destruction ; and, notwithstanding its proud title of the capital of Palestine, it is now no more than a defenceless village," *(baldness has come upon it)* "peopled
by, at most, only two thousand inhabitants."† *It is
forsaken and bereaved of its king.* "The sea-coast,
by which it was formerly washed, is every day re-
moving farther from the *deserted ruins* of Ashkelon."‡
*It shall be a desolation. Ashkelon shall not be inha-
bited.* "Amidst the various successive ruins, those
of Edzoud, (Ashdod) so powerful under the Philistines, are now remarkable for their scorpions." *The
inhabitants shall be cut off from Ashdod.*

  Although the Christian traveller must yield the
palm to Volney,§ as the topographer of Prophecy,

---

and although supplementary evidence be not requisite, yet a place is here willingly given to the following just observations.

" Ashkelon was one of the proudest satrapies of the lords of the Philistines ; now there is not an inhabitant within its walls ; and the prophecy of Zechariah is fulfilled. The king shall perish from Gaza, and Ashkelon shall not be inhabited. When the prophecy was uttered, both cities were in an equally flourishing condition ; and nothing but the prescience of heaven could pronounce on which of the two, and in what manner the vial of its wrath should be poured out. Gaza is truly without a king. The lofty towers of Ashkelon lie scattered on the ground, and the ruins within its walls do not shelter a human being. How is the wrath of man made to praise his Creator ! Hath he not said, and shall he not do it ? The oracle was delivered by the mouth of the prophet more than five hundred years before the Christian era, and we beheld its accomplishment eighteen hundred years after that event."*

Cogent and just as the reasoning is, the facts stated by Volney give wider scope for an irresistible argument. The fate of one city is not only distinguished from that of another ; but the varied aspect of the country itself, the dwellings and cottages for shepherds in one part, and that very region named, the rest of the land destroyed and uninhabited, a desert, and

so very close to the predictions, that his testimony in the relation of positive facts, would have been utterly discredited, and held as purposely adapted to the very words of prophecy, by those who otherwise lent a greedy ear to his utterance of some of the wildest fancies and most gross untruths that ever emanated from the mind of man, or ever entered into a deceitful heart. He who so artfully could pervert the truth, falls the victim of facts stated by himself.

* Richardson's Travels, vol. ii. p. 204.

abandoned to the flocks of the wandering Arabs ; Gaza,
bereaved of a king, a defenceless village, destitute of all
its fortifications ; Ashkelon, a desolation, and without
an inhabitant; the inhabitants also cut off from Ashdod,
as reptiles tenanted it instead of men—form in each
instance a specific prediction, and a recorded fact, and
present such a view of the existing state of Philistia,
as renders it difficult to determine, from the strictest
accordance that prevails between both, whether the
inspired penman or the defamer of Scripture give the
more vivid description.   Nor is there any obscurity
whatever, in any one of the circumstances, or in any
part of the proof.   The coincidence is too glaring,
even for wilful blindness not to discern ; and to all,
the least versed in general history, the priority of the
predictions to the events is equally obvious.   And
such was the natural fertility of the country, and such
was the strength and celebrity of the cities, that no
conjecture possessing the least shadow of plausibility
can be formed in what manner any of these events
could possibly have been thought of, even for many
centuries after " the vision and prophecy " were sealed.   After that period, Gaza defied the power of
Alexander the Great, and withstood for two months a
hard-pressed siege.   The army, with which he soon
afterwards overthrew the Persian empire, having there,
as well as at Tyre, been checked or delayed in the
first flush of conquest, and he himself having been
twice wounded in desperate attempts to storm the city,
the proud and enraged king of Macedon, with all the
cruelty of a brutish heart, and boasting of himself as
a second Achilles, dragged at his chariot-wheels the
intrepid general, who had defended it, twice around
the walls of Gaza.*   Ashkelon was no less celebrated
for the excellence of its wines, than for the strength
of its fortifications.†   And of Ashdod, it is related

---

* Quinti Curtii, lib. iv. cap. 26.   † Relandi Palest. 341, 586.

by an eminent ancient historian, not only that it was
a great city, but that it withstood the longest siege
recorded in history, (it may almost be said, either of
prior, or of later date,) having been besieged for the
space of twenty-nine years by Psymatticus, king of
Egypt.*   Strabo, after the commencement of the
Christian era, classes its citizens among the chief inhabitants of Syria.   Each of these cities, Gaza, Ashkelon, and Ashdod, was the see of a bishop from the
days of Constantine to the invasion of the Saracens.
And, as a decisive proof of their existence as cities
long subsequent to the delivery of the predictions, it
may further be remarked, that different coins of each
of these very cities are extant, and are copied and described in several accounts of ancient coins.†   The
once princely magnificence of Gaza is still attested
by the "ruins of white marble;" and the house of
the present Aga is composed of fragments of ancient
columns, cornices, &c ; and in the court-yard, and
immured in the wall, are shafts and capitals of granite
columns.‡

In short, *cottages for shepherds, and folds for flocks,*
partially scattered along the *sea-coasts,* are now truly
the best substitutes for populous cities, that the once
powerful realm of Philistia can produce ; and the *remnant* of that land, which gave titles and grandeur to
the lords of the Philistines, *is destroyed.*   *Gaza,* the
chief of its satrapies, " the abode of luxury and opulence," now *bereaved of its king and bald* of all its fortifications, is the defenceless residence of a subsidiary
ruler of a devastated province ; and, in kindred degradation, ornaments of its once splendid edifices are now
bedded in a wall that forms an enclosure for beasts.

* Herodot. Hist. lib. ii. cap. 157.
† Relandi Palest. pp. 595, 609, 797.
‡ General Straton's MS.

A handful of men could now take unobstructed
possession of that place, where a strong city opposed
the entrance, and defied, for a time, the power of the
conqueror of the world. The walls, the dwellings,
and the people of *Ashkelon* have all perished; and
though its name was, in the time of the crusades,
shouted in triumph throughout every land in Europe,
it is now literally *without an inhabitant*. And *Ashdod*, which withstood a siege treble the duration of
that of Troy, and thus outrivalled far the boast of
Alexander at Gaza, has, in verification of " the word
of God, which is sharper than any two-edged sword,"
been *cut off*, and has fallen before it to nothing.

There is yet another city which was noted by the
prophets, the very want of any information respecting
which, and the absence of its name from several modern maps of Palestine, while the sites of other ruined
cities are marked, are really the best confirmation of
the truth of the prophecy that could possibly be given.
Ekron shall be rooted up. It is rooted up. It was
one of the chief cities of the Philistines; but though
Gaza still subsists, and while Ashkelon and Ashdod
retain their names in their ruins, the very name of
Ekron is missing.*

The wonderful contrast in each particular, whether
in respect to the land, or to the cities of the Philistines, is the exact counterpart of the literal predic-

---

* In the map prefixed to Dr. Shaw's Travels, Akron is indeed marked; but it is placed close upon the sea-coast,
whereas Ekron was situated in the interior, and was at least
ten miles distant. Shaw did not visit the spot. Dr. Richardson passed some ruins near to Ashdod, and conjectures that
they were *probably Ekron*. But neither does the site of
them correspond with that of Ekron, which, according to
Eusebius, lay between Ashdod and Jamnia, towards the *east*
or inland. Vide Relan. Pal. 77. Any diversity of opinion
respecting its site is not the least conclusive proof that it is
rooted up.

tion ; and, having the testimony of Volney to all the
facts, and also indisputable evidence of the great priority of the predictions to the events, what more complete or clearer proof could there be, that each and
all of them emanated from the prescience of heaven ?

The remaining boundary of Judea was the mountains of LEBANON on the north. Lebanon was celebrated for the extent of its forests, and particularly for the
size and excellency of its cedars.*   It abounded also
with the pine, the cypress and the vine, &c. But, describing what it now is, Volney says, " Towards Lebanon the mountains are lofty, but they are covered
in many places with as much earth as fits them for
cultivation by industry and labour.   There, amid the
crags of the rocks, may be seen the no very magnificent remains of the boasted cedars."†   The words of
the prophets of Israel answer the sarcasm, and con-

---

* Relandi Palest. pp. 320, 379.   Tacit. Hist. lib. v. cap. vi.
† Travels, vol. i. p. 292.—Volney remarks, in a note, that
there are but four or five of those trees which deserve any
notice ; and in a note, it may be added, from the words of
Isaiah,—*the rest of the trees of his forest shall be few, that
a child may write them*, c. x. 19. Could not the infidel
write a brief note, or state a minute fact, without illustrating
a prophecy ?   Maundrell, who visited Lebanon in the end
of the seventeenth century, and to whose accuracy in other
matters all subsequent travellers who refer to him bear witness, describes some of the cedars near the top of the mountain as " very old, and of a prodigious bulk, and others
younger of a smaller size." Of the former he could reckon
only up sixteen. He measured the largest, and found it
above twelve yards in girth. Such trees, however few in
number, show that the *cedars of Lebanon* had once been no
vain boast. But after the lapse of more than a century, not
a single tree of such dimensions is now to be seen. Of those
which now remain, as visited by Captains Irby and Mangles,
there are about fifty in whole on a single small eminence,
from which spot the cedars are the only trees to be seen in
Lebanon. P. 209.

vert it into a testimony of the truth :—" Lebanon is ashamed and hewn down. The high ones of stature shall be hewn down : Lebanon shall fall mightily."* " Upon the mountains, and in all the vallies, his branches are fallen ; to the end that none of all the trees by the water exalt themselves for their height, neither shoot up their top among the thick boughs."† " Open thy doors, O Lebanon, that the fire may devour thy cedars. The cedar is fallen ; the forest of the vintage is come down."‡

Such are the prophecies which explicitly and avowedly referred to the land of Judea, and to the surrounding states. And such are the facts drawn from the narratives of travellers, and given, in general, in their own words, which substantiate their truth ; though without any allusion, but in a few solitary instances, to the predictions which they amply verify. The most unsuspected evidence has been selected ; and the far greater part is so fully corroborated, and illustrated by other testimony, as to bid defiance to scepticism. The prophecies and the proofs of their fulfilment, are so numerous, that it is impossible to concentrate them in a single view, without the exclusion of many ; and they are, upon a simple comparison, so obvious and striking, that any attempt at their farther elucidation must hazard the obscuring of their clearness, and the enfeebling of their force. There is no ambiguity in the prophecies themselves, for they can bear no other interpretation but what is descriptive of the actual events. There can be no question of their genuineness or antiquity, for the countries whose future history they unveiled contained several millions of inhabitants, and numerous

* Isa. xxxiii. 9 ; x. 43, 34.   † Ezek. xxxi. 12, 14.
‡ Zech. xi. 1, 2.

flourishing cities, at a period centuries subsequent to
the delivery, the translation, and publication of the
prophecies, and when the regular and public perusal
of their Scriptures was the law and the practice of the
Israelites; and they have only gradually been reduced
to their existing state of long-prophesied desolation.
There could not possibly have been any human means
of the foresight of facts, so many and so marvellous;
for every natural appearance contradicted, and every
historical fact condemned the supposition; and nothing but continued oppression and a succession of
worse than Gothic desolators,—no government on
earth but the Turkish,—no spoliators but the Arabs,
—could have converted such natural fertility into
such utter and permanent desolation. Could it have
been foreseen, that after the lapse of some hundred
years, no interval of prosperity or peaceful security
would occur throughout many ensuing generations,
to revive its deadened energies, or to rescue from uninterrupted desolation one of the richest, and one of the
most salubrious regions of the world, which the greater part of these territories naturally is? Could the
present aspect of any country, with every alterable
feature changed, and with every altered feature marked, have been delineated by different uninspired mortals, in various ages from 2200 to 3300 years past?
And there could not, so far as all researches have
hitherto reached, be a more triumphant demonstration, from existing facts, of the truth of manifold prophecies. In reference to the complete *historical* truth
of the predictions respecting the successive kings of
Syria and Egypt, Bishop Newton emphatically remarks, (as Sir Isaac Newton's observations had previously proved) that there is not so concise and comprehensive an account of their affairs to be found in
any author of these times; that the prophecy is really
more perfect than any single history, and that no one

historian hath related so many circumstances as the
prophet has foretold : so that "it was necessary to
have recourse to several authors for the better explaining and illustrating the great variety of particulars
contained in the prophecy." The same remark, in
the same words, may, more obviously and with equal
truth, be now applied to the *geographical*, as well as
to the historical proof of the truth of prophecy. Judea,
which, before the age of the prophets, had, from the
uniformity and peculiarity of its government and laws,
remained unvaried in a manner, and to a degree unusual among nations, has since undergone many convulsions, and has for many generations been unceas-
ingly subjected to reiterated spoliation. And now,
after the lapse of more than twenty centuries, travellers see what prophets foretold. Each prediction is
fulfilled in all its particulars, so far as the facts have
(and in almost every case they have) been made
known. But while the recent discoveries of many
travellers have disclosed the state of these countries,
each of their accounts presents only an imperfect delineation ; and a variety of these must be combined
before they bring fully into view all those diversified,
discriminating, and characteristic features of the extensive scene, which were vividly depicted of old, in
all their minute lines, and varied shades, by the pencil of prophecy, and which set before us, as it were,
the history, the land, and the people of Palestine.

Judea trodden down by successive desolators,—remaining uncultivated from generation to generation—
the general devastation of the country,—the mouldering ruins of its many cities,—the cheerless solitude
of its once happy plains,—the wild produce of its
luxuriant mountains,—the land covered with thorns,
—the highways waste and untrodden,—its ancient
possessors scattered abroad,—the inhabitants thereof
depraved in character, few in number, eating their

bread with carefulness, or in constant dread of the
spoiler or oppressor,—the insecurity of property,—
the uselessness of labour,—the poverty of their revenues,—the land emptied and despoiled,—instrumental
music ceased from among them,—the mirth of the
land gone,—the use of wine prohibited in a land of
vines,—and the wine itself bitter unto them that drink
it ;—some very partial exceptions from universal desolation, some rescued remnants, like the gleanings
of a field, and emblems of the departed glory of Judea, the devastation of the land of Ammon, the extinction of the Ammonites—the destruction of all
their cities—their country a spoil to the heathen,
—and a perpetual desolation ;—the desolation of
Moab, its cities without any to dwell therein, and
no city escaped,—the valley perished, the plain destroyed,—the wanderers that have come up against
it, and that cause its inhabitants to wander,—the
manner of the spoliation of the dwellers in Moab,
their danger and insecurity in the plain country, and
flying to the rocks for a refuge and a home—while
flocks lie down among the ruins of the cities—
none there to make them afraid—and the despoiled
and impoverished condition of some of its wretched wanderers : Idumea untrodden and unvisited by
travellers,—the scene of an unparalleled and irre-
coverable desolation,—its cities utterly abandoned
and destroyed,—of the greater part of them no trace
left,—a desolate wilderness, over which the line of
confusion is stretched out,—the country bare,—no
kingdom there,—its princes and nobles nothing, and
empty sepulchres their only memorials,—thistles and
thorns in its palaces,—a border of wickedness—and
yet greatly despised,—wisdom perished from Teman,
and understanding out of the mount of Esau,—abandoned to birds and beasts and reptiles, specified by
name,—its ancient possessors cut off for ever—and

no one remaining of the house of Esau ;—the destruction of the cities of the Philistines—cottages for shepherds and folds for flocks, along the sea-coasts,—the remnant of the plain destroyed and unoccupied by any fixed inhabitant : Lebanon ashamed,—its cedars, few and diminutive, now a mockery instead of a praise ; and finally, the different fate of many cities particularly defined,—the long subjection of Jerusalem to the Gentiles,—the buildings of Samaria cast down into the valley, its foundations discovered, and vineyards in its stead, all so clearly marked both in the prophecy and on the spot, that they serve to fix its site,—Rabbah-Ammon, the capital of the Ammonites, now a pasture for camels, and a couching-place for flocks,—the chief city of Edom brought down,—a court for owls,—and no man dwelling in it,—the forsaken Gaza, bereaved of a monarch, bald of all its fortifications, or defenceless—Ashkelon, desolate, without an inhabitant,—and Ekron rooted up : These are all ancient prophecies, and these are all present facts, which form of themselves a phalanx of evidence which all the shafts of infidelity can never pierce.

Though the countries included in these predictions comprehend a field of prophecy extending over upwards of one hundred and twenty thousand square miles, the existing state of every part of which bears witness of their truth ; yet the prophets, as inspired by the God of nations, foretold the fate of mightier monarchies, of more extensive regions, and of more powerful cities : and there is not a people, nor a country, nor a capital, which was then known to the Israelites, whose future history they did not clearly reveal. And, instead of adducing arguments from the preceding very abundant materials, or drawing those facts already adduced, to their legitimate conclusion, they may be left in their native strength, like the unhewn adamant; and we may pass to other proofs which also show that the temple of Christian faith rests upon a rock that cannot be shaken.

CHAPTER VI.

NINEVEH.

To a brief record of the creation, of the antediluvian world, and of the dispersion and the different settlements of mankind after the deluge, the Scriptures of the Old Testament add a full and particular history of the Hebrews for the space of fifteen hundred years, from the days of Abraham to the era of the last of the prophets. While the historical part of Scripture thus traces, from its origin, the history of the world, the prophecies give a prospective view which reaches to its end. And it is remarkable that profane history, emerging from fable, becomes clear and authentic about the very period when sacred history terminates, and when the fulfilment of these prophecies commences, which refer to other nations besides the Jews.

Nineveh, the capital of Assyria, was for a long time an extensive and populous city. Its walls are said, by heathen historians, to have been a hundred feet in height, sixty miles in compass, and to have been defended by fifteen hundred towers, each two hundred feet high. Although it formed the subject of some of the earliest of the prophecies, and was the very first which met its predicted fate; yet a heathen historian, in describing its capture and destruction, repeatedly refers to an ancient prediction respecting it. Diodorus Siculus relates, that the king of Assyria, after the complete discomfiture of his army, confided in an old prophecy, that Nineveh would not be taken, unless the river should become the enemy of the city;* that after an ineffectual siege of two years, the river, swollen with long-continued and tempestuous torrents, inundated part of the city, and threw down the wall for the space of twenty furlongs; and that the king, deeming the prediction accomplished, despaired of his safety, and erected an immense funeral pile, on which he heaped his wealth, and with which himself, his household and palace, were consumed.† The Book of Nahum was avowedly prophetic of the destruction of Nineveh : and it is therefore told " that the gates of the river shall be opened, and the palace shall be dissolved." " Nineveh of old, like a pool of water—with an overflowing flood he will make an utter end of the place thereof."‡ The historian describes the facts by which the other predictions of the prophet were as literally fulfilled. He relates that the king of Assyria, elated with his former victories, and ignorant of the revolt of the Bactrians, had abandoned himself to scandalous inaction ; had appointed a time of festivity, and supplied his soldiers with abundance of wine ; and that the general of the enemy, apprised, by deserters, of their negligence and drunkenness, attacked the Assyrian army while the whole of them were fearlessly giving way to indulgence, destroyed great part of them, and drove the rest into the city.§ The words of the prophet were hereby verified : " While they

* Diod. Sic. lib. ii. pp. 82, 83.   Ed. Wessel. 1793.
† Ib. p. 84.   ‡ Nahum, ii. 6 ; i.8.
§ Diod. Sic. lib. ii. pp. 81, 84.

be folden together as thorns, and while they are drunken as drunkards, they shall be devoured as stubble full dry."*—The prophet promised much spoil to the enemy: "Take the spoil of silver, take the spoil of gold; for there is no end of the store and glory out of all the pleasant furniture."† And the historian affirms, that many talents of gold and silver, preserved from the fire, were carried to Ecbatana.‡ According to Nahum, the city was not only to be destroyed by an overflowing flood, but the fire also was to devour it;§ and, as Diodorus relates, partly by water, partly by fire, it was destroyed.

The utter and perpetual destruction and desolation of Nineveh were foretold: "The Lord will make an utter end of the place thereof. Affliction shall not rise up the second time. She is empty, void and waste.—The Lord will stretch out his hand against the north, and destroy Assyria, and will make Nineveh a desolation, and dry like a wilderness. How is she become a desolation, a place for beasts to lie down in."‖ In the second century, Lucian, a native of a city on the banks of the Euphrates, testified that Nineveh was utterly perished—that there was no vestige of it remaining—and that none could tell where once it was situated. This testimony of Lucian, and the lapse of many ages during which the place was not known where it stood, render it at least somewhat doubtful whether the remains of an ancient city, opposite to Mosul, which have been described as such by travellers, be indeed those of ancient Nineveh. It is perhaps probable, that they are the remains of the city which succeeded Nineveh, or of a Persian city of the same name, which was built on the banks

---

* Nahum, i. 10; iii. 2.　　† Nahum, ii. 9.
‡ Diod. p. 87.　　§ Nahum, iii. 15.
‖ Nahum, i. 8, 9; ii. 10; iii. 17, 18, 19. Zeph. ii. 13, 14, 15.

of the Tigris by the Persians, subsequently to the
year 230 of the Christian era, and demolished by
the Saracens, in 632.*   In contrasting the then existing great and increasing population, and the accumulating wealth of the proud inhabitants of the
mighty Nineveh, with the utter ruin that awaited it,
—the word of God, (before whom all the inhabitants
of the earth are as grasshoppers,) by Nahum was—
" Make thyself many as the canker-worm, make thyself many as the locusts.   Thou hast multiplied thy
merchants above the stars of heaven : The canker-
worm spoileth and flieth away.   Thy crowned are as
the locusts, and thy captains as the great grasshoppers
which camp in the hedges in the cold day ; but when
the sun riseth, they flee away ; and their place is not
known where they are," or were.   Whether these
words imply that even the site of Nineveh would in
future ages be uncertain or unknown, or as they rather seem to intimate, that every vestige of the palaces of its monarchs, of the greatness of its nobles, and
of the wealth of its numerous merchants, would wholly disappear ; the truth of the prediction cannot be
invalidated under either interpretation.   The avowed
ignorance respecting Nineveh, and the oblivion which
passed over it, for many an age, conjoined with the
meagreness of evidence to identify it still, prove that
the place was long unknown where it stood, and that
even now, it can scarcely with certainty be determined.
And, if the only spot that bears its name, or that
can be said to be the place where it was, be indeed
the site of one of the most extensive of cities on which
the sun ever shone, and which continued for many
centuries to be the capital of Assyria—the " principal mounds," few in number, which " show neither
bricks, stones, nor other materials of building, but are

* *Marshami Can. Chron.* sec. xvii, p. 600, ed. Franeq
1696.

in many places overgrown with grass, and resemble
the mounds left by intrenchments and fortifications
of ancient Roman camps," and the *appearances* of
other mounds and ruins, less marked than even these,
extending for ten miles, and widely spread, and seeming to be " the wreck of former buildings,"* show
that Nineveh is left without one monument of royalty,
without any token whatever of its splendour or
wealth; that their place is not known where they
were; and that it is indeed a desolation—" empty,
void, and waste," its very ruins perished, and less than
the wreck of what it was. " Such an *utter ruin*," in
every view, " has been made of it; and such is the
truth of the divine predictions."†

BABYLON.

If ever there was a city that seemed to bid defiance
to any predictions of its fall, that city was Babylon.
It was for a long time the most famous city in the
whole world.‡   Its walls, which were reckoned among
the wonders of the world, appeared rather like the
bulwarks of nature than the workmanship of man.§

* Buckingham's Travels in Mesopotamia, v. ii. pp. 49, 51, 62.
† See Bishop Newton's Dissertations.
‡ Plinii Hist. Nat. lib. v. cap. 26.
§ The extent of the walls of Babylon is variously stated
by Herodotus at 480 stadia, or furlongs, in circumference;
by Pliny, and Solinius, at sixty Roman miles, or of equal extent; by Strabo at 385 stadia; by Diodorus Siculus, according to the slightly different testimony of Ctesias and Clitar-
chus, both of whom visited Babylon, at 360 or 365; and to
the last of these statements that of Quintus Curtius nearly
corresponds, viz. 368.   The difference of a few stadia rather
confirms than disproves the general accuracy of the three
last of these accounts.   There may have been an error in
the text of Herodotus of 480, instead of 380, which Pliny
and Solinus may have copied.   The variation of 20 or 25
stadia, in excess, may have been caused by the line of mea-

The temple of Belus, half a mile in circumference
and a furlong in height—the hanging gardens, which,
piled in successive terraces, towered as high as the
walls—the embankments which restrained the Euphrates—the hundred brazen gates—and the adjoining artificial lake—all displayed many of the mightiest works of mortals concentrated in a single spot.*
Yet, while in the plenitude of its power, and according to the most accurate chronologers, 160 years before the foot of an enemy had entered it, the voice of
prophecy pronounced the doom of the mighty and unconquered Babylon. A succession of ages brought
it gradually to the dust; and the gradation of its fall
is marked till it sunk at last into utter desolation.
At a time when nothing but magnificence was around
Babylon the great, fallen Babylon was delineated
exactly as every traveller now describes its ruins.—
And the prophecies concerning it may be viewed connectedly from the period of their earliest to that of
their latest fulfilment.

The immense fertility of Chaldea, which retained
also the name of Babylonia till after the Christian
era,† corresponded, if that of any country could vie,
with the greatness of Babylon. It was the most fertile

surement having been the outside of the trench, and not immediately of the wall. And thus the various statements may
be brought nearly to correspond. Major Rennel, estimating
the stadium at 491 feet, computes the extent of the wall at
34 miles, or eight and a half on each side. The opposite
and contradictory statements of the height and breadth of
the wall may possibly be best reconciled on the supposition
that they refer to different periods. Herodotus states the
height to have been 200 cubits, or 300 feet, and the breadth
50 cubits, or 75 feet. According to Curtius, the height was
150 feet, and the breadth 32; while Strabo states the height
at 75 feet, and the breadth at 32 feet.

* Herod. lib. i. c. 178. Diodor. Sic. lib. ii. p. 226. Plin.
lib. v. c. 26. Quinti Curt. lib. v. c. 4.

† Strabo, lib. xvi. p. 743.

region of the whole east.* Babylonia was one vast
plain, adorned and enriched by the Euphrates and
the Tigris, from which, and from the numerous
canals that intersected the country from the one river
to the other, water was distributed over the fields by
manual labour and by hydraulic machines,† giving
rise, in that warm climate and rich exhaustless soil,
to an exuberance of produce without a known parallel,
over so extensive a region, either in ancient or modern
times. Herodotus states, that he knew not how to
speak of its wonderful fertility, which none but eye-
witnesses would credit ; and, though writing in the
language of Greece, itself a fertile country, he expresses his own consciousness that his description of
what he actually saw would appear to be improbable,
and to exceed belief. In his estimation, as well as
in that of Strabo and of Pliny, (the three best ancient
authorities that can be given,) Babylonia was of all
countries the most fertile in corn, the soil never producing less, as he relates, than two hundred fold, an
amount, in our colder regions, scarcely credible, though
Strabo, the first of ancient geographers, agrees with
the " father of history " in recording that it reached
even to three hundred, the grain, too, being of prodigious size.‡ After being subjected to Persia, the
government of Chaldea was accounted the noblest in
the Persian empire.§ Besides supplying horses for
military service, it maintained about seventeen thousand horses for the sovereign's use. And, exclusive
of monthly subsidies, the supply from Chaldea (including perhaps Syria) for the subsistence of the king
and of his army, amounted to a third part of all that
was levied from the whole of the Persian dominions,

---

* Agrum totius orientis fertilissimum. Plin. *Hist. Nat.*
lib. v. c. 26.

† Herod. lib. i. c. 192.   ‡ Ibid. Strabo, lib. xvi. p. 742.
§ Herod. lib. i. c. 192.

which at that time extended from the Hellespont
to India.* Herodotus incidentally mentions that
there were four great towns in the vicinity of Babylon.

Such was the " Chaldee's excellency," that it departed not on the first conquest, nor on the final extinction of its capital, but one metropolis of Assyria
arose after another in the land of Chaldea, when Babylon had ceased to be " the glory of kingdoms."—
The celebrated city of Seleucia, whose ruins attest its
former greatness, was *founded* and *built* by Seleucus
Nicator, king of Assyria, one of the successors of
Alexander the Great, in the year before Christ 293,
—three centuries after Jeremiah prophesied. In the
first century of the Christian era it contained six hundred thousand inhabitants.† The Parthian kings
transferred the seat of empire to Ctesiphon, on the
opposite bank of the Tigris, where they resided in
winter ; and that city, formerly a village, became great
and powerful.‡ Six centuries after the latest of the
predictions, Chaldea could also boast of other great
cities,§ such as Artemita and Sitacene, besides many
towns. When invaded by Julian, it was, as described by Gibbon, a " fruitful and pleasant country."
And at a period equally distant from the time of the
prophets, and from the present day, in the seventh
century, Chaldea was the scene of vast magnificence,
in the reign of Chosroes. " His favourite residence
of Artemita or Destagerd, was situated beyond the
Tigris, about sixty miles to the north of the capital,
(Ctesiphon.) The adjacent pastures," in the words
of Gibbon, " were covered with flocks and herds ; the
paradise, or park, was replenished with pheasants,
peacocks, ostriches, roebucks, and wild boars, and the

* Herod. lib. i. c. 192.   † Plin. lib. v. c. 26.
‡ Strabo, lib. xvi. p. 743.   § Ibid. p. 744.

noble game of lions and tigers was sometimes turned loose for the golden pleasures of the chase. Nine hundred and sixty elephants were maintained for the use and splendour of the great king ; his tents and baggage were carried into the field by twelve thousand great camels, and eight thousand of a smaller size ; and the royal stables were filled with six thousand mules and horses. Six thousand guards successively mounted before the palace gate, and the service of the interior apartments was performed by twelve thousand slaves. The various treasures of gold, silver, gems, silk, and aromatics, were deposited in an hundred subterranean vaults."*—" In the eighth century, the towns of Samarah, Horounieh, and Djasserik, formed, so to speak, one street of twenty-eight miles."† Chaldea, with its rich soil and warm climate, and intersected by the Tigris and Euphrates, was one of the last countries in the world, of which the desolation could have been thought of by man. For to this day " there cannot be a doubt, that if proper means were taken, the *country* would with ease be brought into a high state of cultivation."‡

Manifold are the prophecies respecting Babylon and the land of the Chaldeans ; and the long lapse of ages has served to confirm their fulfilment in every particular, and to render it at last complete. The judgments of heaven are not casual, but sure ; they are not arbitrary, but righteous. And they were denounced against the Babylonians, and the inhabitants

* Gibbon's History, c. 46, v. iv. p. 423.
† Malte-Brun's Geography, vol. ii. p. 119. Historical documents are not wanting to prove that the richness of Chaldea down to the time of the Arabian califs, was such as to give the charm of truth (which, indeed, it is generally admitted that they possess) to many of the splendid descriptions which abound in the otherwise fictitious narratives of the Arabian Nights' Entertainments.
‡ Bombay Philosophical Transactions, vol. i. p. 124.

of Chaldea, expressly because of their idolatry, tyranny, oppression, pride, covetousness, drunkenness, falsehood, and other wickedness. So debasing and brutifying was their idolatry,—or so much did they render the name of religion subservient to their passions,—that practices the most abominable, which were universal among them, formed the very observance of some of their religious rites, of which even heathen writers could not speak but in terms of indignation and abhorrence. Though enriched with a prodigality of blessings, the glory of God was not regarded by the Chaldeans ; and all the glory of man, with which the plain of Shinar was covered, has become, in consequence as well as in chastisement of prevailing vices, and of continued though diversified crimes, the wreck, the ruin, and utter desolation which the word of God (for whose word but his?) thus told from the beginning that the event would be.

" The burden of Babylon, which Isaiah the son of Amos did see : The noise of a multitude in the mountains, like as of a great people ; a tumultuous noise of the kingdoms of nations gathered together ; the Lord of hosts mustereth the host of the battle. They come from a far country, from the end of heaven, even the Lord and the weapons of his indignation, to destroy the whole land.—Behold, the day of the Lord cometh, cruel both with wrath and fierce anger, to lay the land desolate ; and he shall destroy the sinners thereof out of it.—Babylon, the glory of kingdoms, the beauty of the Chaldees' excellency, shall be as when God overthrew Sodom and Gomorrah. It shall never be inhabited, neither shall it be dwelt in from generation to generation; neither shall the Arabian pitch tent there; neither shall the shepherds make their fold there. But wild beasts of the desert shall lie there ; and their houses shall be full of doleful creatures ; and owls shall dwell there, and satyrs shall dance there. And

the wild beasts of the island shall cry in their desolate houses, and dragons in their pleasant palaces."*
" Thou shalt take up this proverb against the king
of Babylon, and say, How hath the oppressor ceased !
the golden city ceased !   Thy pomp is brought down
to the grave, and the noise of thy viols : the worm is
spread under thee, and the worms cover thee.—Thou
shalt be brought down to hell, to the sides of the pit.
Thou art cast out of the grave like an abominable
branch.—I will cut off from Babylon, the name and
remnant, the son and nephew, saith the Lord.   I
will also make it a possession for the bittern and pools
of water: and I will sweep it with the besom of destruction, saith the Lord of hosts."†   " Babylon is
fallen, is fallen ; and all the graven images of her
gods, he hath broken unto the ground."‡   " Thus
saith the Lord, that saith unto the deep, be dry ; and
I will dry up thy rivers ; that saith of Cyrus, he is
my shepherd, and shall perform all my pleasure,—
and I will loose the loins of kings, to open before him
the two-leaved gates ; and the gates shall not be
shut."§   " Bel boweth down," &c.‖   " Come down
and sit in the dust, O virgin daughter of Babylon ;
sit on the ground, there is no throne, O daughter of
the Chaldeans.—Sit thou silent, and get thee into
darkness, O daughter of the Chaldeans ; for thou
shalt no more be called the lady of kingdoms.   Thou
hast said, I shall be a lady for ever—Hear now this,
thou that art given to pleasures, that dwellest carelessly, that sayest in thine heart, I am, and none else
besides me ; I shall not sit as a widow, neither shall
I know the loss of children.   But these two things
shall come to thee in a moment, in one day, the loss

* Isaiah xiii. 1, 4, 5, 9, 19—22.
† Ibid. xiv. 4, 11, 19, 22, 23.   ‡ Ibid. xxi. 9.
§ Ibid. xliv. 27, 28; xlv. 1.   ‖ Ibid. xlvi. 1.

of children, and widowhood : they shall come upon thee in their perfection, for the multitude of thy sorceries, and for the great abundance of thine enchantments. For thou hast trusted in thy wickedness, &c. Therefore shall evil come upon thee ; thou shalt not know from whence it riseth ; and mischief shall come upon thee ; thou shalt not be able to put it off; and desolation shall come upon thee suddenly, which thou shalt not know."*

" I will punish the land of the Chaldeans, and will make it perpetual desolations. And I will bring upon that land all my words which I have pronounced against it, even all that is written in this book which Jeremiah hath prophesied against all the nations. For many nations and great kings shall serve themselves of them also : and I will recompense them according to their deeds, and according to the works of their own hands."† " The word that the Lord spake against Babylon and against the land of the Chaldeans by Jeremiah the prophet. Declare ye among the nations, and publish, and set up a standard ; publish, and conceal not ; say, Babylon is taken, Bel is confounded, Merodach is broken in pieces ; her idols are confounded, her images are broken in pieces. For out of the north there cometh up a nation against her, which shall make her land desolate, and none shall dwell therein ; they shall remove, they shall depart, both man and beast."‡ " For, lo, I will raise and cause to come up against Babylon an assembly of great nations from the north country : and they shall set themselves in array against her ; and from thence she shall be taken ; their arrows shall be as of a mighty expert man ; none shall return in vain. And Chaldea shall be a spoil ; and all that spoil her shall

* Isa. xlvii. 1, 5, 7—11. † Jerem. xxv. 12—14.
‡ Jerem. l. 1, 2, 3.

be satisfied, saith the Lord. Behold the hindermost of the nations a wilderness, a dry land and a desert. Because of the wrath of the Lord it shall not be inhabited, but it shall be wholly desolate: every one that goeth by Babylon shall be astonished, and hiss at all her plagues."* "Her foundations are fallen, her walls are thrown down; for it is the vengeance of the Lord: take vengeance upon her; as she hath done, do unto her. Cut off the sower from Babylon, and him that handleth the sickle in the time of harvest; for fear of the oppressing sword they shall turn every one to his people, and they shall flee every one to his own land."† —"Go up against the land of Merathaim, even against it, and against the inhabitants of Pekod; waste and utterly destroy after them. A sound of battle is in the land, and of great destruction. How is the hammer of the whole earth cut asunder and broken! how is Babylon become a desolation among the nations! I have laid a snare for thee and thou art also taken, O Babylon, and thou wast not aware: thou art found, also caught, because thou hast striven against the Lord. The Lord hath opened his armory, and hath brought forth the weapons of his indignation: for this is the work of the Lord God of Hosts in the land of the Chaldeans. Come against her from the utmost border, open her store-houses; cast her up as heaps, and destroy her utterly, let nothing of her be left."‡ "Let none thereof escape; and the most proud shall stumble and fall, and none shall raise him up: I will kindle a fire in his cities, and it shall devour all round about him."§ —"A sword is upon the Chaldeans, saith the Lord, and upon the inhabitants of Babylon, and upon her princes, and upon her wise men. A sword is upon the liars; a sword is upon her mighty

* Jerem. l. 9—13.   † Ibid. 15, 16.
‡ Ibid 21—26.   § Ibid. 29—32.

men—a sword is upon their horses, and upon their chariots, and upon all the mingled people that are in the midst of her ;—a sword is upon her treasures; and they shall be robbed. A drought is upon her waters; and they shall be dried up; for it is the land of graven images, and they are mad upon their idols. Therefore the wild beasts of the desert, with the wild beasts of the islands, shall dwell there, and the owls shall dwell therein : and it shall be no more inhabited for ever ; neither shall it be dwelt in from generation to generation. As God overthrew Sodom and Gomorrah, and the neighbour cities thereof, saith the Lord ; so shall no more man abide there, neither shall any son of man dwell therein. Behold a people shall come from the north, and a great nation, and many kings shall be raised up from the coasts of the earth. They shall hold the bow and the lance ; they are cruel and will not show mercy ; their voice shall roar like the sea, and they shall ride on horses, every one put in array, like a man to the battle, against thee, O daughter of Babylon.—Behold he shall come up like a lion, from the swelling of Jordan into the habitation of the strong ; but I will make them suddenly run away from her, and who is a chosen man, that I may appoint over her ? For who is like me ? And who will appoint me the time ? And who is that shepherd that will stand before me ? Therefore hear ye the counsel of the Lord, that he hath taken against Babylon ; and his purposes that he hath purposed against the land of the Chaldeans ; surely the least of the flock shall draw them out ; surely he shall make their habitation desolate with them.*—I will send unto Babylon fanners, that shall fan her, and shall empty her land.—The slain shall fall in the land of the Chaldeans.—Babylon is suddenly fallen

---

* Jerem. l. 35—45.

M

and destroyed : howl for her ; take balm for her pain, if so be she may be healed. We would have healed Babylon, but she is not healed ; forsake her, and let us go every one unto his own country ; for her judgment reacheth into heaven, and is lifted up even to the skies.*—The Lord hath raised up the spirit of the kings of the Medes ; for his device is against Babylon to destroy it, &c.—O thou that dwellest upon many waters, abundant in treasures, thine end is come, and the measure of thy covetousness. The Lord of hosts hath sworn by himself, saying, surely I will fill thee with men, as with caterpillars ; and they shall lift up a shout against thee.† Behold I am against thee, O destroying mountain, saith the Lord, which destroyest all the earth ; and I will stretch out mine hand upon thee, and roll thee down from the rocks, and I will make thee a burnt mountain. Set up a standard in the land, blow the trumpet among the nations, prepare the nations against her, call together against her the kingdoms of Ararat, Minni, and Aschenaz ; prepare against her the nations, with the kings of the Medes, the captains thereof, and all the rulers thereof, and all the land of his dominion. And the land shall tremble and sorrow ; *for every purpose* of the Lord shall be performed against Babylon, to make the land of Babylon a desolation without an inhabitant. The mighty men of Babylon have forborne to fight, they have remained in their holds ; their might hath failed ; they became as women ; they have burnt her dwellingplaces ; her bars are broken. One post shall run to meet another, and one messenger to meet another, to show the king of Babylon that his city is taken at one end : and that the passages are stopped.—Thus saith the Lord of hosts, the God of Israel, the daugh-

* Jerem. li. 2, 8, 9.   † Ibid. 11, 13, 14.

ter of Babylon is like a threshing-floor—it is time to
thresh her; yet a little while, and the time of her
harvest shall come:*—I will dry up her sea, and
make her springs dry. And Babylon shall become
heaps, a dwelling-place for dragons, an astonishment,
and an hissing without an inhabitant.—In their heat
I will make their feasts,—that they may sleep a perpetual sleep, and not wake:—how is the praise of the
whole earth surprised! how is Babylon become an astonishment among the nations! The sea is come
upon Babylon: she is covered with the multitude of
the waves thereof. Her cities are a desolation, a dry
land and a wilderness, a land wherein no man dwelleth, neither doth any son of man pass thereby. And
I will punish Bel in Babylon; and I will bring forth
out of his mouth that which he hath swallowed up:
and the nations shall not flow together any more unto
him; yea the wall of Babylon shall fall.—A rumour
shall come one year, and after that in another year
shall come a rumour, and violence in the land, ruler
against ruler. Therefore, behold, the days come that
I will do judgment upon the graven images of Babylon: and her whole land shall be confounded, and all
her slain shall fall in the midst of her, &c.† And I
will make drunk her princes, and her wise men, her
captains, and her rulers, and mighty men: and they
shall sleep a perpetual sleep, and not wake, saith the
King, whose name is the Lord of hosts. Thus saith
the Lord of hosts, the broad walls of Babylon shall
be utterly broken, and her high gates shall be burned
with fire; and the people shall labour in vain, and
the folk in the fire, and they shall be weary.—And
it shall be when thou hast made an end of reading
this book, that thou shalt bind a stone to it, and cast

---

* Jerem. li. 25—33.
† Ibid. li. 36, 37, 39, 41, 42, 43, 44, 45, 47.

it into the midst of Euphrates : and thou shalt say,
thus shall Babylon sink, and shall not rise from the
evil that I will bring upon her.*

The enemies who were to besiege Babylon—the
cowardice of the Babylonians—the manner in which
the city was taken, and all the remarkable circumstances of the siege, were foretold and described by the
prophets as the facts are related by ancient historians.

*Go up, O Elam, (or Persia,) besiege, O Media.
The Lord hath raised up the spirit of the kings of the
Medes, for his device is against Babylon to destroy it.*
The kings of Persia and Media, prompted by a common interest, freely entered into a league against Babylon, and with one accord intrusted the command of
their united armies to Cyrus,† the relative and eventually the successor of them both.—But the taking of
Babylon was not reserved for these kingdoms alone ;
other nations had to be *prepared against her.*

*Set up a standard in the land ; blow the trumpet
among the nations, prepare the nations against her, call
together against her the kingdoms of Ararat, Minni,
and Aschenaz ; Lo, I will raise and cause to come up
against Babylon, an assembly of great nations from
the north country, &c.* Cyrus subdued the Armenians, who had revolted against Media, spared their
king, bound them over anew to their allegiance, by
kindness rather than by force, and incorporated their
army with his own.‡ He adopted the Hyrcanians,
who had rebelled against Babylon, as allies and con-
federates, with the Medes and Persians.§ He conquered the united forces of the Babylonians and Lydians, took Sardis, with Crœsus and all his wealth,
spared his life, after he was at the stake, restored to

---

* Jerem. li. 57, 58, 63, 64.
† Xenoph. Cyrop. lib. i. p. 53.   Ed. Hutch. Glas. 1821.
‡ Xenoph. Cyrop. l. iii. p. 156.   § Ibid. l. iv. pp. 215, 217.

him his family and his household, received him into
the number of his counsellors and friends, and thus
prepared the Lydians, over whom he reigned, and
who were formerly combined with Babylon, for *coming
up against it.** He overthrew also the Phrygians
and Cappadocians, and added their armies in like
manner to his accumulating forces.† And by successive alliances and conquests, by proclaiming liberty
to the slaves, by a humane policy, consummate skill,
a pure and noble disinterestedness, and a boundless
generosity, he changed, within the space of twenty
years, a confederacy which the king of Babylon had
raised up against the Medes and Persians, whose junction he feared, into a confederacy even of the same
nations against Babylon itself,—and thus *a standard
was set up against Babylon in many a land, kingdoms were summoned, prepared, and gathered together
against her ; and an assembly of great nations from
the north,*—including *Ararat and Minni,* or the
greater and lesser Armenia, and *Aschenaz,* or according to Bochart, Phrygia,—*were raised up, and caused to come against Babylon.* Without their aid, and
before they were subjected to his authority, he had
attempted in vain to conquer Babylon ; but when he
had *prepared* and *gathered them* together, it was
taken, though by artifice more than by power.

*They shall hold the bow and the lance—they shall
ride upon horses—let the archer bend his bow—all ye
that bend the bow, shoot at her. They rode upon
horses.* Forty thousand Persian horsemen were armed
from among the nations which Cyrus subdued ; many
horses of the captives were besides distributed among
all the allies. And Cyrus came up against Babylon
with a great multitude of horse ;‡ and also with a

* Xenoph. Cyrop. l. ii. pp. 408—416.
† Ibid. l. iv. pp. 427, 428.   ‡ Ibid. p. 428,

great multitude of archers and javelin-men*—*that held the bow and the lance.*

No sooner had Cyrus reached Babylon, with the nations which he had prepared, and gathered against her, than in the hope of discovering some point not utterly impregnable, accompanied by his chief officers and friends, he rode around the walls, and examined them on every side, after having for that purpose stationed his whole army *round* the city.† *They camped against it round about. They put themselves in array against Babylon round about.*

Frustrated in the attempt to discover, throughout the whole circumference, a single assailable point, and finding that it was not possible, by any attack, to make himself master of walls so strong and so high, and fearing that his army would be exposed to the assault of the Babylonians by a too extended and consequently weakened line,—Cyrus, standing in the middle of his army, gave orders that the heavy armed men should move, in opposite directions, from each extremity towards the centre ; and the horse and light armed men being nearer and advancing first, and the phalanx being redoubled and closed up, the bravest troops thus occupied alike the front and the rear, and the less effective were stationed in the middle.‡ Such a disposition of the army, in the estimation of Xenophon, himself a most skilful general, was well adapted both for fighting and preventing flight ; while the Christian, judging differently of their successive movements, may here see the fulfilment of one prediction after another. For as in this manner " they stood facing the walls," in regular order, and not as a disorderly and undisciplined host, though composed of various nations, *they set themselves in array against Babylon,—every man put in array.*

* Xenoph. Cyrop. p. 129.   † Ibid.   ‡ Ibid. p. 430.

A trench was dug round the city,—towers were erected—Babylon was besieged—the army was divided into twelve parts, that each, monthly by turn, might keep watch throughout the year;*—and though the orders were given by Cyrus, the command of the Lord of Hosts was unconsciously obeyed—*let none thereof escape.*

The mighty men of Babylon have forborne to fight. They have remained in their holds; their might hath failed, they became as women. Babylon had been the hammer of the whole earth, by which nations were broken in pieces, and kingdoms destroyed. Its mighty men carried the terror of their arms to distant regions and led nations captive. But they were *dismayed* according to the word of the God of Israel, whenever the nations which he had stirred up against them stood in array before their walls. Their timidity, so clearly predicted, was the express complaint and accusation of their enemies, who in vain attempted to provoke them to the contest. Cyrus challenged their monarch to single combat, but also in vain;† for *the hands of the king of Babylon waxed feeble.* Courage had departed from both prince and people; and none attempted to save their country from spoliation, or to chase the assailants from their gates. They sallied not forth against the invaders and besiegers, nor did they attempt to disjoin and disperse them, even when drawn all around their walls, and comparatively weak along the extended line. Every gate was still shut; and *they remained in their holds.* Being as unable to rouse their courage, even by a close blockade, and to bring them to the field, as to scale or break down any portion of their stupendous walls, or to force their gates of solid brass,

* Xenoph. Cyrop. pp. 430—434.
† Ibid. l. v. p. 290.

Cyrus reasoned that the greater that was their number, the more easily would they be starved into surrender, and yield to famine, since they would not
contend with arms nor come forth to fight. And
hence arose for the space of two years his only hope
of eventual success. So dispirited became its people,
that Babylon, which had made the world as a wilderness, was long unresistingly a beleaguered town. But,
possessed of many fertile fields and of provisions for
twenty years, which in their timid caution they had
plentifully stored, they derided Cyrus from their impregnable walls within which they *remained*.* Their
profligacy, their wickedness and false confidence were
unabated ; they continued to live carelessly in pleasures, but their might did not return : and Babylon
the great, unlike to many a small fortress and un-
walled town, made not one effort to regain its freedom
or to be rid of the foe.

Much time having been lost, and no progress having been made in the siege, the anxiety of Cyrus
was strongly excited, and he was reduced to great
perplexity, when at last it was suggested and immediately determined on, to turn the course of the
Euphrates. But the task was not an easy one. The
river was a quarter of a mile broad, and twelve feet
deep, and in the opinion of one of the counsellors
of Cyrus, the city was stronger by the river than
by its walls. Diligent and laborious preparation was
made for the execution of the scheme, yet so as
to deceive the Babylonians. And the great trench,
ostensibly formed for the purpose of blockade, which
for the time it effectually secured, was dug around
the walls on every side, in order to drain the Euphrates, and to leave its channel a straight passage into
the city, through the midst of which it flowed. But,

* Xenoph. Cyrop. l. vii. p. 434. Herod. l. i. c. 190.

in the words of Herodotus, " if the besieged had
either been aware of the designs of Cyrus, or had discovered the project before its actual accomplishment,
they might have effected the total destruction of their
troops. They had only to secure the little gates which
led to the river, and to man the embankment on either
side, and they might have enclosed the Persians as in
a net from which they could never have escaped."*
Guarding as much as possibly they could against such
a catastrophe, Cyrus purposely chose, for the execution of his plan, the time of a great annual Babylonish festival, during which, according to their practice, " the Babylonians drank and revelled the whole
night." And while the unconscious and reckless
citizens " were engaged in dancing and merriment,"
the river was suddenly turned into the lake, the
trench and the canals ; and the watchful Persians,
both foot and horse, so soon as the subsiding of the
water permitted, entered by its channel, and were
followed by the allies in array, on the *dry* part of
the river.† " *I will dry up thy sea, and make thy
springs dry. That sayeth to the deep be dry, I will
dry up thy rivers.*"

" One detachment was placed where the river first
enters the city, and another where it leaves it."‡ And
" *one post did run to meet another, and one messenger
to meet another, to show the king of Babylon that his
city is taken at the end, and that the passages are
shut.*" " They were taken," says Herodotus, " by
surprise : and such is the extent of the city, that, as
the inhabitants themselves affirm, they who lived in
the extremities were made prisoners before any alarm
was communicated to the centre of the place,"§

* Herod. lib. i. c. 191.
† Herod. ibid.   Xenoph. Cy op. l. vii. pp. 434—437.
‡ Herod. lib. i. 191.
§ Ibid.

where the palace stood. Not a gate of the city wall was opened; not a brick of it had fallen. But a *snare was laid for Babylon—it was taken and it was not aware; it was found and also caught, for it had sinned against the Lord. How is the praise of the whole earth surprised! For thou hast trusted in thy wickedness, and thy wisdom, and thy knowledge, it hath perverted thee, therefore shall evil come upon thee, and thou shalt not know from whence it riseth, and mischief shall come upon thee, and thou shalt not be able to put it off, &c.—None shall save thee.*

In their heat I will make their feasts, and I will make them drunken, that they may rejoice and sleep a perpetual sleep and not wake, saith the Lord. I will bring them down like lambs to the slaughter, &c. I will make drunken her princes and her wise men, her captains and her rulers, and her mighty men, and they shall sleep a perpetual sleep, &c. Cyrus, as the night drew on, stimulated his assembled troops to enter the city, because in that night of general revel within the walls, many of them were asleep, many drunk, and confusion universally prevailed. On passing, without obstruction or hinderance, into the city, the Persians, slaying some, putting others to flight, and joining with the revellers as if slaughter had been merriment, hastened by the shortest way to the palace, and reached it ere yet a messenger had told the king that his city was taken. The gates of the palace, which were strongly fortified, were shut. The guards stationed before them were *drinking* beside a blazing light, when the Persians rushed impetuously upon them. The louder and altered clamour, no longer joyous, caught the ear of the inmates of the palace, and the bright light showed them the work of destruction, without revealing its cause. And not aware of the presence of an enemy in the midst of Babylon, the king himself (who, as every Christian knows, had been roused from his

revelry by the hand writing on the wall,) excited by
the warlike tumult at the gates, commanded those
within to examine from whence it arose ; and according to the same word, by which *the gates* (leading
from the river to the city) *were not shut, the loins of
kings were loosed to* OPEN *before Cyrus the two-leaved gates.* At the first sight of the opened gates of
the palace of Babylon, the eager Persians sprang
in. *The king of Babylon heard the report of them—
anguish took hold of him,*—he and all who were
about him perished : God had numbered his kingdom and finished it : it was divided and given to the
Medes and Persians ; the lives of the Babylonian
princes, and lords, and rulers, and captains, closed
with that night's festival : the drunken slept a perpetual sleep, and did not wake.*

Her young men shall fall in THE STREETS, *and all
her men of war shall be cut off in that day.* Cyrus
sent troops of horse throughout *the streets*, with orders to slay all who were found there. And he commanded proclamation to be made, in the Syrian language, that all who were in the houses should remain within ; and that, if any one were found abroad,
he should be killed. These orders were obeyed.†
They shall wander every man to his quarter.

I will fill thee with men as with caterpillars. Not
only did the Persian army enter with ease as caterpillars, together with all the nations that had come up
against Babylon, but they seemed also as numerous.
Cyrus, after the capture of the city, made a great display of his cavalry in the presence of the Babylonians,
and in the midst of Babylon. Four thousand guards
stood before the palace gates, and two thousand on
each side. These advanced as Cyrus approached ; two
thousand spearmen followed them. These were suc-

---

* Herod. lib. i. c. 191. Xen. Cyr. l. vii. pp. 434, 439.
† Ibid. p. 439.

cceded by four square masses of Persian cavalry, each
consisting of ten thousand men ; and to these again
were added, in their order, the Median, Arme-
nian, Hyrcanian, Caducian, and Sacian horsemen,—
all, as before, *riding upon horses, every man in array*—with lines of chariots, four abreast, concluding
the train of the numerous hosts.*—Cyrus afterwards
reviewed, at Babylon, the whole of his army, consisting of one hundred and twenty thousand horse,
two thousand chariots, and six hundred thousand
foot.† Babylon, which was taken when not aware,
and within whose walls no enemy, except a captive,
had been ever seen, was also *filled with men as with
caterpillars*, as if there had not been a wall around
it.—The Scriptures do not relate the manner in
which Babylon was taken, nor do they ever allude
to the exact fulfilment of the prophecies. But there
is, in every particular, a strict coincidence between
the predictions of the prophets and the historical narratives, both of Herodotus and Xenophon.

On taking Babylon suddenly, and by surprise, Cyrus, as had been literally prophesied concerning him,
and as the sign by which it was to be known that the
Lord had called him by his name (Isa. xlv. 1—4.‡)
became immediately possessed of the most secret treasures of Babylon. No enemy had ever dared to rise
up against that great city. To take it, seemed not a
work for man to attempt ; but it became the easy prey
of him who was called *the servant of the Lord*. And
as at this day,—from the perfect representation given
by the prophets, of every feature of fallen Babylon,

* Xen. Cyr. l. viii. pp. 494, 495.
† Ibid. p. 532.
‡ Isaiah prophesied above one hundred and sixty years
before the taking of Babylon, two hundred and fifty years
before Herodotus, and nearly three hundred and fifty before
Xenophon.

now at last utterly desolate,—men may know that
God is the Lord, seeing that all who have visited and
describe it, show that the predicted judgments against
it have been literally fulfilled ; so at that time, Cyrus
—who, for two years, could only look on the outer
side of the outer wall of Babylon, and who had begun to despair of reducing it by famine,—was to
know by the *treasures of darkness, and hidden riches
of secret places being given into his hand, that the
Lord, which had called him by his name, was the God
of Israel.* And when the appointed time had come
that the power of their oppressor was to be broken,
Babylon was taken ; and when the similarly prescribed period of the captivity of the Jews, for whose
sake he was called, had expired, Cyrus was their deliverer.

*Thus saith the Lord to his anointed, to Cyrus, whose
right hand I have holden, to* SUBDUE NATIONS *before
him.* Cyrus, commencing his career with a small
army of Persians, not only succeeded to the kingdom
of the Medes and Persians, first united under him,
but the Hyrcanians yielded also voluntarily to his
authority. He subdued the Syrians, Assyrians, Arabs,
Cappadocians, both Phrygias, the Lydians, Carians,
Phenicians, and Babylonians. He governed the
Bactrians, Indians, and Cilicians, and also the Sa-
cians, Paphlagonians and Mariandinians, and other
nations. He likewise reduced to his authority the
Greeks that were in Asia, and the Cyprians, and
Egyptians.* *Nations* were thus *subdued before him.*

*I will stir up the Medes against them, which shall
not regard silver ; and as for gold they shall not delight in it.* He who was called the anointed of the
Lord was free from covetousness. His character is
drawn by Xenophon, (who states that he excelled all

---

* Xen. Cyr. lib. i. 45.

other kings,) as the model of a wise and generous
prince. The liberality of Cyrus was more noble than
the mere possession of immensity of wealth, though
including both the riches of Crœsus and the treasures
of Babylon. He reckoned that his riches belonged
not any more to himself than to his friends.* And
he made as well as pronounced it his object to use and
not to hoard his wealth, and to apply it to the reward
of his servants, and in relief of their wants. So *little*
did he *regard silver* or *delight in gold*, that Crœsus
told him that, by his liberality, he would make himself poor, instead of storing up vast treasures to himself. The Medes possessed, in this respect, the spirit
of their chief, of which an instance, recorded by
Xenophon, is too striking and appropriate to be passed
over.† When Cobryas, an Assyrian governor, whose
son the king of Babylon had slain, hospitably entertained him and his army ; Cyrus appealed to the
chiefs of the Medes and Hyrcanians, and to the
noblest and most honourable of the Persians, whether
giving first what was due unto the gods, and leaving
to the rest of the army their portion, they would not
overmatch his generosity by ceding to him their whole
share of the first and plentiful booty, which they had
won from the land of Babylon. Loudly applauding
the proposal, they immediately and unanimously consented ; and one of them said : " Cobryas may have
thought us poor, because we came not loaded with
golden coins,‡ and drink not out of golden cups ;
but by this he will know, that men can be generous
even without gold."§—*As for gold, they did not delight
in it.*

Cobryas, it may be presumed, was stirred up and
prepared, by gratitude on the one hand, as well as by

* Xen. Cyr. lib. viii. p. 516.   † Ib. lib. viii. p. 452.
‡ Darics.   § Xen. l. v. p. 289.

revenge on the other, to go up against Babylon. And, it may be mentioned, he was afterwards the first to lead the way to the palace; and—for, though a great deep, the judgments of God are altogether righteous,— his hand was among those who slew the murderer of his son.

NONE SHALL RETURN IN VAIN. The walls of Babylon were incomparably the loftiest and the strongest ever built by man. They were constructed of such stupendous size and strength, on very purpose that no possibility might exist of Babylon ever being taken. And, if ever confidence in bulwarks could not have been misplaced, it was when the citizens and soldiery of Babylon, who feared to encounter their enemies in the field—in perfect assurance of their safety and beyond the reach of the Parthian arrow, scoffed from the summit of their impregnable walls the hosts which encompassed them. But though the proud boast of a city so defended, and which had never been taken,— that it would *stand for ever*,—seemed scarcely presumptuous; yet, subsequently to the delivery of the prophecies concerning it, Babylon was not only repeatedly taken, but was never once besieged in vain. Cyrus, indeed, departed, after he first appeared before its walls, but he went to prepare and gather together the nations against it. And he did *not return in vain*. But this prediction, as it is applicable also to all others, is true, not of him only, but also of all who, in after ages, came up against Babylon. It fell before every hand that was raised against it; yet its greatness did not depart, nor was its glory obscured in a day. Cyrus was not its destroyer; but he sought by wise institutions to perpetuate its pre-eminence among the nations. He left it to his successor in all its strength and magnificence. Rebelling against Darius, the Babylonians made preparations for a siege, and bade defiance to the whole power of the Persian empire.

Fully resolved not to yield, and that famine might never reduce them to submission, they adopted the most desperate and barbarous resolution of putting every woman in the city to death, with the exception of their mothers, and one female, the best beloved in every family, to bake their bread. All the rest were *assembled together* and strangled.* *These two things shall come upon thee in a moment, in one day, the loss of children and widowhood, they shall come upon thee in their perfection, for the multitude of thy sorceries, and for the great abundance of thine enchantments. For thou hast trusted in thy wickedness, &c.* They did come upon them in their perfection, when their wives and children were strangled by their own hands; and so suddenly, as before, *in a moment, in one day, did these things come upon them,* that the victims were assembled for the sacrifice; so general was the instant *widowhood,* that fifty thousand women were afterwards taken, in proportionate numbers, from the different neighbouring provinces of the empire, to replace those who had been slain; and the very reservation of their mothers multiplied the lamentations for the *loss of children.* But *trust in their wickedness* brought them no safety. For, while they were thus instrumental in the infliction of one grievous judgment, for which such murderers were ripe; their iniquity was not thereby lessened, and therefore, at however great a price, they procured not any security against another judgment, which also had been denounced against Babylon for its wickedness. They deemed themselves absolutely secure against famine and against assault. The artifice of Cyrus could not again be a snare; and an attempt to renew it was, along with every other, entirely frustrated. But still it was *not in vain* that Darius besieged Babylon.

---

* Herod. l. iii. c. 150. Tom. iii. 160, ed. Foul.

In the twentieth month of the siege a single Persian whose body was covered over with the marks of stripes and with blood, and whose nose and ears had been newly cut off, presented himself at one of the gates of Babylon,—a helpless object of pity, and, if not a great criminal indeed, the obvious victim of wanton and savage cruelty. He had fled, or escaped, from the camp of the enemy. But he was not a common deserter, such as they might not have admitted within their walls,—but it was Zophyrus, who was well known as one of the chief nobles of Persia. He represented to the Babylonians, that, not for any crime, but for the honest advice which he had given to Darius to raise the siege, as the taking of the city seemed to all impossible, the enraged tyrant (his pride wounded, or his fears perhaps awakened, that his army would be discouraged by such counsel,) had inflicted upon him the severest cruelties, caused him to be mutilated as they saw, and to be scourged, of which his whole body bore the marks ;—to one of his proud spirit and high rank, disgrace was worse than suffering, and he came to join the revolters, his soul burning for vengeance against their common tyrant. " And now," addressing them, he said, " I come for the greatest good to you, for the greatest evil to Darius, to his army, and to the Persians. The injuries which I have suffered shall not be unrevenged, for I know, and will disclose all his designs."

On such proofs, and cheered by such hopes, the Babylonians did not doubt the sincerity of Zophyrus, nor his devotion to their cause, identified, as it clearly seemed, with the only hope of revenge against the cruel author of his wrongs, towards whom they could not conceive but that he would cherish an inflexible hatred. He sought but to fight against their enemies. At his request, they gladly and unhesitatingly intrusted him with a military command. Forgiveness

of injuries was not then reckoned a virtue—which it
is too seldom practically accounted even in a Christian land ; and vengeance, still called honour, sleeps
not in an unforgiving breast.   Zophyrus soon satisfied the Babylonians that his wrongs would not long
be unavenged.   To their delight, having watched the
first opportunity, he sallied forth from the gates of
Semiramis, on the tenth day after his entrance into
the city, and falling suddenly on a thousand of the
enemy, slew them every one.   After an interval of
only seven days, twice that number were, in like
manner, slain, near to the Ninian gates.   The men
of Babylon were animated with new vigour and new
hopes ; and the praise of Zophyrus was on every
tongue.   He received a higher command.   But the
Persians, seemingly more wary, were nowhere open
to attack for the space of twenty days.   On the ex-
piry of that period, however, Zophyrus, by a noted
exploit, again proved himself worthy of still greater
authority, by leading out his troops from the Chaldean gates, and killing, in one spot, four thousand
men.   In reward for such services, and such tried
fidelity, skill, and courage, as none, they thought,
could be more worthy of the honour and of the trust,
they not only raised him to the chief command of
their army, but appointed him to the dignified and
most responsible office in Babylon, which it was his
aim to attain, that of (τειχοφυλαξ) guardian of their
walls.*

Darius, as if to be secure against the continued repetition of such desultory carnage of his troops, advanced with all his army to the walls.   They were
manned to repel the assault.   But the treachery of
Zophyrus, however incredible, and unknown and unsuspected, alike by the Babylonians and the Persians,

* Herod. c. 152—157, pp. 166—173.

became immediately apparent. Intrusted as he was, in virtue of his office, with the gates of the city, no sooner had the enemy approached, and the armed citizens ascended the wall, than he opened the Belidian and the Cissian gates, close to which the choicest Persian troops were stationed.* The whole scheme was a preconcerted *snare*, known only to Darius and Zophyrus, and invented solely by the latter, the mutilation of whose body was his own voluntary act. To the glory of the deed were added the greatest gifts and honours, and the governorship of Babylon without tribute, for his reward. The numbers of the different detachments of the Persian troops who fell, their positions, and the precise time of their successive advancements, had all been resolved on and arranged. And Darius as freely sacrificed the lives of seven thousand men, as Zophyrus had inflicted incurable wounds upon himself. " Thus," says Herodotus, " was Babylon a second time taken." And thus was the word of God,—from whom nothing past, present, or future, can be hid,—a second time fulfilled against Babylon—*none shall return in vain.*

Babylon was a third time taken by Alexander the Great. Mazæus, the Persian general, surrendered the city into his hands, and he entered it with his army drawn up, " as if they were marching to battle."† Again was it *filled with men,*—and literally was every man *put in array, like a man to the battle.* The siege of so fortified a city‡ would have been a work of great difficulty and labour, even to the conqueror of Asia. But the inhabitants eagerly flocked upon the walls to see their new king, and exchanged, without a struggle, the Persian for the Macedonian

---

* Herod. c. 158, 159.
† Quadrato agmine, quod ipse ducebat, *velut in aciem irent*, ingredi suos jubet. Quin. Curt. lib. v. c. 2.
‡ —tam munitæ urbis. Ib.

yoke.—Babylon was afterwards successively taken by
Antigonus, by Demetrius, by Antiochus the Great,
and by the Parthians.   But whatever king or nation
came up against it, NONE *returned in vain.*

Each step in the progress of the decline of Babylon
was the accomplishment of a prophecy.   Conquered,
for the first time,* by Cyrus, it was afterwards reduced from an imperial to a tributary city.   *Come
down and sit in the dust, O virgin daughter of Babylon : sit on the ground, there is no throne, O daughter
of the Chaldeans.*—After the Babylonians rebelled
against Darius, the walls were reduced in height, and
all the gates destroyed.†   *The wall of Babylon shall
fall, her walls thrown down.*—Xerxes, after his ignominious retreat from Greece, rifled the temples of
Babylon,‡ the golden images alone in which were
estimated at L.20,000,000, besides treasures of vast
amount.   *I will punish Bel in Babylon, and I will
bring forth out of his mouth that which he has swallowed up ; I will do judgment upon the graven images
of Babylon.*§—Alexander the Great attempted to restore it to its former glory, and designed to make it
the metropolis of an universal empire.   But while
the building of the temple of Belus, and the repara-
tion of the embankments of the Euphrates, were actually carrying on, the conqueror of the world died,
at the commencement of this his last undertaking, in
the height of his power, and in the flower of his age.||
*Take balm for her pain, if so be that she may be
healed.   We would have healed Babylon, but she is not
healed.*¶—The neighbouring city of Seleucia, which

---

* Herod. lib. i. c. 191.   † Herod. lib. iii. c. 150.
    † Herod. lib. i. c. 183.   Arrian. de Expeditione Alex. lib.
vii. c. 17, cited by Bishop Newton.
    § Jer. li. 44, 47, 52.
    || Arrian. lib. vii. c. 17.   Strabo, lib. xvi. p. 738.
    ¶ Jer. li. 8, 9.

was built with that intent, was the chief cause of the
decline of Babylon as a city, and drained it of great
part of its population.*   And at a later period, or
about 130 years before the birth of Christ, Humerus,
a Parthian governor, who was noted as excelling all
tyrants in cruelty, exercised great severities on the
Babylonians, and having burned the forum and some
of the temples, and destroyed the fairest parts of the
city, reduced many of the inhabitants to slavery on
the slightest pretexts, and caused them, together with
all their households, to be sent into Media.† *They
shall remove, they shall depart, both man and beast.*

The " golden city" thus gradually verged, for centuries, towards poverty and desolation.—Notwithstanding that Cyrus resided chiefly at Babylon, and
sought to reform the government and remodel the
manners of the Babylonians, the succeeding kings of
Persia preferred, as the seat of empire, Susa, Perse-
polis, or Ecbatana, situated in their *own country :*
and in like manner the successors of Alexander did
not attempt to complete his purpose of restoring Babylon to its pre-eminence and glory ; but, after the
subdivision of his mighty empire, the very kings of
Assyria, during their temporary residence even in
Chaldea, deserted Babylon, and dwelt in Seleucia.
And thus the foreign inhabitants, first Persians, and
afterwards Greeks, imitating their sovereigns by de-
serting Babylon, acted as if they verily had said,—
*Forsake her, and let us go every man unto his own
country ; for her judgment is reached unto heaven,
and is lifted up even to the skies.*

But kindred judgments—the issue of common
crimes—rested on the land of Chaldea, as well as on
its doomed metropolis ; and the tracing of their ful-

* Plin. Hist. Nat. lib. v. c. 26.
† Diod. Siculi fragmentum, apud Valesium.   Vide Vitrin.
com. in Iesaiam, cap. 13, pp. 420, 421.

filment may best lead to the view of the utter desolation of fallen Babylon.

*They come from a far country, from the end of the
earth, to destroy the whole land. Many nations and
great kings shall serve themselves of thee also, &c.*
The Persians, the Macedonians, the Parthians, the
Romans, the Saracens, and the Turks, are the chief
of the many nations who have unscrupulously and un-
sparingly served themselves of the land of the Chaldeans; and Cyrus and Darius, kings of Persia;
Alexander the Great; and Seleucus, king of Assyria;
Demetrius, and Antiochus the Great; Trajan, Severus, Julian, and Heraclius, emperors of Rome;
the victorious Omar, the successor of Mahomet;—
Holagou, and Tamerlane, are *great kings*, who successively subdued or desolated Chaldea, or exacted
from it tribute to such an extent, as scarcely any other
country ever paid to a single conqueror. And, though
the names of some of these nations were unknown to
the Babylonians, and unheard of in the world at the
time of the prophecy—most of these many nations
and great kings need now but to be named, to show
that, in local relation to Chaldea, *they came from the
utmost border from the coasts of the earth.*

They are CRUEL *both in* ANGER *and fierce wrath to
lay the land* DESOLATE, &c. The Persians vied with
the Parthians in cruelty and fierceness against resisting and against subjugated enemies. Three thousand Babylonians were at once impaled by order of
Darius. Conquest was the object, and kindness was
not in the nature of the Macedonian conquerors of
Babylon. The possession of Chaldea was contested
between Antigonus and Seleucus, and *ruler rose
against ruler.* After its long subjection to the Se-
leucidae, the proverbially cruel Parthians held Babylonia in bondage. In the second century of the
Christian era, the Romans, *coming from afar,*

still maintained the character of the cruel and fierce desolators of Chaldea, and were thus the unconscious instruments of the fulfilment of other prophecies. " Under the reign of Marcus, the Roman generals penetrated *as far* as Ctesiphon and Seleucia. They were received as friends by the Greek colony ; they attacked as enemies the seat of the Parthian kings, yet both cities experienced the same treatment. The sack and conflagration of Seleucia *with the massacre of three hundred thousand of the inhabitants*, tarnished the glory of the Roman triumph.— Seleucia sunk under the fatal blow ; but Ctesiphon, in about thirty-three years, had sufficiently recovered its strength to maintain an obstinate siege against the emperor Severus. Ctesiphon was thrice besieged and thrice taken by the predecessors of Julian."[*] And when attacked by Julian, the *anger* of that Roman emperor and that of his army was not moderated, nor their *cruelty* abated, by the effectual resistance of the citizens of Ctesiphon against sixty thousand besiegers. " The fields of Assyria were devoted by Julian to the calamities of war ; and the philosopher retaliated on a guiltless people the acts of rapine and *cruelty* which had been committed by their haughty master in the Roman provinces. The Persians beheld from the walls of Ctesiphon *the desolation* of the adjacent country."[†] With such violence did he wreak his vengeance on the *inhabitants of Chaldea*, that their *fierce wrath* was conjoined with the *cruelty* of their enemies *to lay the land desolate.* " The extensive region that lies between the river Tigris and the mountains of Media, was filled with villages and towns; and the fertile soil, for the most part, was in a very improved state of cultivation. But on the approach of the Romans, this rich and smiling prospect

[*] Gibbon, v. i. c. viii. p. 212. [†] Ib. v. ii. c xxiv. p 369.

was instantly blasted.   Wherever they moved, the inhabitants deserted the open villages and took shelter
in the fortified towns; the cattle were driven away;
the grass and ripe corn were *consumed with* FIRE;
and as soon as the *flames* had subsided which interrupted the march of Julian, he beheld the melancholy
face of a SMOKING AND NAKED DESERT."* But "the
second city of the province, large, populous, and well
fortified,"—in vain resisted a fierce and desperate assault; and a large breach having been made by a
battering-ram in the walls, "the soldiers of Julian
rushed *impetuously* into the town, and after the full
gratification of every military appetite, Perisabor was
REDUCED TO ASHES; and the engines which assaulted the citadel were planted on the *ruins of the smoking houses.*"† When, in after ages, the Romans,
under Heraclius, penetrated to the royal seat of Destagered, and spread over Chaldea to the gates of
Ctesiphon, "whatever could not be easily transported, *they consumed with fire*, that Chosroes might feel
the *anguish* of those wounds, which he had so often
inflicted on the provinces of the empire; and justice
might allow the excuse," says Gibbon, "if the desolation had been confined to the works of regal luxury, if national *hatred*, military license, and religious
zeal, had not wasted with *equal rage* the habitations
and the temples of the guiltless subjects."‡—The
fierce Abassides, proverbially reckless of committing
murder, which was the very work that their mission-
aries went forth to execute, long reigned over Chaldea; and Bagdad, its new capital, distant about
fifteen miles from Seleucia and Ctesiphon, was their
imperial seat for five hundred years.§—"Their dag-
gers, their only arms, were broken by the sword of

* Gibbon, v. ii. c. xxiv. p. 374.   † Ib. v. ii. p. 361.
‡ Ib. c. 46, v. iv. p. 441.   § Ib. c. 51, vol. v. p. 338.

Holagou, and except the word *assassin*, *not a vestige
is left of the enemies of mankind*,"*—for again and
again has it proved true of the land of Chaldea—*I
will destroy the sinners thereof out of it*. The Mo-
gul Tartars succeeded as the guilty possessors and
cruel desolators of *the land* of Babylon. " Bagdad,
after a siege of two months, was stormed and sacked
by the Moguls, under Holagou Khan, the grandson
of Ghengis Khan."† And Tamerlane, another *great
king*, "reduced to his obedience the whole course of
the Tigris and Euphrates, from the mouth to the
sources of these rivers; and he erected on the ruins
of Bagdad a pyramid of ninety thousand heads."‡
Finally, not with abated, but if possible, with increasing or with more persevering cruelty, the Turks,
aided by Saracens, Coords and Tartars, have become
the weapons of the indignation of the Lord, *brought
forth out of his armory which he hath opened*; *for*
—fearful as a token of judgment, and clear as the
testimony of truth—*this is the work of the Lord God
of Hosts in the land of the Chaldeans—Waste and
utterly destroy after them. A sword is upon the
Chaldeans. A sound of battle is in the land, and of
great destruction. I will kindle a* FIRE *in his* CITIES,
and it shall DEVOUR ALL ROUND ABOUT HIM. *A
sound of great destruction cometh from the land of
the Chaldeans.*

And Chaldea shall be a spoil; ALL *that spoil her
shall be* SATISFIED, *saith the Lord. Come against her
from the utmost border, open her storehouses. A* SWORD
*is upon her treasures, and they shall be robbed. O thou
that dwellest upon many waters,* ABUNDANT *in treasures,
thine end is come, and the measure of thy covetousness.*
On taking Babylon suddenly and by surprise, Cyrus

---

* Gibbon, c. 64, vol. vi. p. 278.   † Ibid.
‡ Ib. c. 65, vol. vi. pp. 312, 322.

became immediately possessed of *the treasures of darkness, and hidden riches of secret places.* On his first publicly appearing in Babylon, all the officers of his army, both of the Persians and allies, according to his command, wore very splendid robes, those belonging to the superior officers being of various colours, all of the finest and brightest dye, and richly embroidered with gold and silver; and thus the *hidden riches of secret places* were openly displayed. And when the treasures of Babylon became the spoil of another great king, Alexander gave six *minæ* (about L.15) to *each* Macedonian horseman, to each Macedonian soldier and foreign horseman two minæ (L.5), and to every other man in his army, a donation equal to two months' pay. Demetrius ordered his soldiers to plunder the land of Babylon for *their own use.** But it is not in these instances alone that Chaldea has been a spoil, and that *all* who spoil her have been *satisfied.* It was the abundance of her treasures which brought successive spoliators. Many nations came from afar, and though they *returned to their own country*, (as in formerly besieging Babylon, so in continuing to despoil the land of Chaldea,) *none returned in vain.* From the richness of the country new treasures were speedily stored up, till again *the sword come upon them, and they were robbed.* The prey of the Persians and of the Greeks for nearly two centuries after the death of Alexander, Chaldea became afterwards the prey chiefly of the Parthians, for an equal period, till a greater nation, the Romans, *came from the coasts of the earth* to pillage it. To be restrained from dominion and from plunder, was the exciting cause, and often the shameless plea, of the anger and fierce wrath of these famed, but cruel, conquerors of the world. Yet within

---

* Plutarch, Life of Demetrius.

the provinces of their empire, it was their practice,
on the submission of the inhabitants, to protect and
not to destroy. But Chaldea, from its extreme distance, never having yielded permanently to their
yoke, and the limits of their empire having been
fixed by Hadrian on the western side of the Euphrates, or on the very borders of Chaldea, that hap-
less country obtained not their protection, though repeatedly the scene of ruthless spoliation by the Romans. The authority of Gibbon, in elucidation of
Scripture, cannot be here distrusted any more than
that of heathen historians. To use his words, "a
hundred thousand captives, and a *rich booty*, rewarded the fatigues of the Roman soldiers,"* when
Ctesiphon was taken, in the second century, by the
generals of Marcus. Even Julian, who, in the
fourth century, was forced to raise the siege of
Ctesiphon, came not in vain to Chaldea, and failed
not to take of it a spoil ; nor, though an apostate,
did he fail to verify by his acts the truth which he
denied. After having given Perisabor to the flames,
"the plentiful magazines of corn, of arms, and of
splendid furniture, were partly distributed among the
troops, and partly reserved for the public service ;
the *useless stores* were destroyed by fire, or thrown
into the streams of the Euphrates."† Having also
rewarded his army with a hundred pieces of silver,
to each soldier, he thus stimulated them (when still
dissatisfied) to fight for greater spoil—" Riches are
the object of your desires ? those riches are in the
hands of the Persians, and the *spoils* of this fruitful country are proposed as the prize of your valour
and discipline."‡ The enemy being defeated after

* Gibbon, c. viii. v. i. p. 211.
† Ib. c. xxiv. v. ii. p. 361.
‡ Ib. p. 364.

6

an arduous conflict, "the *spoil* was such as might be expected from the riches and luxury of an oriental camp ; *large quantities of silver and gold*, splendid arms and trappings, and beds and tables of massy silver."*

When the Romans under Heraclius, ravaged Chaldea, " though much of the treasure had been removed from Destagered, and much had been expended, the *remaining wealth* appears to have *exceeded their hopes*, and even to have SATIATED their avarice."†

While the deeds of Julian and the words of Gibbon show how Chaldea was *spoiled*—how a *sword* continued to be on her *treasures*—and how, *year after year*, and age after age, there was *rumour on rumour*, and *violence in her land, and that all that spoil her would be* SATISFIED—more full illustrations remain to be given of the truth of the same prophetic word. And as a painter of great power may cope with another by drawing as closely to the life as he, though the features be different, so Gibbon's description of the sack of Ctesiphon, as previously he had described the sack and conflagration of Seleucia, (cities, each of which may aptly be called " the daughter of Babylon," having been, like it, the capital of Chaldea,) is written as if, by the most graphic representation of facts, he had been aspiring to rival Volney as an illustrator of Scripture prophecy. " The capital was taken by assault ; and the disorderly resistance of the people gave a keener edge to the *sabres* of the Moslems, who shouted with religious transport, ' This is the white palace of Chosroes ; this is the promise of the apostle of God.' The naked *robbers* of the desert were suddenly en-

---

* Gibbon, p. 369.   † Ibid.

riched beyond the measure of their hope or knowledge. Each chamber revealed a new *treasure*,
secreted with art, or ostentatiously displayed; the
gold and silver, the various wardrobes and precious
furniture, surpassed (says Abulfeda) the estimate of
fancy or numbers; and another historian defines the
untold and almost infinite mass by the fabulous
computation of three thousands of thousands of
thousands of pieces of gold. One of the apartments
of the palace was decorated with a carpet of silk
sixty cubits in length, and as many in breadth,
(90 feet); a paradise, or garden was depicted on
the ground; the flowers, fruits, and shrubs were
imitated by the figures of the *gold* embroidery, and
the colours of the *precious stones;* and the ample
square was encircled by a variegated and verdant
border. The rigid Omar *divided the prize* among
his brethren of Medina; the picture was destroyed;
but such was the intrinsic value of the materials, that
the share of Ali alone was sold for 20,000 drachms.
A mule that carried away the tiara and cuirass, the
belt and bracelets of Chosroes, was overtaken by the
pursuers; the gorgeous trophy was presented to the
commander of the faithful, and the gravest of the
companions condescended to smile when they beheld
the white beard, hairy arms, and uncouth figure of
the veteran who was invested with the *spoil* of the
great king."*

Recent evidence is not wanting to show, that,
wherever a *treasure* is to be found, a sword, in the
hand of a *fierce* enemy, is upon it, and spoliation has
not ceased in the land of Chaldea.

" On the west of Hillah, there are two towns, which,
in the eyes of the Persians and all the Shiites, are rendered sacred by the memory of two of the greatest

---

* Gibbon, c. li. pp. 111, 451.

martyrs of that sect. " These are Meshed Ali and
Meshed Housein, lately filled with riches, accumulated by the devotion of the Persians, but carried off
by the *ferocious* Wahabees to the middle of their deserts."*

And, after the incessant spoliation of ages, now
that *the end is come* of the treasures of Chaldea, the
earth itself fails not to disclose its *hidden treasures*, so
as to testify that they once were *abundant*. In proof
of this an instance may be given. At the ruins of
Hoomania, near to those of Ctesiphon, pieces of silver
having, (on the 5th of March 1812,) been accident-
ally discovered, edging out of the bank of the Tigris,
" on examination, there were found and brought
away," by persons sent for that purpose by the Pasha
of Bagdad's officers, " between six and seven hundred
ingots of silver, each measuring from one to one and
a half feet in length ; and an earthen jar, containing
upwards of two thousand Athenian coins, all of silver.
Many were purchased at the time by the late Mr.
Rich, formerly the East India Company's resident at
Bagdad, and are now in his valuable collection,
since bought by government, and deposited in the
British Museum."† Amidst the ruins of Ctesiphon
" the natives often pick up coins of gold, silver, and
copper, for which they always find a ready sale in
Bagdad. Indeed, some of the wealthy Turks and
Armenians, who are collecting for several French and
German consuls, hire people to go and search for
coins, medals, and antique gems ; and I am assured
they never return to their employers empty-handed,"‡
—as if *all who spoil Chaldea shall be satisfied*, till
even the ruins be spoiled unto the uttermost.

---

* Malte-Brun's Geogr. vol. ii. p. 119. Buckingham's Travels in Mesopotamia, v. ii. p. 246.
† Captain Mignan's Travels, p. 53.   ‡ Ibid. p. 74.

The past history of the land of the Chaldeans may be briefly closed in the language of prophecy; for the prophets, in their visions, saw it as it is; although historians knew not, even after its grandeur was partially gone, how to tell of its fertility, which they witnessed, and hope to be believed. Those who recorded *the word that the Lord spake against Babylon and against the land of the Chaldeans*, had no such fear, though two thousand four hundred years have elapsed since they described what is now only at last to be seen.

I will punish the land of the Chaldeans, and will make it perpetual desolations ; cut off the sower from Babylon, and him that handleth the sickle in the time of harvest. A drought is on her waters, and they shall be dried up. Behold the hindermost of the nations, a dry land and a desert. Her cities are a desolation, a dry land and a wilderness, a land where no man dwelleth, neither doth son of man pass thereby. I will send unto Babylon fanners that shall fan her, and empty her land. The land shall tremble and sorrow ; for every purpose of the Lord shall be performed against Babylon, to make the land of Babylon a desolation without an inhabitant. The land of the Chaldeans was to be made *perpetual*, or long continued *desolation.*—Ravaged and spoiled for ages, the Chaldees' excellency finally disappeared, and the land became desolate, as still it remains. Rauwolff, who passed through it in 1574, describes the country as bare, and " so dry and barren that it cannot be tilled."* And the most recent travellers all concur in describing it in similar terms.

The land of Babylon was to be fanned and emptied,

---

* Rauwolff's Travels, in Ray's Collection of Travels, 1693, p. 164.

—to be a dry land, a wilderness, and a desert, &c.—
On the one side, near to the site of Opis, " the country all around appears to be one wide desert of sandy
and barren soil, thinly scattered over with brushwood
and tufts of reedy grass."* On the other, between
Bussorah and Bagdad, " immediately on either bank
of the Tigris, is the *untrodden desert.* The absence
of all cultivation,—the sterile, arid, and wild character of the whole scene, formed a contrast to the rich
and delightful accounts delineated in Scripture. The
natives, in travelling over these *pathless deserts,* are
compelled to explore their way by the stars."† " The
face of the country is open and flat, presenting to the
eye one vast level plain where nothing is to be seen
but here and there a herd of half-wild camels. This
immense tract is very rarely diversified with any trees
of moderate growth, but is an immense wild bounded
only by the horizon."‡ In the intermediate region,
" the whole extent from the foot of the wall of Bagdad is a barren waste without a blade of vegetation of
any description ;" on leaving the gates, the traveller
has before him " the prospect of a bare *desert,*—a flat
and barren country."—" The whole country between
Bagdad and Hillah is a perfectly flat and (with the
exception of a few spots as you approach the latter
place) *uncultivated waste.*"§ " That it was at some former period in a far different state, is evident from the
number of canals by which it is traversed, now *dry*
and neglected ; and the quantity of heaps of earth
covered with fragments of brick and broken tiles, which
are seen in every direction,—the indisputable traces

---

* Buckingham's Travels in Mesopotamia, vol. ii. p. 155.
† Mignan's Travels, p. 5.
‡ Ibid. pp. 31, 32. Keppel's Nar. vol. i. p. 260. Bucking-
ham's Travels, p. 242. Kinnier's Memoirs of Persia, p. 279,
§ Rich's Memoir, p. 4.

of former population. At present the only inhabitants of the tract are the Sobeïde Arabs."* "Around,
as far as the eye can reach, is a *trackless desert*."†
"The abundance of the country has vanished as clean
away as if the 'besom of desolation' had swept it from
north to south; the whole land from the outskirts of
Babylon to the farthest stretch of sight lying a melancholy waste. *Not a habitable spot* appears for countless miles."‡ *The land of Babylon is desolate without
an inhabitant.* The Arabs traverse it; and every man
met with in the desert is looked on as an enemy.
Wild beasts have now their home in the land of Chaldea; but the traveller is less afraid of them,—even of
the lion,—then of "the wilder animal, the desert
Arab." The country is frequently "totally impassable." "Those splendid accounts of the Babylonian
lands, yielding crops of grain two or three hundred
fold, compared with the modern face of the country, afford a remarkable proof of the *singular desolation* to which it has been subjected. The canals at present can only be traced by their decayed
banks."§

"The soil of this desert," says Captain Mignan, who
traversed it on foot, and who, in a single day, crossed
forty water-courses, "consists of a hard clay, mixed
with sand, which at noon became so heated with the
sun's rays that I found it too hot to walk over it with
any degree of comfort. Those who have crossed those
desert wilds, are already acquainted with their dreary
tediousness even on horseback: what it is on foot they
can easily imagine."‖

* Transactions of the Literary Society, Bombay, vol. i.
pp. 123, 138. Captain Frederick on the State of Babylon.
 † Keppel's Nar. p. 87.
 ‡ Sir R. K. Porter's Travels in Babylonia, &c. vol. ii.
p. 285.
 § Mignan's Travels, p. 2.   ‖ Ibid. pp. 2, 31—34.

Where astronomers first registered eclipses, and marked the motions of the planetary bodies, the natives, as in the deserts of Africa, or as the mariner without a compass on the pathless ocean, can now direct their course only by the stars, over the pathless desert of Chaldea. Where cultivation reached its utmost height, and where two hundred fold was stated as the common produce, there is now one wide and uncultivated waste ; and *the sower and reaper are cut off from the land of Babylon.* Where abundant stores and treasures were laid up, and annually renewed and increased, *fanners* have *fanned*, and *spoilers* have *spoiled* them till they have *emptied* the land. Where labourers, shaded by palm-trees a hundred feet high, irrigated the fields till all was plentifully watered from numerous canals, the wanderer, without an object on which to fix his eye but " stinted and short-lived shrubs," can scarcely set his foot without pain, after the noon-day heat, on the " arid and parched ground," in plodding his weary way through *a desert, a dry land, and a wilderness.* Where there were crowded thoroughfares from city to city, there is now " silence and solitude ;" for the ancient *cities* of Chaldea are *desolations,—where no man dwelleth, neither doth any son of man pass thereby.**

* Sin has wrought desolation in Chaldea, as finally, if unrepented of, it must in any, and in every land. But justice shall yet dwell in the wilderness, and righteousness *remain* in the fruitful field. And—not in Judea alone, on the restoration and conversion of all the house of Israel, but throughout all nations, when enlightened by the word of God, and renewed by his Spirit, moved by whom the prophets spake,—the work of righteousness shall be peace ; and the effect of righteousness, quietness and assurance for ever, (Isa. xxxii. 15—17): And it is pleasing to pause for a moment, and to turn from the direful retrospect of sin, judgment, and desolation, which the past history of Chaldea holds up to view, to a word of Scripture, (one word, if rightly interpreted, is enough,) which, like a bright star

Her cities are desolations. The course of the Tigris through Babylonia, instead of being adorned, as of old, with cities and towns, is marked with the sites of " ancient ruins."* Sitace, Sabata, Narisa, Fuchera, Sendia, " no longer exist."† A succession of longitudinal mounds, crossed at right angles by others, mark the supposed site of Artemita, or Destagered. Its once luxuriant gardens are covered with grass ; and a higher mound distinguishes " the royal residence" from the ancient streets.‡ Extensive ridges and mounds (near to Houmania,) varying in height and extent, are seen branching in every di-

in the east, shines as the harbinger of a brighter day, after the long night of darkness which has rested on that land which was full of wickedness, and therefore has been *emptied* in judgment. And seemingly commencing convulsions, in the war and the trial of principles, throughout the wide world, that must come,—the rising " hurricane" which, controlled by the Lord, shall yet sweep every moral " pestilence" from the earth—seem in their beginning, to betoken, that the time may not be distant, when the effect of the vision shall be seen. *Then said I to the angel that talked with me*, (Zechariah v. 10, 11.) *whither do these bear the ephah? And he said unto me, To build it an house in the land of Shinar ; and it shall be established, and set there on its own base*,—in the *land* of Shinar, but it is not said, in the city of Babylon. Building, establishing, and setting, all appear to be significative of blessing—of reconstruction, on a new base, and not reducible to *heaps*—and though the previous vision be of judgment, he whose name is THE BRANCH, is immediately after spoken of ; and, in " building the temple of the Lord," his office is redemption. But, without a metaphor, it is said, and, without a doubt, it shall prove true—All the ends of the earth shall see the salvation of the Lord. The whole earth shall rejoice,—the *wilderness* and the *solitary places* shall be glad for them ; and the *desert* shall rejoice, and blossom as the rose.

* See Chart prefixed to Major Keppel's Narrative.

† Plan of the Environs of Babylon, &c. in Major Rennell's Geography of Herodotus, p. 335.

‡ Keppel's Narrative, v. i. p. 267.

rection."* A wall, with sixteen bastions, is the only
memorial of Apollonia.† The once magnificent Seleucia is now a scene of desolation. There is not a
single building, but the country is strewed for miles
with fragments of decayed buildings. "As far,"
says Major Keppel, "as the eye could reach, the horizon presented a broken line of mounds ; the whole
of this place was a desert flat."‡ On the opposite
bank of the Tigris, where Ctesiphon its rival stood,
besides fragments of walls and broken masses of brick-
work, and remains of vast structures encumbered
with heaps of earth, there is one magnificent monument of antiquity, "in a remarkably perfect state
of preservation," "a large and noble pile of building, the front of which presents to view a wall
three hundred feet in length, adorned with four
rows of arched recesses, with a central arch, in span
eighty-six feet, and above an hundred feet high, supported by walls sixteen feet thick, and leading to a hall
which extends to the depth of one hundred and fifty-
six feet," the width of the building.§ A great part
of the back wall, and of the roof, is broken down ; but
that which remains "still appears much larger than
Westminster Abbey."‖ It is supposed to have been
the lofty palace of Chosroes ; but there desolation now
reigns. "On the site of Ctesiphon, the smallest in-
sect under heaven would not find a single blade of
grass wherein to hide itself, nor one drop of water to
allay its thirst."¶ In the rear of the palace and
attached to it, are mounds two miles in circumference,
indicating the utter desolation of buildings, formed
to minister to luxury. But, in the words of Captain
Mignan, "such is the extent of the irregular mounds

---

* Mignan's Travels, p. 49.   † Keppel, p. 273.
‡ Keppel's Narrative, p. 125.   § Ibid. p. 130.
‖ Mignan's Travels, p. 79.   ¶ Buck. p. 441.

and hillocks that overspread the sites of these renowned cities, that it would occupy some months to
take the bearings and dimensions of each with accuracy."*

While the ancient *cities of Chaldea* are thus *desolate*, the sites of others cannot be discovered, or have
not been visited, as none pass thereby ; the more
modern cities, which flourished under the empire of
Califs, " are all in ruins."† The second Bagdad
has not indeed yet shared the fate of the first. And
Hillah,—a town of comparatively modern date, near
to the site of Babylon, but in the gardens of which
there is not the least vestige of ruins—yet exists.
But the former, " ransacked by massacre, devastation, and oppression, during several hundred years,"
has been " gradually reduced from being a rich and
powerful city to a state of comparative poverty, and
the feeblest means of defence."‡ And of the inhabitants of the latter, about eight or ten thousand, it
is said that " if any thing could identify the modern
inhabitants of Hillah as the descendants of the ancient Babylonians, it would be their extreme profligacy, for which they are notorious even amongst
their immoral neighbours."§ They give no sign of
repentance and reformation to warrant the hope that
judgment, so long continued upon others, will cease
from them ; or that they are the people that shall
escape. Twenty years have not passed since towns
in Chaldea have been ravaged and pillaged by the
Wahabees ; and so lately as 1823, the town of Shehre-
ban " was sacked and ruined by the Coords," and
reduced to desolation.‖ Indications of ruined cities,
whether of a remote or more recent period, abound
throughout the land. The process of destruction is

---

* Mignan's Travels, p. 81.   † Ibid. p. 82.
‡ Sir R. K. Porter's Travels, vol. ii. pp. 265, 266.
§ Keppel's Narrative, v. i. 182, 183. ‖ Ibid. pp. 272, 278.

4

still completing. Gardens which studded the banks
of the Tigris have very recently disappeared, and
mingled with the desert,—and concerning the *cities*
also of *Chaldea*, the word is true that they *are deso-
lutions.* For " the whole country is strewed over with
the debris of Grecian, Roman, and Arabian towns,
confounded in the same mass of rubbish."*

But while these lie in indiscriminate ruins, the
chief of the cities of Chaldea, the first in name and
in power that ever existed in the world, bears many
a defined mark of the judgments of heaven.

The progressive and predicted decline of Babylon
the Great, till it ceased to be a city, has already
been briefly detailed. About the beginning of the
Christian era a small portion of it was inhabited, and
the far greater part was cultivated.† It diminished
as Seleucia increased, and the latter became the
greater city. In the second century nothing but the
walls remained. It became gradually a great desert ;
and, in the fourth century, its walls, repaired for that
purpose, formed an enclosure for wild beasts, and
Babylon was converted into a field for the chase—a
hunting-place for the pastime of the Persian monarchs. The name and the remnant were cut off
from Babylon ; and there is a blank, during the interval of many ages, in the history of its mutilated
remains and of its mouldering decay. It remained
long in the possession of the Saracens ; and abundant evidence has since been given, that every feature of its prophesied desolation is now distinctly
visible—for the most ancient historians bore not a
clearer testimony to facts confirmatory of the prophecies relative to its first siege and capture by Cyrus,
than the latest travellers bear to the fulfilment of

---

* Malte-Brun's Geography, v. ii. p. 119.
† Diod. Sic. tom. ii. p. 35.

those which refer to its final and permanent ruin.
The identity of its site has been completely established.* And the truth of every general and every particular prediction is now so clearly demonstrated, that
a simple exhibition of the facts precludes the possibility of any cavil, and supersedes the necessity of any
reasoning on the subject.

It is not merely the general desolation of Babylon
—however much that alone would have surpassed all
human foresight,—which the Lord declared by the
mouth of his prophets. In their *vision*, they saw not
more clearly, nor defined more precisely, the future
history of Babylon, from the height of its glory to
the oblivion of its name, than they saw and depicted
fallen Babylon as now it lies, and as, in the nineteenth
century of the Christian era, it has, for the first time,
been fully described.† And now when *an end has
come upon Babylon*, after a long succession of ages
has wrought out its utter desolation, both the pen and
the pencil of travellers, who have traversed and inspected its ruins, must be combined, in order to delineate what the word of God, by the prophets, told
from the beginning that that end would be.

Truth ever scorns the discordant and encumbering
aid of error: but to diverge in the least from the
most precise facts, would here weaken and destroy the
argument; for the predictions correspond not closely
with any thing, except alone with the express and
literal reality. To swerve from it is, in the same

---

* Rennell's Geography of Herodotus, p. 349. Keppel's
Narrative, p. 171.

† Niebuhr, Ives, Irwin, Ottar, Evirs, Thevenot, Della
Valle, Texeira, Edrisi, Abulfeda, and Balbi, were consulted
by Major Rennell—to these may now be added—Mr. Rich,
Sir Robert Ker Porter, Captain Frederick, the Hon. Major
Keppel, Colonel Kinnier, Mr. Buckingham, and Captain
Mignan,—most of whom were accompanied by others.

degree, to vary from them: and any misrepresentation would be no less hurtful than iniquitous. But the actual fact renders any exaggeration impossible, and any fiction poor. Fancy could not have feigned a contrast more complete, nor a destruction greater than that which has come from the Almighty upon Babylon. And though the greatest city on which the sun ever shone be now a *desolate wilderness*, there is scarcely any spot on earth more clearly defined—and none could be more accurately delineated by the hands of a draftsman—than the scene of Babylon's desolation is set before us in the very words of the prophets; and no words could now be chosen like unto those, which, for two thousand five hundred years have been its "burden"—the burden which now it bears.

Such is the multiplicity of prophecies and the accumulation of facts, that the very abundance of evidence increases the difficulty of arranging, in a condensed form, and thus appropriating its specific fulfilment to each precise and separate prediction, and many of them may be viewed connectedly. All who have visited Babylon, concur in acknowledging or testifying that the desolation is exactly such as was foretold. They, in general, apply the more prominent predictions; and, in minute details, they sometimes unconsciously adopt, without any allusion or reference, the very words of inspiration.

Babylon is wholly desolate. It has become heaps —it is cut down to the ground—brought down to the grave—trodden on—uninhabited—its foundations fallen—its walls thrown down, and utterly broken—its loftiest edifices rolled down from the rocks—the golden city has ceased—the worms are spread under it, and the worms cover it, &c. There the Arabian pitches not his tent; there the shepherds make not their folds; but wild beasts of the desert lie there, and

SITE OF THE RUINS OF BABYLON

Engraved by permission, from a print in the Travels of Sir Robert Ker Porter.

Eng.ᵈ by W.H.Lizars

Babylon is fallen _ Isaiah XXI _ 9   I will sweep it with the besom
of destruction saith the Lord of Hosts _ Isaiah XIV. 23
Babylon shall become heaps without an inhabitant _ Jer LI. 37

PUBLISHED BY WAUGH & INNES, EDINBURGH.

their houses are full of doleful creatures, and owls dwell there, &c. It is a possession for the bittern, and a dwelling-place for dragons—a wilderness, a dry land and a desert—a burnt mountain—pools of water —spoiled—empty—nothing left—utterly destroyed —every one that goeth by it is astonished, &c.

Babylon shall become heaps. Babylon the glory of kingdoms is now the greatest of ruins. " Immense tumuli of temples, palaces, and human habitations of every description," are everywhere seen, and form " long and varied lines of ruins," which, in some places, " rather resemble natural hills than *mounds* which cover the remains of great and splendid edifices."* Those buildings which were once the labour of slaves and the pride of kings, are now mis-shapen heaps of rubbish. " The whole face of the country is covered with vestiges of building, in some places consisting of brick-walls surprisingly fresh, in others, merely a *vast succession of mounds* of rubbish, of such indeterminate figures, variety and extent, as to involve the person who should have formed any theory in inextricable confusion."† " Long mounds running from north to south, are crossed by others from east to west;" and are only distinguished by their form, direction, and number, from the decayed banks of canals. " The greater part of the mounds are certainly the remains of buildings, originally disposed in streets, and crossing each other at right angles."‡ The more distinct and prominent of these " heaps" are double, or lie in parallel lines, each exceeding twenty feet, and " are intersected by cross passages, in such a manner as to place beyond a doubt, the fact of their being rows of houses or streets fallen to decay."§ Such was the form of the streets of Baby-

* Porter's Travels, vol. ii. pp. 294, 297.
† Rich's Memoirs, p. 2.
‡ Buckingham's Travels in Mesopotamia, vol. ii. p. 298.
§ Ibid. p. 299.

lon, leading towards the gates ; and such are now the
lines of its heaps—" There are also, in some places,
two hollow channels, and three mounds, running parallel to each other for a considerable distance, the
central mound being, in such cases, a broader and
flatter mass than the other two, as if there had been
two streets going parallel to each other, the central
range of houses which divided them being twice the
size of the others, from their being double residences,
with a front and door of entrance to face each avenue."* " Irregular hillocks and mounds, *formed
over* masses of ruins, present at every step memorials
of the past."†

From the temple of Belus and the two royal palaces, to the streets of the city and single dwellings,
all have *become heaps ;* and the only difference or gradation now is from the vast and solid masses of ruins
which look like mountains, to the slight mound that
is scarcely elevated above the plain. *Babylon is fallen,*
literally FALLEN to such a degree that those who
stand on its site and look on numerous parallel mounds,
with a hollow space between, are sometimes at a loss
to distinguish between the remains of a street or a
canal, or to tell where the crowds frequented or where
the waters flowed. *Babylon is fallen ;* till its ruins
cannot fall lower than they lie. *It is cut down to the
ground. Her foundations are fallen ;* and the ruins
rest not on them. Its palaces, temples, streets and
houses, lie " *buried* in shapeless heaps."‡ And " the
view of Babylon," as taken from the spot, is truly a
picture of utter desolation, presenting its *heaps* to the
eye, and showing how, as if literally buried under
them, *Babylon is brought down to the grave.*

* Buckingham's Travels in Mesopotamia, vol. ii. p. 299.
† Mignan's Travels, vol. ii. p. 116.
‡ Porter's Travels, p. 294.

Cast her up as heaps. Mr. Rich, in describing a grand heap of ruins, the shape of which is nearly a square of seven hundred yards length and breadth, states that the workmen pierce into it in every direction, in search of bricks, " hollowing out deep ravines and pits, and *throwing up* the rubbish *in heaps* on the surface."* " The summit of the Kasr," (supposed to have been the lesser palace) is in like manner " covered with *heaps of rubbish.*"

Let nothing of her be left. " Vast heaps constitute *all that now remains* of ancient Babylon."† All its grandeur is departed ; all its treasures have been spoiled ; all its excellence has utterly vanished ; the very heaps are searched for bricks when nothing else can be found ; even these are *not left* wherever they can be taken away, and Babylon has for ages been " a quarry above ground," ready to the hand of every successive despoiler. Without the most remote allusion to this prophecy, Captain Mignan describes a mound attached to the palace, ninety yards in breadth by half that height, the whole of which is deeply furrowed in the same manner as the generality of the mounds. " The ground is extremely soft, and tiresome to walk over, and appears *completely exhausted* of all its building materials : *nothing now is left* save one towering hill, the earth of which is mixed with *fragments* of broken brick, red varnished pottery, tile, bitumen, mortar, glass, shells, and pieces of mother of pearl,"‡—worthless fragments, of no value to the poorest. *From thence shall she be taken—let nothing of her be left.* One traveller, towards the end of last century, passed over the site of ancient Babylon, without being conscious of having traversed it.§

* Rich's Memoirs, p. 22.   † Keppel's Narrative, p. 196.
‡ Mignan's Travels, pp. 190, 200.
§ Transactions of the Literary Society at Bombay, v. i. p. 130. Note Cunningham's Journey to India, 1785.

Babylon shall be pools of water. While the work-men *cast her up as heaps* in piling up the rubbish while excavating for bricks, that they may *take* them *from thence,* and that *nothing may be left ;* they la-bour more than trebly in the fulfilment of prophecy, for the numerous and deep excavations form *pools of water,* on the overflowing of the Euphrates, and, an-nually filled, they are not dried up throughout the year. " Deep cavities are also formed by the Arabs, when digging for hidden treasure."* " The ground is sometimes covered with *pools of water* in the hol-lows."†

Sit on the dust, sit on the ground, O daughter of the Chaldeans. The *surface* of the mounds, which form all that remains of Babylon, consists of decom-posed buildings, reduced to dust ; and over all the ancient streets and habitations, there is literally no-thing but the dust or the ground on which to sit.

Thy nakedness shall be uncovered. " Our path," says Captain Mignan, " lay through the great mass of ruined heaps on the site of ' shrunken Babylon.' And I am perfectly incapable of conveying an ade-quate idea of the dreary, lonely nakedness that appear-ed before me."‡

Sit thou silent, and get thee into darkness. There reigns throughout the ruins " a silence profound as the grave."§ Babylon is now a " silent scene, a su-blime solitude."||

It shall never be inhabited, nor dwelt in from genera-tion to generation. From Rauwolff's testimony it ap-pears that in the sixteenth century " there was not a

---

* Mignan's Travels, p. 213.
† Buckingham's Travels, vol. ii. p. 296. Keppel's Travels, vol. i. p. 125.
‡ Mignan's Travels, p. 116.
§ Porter's Travels, v. ii. p. 294. || Ib. p. 407.

house to be seen."* And now " the eye wanders over a *barren desert*, in which the ruins are nearly the only indication that it had ever been inhabited." " It is impossible," adds Major Keppel, " to behold this scene and not to be reminded how exactly the predictions of Isaiah and Jeremiah have been fulfilled, even in the appearance Babylon was doomed to present, that *she should never be inhabited*; that the ' Arabian should not pitch his tent there ;' that she should ' become heaps ;' that her cities should be ' a desolation, a dry land, and a wilderness.' "† " Babylon is spurned alike by the heel of the Ottomans, the Israelites and the sons of Ishmael."‡ It is " a *tenantless* and desolate metropolis."§ *It shall not be inhabited, but wholly desolate.*

Neither shall the Arabian pitch tent there ; neither shall the shepherds make their folds there. It was prophesied of Ammon that it should be a stable for camels and a couching-place for flocks ; and of Philistia, that it should be cottages for shepherds, and a pasture of flocks. But Babylon was to be visited with a far greater desolation, and to become unfit or unsuiting even for such a purpose. And that neither a tent would be pitched there, even by an Arab, nor a fold made by a shepherd, implies the last degree of solitude and desolation. " It is common in these parts for shepherds to make use of ruined edifices to shelter their flocks in."‖ But Babylon is an exception. Instead of taking the bricks *from thence*, the shepherd might with facility erect a defence from wild beasts, and make a fold for his flock amidst the heaps of Babylon ; and the Arab who fearlessly traverses it by day, might pitch his tent by night. But neither the one nor the other could now be persuaded to re-

* Porter's Travels, v. ii. p. 174.
† Keppel's Nar. vol. i. p. 197. ‡ Mignan's Travels, p. 108.
§ Ibid. 234.   ‖ Ibid. p. 235.

main a single night among the ruins. The superstitious dread of evil spirits, far more than the natural terror of the wild beasts, effectually prevents
them. Captain Mignan was accompanied by six
Arabs, completely armed, but he " could not induce
them to remain towards night, from the apprehension
of evil spirits. It is impossible to eradicate this idea
from the minds of these people, who are very deeply
imbued with superstition." And when the sun sunk
behind the Mujelibé, and the moon would have still
lighted his way among the ruins, it was with infinite
regret that he obeyed " *the summons of his guides.*"*
" *All the people of the country assert* that it is extremely dangerous to *approach* this mound after night-
fall, on account of the multitude of evil spirits by
which it is haunted."† *Neither shall the Arabian
pitch tent there ; neither shall the shepherds make
their folds there.* But

*Wild beasts of the desert shall lie there, and their
houses shall be full of doleful creatures ; and owls shall
dwell there, and satyrs* (goats) *shall dance there, &c.*
" There are many dens of wild beasts in various parts.
There are quantities of porcupine quills" (kephud ?).
And while the lower excavations are often pools of
water, " in most of the cavities are numbers of bats
and *owls.*"‡ " These souterrains (caverns) over which
the chambers of majesty may have been spread, are
now the refuge of jackalls and other savage animals.
The mouths of their entrances are strewed with the
bones of sheep and *goats ;* and the loathsome smell
that issues from most of them is sufficient warning
not to proceed into the den."§ The king of the forest
now ranges over the site of that Babylon which Nebuchadnezzar built for his own glory. And the tem-

---

* Travels, pp. 201, 235.

† Rich's Mem. p. 27.   Buckingham's Travels, v. ii. p. 397.

‡ Ibid. p. 30.   § Sir R. K. Porter's Travels, v. ii. p. 342.

ple of Belus, the greatest work of man, is now like
unto a natural den of lions. " Two or three majestic lions" were seen upon its heights, by Sir Robert
Ker Porter, as he was approaching it ; and " the
broad prints of their feet were left plain in the clayey
soil."* Major Keppel saw there a similar foot-print
of a lion. It is also the unmolested retreat of jackalls, hyenas, and other noxious animals.† Wild
beasts are " numerous" at the *Mujelibé*, as well as
on *Birs Nimrood.* " The mound was full of large
holes ; we entered some of them, and found them
strewed with the carcasses and skeletons of animals recently killed. The ordure of wild beasts was so
strong that prudence got the better of curiosity, for
we had no doubt as to the savage nature of the inhabitants. Our guides, indeed, told us that all the
ruins abounded in lions and other wild beasts ; so literally has the divine prediction been fulfilled, that
wild beasts of the desert should lie there, and their
houses be full of doleful creatures ; that the wild beast
of the islands should cry in their desolate houses."‡

*The sea is come upon Babylon. She is covered with
the multitude of the waves thereof.* The traces of the
western bank of the Euphrates are now no longer dis-
cernible. The river overflows unrestrained ; and the
very ruins, " with every appearance of the embankment," have been swept away. " The ground there
is low and marshy, and presents not the slightest vestige of former buildings, of any description whatever."§
" Morasses and ponds tracked the ground in various
parts. For a long time after the general subsiding of
the Euphrates, great part of this plain is little better

* Sir R. K. Porter's Travels, p. 387.
† Kinnier's Memoirs, p. 279.
‡ Keppel's Narrative, vol. i. pp. 179, 180.
§ Buckingham's Travels, vol. ii. p. 278.

than a swamp," &c.* "The ruins of Babylon are then *inundated*, so as to render many parts of them inaccessible, by converting the vallies among them into morasses."† But while Babylon *is thus covered with the multitude of waves and the waters come upon it*, yet, in striking contrast and seeming contradiction to such a feature of desolation, (like the formation of *pools of water*, from the *casting up of heaps*) at all times the elevated sun-burnt ruins, which the waters do not overflow, and generally throughout the year, the "dry waste and parched and burning plain,"‡ on which the heaps of Babylon lie, equally prove that it is *a desert, a dry land, and a wilderness*. One part, even on the western side of the river, is "low and *marshy*, and another an *arid* desert."§

It shall never be inhabited. It shall be utterly desolate. "Ruins composed, like those of Babylon, of heaps of rubbish impregnated with nitre, cannot be cultivated."‖ "The decomposing materials of a Babylonian structure doom the earth on which they perish to lasting sterility.—On this part of the plain, both where traces of buildings were left, and where none had stood, all seemed equally *naked* of vegetation; the whole ground appearing as if it had been washed over and over again, by the coming and receding waters, till every bit of genial soil was swept away; its half-clay, half-sandy surface being left in ridgy streaks, like what is often seen on the flat shores of the sea after the retreating of the tide."¶ Babylon, which in its pride did say, I shall be a lady for ever, is no more called the lady of kingdoms, but is *desolate for ever*.

* Sir R. K. Porter's Travels, vol. ii. pp. 389, 390.
† Rich's Memoir, p. 13.
‡ Buckingham's Travels, vol. ii. pp. 302, 305.
§ Mignan's Travels, 139, Plan. ‖ Rich's Memoir, p. 16.
¶ Sir R. K. Porter's Travels, vol. ii. p. 392.

Bel boweth down. The temple of Belus or Baal, here evidently spoken of, was a stadium, or furlong, in height, computed by Major Rennell at five hundred, and by Prideaux at six hundred feet. By the lowest computation it was higher than the greatest of the pyramids. The *highest* of the heaps which now constitute fallen Babylon, is the Birs Nimrood, generally supposed to have been the temple of Belus. The heap occupies a larger space of ground than that on which the temple stood, having spread, in falling down, beyond its original base. It rests not now upon its ancient foundations, but lies upon the earth, an enormous mass of ruin. "At first sight it presents the appearance of a hill, with a castle at the top,"[*] so as not only to deceive the eye in beholding it at a distance, or in looking on its picture ; but, "incredible as it may seem, the ruins on the summit of it are actually those spoken of by Pere Emanuel, who takes no sort of notice of the prodigious mound on which they are elevated. It is almost needless to observe, that the whole of the mound is itself a ruin ;"[†] and it is altogether needless to add another word, to show that it is *bowed down*, as may be seen by the sketch here inserted, of the comparative ancient and modern height annexed to the plan of Birs Nimrood, in Sir Robert K. Porter's Travels.[‡]

[*] Mignan's Travels, p. 192.   [†] Rich's Memoir, p. 37.
[‡] Vol. ii. p. 323.

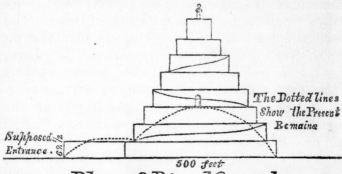

Elevation of Birs Nimrood (North face) according to Strabo and Herodotus

The Dotted lines Show the Present Remains

Supposed Entrance.

500 feet

Plan of Birs Nimrood

Bel is confounded. Originally constructed of eight successive towers, one rising above another, it is now consolidated into one irregular hill, presenting a different aspect, and of different altitudes on every side, —a confused and misshapen mass. " The eastern face presents two stages of hill ; the first showing an elevation of about sixty feet cloven in the middle into a deep ravine, and intersected in all directions by furrows channelled there by the descending rains of succeeding ages. The summit of this first stage stretches in rather a flattened sweep to the base of the second ascent, which springs out of the first in a steep and abrupt conical form, terminated on the top by a solitary standing fragment of brick-work, like the ruin of a tower. From the foundation of the whole pile to the base of this piece of ruin, measures about two hundred feet ; and from the bottom of the ruin to its shattered

Eng.^d by Wm Lizars

Bel (the temple of Belus) boweth down _ Isaiah XLVI. 1

Bel is confounded _ Jer L. 2

I will roll thee down from the rocks & make thee a burnt mountain _ Jer LI. 25

top, are thirty-five feet. On the western side, the entire mass rises at once from the plain in one stupendous, though irregular, pyramidal hill, broken, in the slopes of its sweeping acclivities, by the devastations of time and rougher destruction. The southern and northern fronts are particularly abrupt."* Such, and so *confounded* is now the temple of Belus.

I will stretch out mine hand upon thee, and roll thee down from the rocks, and will make thee a burnt-mountain. On the summit of the hill are " immense fragments of brick-work of no determinate figures, tumbled together, and converted into solid vitrified masses."† " Some of these huge fragments measured twelve feet in height, by twenty-four in circumference ; and from the circumstance of the standing brick-work having remained in a perfect state, the change exhibited in these is only accountable from their having been exposed to the *fiercest fire, or rather, scathed by lightning.*"‡ " They are completely molten—a strong presumption that fire was used in the destruction of the tower, which in parts resembles what the Scriptures prophesied it should become, ' a burnt mountain.' In the denunciation respecting Babylon, fire is particularly mentioned as an agent against it. To this Jeremiah evidently alludes, when he says that it should be, ' as when God overthrew Sodom and Gomorrah,' on which cities it is said, ' the Lord rained brimstone and fire.'—' Her high gates shall be burned with fire, and the people shall labour in vain, and the folk in the fire, and they shall be weary.' "§ " In many of these immense unshapen masses, might be traced the gradual effects of the

---

* Sir R. K. Porter's Travels, vol. ii. p. 310.
† Rich's Memoir, p. 36.
‡ Mignan's Travels, p. 207.
§ Keppel's Narrative, pp. 194, 195.

consuming power, which had produced so remarkable
an appearance ; exhibiting parts burnt to that variegated dark hue, seen in the vitrified matter lying
about in glass manufactories ; while, through the
whole of these awful testimonies of the fire (whatever
fire it was !) which, doubtless, hurled them from their
original elevation," *(I will roll thee down from the
rocks,)* "the regular lines of the cement are visible,
and so hardened in common with the bricks, that
when the masses are struck they ring like glass. On
examining the base of the standing wall, contiguous
to these huge transmuted substances, it is found tolerably free from any similar changes, in short, quite
in its original state ; hence," continues Sir Robert Ker
Porter, " I draw the conclusion, that the consuming
power acted from above, and that the scattered ruin
fell from some higher point than the summit of the
present standing fragment. The heat of the fire
which produced such amazing effects, must have burned with the force of the strongest furnace ; and from
the general appearance of the cleft in the wall, and
these vitrified masses, I should be induced to attribute
the catastrophe to lightning from heaven. Ruins,
by the explosion of any combustible matter, would
have exhibited very different appearances."*

" The fallen masses bear evident proof of the operation of fire having been continued on them, as well
after they were broken down as before, since every
part of their surface has been so equally exposed to
it, that many of them have acquired a rounded form,
and in none can the place of separation from its adjoining one be traced by any appearance of superior
freshness, or any exemption from the influence of the
destroying flame."†

* Sir Robert Ker Porter's Travels, vol. ii. pp. 312, 313.
† Buckingham's Travels, vol. ii. p. 375.

WATER GAP
Marina Pa

The high gates of the temple of Belus, which were standing in the time of Herodotus, have been *burnt with fire;* the vitrified masses which fell when *Bel bowed down,* rest on the top of its stupendous ruins. *The hand of the Lord has been stretched upon it; it has been rolled down from the rocks, and has been made a burnt mountain,*—of which it was farther prophesied,

They shall not take of thee a stone for a corner, nor a stone for foundations, but thou shalt be desolate for ever, saith the Lord. The old wastes of Zion shall be built; its former desolations shall be raised up; and Jerusalem shall be inhabited again in her own place, even in Jerusalem. But it shall not be with Bel as with Zion, nor with Babylon as with Jerusalem. For as the " heaps of rubbish, impregnated with nitre," which cover the site of Babylon, " cannot be cultivated,"* so the vitrified masses on the summit of Birs Nimrood cannot be rebuilt. Though still they be of the hardest substance, and indestructible by the elements, and though once they formed the highest pinnacles of Belus, yet incapable of being hewn into any regular form, they neither are, nor can now be taken *for a corner or for foundations.* And the bricks on the solid fragments of wall, which rest on the summit, though neither scathed nor molten, are so firmly cemented, that, according to Mr. Rich, " it is nearly impossible to detach any of them whole,"† or as Captain Mignan still more forcibly states, " they are so firmly cemented, that it is utterly impossible to detach any of them."‡ " My most violent attempts," says Sir Robert Ker Porter, " could not separate them,"§ and Mr. Buckingham, in assigning reasons for lessening the wonder at the total dis-

* Rich's Memoir, p. 16.   † Ibid. p. 36.
‡ Mignan's Travels, p. 206.   § Travels, vol. ii. p. 311.

appearance of the walls at this distant period, and
speaking of the Birs Nimrood generally, observes,
" that the burnt bricks (the only ones sought after)
which are found in the Mujelibé, the Kasr, and the
Birs Nimrood, the only three *great monuments* in
which there are any traces of their having been used,
are so difficult, in the two last indeed so impossible, to
be extracted whole, from the tenacity of the cement in
which they are laid, that they could never have been
resorted to while any considerable portion of the walls
existed to furnish an easier supply ; even now, though
some portion of the mounds on the eastern bank of
the river" (the Birs is on the western side) " are occasionally dug into for bricks, they are not extracted
without a comparatively great expense, and very few
of them whole, in proportion to the great number of
fragments that come up with them."* Around the
tower there is not a single whole brick to be seen.†

These united testimonies, given without allusion
to the prediction, afford a better than any conjectural
commentary, such as previously was given without
reference to these facts.

While of Babylon, in general, it is said that it
would be *taken from thence ;* and while, in many
places *nothing is left*, yet, of the *burnt mountain*,
which forms an accumulation of ruins enough in magnitude to build a city, men do not take a stone for
foundations nor a stone for a corner. Having undergone the action of the fiercest fire, and being completely molten, the masses on the summit of Bel, on
which the hand of the Lord has been stretched, cannot be reduced into any other form or substance, nor
be built up again by the hand of man. And the
tower of Babel, afterwards the temple of Belus, which

* Buckingham's Travels, vol. ii. p. 332.
† Porter's Travels, vol. ii. p. 329.

witnessed the first dispersion of mankind, shall itself
be witnessed by the latest generation, even as now it
stands, *desolate for ever*,—an indestructible monument of human pride and folly, and of divine judgment and truth. The greatest of the ruins, as once
of the edifices of Babylon, is rolled down into a vast,
indiscriminate, cloven, confounded, useless, and
blasted mass, from which fragments might be hurled
with as little injury to the ruined heap, as from a
bare and rocky mountain's side. Such is the triumph
of the word of the living God over the proudest of the
temples of Baal.

Merodach is broken in pieces. Merodach was a
name or a title common to the princes and kings of
Babylon, of which, in the brief Scriptural references
to their history, two instances are recorded, viz. Me-
rodach-baladan the son of Baladan, king of Babylon,
who exercised the office of government, and Evil-
Merodach who lived in the days of Jeremiah. From
Merodach being here associated with Bel, or the
temple of Belus, and from the similarity of their
judgments—the one *bowed down* and *confounded*, and
the other *broken in pieces*—it may reasonably be inferred that some other famous Babylonian building
is here also denoted ; while, at the same time, the
express identity of the name with that of the kings of
Babylon, and even with Evil-Merodach, then residing there, it may with equal reason be inferred that,
under the name of Merodach, the palace is spoken of
by the prophet. And next to the idolatrous temple,
as the seat of false worship which corrupted and destroyed the nations, it may well be imagined that the
royal residence of the despot who oppressed the people
of Israel, and made the earth to tremble, would be
selected as the marked object of the righteous judgments of God. And secondary only to the Birs Nimrood, in the greatness of its ruins, is the Mujelibé,

or Makloube, generally understood and described by travellers as the remains of the chief palaces of Babylon.

The palace of the king of Babylon almost vied with the great temple of their God. And there is now some controversy, in which of the principal mountainous heaps the one or the other lies buried. But the *utter desolation* of both leaves no room for any debate on the question,—which of the twain is *bowed down and confounded*, and which of them is *broken in pieces*.

The two palaces, or castles, of Babylon were strongly fortified. And the larger was surrounded by three walls of great extent.* When the city was suddenly taken by Demetrius, he seized on one of the castles by surprise, and displaced its garrison by seven thousand of his own troops, whom he stationed within it.† Of the other he could not make himself master. Their extent and strength, at a period of three hundred years after the delivery of the prophecy, are thus sufficiently demonstrated. The solidity of the structure of the greater, as well as of the lesser palace, might have warranted the belief of its unbroken durability for ages. And never was there a building whose splendour and magnificence were in greater contrast to its present desolation. The vestiges of the walls which surrounded it are still to be seen, and serve with other circumstances to identify it with the Mujelibé, as the name Merodach is identified with the palace. *It is broken in pieces*, and hence its name Mujelibé, signifying overturned, or turned upside down. Its circumference is about half a mile; its height one hundred and forty feet. But it is " a mass of confusion, none of its members being distinguish-

---

* Diodor. Sic. lib. ii.   Herod. lib. i. c. 181.
† Plutarch's Life of Demetrius.

able."* The existence of chambers, passages, and cellars, of different forms and sizes, and built of different materials, has been fully ascertained.† It is the receptacle of wild beasts, and full of doleful creatures: wild beasts cry in the desolate houses, and *dragons in the pleasant palaces*—"venomous reptiles being very numerous throughout the ruins."‡ "All the sides are worn into furrows by the weather, and in some places where several channels of rain have united together, these furrows are of great depth, and penetrate a considerable way into the mound."§ "The *sides* of the ruin exhibit *hollows* worn partly by the weather."‖ *It is brought down to the grave, to the sides of the* PIT.

They that see thee shall narrowly look upon thee, and consider thee, saying, is this the man that made the earth to tremble, that did shake kingdoms? Narrowly to look on and to consider even the view of the Mujelibé, is to see what the palace of Babylon, in which kings, proud as "Lucifer," boasted of exalting themselves above the "stars of God," has now become, and how, cut down to the ground, it is *broken in pieces.*¶

* Della Valle. Buckingham's Travels, vol. ii. p. 273.
† Ibid. p. 274.   ‡ Mignan's Travels, p. 168.
§ Rich's Memoir, p. 29.   ‖ Mignan's Travels, p. 167.
¶ By the kindness of Sir Robert Ker Porter's family, in his absence abroad, the author was presented with the original drawings of the Birs Nimrood and Mujelibé, for engravings, as here inserted. His *Travels in Persia, Babylonia, &c.* contain four views of each, which show how, on every side, they are *bowed down and broken in pieces.* Small engravings of them are also inserted in *Mines de l' Orient, Vienne;* in Rich's Memoirs on the Ruins of Babylon, and in Mr. Buckingham's Travels. There is a view of each in Captain Mignan's Travels. The curious reader may contrast the Mujelibé with Martin's splendid picture of "Belshazzar's Feast." The place, no longer a palace, is the same Every child is familiar with the common picture of the temple of Belus, the ancient magnificence of which could no:

" On pacing over the loose stones and fragments
of brick-work which lay scattered through the immense fabric, and surveying the sublimity of the
ruins," says Captain Mignan, " I naturally recurred
to the time when these walls stood proudly in their
original splendour,—when the halls were the scenes
of festive magnificence, and when they resounded to
the voices of those whom death has long since swept
from the earth.   This very pile was once the seat of
luxury and vice ; now abandoned to decay, and exhibiting a melancholy instance of the retribution of
heaven.   It stands alone ;—the solitary habitation of
the goat-herd marks not the forsaken site."* *Thy
pomp is brought down to the grave, and the noise of
thy viols ; the worms are spread under thee, and the
worms cover thee.*

*Thou art cast out of thy grave like an abominable
branch, and as the raiment of those that are slain,
thrust through with a sword, that go down to the stones
of the pit ; as a carcase trodden under feet.* " Several
deep excavations have been made in different places,
into the sides of the Mujelibé ; some probably by the
wearing of the seasons ; but many others have been
dug by the rapacity of the Turks, tearing up its
bowels in search of hidden treasure,"—*as if the palace of Babylon were cast out of its grave.* " Several *penetrate very far* into the body of the structure,"
till it has become *as the raiment of those that are
slain, thrust through with a sword.* " And some it
is likely have never yet been explored, the *wild beasts
of the desert* literally keeping guard over them."†

well be exaggerated, any more than the faintest resemblance
to it could be recognised in what it now is—the Birs Nimrood.

  * Mignan's Travels, pp. 172, 173.
  † Sir R. K. Porter's Travels, vol. ii. p. 342.

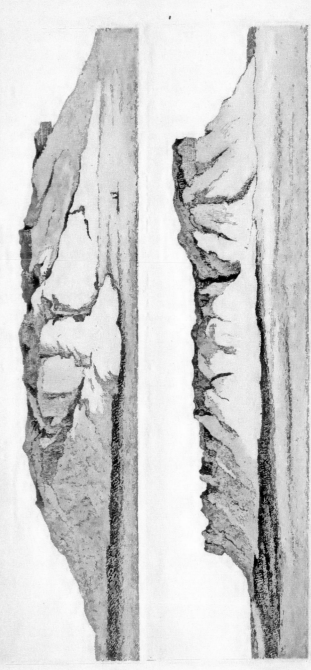

Engravd by W.H. Lizars

Merodach (the palace) is broken in pieces ——— for i. 2

Thy pomp is brought down to the grave &c.

Thou shalt be brought down to the sides of the pit.   Isa. XIV. 11.15

PUBLISHED BY WAUGH & INNES EDINBURGH

" The mound was full of large holes"*—*thrust
through.*

Near to the Mujelibé, on the supposed site of the
hanging gardens which were situated within the walls
of the palace, " the ruins are so *perforated,* in consequence of the digging for bricks, that the original
design is entirely lost. All that could favour any
conjecture of gardens built on terraces, are two *subterranean* passages.—There can be no doubt that both
passages are of vast extent, they are lined with bricks
laid in with bitumen and *covered over with large
masses of stone.* This is nearly the only place where
stone is observable."† Arches built upon arches raised the hanging gardens from terrace to terrace, till
the highest was on a level with the top of the city
walls. Now they *are cast out like an abominable
branch*—and *subterranean* passages are disclosed,—
down to the stones of the pit.

As a carcase trodden under feet. The streets of
Babylon were parallel, crossed by others at right
angles, and abounded with houses three and four
stories high ;‡ and none can now traverse the site of
Babylon, or find any other path, without *treading
them under foot.* The traveller directs his course to
the highest mounds ; and there are none, whether
temples or palaces, that are not *trodden on.* The
Mujelibé " rises in a steep ascent, *over which* the
passengers can only go up by the winding paths *worn*
by frequent visits to the ruined edifice."§

*Her idols are confounded, her images are broken
in pieces : all the graven images of her gods he hath
broken unto the ground.* " This place (says Beau-

---

* Keppel's Travels, vol. i. p. 179.
† Keppel's Travels, vol. i. p. 205.
‡ Herod. lib. i. c. 180.
§ Buckingham's Travels, vol. ii. p. 258.

champ, quoted by Major Rennell), and the mount of Babel, are commonly called by the Arabs Makloube, that is, turned *topsy-turvy.* I was informed by the master mason, employed to dig for bricks, that the places from which he procured them were large thick walls, and sometimes chambers. He has frequently found earthen vessels, *engraved marbles,* and about eight years ago, a *statue* as large as life, which he *threw among the rubbish.* On one wall of the chamber, he found the figure of a cow, and of the sun and moon, formed of varnished bricks. Sometimes *idols* of clay are found, representing human figures."* " Small figures of brass or copper are found at Babylon."† " Bronze antiquities, generally much corroded with rust, but exhibiting small figures of men and animals, are *often* found among the ruins."‡

The broad walls of Babylon shall be utterly broken. They were so broad, that, as ancient historians relate, six chariots could be driven on them abreast ; or a chariot and four horses might pass and turn. They existed, as walls, for more than a thousand years after the prophecy was delivered ; and long after the sentence of utter destruction had gone forth against them, they were numbered among " the seven wonders of the world." And what can be more wonderful now, or what could have been more inconceivable by man, when Babylon was in its strength and glory, than that the broad walls of Babylon should be so utterly broken, that it cannot be determined with certainty that even the slightest vestige of them exists ?

" All accounts agree," says Mr. Rich, " in the height of the walls, which was fifty cubits, having been reduced to these dimensions from the prodigious

---

* Rennell's Geography of Herodotus, p. 365.
† Rich's Second Memoir, p. 58.
‡ Mignan's Travels, p. 229.

height of three hundred and fifty feet," (formerly
stated, by the lowest computation of the length of the
cubit, at three hundred feet,) " by Darius Hystaspes,
after the rebellion of the town, in order to render it
less defensible. I have not been fortunate enough to
discover the *least trace* of them in *any part* of the
ruins at Hillah ; which is rather an unaccountable
circumstance, considering that they survived the final
ruin of the town, long after which they served as an
enclosure for a park ; in which comparatively perfect
state St. Jerome informs us they remained in his
time."*

In the sixteenth century they were seen for the last
time by an European traveller, (so far as the author
has been able to trace,) before they were finally so
utterly broken as totally to disappear. And it is interesting to mark both the time and the manner in
which the walls of Babylon, like the city of which
they were the impregnable yet unavailing defence,
were brought down to the grave, to be seen no more.

" The mean while," as Rauwolff describes them,
" when we were lodged there, I considered and viewed this ascent, and found that there were two behind
one another," (Herodotus states that there was both
an inner, or inferior, and outer wall) " distinguished
by a ditch, and extending themselves like unto two
parallel *walls* a great way about, and that they were
open in some places, where one might go through like
gates ; wherefore I believe that they were the wall of
the old town that went about them; and that the places
where they were open have been anciently the gates
(whereof there were one hundred) of that town. And
this the rather because I saw in some places under the
sand (wherewith the two ascents were *almost covered)*
the *old wall* plainly appear."†

* Rich's Memoirs, pp. 43, 44.
† Ray's Collection of Travels, pp. 177, 178.

The cities of Seleucia, Ctesiphon, Destagered, Kufa, and anciently many others in the vicinity, together with the more modern towns of Mesched Ali, Mesched Hussein, and Hillah, " with towns, villages and caravansaries without number,"* have, in all probability, been chiefly built out of the walls of Babylon. Like the city, the walls have been *taken from thence*, till none of them are *left*. The rains of many hundred years, and the waters coming upon them annually by the overflowing of the Euphrates, have also, in all likelihood, washed down the dust and rubbish from the broken and dilapidated walls into the ditch from which they were originally taken, till at last the sand of the parched desert has smoothed them into a plain, and added the place where they stood to the wilderness, so that the *broad walls of Babylon are utterly broken*. And now, as the subjoined evidence, suppletory of what has already been adduced, fully proves, —it may verily be said that the loftiest walls ever built by man, as well as the " greatest city on which the sun ever shone," which these walls surrounded, and the most fertile of countries, of which Babylon the great was the capital and the glory,—have all been *swept by the Lord of Hosts with the besom of destruction.*

A chapter of sixty pages in length, of Mr. Buckingham's Travels in Mesopotamia, is entitled, "Search after the walls of Babylon." After a long and fruitless search, he discovered on the eastern boundary of the ruins, on the *summit* of an *oval mound* from seventy to eighty feet in height, and from three to four hundred feet in circumference, " a mass of solid wall, about thirty feet in length, by twelve or fifteen in thickness, yet evidently once of much greater dimensions each way, the work being, in its present state,

* Sir R. K. Porter's Travels, vol. ii. p. 338.

broken and incomplete *in every part :*"* and this heap
of ruin and fragment of wall he conjectured to be a
part—the only part, if such it be, that can be discovered—of the walls of Babylon, *so utterly* are *they
broken.* Beyond this there is not even a pretension
to the discovery of any part of them.

Captain Frederick, of whose journey it was the
" principal object to search for the remains of the wall
and ditch that had compassed Babylon," states, that
" neither of these have been seen by any modern traveller. All my inquiries among the Arabs," he adds,
" on this subject, completely failed in producing the
smallest effect. Within the space of twenty-one miles
in length, along the banks of the Euphrates, and
twelve miles across it in breadth, I was unable to perceive any thing that could admit of my imagining
that either a wall or a ditch had existed within this
extensive area. If any remains do exist of the walls,
they must have been of greater circumference than is
allowed by modern geographers. I may possibly have
been deceived ; but I spared no pains to prevent it.
I never was employed in riding and walking less than
eight hours for six successive days, and upwards of
twelve on the seventh."†

Major Keppel relates, that he and the party who
accompanied him, " in common with other travellers,
had totally failed in discovering any trace of the city
walls," and he adds, " the divine predictions against
Babylon have been so literally fulfilled in the appearance of the ruins, that I am disposed to give the fullest
signification to the words of Jeremiah,—*the broad
walls of Babylon shall be utterly broken.*"‡

Babylon shall be an astonishment—Every one that

---

* Buckingham's Travels, vol. ii. pp. 306, 307.

† Transactions of the Literary Society, Bombay, vol. i.
pp. 130, 131.

‡ Keppel's Narrative, vol. i. p. 175. Jer. li. 58.

goeth by Babylon shall be astonished. It is impossible to think on what Babylon was, and to be an eye-witness of what it is, without *astonishment.* On first entering its ruins, Sir Robert Ker Porter thus expresses his feelings, " I could not but feel an indescribable awe in thus passing, as it were, into the gates of fallen Babylon."* " I cannot pourtray," says Captain Mignan, " the overpowering sensation of reverential awe that possessed my mind, while contemplating the extent and magnitude of ruin and devastation on every side."†

How is the hammer of the whole earth cut asunder! How is Babylon become a desolation among the nations!—The following interesting description has lately been given from the spot. After speaking of the ruined embankment, divided and subdivided again and again, like a sort of tangled net-work, over the apparently interminable ground—of large and wide-spreading morasses—of ancient foundations—and of chains of undulated heaps—Sir Robert Ker Porter emphatically adds :—" The whole view was particularly solemn. The majestic stream of the Euphrates, wandering in solitude, like a pilgrim monarch through the silent ruins of his devastated kingdom, still appeared a noble river under all the disadvantages of its desert-tracked course. Its banks were hoary with reeds ; and the grey osier willows were yet there on which the captives of Israel hung up their harps, and, while Jerusalem was not, refused to be comforted. But how has the rest of the scene changed since then! At that time those broken hills were palaces—those long undulating mounds, streets—this vast solitude filled with the busy subjects of the proud daughter of the east.—Now wasted with misery, her *habitations are not to be*

* Sir Robert Ker Porter's Travels, vol. ii. p. 294.
† Mignan's Travels, p. 117.

found—and for herself, *the worm is spread over her.**

From palaces converted into broken hills ;—from streets to long lines of heaps ;—from the throne of the world to sitting on the dust ;—from the hum of mighty Babylon to the death-like silence that rests upon the grave to which it is brought down ;—from the great storehouse of the world, where treasures were gathered from every quarter, and the prison-house of the captive Jews, where, not loosed to return homewards, they served in a hard bondage, to Babylon the spoil of many nations, itself taken from thence, and nothing left ;—from a vast metropolis, the place of palaces and the glory of kingdoms, whither multitudes ever flowed, to a dreaded and shunned spot, not inhabited nor dwelt in from generation to generation, where even the Arabian, though the son of the desert, pitches not his tent, and where the shepherds make not their folds ;—from the treasures of darkness, and hidden riches of secret places, to the taking away of bricks, and to an uncovered nakedness ;—from making the earth to tremble, and shaking kingdoms, to being cast out of the grave like an abominable branch ;—from the many nations and great kings from the coasts of the earth, that have so often come up against Babylon, to the workmen that still cast her up as heaps, and add to the number of pools in the ruins ;—from the immense artificial lake, many miles in circumference, by means of which the annual rising of the Euphrates was regulated and restrained, to these pools of water, a few yards round, dug by the workmen, and filled by the river ;—from the first and greatest of temples to a burnt mountain desolate for ever ;—from the golden image, forty feet in height,

* Sir Robert Ker Porter's Travels, v. ii. p. 207.

which stood on the top of the temple of Belus, to all the graven images of her gods that are broken unto the ground and mingled with the dust ;—from the splendid and luxuriant festivals of Babylonian monarchs, the noise of the viols, the pomp of Belshazzar's feast, and the godless revelry of a thousand lords drinking out of the golden vessels that had been taken from Zion, to the cry of wild beasts, the creeping of doleful creatures of which their desolate houses and pleasant palaces are full, the nestling of owls in cavities, the dancing of wild goats on the ruinous mound as on a rock, and the dwelling-place of dragons and of venomous reptiles ;—from arch upon arch, and terrace upon terrace, till the hanging gardens of Babylon rose like a mountain, down to the stones of the pit, now disclosed to view ;— from the palaces of princes who sat on the mount of the congregation, and thought in the pride of their hearts to exalt themselves above the stars of God, to heaps cut down to the ground, perforated as the raiment of those that are slain, and as a carcase trodden under feet ;—from the broad walls of Babylon, in all their height, as Cyrus camped against them round about, seeking in vain a single point where congregated nations could scale the walls or force an opening, to the untraceable spot on which they stood, where there is nothing left to turn aside, or impede in their course, the worms that cover it ;—and finally, from Babylon the great, the wonder of the world, to fallen Babylon, the astonishment of all who go by it ; in extremes like these, whatever changes they involve, and by whatever instrumentality they may have been wrought out, there is not to this hour, in this most marvellous history of Babylon, a single fact that may not most appropriately be ranked under a prediction, and that does not tally entirely with its express and precise fulfilment, while at the same time they all united show, as may now be seen,—reading the judgments to the very letter, and looking to the facts as they are,—the destruction which has come from the Almighty upon Babylon.

Has not every purpose of the Lord been performed against Babylon? And having so clear illustrations of the facts before us, what mortal shall give a negative answer to the question, subjoined by their omniscient Author to these very prophecies?—" Who hath declared this from ancient time? Who hath told it from that time? Have not I the Lord? and there is no god beside me ;—declaring the end from the beginning, and from ancient times the things that are not yet done—saying, my counsel shall stand, and I will do all my pleasure." Is it possible that there can be any attestation of the truth of prophecy, if it be not witnessed here? Is there any spot on earth which has undergone a more complete transformation? " The records of the human race," it has been said with truth, " do not present a contrast more striking than that between the primeval magnificence of Babylon and its long desolation."* Its ruins have of late been carefully and scrupulously examined by different natives of Britain, of unimpeached veracity, and the result of every research is a more striking demonstration of the literal accomplishment of every prediction. How few spots are there on earth of which we have so clear and faithful a picture, as prophecy gave of fallen Babylon at a time when no spot on earth resembled it less than its present desolate solitary site ! Or could any prophecies respecting any single place have been more precise or wonderful, or numerous, or true,—or more gradually accomplished throughout many generations? And when they look at what Babylon was, and what it is, and perceive

* Edinburgh Review, No. 50, p. 439.

the minute realization of them all—may not nations learn wisdom—may not tyrants tremble—and may not sceptics think?

TYRE.

Tyre was the most celebrated city of Phœnicia, and the ancient emporium of the world. Its colonies were numerous and extensive. " It was the theatre of an immense commerce and navigation—the nursery of arts and science, and the city of perhaps the most industrious and active people ever known."* The kingdom of Carthage, the rival of Rome, was one of the colonies of Tyre. While this mart of nations was in the height of its opulence and power, and at least one hundred and twenty-five years before the destruction of old Tyre, Isaiah pronounced its irrevocable fall. Tyre on the island succeeded to the more ancient city on the continent: and,—being inhabited by the same people, retaining the same name, being removed but a little space, and perhaps occupying in part the same ground,—the fate of both is included in the prophecy. The pride and the wickedness of the Tyrians —their exultation over the calamities of the Israelites—and their cruelty in selling them to slavery, are assigned as the reasons of the judgments that were to overtake them, or as the causes of the revelation of the destiny of their city. And the whole fate of Tyre was foretold.

Bishop Newton shows, at length, how the following prophecies were all exactly fulfilled, as well as clearly foretold, viz. that Tyre was to be taken and destroyed by the Chaldeans, who were, at the time

* Volney's Travels, vol. ii. p. 210. Steph. Dic. p. 2039. Mars. Can. Ch. p. 304, &c.—Strabo.

of the delivery of the prophecy, an inconsiderable people, and particularly by Nebuchadnezzar, king of Babylon;—that the inhabitants should fly over the Mediterranean into the island and countries adjoining, and even then should not find a quiet settlement; that the city should be restored after seventy years, and return to her gain and merchandize; that the people should in time forsake their idolatry, and become converts to the true religion and worship of God;—and finally, that the city should be totally destroyed, and become a place only for fishers to spread their nets upon.

But, instead of reviewing the whole of these, a few of the most striking predictions which were accomplished after the era of the last of the Old Testament prophets, and the fulfilment of which rests on the most unexceptionable testimony, shall be selected.

One of the most singular events in history was the manner in which the siege of Tyre was conducted by Alexander the Great. Irritated that a single city should alone oppose his victorious march, enraged at the murder of some of his soldiers, and fearful for his fame,—even his army's despairing of success could not deter him from the siege. And Tyre was taken in a manner, the success of which was more wonderful than the design was daring; for it was surrounded by a wall one hundred and fifty feet in height, and situated on an island half a mile distant from the shore. A mound was formed from the continent to the island; and the ruins of old Tyre,* two hundred and forty years after its demolition, afforded ready materials for the purpose. Such was the work, that the attempts at first defeated the power of an Alexander. The enemy consumed and the storm destroyed it. But

---

* Magna vis saxorum ad manum erat, Tyro vetere præbente. *Quint. Cur.* lib. iv. cap. 9.

7

its remains, buried beneath the water, formed a barrier which rendered successful his renewed efforts. A vast mass of additional matter was requisite. The soil and the very rubbish were gathered and heaped. And the mighty conqueror, who afterwards failed in raising again any of the ruins of Babylon, cast those of Tyre into the sea, and took her very DUST* from off her. He left not the remnant of a ruin—and the site of *ancient* Tyre is now unknown.† Who then taught the prophets to say of Tyre—" *They shall lay thy stones, and thy timber, and thy dust, in the midst of the water—I will also* SCRAPE HER DUST *from her. I will make thee a terror, and thou shalt be no more. Thou shalt be sought for, yet thou shalt never be found again.*"‡

After the capture of Tyre, the conqueror ordered it to be set on fire. Fifteen thousand of the Tyrians escaped in ships. And, exclusive of multitudes that were cruelly slain, thirty thousand were sold into slavery. Each of these facts had been announced for centuries :—" *Behold the Lord will cast her out—he will smite her power in the sea, and she shall be devoured with fire.—I will bring forth a fire from the midst of thee—I will bring thee to ashes upon the earth. Pass ye over to Tarshish—pass over to Chittim. The isles that are in the sea shall be troubled at thy departure.—Thou shalt die the death of them that are slain in the midst of the sea. The children of Israel also, and the children of Judah have ye sold. I will return the recompense upon your own head.*"

But it was also prophesied of the greatest commer-

---

* HUMUS aggerabatur, ib. cap. 11. *Arrian. de Exp. Al.* lib. ii. c. 21—24. *Quint. Cur.* lib. iv. c. 7—19.

† Volney's Travels, vol. ii. Pococke's Descrip. of the East, b. i. c. 20. Buckingham's Travels, p. 46.

‡ Ezek. xxiv. 4, 12, 21.

cial city of the world, whose merchants were princes,
—whose traffickers were the honourable of the earth :—
" *I will make thee like the top of a rock. Thou shalt
be a place to spread nets upon.*"* The same prediction is repeated with an assurance of its truth :—" *I
will make her like the top of a rock ; it shall be a
place for the spreading of nets in the midst of the sea,
for I have spoken it.*"†

Tyre, though deprived of its former inhabitants,
soon revived as a city, and greatly regained its commerce. It was populous and flourishing at the beginning of the Christian era. It contained many
disciples of Jesus, in the days of the apostles. An
elegant temple and many churches were afterwards
built there. It was the see of the first archbishop under
the patriarch of Jerusalem. Her merchandize and her
hire, according to the prophecy, were holiness to the
Lord. In the seventh century Tyre was taken by the
Saracens. In the twelfth by the Crusaders—at which
period it was a great commercial city. The Mamelukes succeeded as its masters ; and it has now remained for three hundred years in the possession of
the Turks. But it was not excluded from among the
multitude of cities and of countries whose ruin and
devastation, as accomplished by the cruelties and ravages of Turkish barbarity and despotism, were foretold nearly two thousand years before the existence of
that nation of plunderers. And although it has more
lately, by a brief respite from the greatest oppression,
risen somewhat from its ruins, the last of the predictions respecting it has been literally fulfilled, according to the testimony of many witnesses. But that
of Maundrell, Shaw, Volney, and Bruce, may suffice :—

" You find here no similitude of that glory for

Ezek. xxvi. 14, 15.　　　　† Ib. 5.

which it was so renowned in ancient times. You
see nothing here but a mere Babel of broken walls,
pillars, vaults, &c. Its present inhabitants are only
a few poor wretches, harbouring themselves in the
vaults, and subsisting chiefly upon fishing, who seem
to be preserved in this place by divine providence, as
a visible argument how God hath fulfilled his word
concerning Tyre."* " The port of Tyre, small as it
is at present, is choked up to that degree with sand
and rubbish, that the boats of those fishermen who
now and then visit this once renowned emporium,
and dry their nets upon its rocks and ruins, can with
great difficulty only be admitted."† And even Volney, after quoting the description of the greatness of
Tyre, and the general description of the destruction
of the city, and the annihilation of its commerce,
acknowledges that " the vicissitudes of time, or
rather the barbarism of the Greeks of the Lower Empire and the Mahometans have accomplished this prediction.   Instead of that ancient commerce, so active
and so extensive, Sour, (Tyre,) reduced to a miserable village, has no other trade than the exportation
of a few sacks of corn and raw cotton ; nor any merchant but a single Greek factor, in the service of the
French of Saide, who scarcely makes sufficient profit
to maintain his family." But though he overlooks
the fulfilment of minuter prophecies, he relates facts
more valuable than any opinion, and more corroborative of their truth :—" The whole village of Tyre
contains only fifty or sixty poor families, who live
obscurely on the produce of their little ground and a
trifling fishery. The houses they occupy are no
longer, as in the time of Strabo, edifices of three or
four stories high,—but wretched huts, ready to crum-

* Maundrell's Journey from Aleppo to Jerusalem, p. 82.
† Shaw's Travels, vol. ii. p. 31.

ble into ruins."* Bruce describes Tyre as "a rock whereon fishers dry their nets."

It matters not by what means these prophecies have been verified; for the means were as inscrutable, and as impossible to have been foreseen by man, as the event. The fact is beyond a doubt that they have been literally fulfilled—and therefore the PROPHECIES ARE TRUE. They may be overlooked—but no ingenuity can pervert them. No facts could have been more unlikely or striking—and no predictions respecting them could have been more clear.

EGYPT.

Egypt was one of the most ancient and one of the mightiest of kingdoms, and the researches of the traveller are still directed to explore the unparalleled memorials of its power. No nation, whether of ancient or of modern times, hath ever erected such great and durable monuments. While the vestiges of other ancient monarchies can hardly be found amidst the mouldered ruins of their cities, those artificial mountains, visible at the distance of thirty miles, the pyramids of Egypt, without a record of their date, have withstood, unimpaired, all the ravages of time. The dynasty of Egypt takes precedence, in antiquity, of every other. No country ever produced so long a catalogue of kings. The learning of the Egyptians was proverbial. The number of their cities,† and the population of their country, as recorded by ancient historians, almost surpass credibility. Nature

---

* Volney's Travels, vol. ii. p. 212.
† Twenty thousand.—Herod. lib. ii. c. 177.

and art united in rendering it a most fertile region.
It was called the granary of the world. It was divided into several kingdoms, and their power often
extended over many of the surrounding countries.*
Yet the knowledge of all its greatness and glory de-
terred not the Jewish prophets from declaring, that
Egypt should become *a base kingdom, and never exalt itself any more among the nations.* And the *literal* fulfilment of every prophecy affords as clear a
demonstration as can possibly be given, that each and
all of them are the dictates of inspiration.

Egypt was the theme of many prophecies, which
were fulfilled in ancient times; and it bears to the
present day, as it has borne throughout many ages,
every mark with which prophecy had stamped its
destiny :—

"They shall be a base kingdom. It shall be the
basest of kingdoms. Neither shall it exalt itself any
more among the nations : for I will diminish them
that they shall no more rule over the nations.† The
pride of her power shall come down. And they shall
be desolate in the midst of the countries that are
desolate, and her cities shall be in the midst of the
cities that are wasted. I will make the land of Egypt
desolate, and the country shall be desolate of that
whereof it was full. I will sell the land into the
hand of the wicked. I will make the land waste and
all that is therein, by the hand of strangers. I the
Lord have spoken it. And there shall be no more a
prince of the land of Egypt."‡

Egypt became entirely subject to the Persians
about three hundred and fifty years previous to the
Christian era. It was afterwards subdued by the Ma-

---

* Marshami *Can. Chron.* pp. 239, 242.
† Ezek. xxix. 14, 15.
‡ Ezek. xxx. 6, 7, 12, 13 ; xxxii. 15.

cedonians, and was governed by the Ptolemies for the
space of two hundred and ninety-four years; until
about thirty years before Christ, it became a province
of the Roman empire. It continued long in subjection to the Romans—tributary first to Rome, and
afterwards to Constantinople. It was transferred,
A.D. 641, to the dominion of the Saracens. In
1250 the Mamelukes deposed their rulers, and usurped the command of Egypt. A mode of government
the most singular and surprising that ever existed on
earth, was established and maintained. Each successive ruler was raised to supreme authority, from
being a *stranger* and a slave. No son of the former
ruler—no native of Egypt succeeding to the sovereignty; but a chief was chosen from among a new
race of imported slaves. When Egypt became tributary to the Turks in 1517, the Mamelukes retained much of their power, and every Pasha was an oppressor and a stranger. During all these ages, every
attempt to emancipate the country, or to create a
prince of the land of Egypt, has proved abortive, and
has often been fatal to the aspirant. Though the facts
relative to Egypt form too prominent a feature in the
history of the world to admit of contradiction or doubt,
yet the description of the fate of that country, and of
the form of its government, shall be left to the testimony of those whose authority no infidel will question,
and whom no man can accuse of adapting their descriptions to the predictions of the event. Gibbon
and Volney are again our witnesses of the facts.

" Such is the state of Egypt. Deprived twenty-
three centuries ago of her natural proprietors, she has
seen her fertile fields successively a prey to the Persians, the Macedonians, the Romans, the Greeks,
the Arabs, the Georgians, and, at length, the race
of Tartars distinguished by the name of Ottoman
Turks. The Mamelukes, purchased as slaves and

introduced as soldiers, soon usurped the power and elected a leader. If their first establishment was a singular event, their continuance is not less extraordinary. They are replaced by slaves *brought from their original country*. The system of oppression is methodical. Every thing the traveller sees or hears, reminds him he is in the country of slavery and tyranny."* "A more unjust and absurd constitution cannot be devised than that which condemns the natives of a country to perpetual servitude, under the arbitrary dominion of *strangers* and slaves. Yet such has been the state of Egypt above five hundred years. The most illustrious sultans of the Baharite and Borgite dynasties, were themselves promoted from the Tartar and Circassian bands ; and the four and twenty Beys or military chiefs, have ever been succeeded, not by their sons, but by their servants."† These are the words of Volney and of Gibbon ;—and what did the ancient prophets foretell ? "*I will lay the land waste, and all that is therein by the hands of strangers. I the Lord have spoken it.—And there shall be no more a prince of the land of Egypt.—The sceptre of Egypt shall depart away.*" The prophecy adds,—"*they shall be a base kingdom—it shall be the basest of kingdoms.*" After the lapse of two thousand and four hundred years from the date of this prophecy, a scoffer at religion, but an eye-witness of the facts, thus describes the self-same spot. "In Egypt there is no middle class, neither nobility, clergy, merchants, landholders. An universal air of misery, manifest in all the traveller meets, points out to him the rapacity of oppression and the distrust attendant upon slavery. The profound ignorance of the inhabitants equally prevents them from perceiving the causes of

* Volney's Travels, vol. i. pp. 74, 103, 110, 198.
† Gibbon's History, vol. vi. pp. 109, 110. Dublin ed. 1789.

2

their evils, or applying the necessary remedies. Ignorance, diffused through every class, extends its effects to every species of moral and physical knowledge. Nothing is talked of but intestine troubles, the public misery, pecuniary extortions, bastinadoes, and murders. Justice herself puts to death without formality."* Other travellers describe the most execrable vices as common, and represent the moral character of the people as corrupted to the core. As a token of the desolation of the country, mud-walled cottages are now the only habitations where the ruins of temples and palaces abound. Egypt is surrounded by the dominions of the Turks and of the Arabs; and the prophecy is literally true which marked it in the midst of desolation :—" *They shall be desolate in the midst of the countries that are desolate, and her cities shall be in the midst of the cities that are wasted.*" The systematic oppression, extortion, and plunder, which have so long prevailed, and the price paid for his authority and power by every Turkish Pasha, have rendered the country *desolate of that whereof it was full*, and still show both how *it has been wasted by the hands of strangers*, and how *it has been sold into the hand of the wicked*.

Can any words be more free from ambiguity, or could any events be more wonderful in their nature, or more unlikely or impossible to have been foreseen by man, than these prophecies concerning Egypt? The long line of its kings commenced with the first ages of the world, and, while it was yet unbroken, its final termination was revealed. The very attempt once made by infidels to show, from the recorded number of its monarchs and the duration of their reigns, that Egypt was a kingdom previous to the Mosaic era of the deluge, places the wonderful nature of these predictions respecting it in the most striking

* Volney's Travels, vol. i. pp. 190, 198.

view. And the previous experience of two thousand
years, during which period Egypt had never been
without a prince of its own, seemed to preclude the
possibility of those predicted events which the experience of the last two thousand years has amply verified. Though it had often tyrannized over Judea
and the neighbouring nations, the Jewish prophets
foretold that its own sceptre should depart away ; and
that that country of kings (for the number of its
cotemporary as well as successive monarchs may warrant the appellation) would never have a prince of its
own : and that it would be laid waste by the hands
of strangers. They foretold that it should be a base
kingdom—the basest of kingdoms—that it should be
desolate itself and surrounded by desolation—and
that it should never exalt itself any more among the
nations. They described its ignominious subjection
and unparalleled baseness, notwithstanding that its
past and present degeneracy bears not a more remote
resemblance to the former greatness and pride of its
power than the frailty of its mud-walled fabrics now
bears to the stability of its imperishable pyramids.
Such prophecies accomplished in such a manner,
prove, without a comment, that they must be the
revelation of the Omniscient Ruler of the Universe.*

* Egypt has, indeed, lately risen, under its present spirited
but despotic Pasha, who is both an *oppressor* and a *stranger*,
to a degree of political importance and power unknown to
it for many past centuries. Yet this fact, instead of militating against the truth of prophecy, may, possibly at no distant period, serve to illustrate another prediction, which implies that, however base and degraded it might continue to
be throughout many generations, it would, notwithstanding,
have strength sufficient to be looked to for aid or protection, even at the time of the restoration of the Jews to Judea, who will seek "to strengthen themselves in the
strength of Pharaoh, and trust in the shadow of Egypt."
Other prophecies respecting it await their fulfilment. Yet,
whatever its present apparent strength may be, it is still but

On a review of the prophecies relative to Nineveh, Babylon, Tyre, and Egypt, may we not, by the plainest induction from indisputable facts, conclude that the fate of these cities and countries, as well as of the land of Judea and the adjoining territories, demonstrates the truth of all the prophecies respecting them? And that these prophecies, ratified by the events, give the most powerful of testimonies to the truth of the Christian religion? The desolation was the work of man, and was effected by the enemies of Christianity; and would have been the same as it is, though not a single prophecy had been uttered. It is the prediction of these facts, in all their particulars, infinitely surpassing human foresight, which is the word of God alone. And the *ruin of these empires*, while it substantiates the truth of every iota of these predictions, is thus a miraculous confirmation and proof of the inspiration of the Scriptures. By what fatality is it, then, that infidels should have chosen for the display of their power this very field, where, without conjuring, as they have done, a lying spirit from the ruins, they might have read the fulfilment of the prophecies on every spot? Instead of disproving the truth of every religion, the greater these ruins are, the more strongly do they authenticate the scriptural prophecies; and it is not, at least, on this stronghold of the faith that the standard of infidelity can be erected. Every fact related by Volney is a witness against all his speculation—and out of his own mouth is he condemned. Can any purposed decep-

---

"the shadow of Egypt." Isa. xxx. 2; xxxi. 1. The whole earth shall yet rejoice; and Egypt shall not be for ever *base*. *The Lord shall smite Egypt; he shall smite and heal it; and they shall return to the Lord, and he shall be entreated of them, and shall heal them. In that day shall Israel be the third with Egypt and with Assyria, even a blessing in the midst of the land, &c.* Isa. xix. 19—25.

tion be more glaring or great, than to overlook all
these prophecies, and to raise an argument against
the truth of Christianity from the very facts by which
they have been fulfilled? Or can any evidence of
divine inspiration be more convincing and clear, than
to view, in conjunction, all these marvellous predictions, and their exact completion?

CHAPTER VII.

THE ARABS.

THE history of the Arabs, so opposite in many re-
spects to that of the Jews, but as singular as theirs,
was concisely and clearly foretold. It was prophesied
concerning Ishmael :—" He will be a wild man ;
his hand will be against every man, and every man's
hand will be against him : and he shall dwell in the
presence of all his brethren. I will make him
fruitful, and multiply him exceedingly ; and I will
make him a great nation."* The fate of Ishmael is
here identified with that of his descendants ; and the
same character is common to them both. The historical evidence of the fact, the universal tradition, and
constant boast of the Arabs themselves, their language, and the preservation for many ages of an
original rite, derived from him as their primogenitor,
confirm the truth of their descent from Ishmael.
The fulfilment of the prediction is obvious. Even
Gibbon, while he attempts from the exceptions which

* Genesis xvi. 12 ; xvii. 20.

he specifies, to evade the force of the fact, that the
Arabs have maintained a perpetual independence, acknowledges that these exceptions are temporary and
local; that the body of the nation has escaped the
yoke of the most powerful monarchies; and that
" the arms of Sesostris and Cyrus, of Pompey and
Trajan, could never achieve the conquest of Arabia."*
But even the exceptions which he specifies, though
they were justly stated, and though not coupled with
such admissions as invalidate them, would not detract
from the truth of the prophecy. The independence
of the Arabs was proverbial in ancient as well as in
modern times; and the present existence as a free
and independent nation, of a people who derive their
descent from so high antiquity, demonstrates that they
have never been wholly subdued, as all the nations
around them have unquestionably been; and that they
had ever dwelt in the presence of their brethren.
They not only subsist unconquered to this day, but
the prophesied and primitive wildness of their race,
and their hostility to all, remain unsubdued and unaltered. " *They are a wild people: their hand is
against every man, and every man's hand is against
them.*" In the words of Gibbon, which strikingly
assimilate with those of the prophecy, they are " *armed against mankind.*" Plundering is their profession. Their alliance is never courted, and can never
be obtained; and all that the Turks, or Persians,
or any of their neighbours, can stipulate for from
them, is a partial and purchased forbearance. Even
the British, who have established a residence in almost every country, have entered the territories of the
descendants of Ishmael to accomplish only the pre-
meditated destruction of a fort, and to retire. It cannot be alleged, with truth, that their peculiar cha-

* Gibbon's Hist. vol. v. p. 144.

racter and manner, and its uninterrupted permanency,
are the necessary result of the nature of their country.
They have continued wild or uncivilized, and have
retained their habits of hostility towards all the rest
of the human race, though they possessed for three
hundred years countries the most opposite in their
nature from the mountains of Arabia. The greatest
part of the temperate zone was included within the
limits of the Arabian conquests;* and their empire
extended from India to the Atlantic, and embraced a
wider range of territory than ever was possessed by the
Romans, those boasted masters of the world. The
period of their conquest and dominion was sufficient,
under such circumstances, to have changed the manners of any people; but whether in the land of Shinar or in the vallies of Spain, on the banks of the
Tigris or the Tagus, in Araby the blessed, or Araby
the barren, the posterity of Ishmael have ever maintained their prophetic character: They have remained, under every change of condition, a wild people;
their hand has still been against every man, and every
man's hand against them.

The natural reflection of a recent traveller, on examining the peculiarities of an Arab tribe, of which he
was an eye-witness, may suffice, without any art of
controversy, for the illustration of this prophecy:—
" On the smallest computation, such must have been
the manners of those people for more than three thousand years: Thus in all things verifying the prediction given of Ishmael at his birth, that he, in his posterity should be a wild man, and always continue to
be so, though they shall dwell for ever in the presence of their brethren. And that an acute and active people, surrounded for ages by polished and lux-
urious nations, should from their earliest to their

* Gibbon, vol. v. pp. 226, 317.

latest times, be still found a wild people, dwelling in the presence of all their brethren, (as we may call these nations,) unsubdued and unchangeable, is, indeed, a standing miracle—one of those mysterious facts which establish the truth of prophecy."*

Recent discoveries have also brought to light the miraculous preservation and existence, as a distinct people, of a less numerous, but not less interesting race—" a plant which grew up under the mighty cedar of Israel, but was destined to flourish when that proud tree was levelled to the earth."† " Thus saith the Lord of Hosts, the God of Israel, Jonadab, the son of Rechab, shall not want a man to stand before me for ever."‡ The Beni Rechab, sons of Rechab, still exist, a "distinct and easily distinguishable" people. They boast of their descent from Rechab, profess pure Judaism, and all know Hebrew. Yet they live in the neighbourhood of Mecca, the chief seat of Mahometanism, and their number is stated to be sixty thousand. The account given of them by Benjamin of Tudela in the twelfth century,§ has very recently been confirmed by Mr. Wolff; and, as he witnessed, and heard from an intrepid " Rechabite cavalier," there is not a man wanting to stand up as a son of Rechab.

* Sir R. K. Porter's Travels, p. 304.
† Quarterly Review, No. lxxv. p. 142.
‡ Jer. xxxv. 19.
§ Basnage's History, p. 620.

SLAVERY OF THE AFRICANS—EUROPEAN COLONIES
IN ASIA.

NOT only do the different countries and cities, which
form the subjects of prophecy, exhibit to this day
their predicted fate, but there is also a prophecy recorded as delivered in an age coeval with the deluge, when the members of a single family included
the whole of the human race—the fulfilment of which
is conspicuous even at the present time.   And while
the fate of the Jews and of the Arabs, throughout many
ages, has confirmed in every instance in which the
period of their prediction is already past, the prophecies relative to the descendants of Isaac and of Ishmael—existing facts, which are prominent features
in the history of the world, are equally corroborative
of the predictions respecting the sons of Noah.   The
unnatural conduct of Ham, and the dutiful and re-
spectful behaviour of Shem and Japheth towards their
aged father, gave rise to the prediction of the future
fate of their posterity, without being at all assigned
as the cause of that fate.   But whatever was the occasion on which it was delivered, the truth of the
prophecy must be tried by its completion :—" Curs-
ed be Canaan ; a servant of servants shall he be unto
his brethren. Blessed be the Lord God of Shem, and
Canaan shall be his servant.   God shall enlarge
Japheth, and he shall dwell in the tents of Shem, and
Canaan shall be his servant."*

The historical part of Scripture, by its describing
so particularly the respective settlements of the descendants of Noah, " after their generations in their

* Gen. ix. 25, 26, 27.

nations," affords, to this day, the means of trying
the truth of the prediction, and of ascertaining whether the prophetic character, as given by the patriarch of the postdiluvian world, be still applicable to
the inhabitants of the different regions of the earth
which were peopled by the posterity of Shem, of
Ham, and of Japhet. The *Isles of the Gentiles,**
or the countries beyond the Mediterranean, to which
they passed by sea, *viz.* those of Europe, were divided by the sons of Japhet. The descendants of Ham
inhabited Africa and the south-western parts of Asia.†
The families of the Canaanites were spread abroad.
The border of the Canaanites was from Sidon.‡ The
city of Tyre was called the daughter of Sidon ; and
Carthage, the most celebrated city of Africa, was
peopled from Tyre. And the dwellings of the sons
of Shem were *unto the east,*§ or Asia. The particular allotment, or portion of each, " after their families, after their tongues, in their countries, and in
their nations,"‖ is distinctly specified. And although
the different nations, descended from any one of the
sons of Noah, have intermingled with each other, and
undergone many revolutions, yet the three great divisions of the world have remained distinct, as separately
peopled and possessed by the posterity of each of the
sons of Noah. On this subject the earliest commentators are agreed, before the existence of those facts which
give to the prophecy its fullest illustration. The facts
themselves by which the prediction is verified, are so
notorious and so applicable, that the most brief and
simple statement may suffice. Before the propagation of Christianity, which first spoke peace to earth,
taught a law of universal love, and called all men
brethren, slavery everywhere prevailed, and the

* Gen. x. 5.   † Ib.   ‡ Ib. x. 6, 18, 19.
§ Ib. x. 30.   ‖ Ib. 31, 32.—See Mede. Dic. L. p. 277, &c.

greater part of the human race, throughout all the world, were born to slavery, and unredeemed for life. Man can now boast of a nobler birthright. But, though long banished from almost all Europe, slavery still lingers in Africa. That country is distinguished above every other as the land of slavery. Slaves at home, and transported for slavery, the poor Africans, the descendants of Ham, are the servants of servants, or slaves to others. Yet so unlikely was this fact to have been foreseen by man, that, for centuries after the close of the Old Testament History, the inhabitants of Africa disputed with the Romans the empire of the world. But Hannibal, who was once almost master of Rome and of Europe, was forced to yield to and to own the fate of Carthage.*

"God shall enlarge Japheth, and he shall dwell in the tents of Shem." Some of the ablest interpreters of prophecy, of a former age, conceived that this prediction was fulfilled, not only by the conquests which the Macedonians and the Romans obtained over many of the countries of Asia, but that the promise or blessing of enlargement to Japhet was also verified in a metaphorical sense, by the extension of the knowledge of true religion to the nations of Europe. But it stands not now in need of any questionable interpretation, having received a literal accomplishment. What is at present the relative situation or connexion of the inhabitants of Europe and of Asia, the descendants of Japhet and of Shem? May not the former be said literally to dwell in the tents of the latter? Or what simile, drawn from the simplicity of primeval ages, could be more strikingly graphic of the numerous and extensive European colonies in Asia? And how much

---

* Liv. i. 27.

have the posterity of Japhet been enlarged within
the regions of the posterity of Shem ?   In how many
of their ancient cities do they dwell ?   How many
settlements have they established ?—while there is
not a single spot in Europe the colony or the property of any of the nations whom the Scriptures represent as descended from Shem, or who inhabit any
part of that quarter of the world which they possessed.   And it may be said, in reference to our own
island, and to the immense extent of the British
Asiatic dominions, that the natives *of the Isles of
the Gentiles dwell in the tents of the East !*   From
whence, then, could such a prophecy have emanated,
but from inspiration by Him whose presence and
whose prescience are alike unlimited by space or by
time ?

Whatever events the prophecies reveal, they never
sanction any iniquity or evil.   The wrath of man
worketh not the righteousness of God, though it be
made to praise him.   And any defence or attempted
justification of slavery, or of man having any moral
right of property in man, must be sought in vain
from the fulfilment of this prediction.   Nebuchadnezzar was the guilty instrument of righteous judgments ; and although, in the execution of these, he
was the servant of the Lord, it was his own gain
and glory which he sought, and after having subdued nations not a few, he was driven from men, and
had his dwelling with the beasts.   Never were judgments more clearly marked than those which have
rested on the Jews in every country under heaven.
Yet he that toucheth them toucheth the apple of his
eye ; and the year of recompenses for the controversy
of Zion shall be the day of the Lord's vengeance, when
he will plead with all flesh for his people and for his
heritage.   And if these examples suffice not to show
that it is a wresting of Scripture to their destruction,

1

for any to seek from them the vindication of slavery, because Canaan was to be the servant of servants unto his brethren, yet they who profess to look here to the *holy* Scriptures for a warrant, because that fact was foretold, should remember, that though Christ was delivered into the hands of his enemies " by the *determinate counsel and foreknowledge* of God ; it was by *wicked hands* that he was crucified and slain." God hath made of one flesh all the nations of the earth.   And, were the gospel universally and rightly appealed to, no other bond would be known among men but that of Christian brotherhood.

CHAPTER VIII.

THE SEVEN CHURCHES OF ASIA.

INCOMPLETE as has been the view given in the foregoing pages of the Evidence of Prophecy, yet do not the joint clearness of the prophecies themselves, and the profusion of precise facts which show their literal fulfilment, bid defiance to the most subtle sceptic to forge or feign the shadow of a just reason to prove how they could all have been spoken, except by inspiration of God ?   The sure word of prophecy has indeed unfolded many a desolation which has come upon the earth ; but while it thus reveals the operation, in some of its bearings, of the " mystery of iniquity," it forms, itself, a part of the " mystery of godliness :" and it is no less the testimony of Jesus, because it shows, as far as earthly ruins can reveal, the progress and the issue of the dominion of " other lords" over the hearts of the children of men. The sins of men have caused, and the cruelty of men has effected, the dire desolations which the word of God foretold.   Signs and tokens of his judgments there indeed have been, but they are never to be found but where iniquity first prevailed. And though all other warnings were to fail, the sight of his past judgments, and the sounding of those that are to come, might teach the unrepenting and unconverted sinner to give heed to the threatenings of His word and to the terrors of the Lord, and to try his ways and turn unto God, while space for repentance may be found, ere, as death leaves him, judgment shall find him. And may not the desolations which God has wrought upon the earth, and that accredit his word, wherein life and immortality are brought to light, teach the man whose God is the world, to cease to account it worthy of his worship and of his love, and to abjure that " covetousness, which is idolatry," till the idol of mammon in the temple within shall fall, as fell the image of Dagon before the ark of the Lord, in which " the testimony" was kept ?

But naming, as millions do, the name of Christ, without departing from iniquity, there is another warning voice that may come more closely to them all. And it is not only from the desolate regions where heathens dwelt, which show how holy men of old spake as they were moved by the Holy Ghost ; but also from the ruins of some of the cities where churches were formed by apostles, and where the religion of Jesus once existed in its purity, that all may learn to know that God is no respecter of persons, and that he will by no means clear the guilty. " He that hath an ear let him hear what the Spirit saith unto the churches."

What church could rightfully claim or ever seek a higher title than that which is given in Scripture to the seven churches of Asia, the angels of which were the seven stars in the right hand of Him, who is the first and the last—of Him that liveth and was dead and is alive for evermore, and that hath the keys of hell and of death ; and which themselves were the seven golden candlesticks in the midst of which HE walked ? And who that hath an ear to hear, may not humbly hear and greatly profit by what the Spirit said unto them ?*

The CHURCH OF EPHESUS, after a commendation of their first works, to which they were commanded to return, were accused of having left their first love, and threatened with the removal of their candlestick out of its place, except they should repent.† Ephesus is situated nearly fifty miles north of Smyrna. It was the metropolis of Ionia, and a great and opulent city, and (according to Strabo) the greatest emporium of Asia Minor. It was chiefly famous for the temple of Diana, " whom all Asia worshipped," which was adorned with one hundred and twenty-seven columns of Parian marble, each of a single shaft, and sixty feet high, and which formed one of the seven wonders of the world. The remains of its magnificent theatre in which it is said that twenty thousand people could easily have been seated, are yet to be seen.‡ But " a few heaps of stones, and some miserable mud cottages, occasionally tenanted by Turks, without one Christian residing there,§ are all the remains of ancient Ephesus." It is, as described by different travellers, a solemn and most forlorn spot. The Epistle to the Ephesians is read throughout the world : but there is

---

* Rev. ii. and iii.　　　　　† Rev. ii. 5.
‡ Acts xix. 29.
§ Arundel's Visit to the Seven Churches of Asia, p. 27.

none in Ephesus to read it now. They left their first
love, they returned not to their first works. Their
candlestick has been removed out of its place; and
the great city of Ephesus is no more.

The CHURCH OF SMYRNA was approved of as "rich,"
and no judgment was denounced against it. They
were warned of a tribulation of ten days, (the ten
years' persecution by Diocletian,) and were enjoined
to be faithful unto death, and they would receive a
crown of life.* And, unlike to the fate of the more
famous city of Ephesus, Smyrna is still a large city,
containing nearly one hundred thousand inhabitants,
with several Greek churches; and an English and
other Christian ministers have resided in it. The
light has indeed become dim, but the candlestick has
not been wholly removed out of its place.

The CHURCH OF PERGAMOS is commended for holding fast the name of the Lord, and not denying his
faith, during a time of persecution, and in the midst
of a wicked city. But there were some in it who
held doctrines, and did deeds, which the Lord hated.
Against them He was to fight with the sword of his
mouth; and all were called to repent. But it is not
said as of Ephesus, that their candlestick would be
removed out of its place.† Pergamos is situated to
the north of Smyrna, at a distance of nearly sixty-
four miles, and "was formerly the metropolis of Hel-
lespontic Mysia." It still contains at least fifteen
thousand inhabitants, of whom fifteen hundred are
Greeks, and two hundred Armenians, each of whom
have a church.

In the CHURCH OF THYATIRA, like that of Pergamos, some tares were soon mingled with the wheat.
He who hath eyes like unto a flame of fire discerned
both. Yet happily for the souls of the people, more

* Rev. ii. 8—11.   † Ib. ii. 12—16.

than for the safety of the city, the general character of
that church, as it then existed, is thus described : " I
know thy works, and charity, and service, and faith,
and thy patience, and thy works ; and the last to be
more than the first."* But against those, for such
there were among them, who had committed fornication, and eaten things sacrificed unto idols, to whom
the Lord gave space to repent of their fornication, and
they repented not, great tribulation was denounced ;
and to every one of them was to be given according to
their works. These, thus warned while on earth in
vain, have long since passed, where all are daily
hastening, to the place where no repentance can be
found, and no work be done. " But unto the rest in
Thyatira (as many as have not known the depths of
Satan) I will put upon you, saith the Lord, none
other burden."† There were those in Thyatira who
could save a city. It still exists, while greater cities
have fallen. Mr. Hartley, who visited it in 1826,
describes it as " embosomed in cypresses and poplars.
The Greeks are said to occupy three hundred houses,
and the Armenians thirty. Each of them have a
church."

The Church of Sardis differed from those of Pergamos and Thyatira. They had not denied the faith ;
but the Lord had a few things against them, for there
were some evil doers among them, and on those, if they
repented not, judgment was to rest. But in Sardis,
great though the city was, and founded though the
church had been by an apostle, there were only a few
names which had not defiled their garments. And to
that church the Spirit said, " I know thy works, that
thou hast a name, that thou livest and art dead." But
the Lord is long-suffering, not willing that any should
perish, but that all should come to repentance. And

* Rev. ii. 19.　　　　　† Ib. v. 24.

the church of Sardis was thus warned—" Be watchful, and strengthen the things which remain, that are ready to die, for I have not found thy works perfect before God. Remember, therefore, how thou hast received and heard, and hold fast and repent. If therefore thou shalt not watch, I will come on thee as a thief, and thou shalt not know what hour I shall come upon thee."*

The state of Sardis now is a token that the warning was given in vain ; and shows that the threatenings of the Lord, when disregarded, become certain judgments. Sardis, the capital of Lydia, was a great and renowned city, where the wealth of Crœsus, its king, was accumulated, and became even a proverb. But now a few wretched mud huts, " scattered among the ruins," are the only dwellings in Sardis, and form the lowly home of Turkish herdsmen, who are its only inhabitants. As the seat of a Christian church, it has lost—all it had to lose—the name. " No Christians reside on the spot."

" And to the angel of the CHURCH IN PHILADELPHIA, write, These things saith He that is holy, He that is true, He that hath the key of David, He that openeth and no man shutteth ; and shutteth and no man openeth :—I know thy works ; behold I have set before thee an open door, and no man can shut it ; for thou hast a little strength, and hast kept my word, and hast not denied my name.— Because thou hast kept the word of my patience I also will keep thee from the hour of temptation, which shall come upon all the world."† The promises of the Lord are as sure as his threatenings. Philadelphia alone long withstood the power of the Turks, and in the words of Gibbon, " at length capitulated with the proudest of the Ottomans. Among

* Rev. iii. 3, 4. † Ib. iii. 8, 10.

the Greek colonies and churches of Asia," he adds,
" Philadelphia is still erect ; a column in a scene
of ruins."* " It is indeed an interesting circumstance," says Mr. Hartley, " to find Christianity
more flourishing here than in many other parts of
the Turkish empire ; there is still a numerous
Christian population ; they occupy three hundred
houses. Divine service is performed every Sunday
in five churches." Nor is it less interesting, in
these eventful times, and notwithstanding the general degeneracy of the Greek church, to learn that
the present bishop of Philadelphia accounts " the
Bible the only foundation of all religious belief ;"
and that he admits that " abuses have entered
into the church, which former ages might endure ;
but the present must put them down." It may well
be added, as stated by Mr. Hartley,† " the circumstance that Philadelphia is now called Allah-Shehr,
the city of God, when viewed in connexion with the
promises made to that church, and especially with
that of writing the name the city of God upon its
faithful members, is, to say the least, a singular con-
currence. From the prevailing iniquities of men
many a sign has been given how terrible are the
judgments of God. But from the fidelity of the
church in Philadelphia of old in keeping his word, a
name and memorial of his faithfulness has been left
on earth, while the higher glories, promised to those
that overcame, shall be ratified in heaven ; and towards them, but not them only, shall the glorified
Redeemer confirm the truth of his blessed words,
" Him that overcometh will I make a pillar in the
temple of my God ;" even as assuredly as Philadelphia, when all else fell around it, " stood erect,"

* Gibbon, lxiv.
† Missionary Register, June 1827.

our enemies themselves being judges, "a column in a scene of ruins."

"And unto the angel of the CHURCH OF THE LAODICEANS write,—These things saith the Amen, the faithful and true witness, the beginning of the creation of God.—I know thy works, that thou art neither cold nor hot; I would thou wert cold or hot. So then because thou art lukewarm, and neither cold nor hot, I will spue thee out of my mouth. Because thou sayest, I am rich and increased with goods, and have need of nothing; and knowest not that thou art wretched, and miserable, and poor, and blind, and naked: I counsel thee to buy of me gold tried in the fire that thou mayest be rich, and white raiment that thou mayest be clothed, and that the shame of thy nakedness do not appear; and anoint thine eyes with eye-salve that thou mayest see."* All the other churches were found worthy of some commendation; and there were some blessing in them all. The church of Ephesus had laboured and had not fainted, though she had forsaken her first love; and the threatened punishment, except she repented, was the removal of her candlestick out of its place. A faithless and wicked few polluted the churches of Pergamos and Thyatira by their doctrines or by their lives; but the body was sound; and the churches had a portion in Christ. Even in Sardis, though it was dead, there was life in a few, who had not defiled their garments; "and they shall walk with me in white, said the Lord, for they are worthy."

But in what the Spirit said to the Church in Laodicea, there was not one word of approval; it was lukewarm, without exception; and therefore it was wholly loathed. The religion of Jesus had become to them as an ordinary matter. They would attend to it just

* Rev. iii. 14, &c.

as they did to other things, which they loved as well. The sacrifice of the Son of God upon the cross was nothing thought of more than a common gift by man. They were not constrained by the love of Christ more than by other feelings. They could repeat the words of the first great commandment of the law, and of the second that is like unto it; but they showed no sign that the one or the other was truly a law to them. There was no Dorcas among them, who, out of pure Christian love, made clothes for the poor. There was no Philemon to whom it could be said, "The church in thy house," and who could look on a servant as a "brother beloved." There was no servant who looked to the eye of his Father in heaven more than to that of his master on earth, and to the recompense of eternal reward more than to the hireling wages of a day; and who, by shewing all good fidelity, sought to adorn the doctrine of God his Saviour in all things. There was nothing done as every thing should be, heartily, as to the Lord, and not unto men.

They neither felt nor lived as if they knew that whatsoever is not of faith is sin. Their lukewarmness was worse, for it rendered their state more hopeless than if they had been cold. For sooner would a man in Sardis have felt that the chill of death was upon him, and have cried out for life, and called to the physician, than would a man of Laodicea, who could calmly count his even pulse, and think his life secure, while death was preying on his vitals. The character of lukewarm Christians, a self-contradicting name, is the same in every age. Such was the church of the Laodiceans.—But what is that city now, or how is it changed from what it was!

Laodicea was the metropolis of the Greater Phrygia; and as heathen writers attest, it was an extensive and very celebrated city. Instead of then verg-

ing to its decline, it arose to its eminence only about
the beginning of the Christian era. " It was the
mother-church of sixteen bishoprics." Its three theatres, and the immense circus, which was capable of
containing upwards of thirty thousand spectators, the
spacious remains of which (with other ruins buried
under ruins) are yet to be seen, give proof of the
greatness of its ancient wealth and population, and
indicate too strongly, that in that city where Christians were rebuked, without exception, for their lukewarmness, there were multitudes who were lovers of
pleasure more than lovers of God. The amphitheatre
was built after the Apocalypse was written, and the
warning of the Spirit had been given to the church
of the Laodiceans to be zealous and repent ; but whatever they there may have heard or beheld, their hearts
would neither have been quickened to a renewed zeal
for the service and glory of God, nor turned to a deeper
sorrow for sin, and to a repentance not to be repented
of. But the fate of Laodicea, though opposite, has
been no less marked than that of Philadelphia. There
are no sights of grandeur, nor scenes of temptation
around it now. Its own tragedy may be briefly told.
It was lukewarm and neither cold nor hot, and therefore it was loathsome in the sight of God. It was
loved, and rebuked, and chastened in vain. And it
has been blotted from the world. It is now as desolate as its inhabitants were destitute of the fear and
the love of God, and as the church of the Laodiceans
was devoid of true faith in the Saviour, and zeal in
his service. It is, as described in his Travels by Dr.
Smith, " utterly desolated, and without any inhabitant, except wolves and jackals, and foxes." It can
boast of no human inhabitants, except occasionally
when wandering Turkomans pitch their tents in its
spacious amphitheatre. The " finest sculptured fragments " are to be seen at a considerable depth, in

Q

excavations which have been made among the ruins.*
And Colonel Leake observes,† " there are few ancient cities more likely than Laodicea to preserve
many curious remains of antiquity beneath the surface of the soil.   Its opulence, and the earthquakes
to which it was subject, rendering it probable that
valuable works of art were often there buried beneath the ruins of the public and private edifices."
A fearful significancy is thus given to the terrific
denunciation, " Because thou art lukewarm, and neither cold nor hot, I will spue thee out of my mouth."

" He that hath ears to hear let him hear what the
Spirit saith unto the churches."   The Spirit searcheth
all things, yea the deep things of God.   Each church,
and each individual therein, was weighed in the ba-
lance of the sanctuary according to their works.   Each
was approved of according to its character, or rebuked
and warned according to its deeds.   Was the church
itself pure, the diseased members alone were to be cut
off.   Was the church itself dead, yet the few names,
in which there were life, were all written before God,
and not one of those who overcame would be blotted
out of the book of life.   All the seven churches were
severally exhorted by the Spirit according to their
need.   The faith delivered to the saints was preached
unto them all ; and all, as Christian churches, possessed the means of salvation.   The Son of man walked in the midst of them, beholding those who were,
and those who were not his.

By the preaching of the gospel, and by the written
word, every man, in each of the churches, was warned,
and every man was taught in all wisdom, that every
man might be presented perfect in Christ Jesus.   And
in what the Spirit said unto each, and all of the
churches, which he that hath ears to hear was com-

* Arundel's Travels, p. 85.   † Journal, p. 252.

manded to hear, the promise of everlasting blessedness, under a variety of the most glorious representations, was given without exception, restriction, or reservation to him that overcometh. The language of love, as well as of remonstrance and rebuke, was urged even on the lukewarm Laodiceans. And if any Christian fell, it was from his own resistance and quenching of the Spirit; from his choosing other lords than Jesus to have dominion over him; from his lukewarmness, deadness, and virtual denial of the faith; and from his own wilful rejection of freely offered and dearly purchased grace; sufficient, if sought and cherished, and zealously used, to have enabled him to overcome and triumph in that warfare against spiritual wickedness to which Christ hath called his disciples; and in which, as the finisher of their faith, he is able to make the Christian more than conqueror.

But if such, as the Spirit described them and knew them to be, were the churches, and Christians then, what are the churches, and what are Christians now? Or, rather, we would ask of the reader, what is your own hope towards God, and what the work of your faith? If, while Christianity was in its prime, and when its divine truths had scarcely ceased to reach the ears of believers from the lips of Apostles, on whose heads the Spirit had visibly descended, and cloven tongues, like as of fire, had sat; if, even at that time, one of the seven churches of Asia had already departed from its first love; if two others were partially polluted by the errors in doctrine, and evils in the practice, of some of their members; if another had only a few names that were worthy, and yet another none: and if they, who formed the last and worst of these, thought themselves rich and increased with goods, and that they had need of nothing; and knew not, that, being lukewarm, they were wretched, and miserable, and poor, and blind, and naked; have you an ear to hear or a heart to understand such knowledge? and do you, professing yourself a Christian, as they also did, see no cause or warning here to question and examine yourself; even as the same Spirit would search and try you, of your works, and charity, and service, and faith, and patience, and thy works, and the last more than the first?

What is your labour of love, or wherein do you labour at all for His name's sake, by whose name you are called? What trials does your faith patiently endure, what temptations does it triumphantly overcome? Is Christ in you the hope of glory, and is your heart purified through that blessed hope? To a church, we trust, you belong; but whose is the kingdom within you? What principles ever actuate you which Christ and his apostles taught? Where, in your affections and life, are the fruits of the Spirit—love, joy, peace, long-suffering, gentleness, goodness, meekness, temperance? Turn the precepts of the gospel into questions, and ask thus, what the Spirit would say unto you, as he said unto the churches?

What the Spirit said unto primitive and apostolic churches, over which " the beloved disciple " personally presided, may suffice to prove that none who have left their first love, if ever they have truly felt the love of Jesus—that none who are guilty of seducing others into sin and uncleanness—that none who have a name that they live and are dead—and that none who are lukewarm, are worthy members of any Christian communion; and that, while such they continue, no Christian communion can be profitable to them. But unto them is " space to repent " given. And to them the word and Spirit speak in entreaties, encouragements, exhortations, and warnings; that they may turn from their sins to the Saviour, and that they may live and not die.

4

But were there one name in Sodom, or a few in
Sardis, that are the Lord's, He knows and names
them every one; and precious in his sight is the
death of his saints. Some, on the other hand, may
be sunk into the depths of Satan, though in outward
fellowship with a church, were such to be found, as
pure as once was that of Thyatira. Whatever, therefore, the profession of your faith may be, seek the
kingdom of God and his righteousness; that kingdom which is righteousness and peace, and joy in
the Holy Ghost, and that righteousness which is
through faith in Christ, who gave himself for the
church that he might sanctify and cleanse it. And
whatever dangers may then encompass you around,
fear not—only believe; all things are possible to
him that believeth.

It was by keeping the word of the Lord, and not
denying his faith, by hearing what the Spirit said,
that the church of Philadelphia held fast what they
had, and no man took their crown, though situated
directly between the church of Laodicea, which was
lukewarm, and Sardis, which was dead. And dead
as Sardis was, the Lord had a few names in it which
had not defiled their garments—Christians, worthy
of the name, who lived, as you yourself should ever
live, in the faith of the Lord Jesus—dead unto sin,
and alive unto righteousness; while all around them,
though naming the name of Jesus, were dead in
trespasses and sins. Try your faith by its fruits;
judge yourselves that you be not judged; examine
yourselves whether you be in the faith; prove your
own selves; and, with the whole counsel of God, as
revealed in the gospel, open to your view, let the rule
of your self-scrutiny be what the Spirit said unto the
churches.

If you have seen any wonderful things out of the
law of the Lord, and have looked, though from afar

off, on the judgments of God that have come upon the earth, lay not aside the thought of these things when you now lay down this little book. Treat them not as if they were an idle tale, or as if you yourself were not to be a witness—and more than a witness— of a far greater judgment which shall be brought nigh unto you, and shall be your own.

If, in traversing some of the plainest paths of the field of prophecy, you have been led by a way which you knew not of before, let that path lead you to the well of living waters, which springeth up into ever-lasting life to every one that thirsts after it and drinks. Let the words of our Lord and Saviour Jesus Christ be to you this well-spring of the Christian life. Let the word of God enlighten your eyes, and it will also rejoice your heart. Search the Scriptures, in them are no lying divinations; they testify of Jesus, and in them you will find eternal life. Pray for the teaching and the aid of that Spirit by whose inspiration they were given. And above all Christian virtues, that may bear witness of your faith, put on charity, love to God, and love to man, the warp and woof of the Christian's new vesture without a seam; even that charity, or love, by which faith worketh; which is the fruit of the Spirit, the end of the commandment, the fulfilling of the law, the bond of perfectness, and a better gift and a more excellent way than speaking with tongues, or inter-preting or prophesying; and without which you would be as nothing, though you understood all mystery and all knowledge. From the want of this the earth has been covered with ruins. Let it be yours, and, however poor may be your earthly por-tion, it will be infinitely more profitable to you than all the kingdoms of the world, and all their glory. Prophecies shall fail; tongues shall cease; know-ledge shall vanish away; the earth and the works

that are therein shall be burned up; but charity
never faileth.

If you have kept the word of the Lord, and have
not denied His name, hold that fast which thou hast,
that no man take thy crown.   But if heretofore you
have been lukewarm, and destitute of Christian faith
and zeal, and hope, and love, it would be vain, in
closing a chapter on such a subject, to leave you
with any mortal admonition; hear what the Spirit
saith, and harden not your heart against the heavenly counsel, and the glorious encouragement given
unto you by that Jesus, of whom all the prophets
bear witness, and unto whom all things are now committed by the Father.—" I counsel thee to buy of
me gold tried in the fire, that thou mayest be rich;
and white raiment, that thou mayest be clothed, and
that the shame of thy nakedness do not appear; and
anoint thine eyes with eye-salve, that thou mayest
see.   As many as I love I rebuke and chasten; be
zealous, therefore, and repent.   Behold I stand at
the door and knock: if any man hear my voice, and
open the door, I will come in to him, and will sup
with him, and he with me.   To him that overcometh will I grant to sit with me in my throne,
even as I also overcame, and am sat down with my
Father in his throne.   He that hath an ear to
hear, let him hear what the Spirit saith unto the
churches."

CHAPTER IX.

DANIEL'S PROPHECY OF THE THINGS NOTED IN THE SCRIPTURE OF TRUTH.

THERE is a connected series of predictions, emphatically denominated the Things noted in the Scripture of Truth, which forms a commentary upon some of the more obscure prophecies—which give a condensed but precise account of the history of many kings—which marks the propagation, the persecution, the establishment, and the corruptions of Christianity—and which, while it commences with the reign of Cyrus, who delivered the Jews from their first captivity, describes, with the utmost precision, the rise, extent, and fall of that power which was to possess Judea in the latter times, previous to their final restoration. The prophecy is both local and chronological. It is descriptive of the government of the same identical region, and of the chief facts which relate to it, for many successive ages, and also of the spiritual tyranny which reigned for so long a period over Christendom. The events follow in succession, in the exact order of the prediction. They are not shadowed under types or figures, but foretold, in general, with the plainness of a narrative, and with the precision of facts. And Daniel relates them, not as delivered by him to others, but as declared in a vision to himself by an angel. These claims upon attention might well command it, even although the prophecy referred not, as it does, to a subject peculiarly interesting at the present critical period of the history of the world.

To enumerate all the particulars would be to transcribe all the words of the prophecy ;—but they afford too conclusive an evidence to be passed over in silence. The observations of Sir Isaac Newton on this prophecy contain a circumstantial detail of the historical events, and of their application to the prediction.* A succinct and general view may be here given. The prophecy includes the whole of the eleventh chapter of Daniel :—" *And now I will show thee the truth. Behold there shall stand up three kings in Persia :* (Cambyses, Smerdis, and Darius Hystaspes,) *and the fourth* (Xerxes) *shall be far richer than they all : and by his strength through his riches he shall stir up all against the realm of Grecia. And a mighty king* (Alexander the Great,) *shall stand up, that shall rule with great dominion, and do according to his will. And when he shall stand up, his kingdom shall be broken, and shall be divided towards the four winds of heaven ; and not to his posterity, nor according to his dominion which he ruled : for his kingdom shall be plucked up even for others besides those.*"†

Soon after the death of Alexander the Great, his kingdom was divided towards the four winds of heaven, but not to his posterity ; four of his captains, Ptolemy, Antigonus, Lysimachus, and Cassander, reigned over Egypt, Syria, Thrace and Greece. The kingdoms of Egypt and of Syria became afterwards the most powerful : they subsisted as independent monarchies for a longer period than the other two ; and, as they were more immediately connected with the land of Judea, which was often reduced to their dominion, they form the subject of the succeeding predictions ‡ Bishop Newton gives even a more copious illustration of the historical facts, which verify the whole of this prophecy, than that which had previously been given by

---

* See Appendix III.　　　† Dan. xi. 2, 3, 4.
‡ Dan. v. 5, 30.

his illustrious predecessor of the same name—who
has rendered that name immortal. He quotes or
refers to authorities in every instance : and his disser-
tation on that part of the prophecy which relates to
the kingdoms of Syria and Egypt, is wound up in
these emphatic words : " It may be proper to stop
here, and reflect a little how particular and circumstantial this prophecy is concerning the kingdoms of
Egypt and Syria, from the death of Alexander to the
time of Antiochus Epiphanes. There is not so complete and regular a series of their kings—there is not
so concise and comprehensive an account of their
affairs to be found in any author of these times. The
prophecy is really more perfect than any history. No
one historian hath related so many circumstances,
and in such exact order of time, as the prophet hath
foretold them ; so that it was necessary to have re
course to several authors, Greek and Roman, Jewish
and Christian ; and to collect here something from
one, and to collect there something from another, for
better explaining and illustrating the great variety of
particulars contained in this prophecy." So close is
the coincidence between the prophetic and the real
history of the kings of Egypt and of Syria, that
Porphyry, one of the earliest opponents of Christianity, laboured to prove its extreme accuracy, and
alleged, from thence, that the events must have preceded the prediction. The same argument is equally
necessary, at the present hour, to disprove the subsequent parts of the same prophecy—though none
can urge it now. The last of those facts to which it
refers, the accomplishment of which is already past,
are unfolded with equal precision and truth as the
first—and the fulfilment of the whole is yet incomplete. The more clearly that the event corresponds
to the prediction, instead of being an evidence against
the truth, the more conclusive is the demonstration

that it is the word of Him who hath the times and the seasons in his own power.

The subject of the prophecy is represented in these words :—" I am come to make thee understand what shall befall thy people in the latter days ; for the vision is for many days."* And that which is noted in the Scripture of Truth terminates not with the reign of Antiochus. At that very time the Romans extended their conquests towards the East. Macedonia, the seat of the empire of Alexander the Great, became a province of the Roman empire. And the prophecy, faithfully tracing the transition of power, ceases to prolong the history of the kings of Egypt and of Syria—and becomes immediately descriptive of the progress of the Roman arms. The very term *(shall stand up,)* which previously marked the commencement of the Persian and of the Macedonian power, is here repeated, and denotes the commencement of a third era or a new power. The word, in the original, is the same in each. And *arms* (an epithet sufficiently characteristic of the extensive military power of the Romans,) *shall stand up, and they shall pollute the sanctuary of strength, and shall take away the daily sacrifice, and they shall place the abomination that maketh desolate.†* All these things, deeply affecting the Jewish state, the Romans did—and they finally rendered the country of Judea " desolate of its old inhabitants." The propagation of Christianity—the succeeding important event—is thus represented :—*The people that do know their God shall be strong and do exploits. And they that understand among the people shall instruct many.* The persecutions which they suffered are as significantly described :—*Yet they shall fall by the sword and by flame, by captivity and by spoil*

---

* Dan. x. 14.   † Ib. xi. 31.

many days. Now, when they shall fall, they shall be holpen with a little help, and many shall cleave to them with flatteries. And such was Constantine's conversion and the effect which it produced. No other government but that of the Romans *stood up*—but the mode of that government was changed. After the days of Constantine, Christianity became gradually more and more corrupted. Previously to that period, there had existed no system of dominion analogous to that which afterwards prevailed. The greatest oppressors had never extended their pretensions beyond human power, nor usurped a spiritual tyranny. But, in contradiction to every other, and *diverse* from that of the ten kingdoms into which the Roman empire was subdivided, and peculiarly marked by its persecuting spirit, (Dan. vii. 24, 25,) the next succeeding form of government, unparalleled in its nature, in the annals of despotism or of delusion, is thus characterised by the prophet :—*And the king* (the ruling power, signifying any government, state, or potentate)† *shall do according to his will ; and he shall exalt himself and magnify himself above every god, and shall speak marvellous things against the God of gods, and shall prosper till the indignation be accomplished.*‡ The papal power of Rome gradually succeeded to the imperial ; and the pretension of the popes, and the prerogatives which they actually exercised during many ages, far exceeded that of the Cæsars, or of any earthly potentates whatever. They claimed and exercised a sovereignty of a higher order, over the minds as well as over the bodies of men, than kings ever ventured to assume. They dispensed with, alike, and altered at

* Dan xi. 32, 33, 34, 35.
† See Bishop Newton on this Prophecy.
‡ Dan. xi. 36, &c.

their pleasure, the laws both of God and of man, wherever these would have otherwise limited their authority, or controlled their *will*. They claimed supremacy and infallibility as inalienably their own. " The commandments of the church" were not only held of equal authority with the word of God, but the interpretation given to them by the church was held as the only rule of faith ; and the Bishop of Rome suppressed the propagation of the gospel. A bull, or edict of the pope, once sufficed throughout Christendom for the deposition of monarchs ; and millions were released from their allegiance by a word. By dispensations from the pope, oaths lost their validity, and sin its guilt. He did according to his will, and exalted and magnified himself above every god, and spake marvellous things against the God of gods ; and long did he continue to *prosper*. But the recent termination of his power may show that the *indignation*, if not already in progress, is about to be accomplished.

The prevalence of superstition, the prohibition, or discouragement of marriage, and the worship of saints, as characteristic of the same period and of the same power, are thus prophetically described :—" *Neither shall he regard the God of his fathers nor the desire of women* (or matrimony,) *neither shall he regard any God.** *But in his estate shall he honour the God of forces*"—MAHUZZIM—protectors or guardians, a term so applicable to the worship of saints, and to the confidence which was reposed in them, that expressions exactly synonymous are often used by many ancient writers in honour of them—of which Mede and Sir Isaac Newton have adduced a multiplicity of instances. Mahuzzim were the *tutelary saints* of the Greek and Romish churches. The subserviency, which long existed, of spiritual power to temporal

* Dan. xi. 37, 38.

aggrandizement, is also noted in the prophecy :—
*and he shall cause them to rule over many, and shall
divide the land for gain.** And that the principal
teachers and propagators of the worship of *Mahuzzim*
—" the bishops, priests and monks, and religious orders, have been honoured and reverenced, and esteemed in former ages ; that their authority and jurisdic-
tion have extended over the purses and consciences of
men ; that they have been enriched with noble buildings and large endowments, and have had the choicest
of the lands appropriated for church-lands ;—are
points of such notoriety that they require no proof,
and will admit of no denial."†

Having thus described the Antichristian Power,
which prospered so long and prevailed so widely, the
prophecy next delineates, in less obscure terms, the
manner in which that power was to be humbled and
overthrown, and introduces a more particular definition of the rise, extent, and fall of that kingdom
which was to oppress and supplant it in the latter
days. *And at the time of the end shall the king of the
south push at him.*‡ The Saracens extended their conquests over great part of Asia and of Europe : They
penetrated the dominions of the Grecian empire, and
partially subdued, though they could not entirely sub-
vert it, nor obtain possession of Constantinople the capital city. The prediction, however brief, significantly
represents their warfare which was desultory, and their
conquest which was incomplete. And Arabia is situated
to the south of Palestine. The Turks, the next and the
last invaders of the Grecian empire, were of Scythian
extraction, and came from the North.§ And, while
a single expression identifies the Saracen invasion—
the irruption of the Turks being of a more fatal cha-

---

* Dan. v. 39.   † Bishop Newton.   ‡ Dan. xi. 40.
§ Gibbon's Hist. vol. iv. 136—vol. v. 527.

racter and more permanent in its effects, is fully described. Every part of the description is most faithful to the facts. Their local situation, the impetuosity of their attack, the organization of their armies, and the success of their arms, form the first part of the prediction respecting them. *And the king of the north shall come against him like a whirlwind, with chariots and with horsemen and with many ships ; and he shall enter into the countries, and shall overflow and pass over.** Although the Grecian empire withstood the predatory warfare of the Saracens, it gave way before the overwhelming forces of the Turks, whose progress was tracked with destruction, and whose coming was indeed like a whirlwind. Chariots and horsemen were to be the distinguishing marks of their armies, though armies in general contain the greatest proportion of foot soldiers. And, in describing their first invasion of the Grecian territory, Gibbon relates, that "the myriads of Turkish horse overspread a frontier of six hundred miles, from Taurus to Arzeroum, and the blood of one hundred and thirty thousand Christians was a grateful sacrifice to the Arabian prophet.† The Turkish armies at first consisted so exclusively of horsemen, that the stoutest of the youths of the captive Christians were afterwards taken and trained as a band of infantry, and called janisaries, (yengi cheri) or new soldiers."‡ In apparent contradiction to the nature of their army, they were also to possess many ships. And Gibbon again relates, that "a fleet of two hundred ships was constructed by the hands of the captive Greeks."§ But no direct evidence is necessary to prove, that many ships must have been re-

* Dan. xi. 40.
† Gibbon's Hist. vol. v. p. 538, c. 57.
‡ Ib. vi. p. 297, c. 64.
§ Gibbon's Hist. vol. v. p. 553.

quisite for the capture of so many islands, and the destruction of the Venetian naval power, which was once the most celebrated in Europe. "The words, *shall enter into the countries and overflow and pass over*, give us an exact idea of their *overflowing* the western parts of Asia, and then passing over into Europe."*

He shall enter also into the glorious land, and many countries *shall be overthrown.†* This expression, *the glorious land*, occurs in the previous part of this prophecy, (v. 16,) and in both cases, it evidently means the land of Israel; and such the Syriac translation renders it. The Holy Land formed part of the earliest conquests of the Turks, before their career of conquest was suspended. *And many* countries *shall be overthrown*, or, according to the original, *many shall be overthrown*. The entrance of the Turks into Palestine led the way to the Crusades, which, as much as any event in the history of man, was marked by the overthrow of many. The king of the north, or the Turkish sultan, *entered into the countries and overflowed them*, before his conquests extended to Judea; and after the crusades had ceased, he stretched his hand anew over the *countries*. In the intervening period *many were overthrown.‡* "The recovery of the Holy Land," was deemed an adequate recompense for the sacrifice of the lives of many thousands; and Europe contended with Asia for the possession of Palestine, which it could not ultimately rescue from the Turks. Yet, while Europe could not wrest from them one portion of Syria, another did escape out of their hands, though that region partially intersects the Turkish dominions, and divides one portion of them

* Bishop Newton.
† Dan xi. 41.
‡ The writer has entered more fully into the prophetical history of the Turks in a separate publication.

from another, forming a singular contrast to the general continuity of kingdoms. And, while every particular prediction respecting these separate states has been fully verified, their escaping out of the hands of the Turks has been no less marvellously fulfilled. *But these shall escape out of his hand, even Edom and Moab, and the chief of the children of Ammon.*[*] Mede, Sir Isaac and Bishop Newton, in applying this prophecy to the Turkish empire, could only express, in general terms, that the Arabs possessed these countries, and exacted tribute from the Turks for permitting their caravans to pass through them. But recent travellers, among whom Volney has to be numbered, have unconsciously given the most satisfactory information, demonstrative of the truth of all the minutiæ of the prediction. Volney described these countries in part—Burckhardt traversed them all—and they have since been visited by other travellers. Edom and Moab are in possession of the Bedouin (or wandering) Arabs. The Turks have often attempted, in vain, to subjugate them. The partial escape of Ammon from their dominion is not less discriminating than just. For, although that territory lies in the immediate vicinity of the Pachalic of Damascus, to which part of it is subjected,—though it be extremely fertile by nature,—though its situation and its soil have thus presented, for several centuries, the strongest temptation to Turkish rapacity—though they have often attempted to subdue it,—yet no fact could have been more explicitly detailed, or more incidentally communicated, than that the inhabitants of the greater part of that country, particularly what adjoins the ancient but now desolate city of Ammon, " live in a state of complete independence of the Turks."[†]

---

[*] Dan. xi. 41.
[†] Buckingham's Travels, pp. 325, 329, 337. Burckhardt's

*He shall stretch forth his hand also upon the countries.** How significantly do these words represent the vast extent of the Turkish empire, which alone has stretched its dominion over many countries of Asia, of Europe, and of Africa. Ill-fated Egypt was not to escape from subjection to such a master. *And the land of Egypt shall not escape; but he shall have power over the treasures of gold and of silver, and over all the precious things of Egypt.*† The Turks have drained Egypt of its wealth, of its gold, and of its silver, and of its precious things : and such power have they exercised over them, that the kingdom of the Pharaohs, the land where everlasting pyramids were built, despoiled to the utmost, is now one of the poorest, as it has long been the basest of the kingdoms. *The Lybians and Ethiopians shall be at his steps.*‡ These form the extremities of the Turkish empire, and were partially subject to its power. " After the conquest of Egypt, the terror of Selim's victories," says the historian, " spreading wide, the kings of Africa, bordering upon Cyrenaica, sent their ambassadors, with offers to become his tributaries. Other more remote nations also towards Ethiopia were easily induced to join in amity with the Turks."§ Such is the prophetic description of the rise and extent of that power which was to possess Judea in the latter days ; and it is a precise delineation of the rise and extent of the Turkish Empire to which Judea has been subject for centuries.

Travels in Nubia, p. 44th of Memoir. Letter to Sir Joseph Banks. Burckhardt's Travels in Syria, pp. 349, 355.
* Dan. xi. 42.   † Ibid. 43.   ‡ Ibid.
§ Pauli Jovi Hist. quoted by Bishop Newton.

But other events seem to be rising up to view—
and the time would also seem to be drawing nigh—
when that which *shall befall the* Jews *in the latter
days*, shall become the subject of history, and when
the last part of the vision shall be unsealed.

CONCLUSION.

THE whole of the preceding brief and imperfect
sketch forms little else than an enumeration of some
of the more striking prophecies, and of facts which
demonstrate their fulfilment ; and a recapitulation
of all the particulars would be an unnecessary repetition. The numerous obscure prophecies which
contain much and striking evidence, have hitherto been omitted, that the charge of ambiguity, too
generally and indiscriminately attached to them all,
might be proved to be unfounded. But, having
seen, in hundreds of instances, that prophecies which
were plainly delivered, have been as clearly fulfilled,
comprehending them all in a single argument, and
leaving the decision to the enemies of Christianity,
or to those who are weak in the faith, and appealing
to their reason without bespeaking their favour,—
may it not, in the first instance, be asked if it be an
easy task which is assigned them, to disprove even
this part of the POSITIVE EVIDENCE to the truth of

the religion of Jesus ? If they have ever staggered at the promises or threatenings of the Scriptures because of unbelief—discrediting all *revelation* from on high —can they not here discern supernatural evidence in confirmation of supernatural truths ? May not *sight* lead them to *faith ?* Must they not concede that the Christian has some reason for the hope that is in him ? And may they not, at the very least, be led from thence to the calm and unprejudiced investigation, not only of the other prophecies, but of all the evidence which Christianity presents?

It cannot be alleged, with truth, that the prophecies which have been selected are ambiguous ; that they bear the character of those auguries which issued from the cloud that always overhung the temple of Apollo, or of those pretended inspirations which emanated from the cave of Hera. It cannot be denied, that they were all foretold hundreds or thousands of years before the events, which even at the present day demonstrate their fulfilment, though every other oracle has ceased for ages to appeal to a single fact. And the historical and geographical facts, which were so clearly foretold, are, in general, of so wonderful a nature, that the language of prophecy, though expressive of literal truths, seems at first sight to be hyperbolical ; and the prophecies of Isaiah, in particular, have been charged with being " full of extravagant metaphor ;"* the more extrava-

---

* Were it not for the impiety with which they are conjoined, the remarks of Paine on the prophecies would, to those who have studied these at all, be sufficiently amusing. He characterises the book of Isaiah as " one continued bombastical rant, full of extravagant metaphor, without application, and destitute of meaning." The predictions respecting Babylon, Moab, &c. are forsooth compared " to the story of the Knight of the Burning Mountain, the story of Cin-

gant the metaphor, or the more remarkable the predicted fact, the farther are the prophecies removed from all possibility of their having been the words of human invention.

The following comprehensive and luminous statement of the argument, extracted from a review of the former edition of this treatise, is here so apposite, that no apology need be offered for inserting it at length.

" This geographical argument (viz. the fulfilment of those prophecies which describe the future fate of particular nations, and the future aspect of their countries,) has always appeared to us one of the most impregnable strongholds of Christian prophecy ; or rather one of the most resistless and wide-ranging instruments of aggressive evidence. There is no obscurity in the language of the prophet.

derella," and such like. Isaiah, in short, " was a lying prophet and impostor." And " what can we say," he asks, " of these prophets, but that they were all impostors and liars ?" Such words are not merely harmless ; they may be also useful, as they show, that while every possible corroboration from history, fact, reason, and even the unconscious testimony of infidels themselves, is given to the truth of the prophecies ; nothing can be alleged on the other hand but what in the sight of all men manifestly is " bombastical rant, and extravagant metaphor, without application, and destitute of meaning. And since both speak not the truth, who is the liar ?" Isaiah the prophet or Paine the infidel ? And " what can we say " of this staunch assertor of rights, but that *his* right to the title is undisputed, and that these very words of his, were others wanting, must in every " age of reason" rivet to his unblest memory the foul aspersions he so falsely applied ? Argument in such a case would be an idle waste of words. But while it would be an act of mere prodigality and folly to cast pearls before swine, the filth which they have snorted out may well be cast into their own kennel again, that they and their kind may partake of what pertains to them.

There is no variety of opinion with regard to the object in his view. There is no denying of the change which he predicts. There is no challenging of the witnesses who prove the facts of the case. The former glory of these regions and kingdoms is recorded by ancient heathen historians, who knew nothing of the fall foretold. Their present state is described by recent and often infidel travellers, who knew often as little of the predictions which they were verifying by their narratives. It is not a particular event which has passed away, or a particular character who has perished, for whose era we must search in the wide page of history, and of whose description we may find so many resemblances as to become perplexed in our application. The places and the people are named by the prophet, and the state in which they now exist is matter of actual observation. The fulfilment of the prediction is thus inscribed as upon a public monument, which every man who visits the countries in question may behold with his own eyes; and is expressed in a language so universally intelligible, that every man may be said to read it in his own tongue. To these scenes of Scripture prophecy we may point with triumph as to ocular demonstration; and say to the sceptical inquirer, in the words of the evangelist, ' Come and see.' The multitude of travellers who have recently visited the Holy Land and the adjacent regions, have furnished ample and authentic materials for the construction of so irrefragable an argument. Many of these travellers have discovered no intention of advocating by their statements the cause of revealed truth; and some of them have been obviously influenced by hostility to its claims. Yet in spite of these prejudices, and altogether unconsciously on their part, they have recorded the most express confirmation of the Scripture prophecies, frequently employing in their descriptions the very language of inspiration, and bringing into view (though evidently without design) those features of the scene which form the precise picture painted in the visions of the prophet."

Willingly might the Christian here rest his assurance " in the faith once delivered to the saints," and leave to the unbeliever his hopeless creed. But the reasonings of one class of infidels must be combined with the researches of another to give full force to the *Evidence of Prophecy :* and they jointly supply both the clearest facts and the strongest arguments, and have made ready the means which need only to be applied for bringing the controversy with them, in its various bearings, and in their own words, to a short issue.

The metaphysical speculations of Hume,* and the mathematical demonstrations of La Place, which have

---

* It may not be here amiss to allude to that kind and courteous admonition to Christian writers, so meekly given, and with wisdom rivalling its modesty, by this great master of *ideal* philosophy, in which, in order perhaps to bring their arguments to cope the better with his own, he prescribes to them, as best suited to their cause, the total rejection of reason ! After quoting a passage from Lord Bacon's Works, which has a very different application, he adds,— *This method of reasoning* (about monsters, magic, and alchymy, &c.) *may serve to confound those dangerous friends or disguised enemies of the Christian religion, who have undertaken to defend it by the principles of human reason,* (of whom, by the bye, Lord Bacon was one, and Sir Isaac Newton another.) *Our most holy religion is founded on faith, not on reason ; and it is a sure method of exposing it to put it to such a trial as it is by no means fitted to endure. (Hume's Essays, § 10. v. ii. pp. 136, 7. Ed. Edin. 1800.)* If these words may not justly be retorted against the " unbeliever's creed," excluding the epithet of holy ; or *if* Mr. David Hume was better acquainted with the principles of the Christian Religion than the Author of it, who appealed to the *reason* of men, and

been directed against the credibility of the miracles, rest entirely on the " *Theory of Probability.*" Assuming its logical and ligitimate application to the testimony of any supernatural evidence of a divine revelation, it is argued that the *improbabilities* of the occurrence of miracles, being contradictory to uniform experience, are so extreme as to destroy entirely the

asked them why they did not of themselves judge that which was right, and than the apostles Peter and Paul, who enjoin Christians to try all things, and to hold fast to that which is good, and to be able to give an answer to every one that asketh them a *reason* of the hope that is in them; then the writer of this treatise having only the hard alternative of being either " a dangerous friend or a disguised enemy of the Christian religion," would, with whatever reluctance, prefer the former, and has to lament the evil he has done, and the " sure method" he has taken " of exposing it." And although he may hope that Christians in their charity will forgive him, he must yet leave to unbelievers the comfort and the joy of the triumph, which, in the exercise of that reason which they have monopolized, these pages must necessarily give them. Or if, on the other hand, in somewhat stricter accordance with the truths of Scripture, the author of the Essay on *Human Nature* supplies, by the prefixed words, as clear practical proof, in his " Academical Philosophy," or Scepticism in Theory, that it is one of the characteristics of the *heart of man* to be *deceitful above all things*, as mere worldly wisdom and infidelity in practice too frequently demonstrate that it is also *desperately wicked:* and if Scripture prophecy can " endure the trial of reason," and its evidence be rejected—then the disciples of Hume, the traducers of the Christian religion as not founded on reason, holding to " human nature" as of itself it is, and deriding the idea of its proffered ransom from the guilt and rescue from the power of sin, have need, without exhausting their reason in abstract speculations, to look to their own harder alternative, and (if both be not possibly conjoined) to choose between the incomparable deceitfulness and desperate wickedness of the heart within—evils greater far than all that the Christian can ever fear for himself from all the sneers of the sophist, or the railings of the ungodly.

validity of *any* testimony to their truth which has been transmitted through so many ages. " And upon the whole, we may conclude," says Hume, " that the Christian religion, even at this day, cannot be believed by any reasonable person without a miracle." What then is the evidence, that, even at this day, there are subsisting miracles which must command the belief of every person to the truth of the Christian religion, who is not so utterly unreasonable, and his mind so steeled against conviction, as not to be persuaded even by miraculous demonstration ? And in what better or less exceptionable " method " can this evidence be meted out than according to the very " measure of probability " in use with unbelievers ; and by means of which they profess to have discovered the deficiency of testimony to the truth of ancient miracles ?

Archimedes demanded only a spot whereon to stand that he might move the world. If the most reasonable concession from the infidel be not as impossible to be obtained as the demand of Archimedes ; and if he will admit either the truth of his own principles, or the force of mathematical proof, or if his prejudices be not immoveable as a world, the existing and obvious fulfilment of a multiplicity of prophecies might well excite his attention, and convince him of the truth.

The *doctrine of chances*, or calculation of probabilities, has been reduced into a science, and is now in various ways of great practical use, and securely acted upon in the affairs of life. But it is altogether impossible that short-sighted man could select, from the infinite multitude of the possible contingencies of distant ages, any one of such particular facts as abound in the prophecies ; and it is manifest that, upon the principle of probabilities, the chance would be incalculable against the success of the attempt, even in a

single instance. Each accomplished prediction is a
miracle. But the advocate for Christianity may safely concede much, and reduce his data to the lowest
terms. And if the unbeliever reckon not his own
cause utterly hopeless, and " by no means fitted to
endure the trial of reason," he must grant that there
was as great a probability that *each* prediction would
not as that it *would* have been fulfilled ; or that the
probabilities were *equal* for and against the occurrence
of *each* predicted event. The Christian may fearlessly descend to meet him even on this very lowly
ground. And without enumerating all the particulars
included in the volume of prophecy respecting the life
and character and death of Christ—the nature and extent of Christianity, &c.—the destruction of Jerusalem—the fate of the Jews in every age and nation—
the existing state of Judea, of Ammon, Moab, Edom,
Philistia, Babylon, Tyre, Egypt, the Arabs, &c. the
Church of Rome, and the prophetic history which
extends throughout two thousand three hundred
years ; may it not be assumed (though fewer would
suffice, and though incontestable evidence has been
adduced to prove more than double the number) that
a *hundred* different particulars have been foretold
and fulfilled ? What, then, even upon these data,
is the *chance*, on a calculation of probabilities, that
all of them would have proved true,—the chance di-
minishing one-half for every number, (or what, in
other words, is the hundredth power of two to
unity ?)* Such is the desperate hazard to which the
unbeliever would trust, that even from these premises,
it is *mathematically demonstrable* that the number of
chances is far greater against him than the number of

* Essai Philosophique sur les Probabilités, par. M. Le
Comte La Place. Emerson on Chances, prop. 3. Hutton's
edit. of Ozanam's Mathemat. Recr. v. i.

drops in the ocean, although the whole world were one globe of water. Let the chance at least be counted before it be confided in. But who would risk a single mite against the utmost possible gain, at the stake on which unbelievers here recklessly put to certain peril the interests of eternity?

But each prediction recorded in Scripture, being a *miracle of knowledge*, is equal to any miracle of power, and could have emanated only from the Deity. "All prophecies are real miracles, and as such only can be admitted as proof of any revelation."* They may even be said to be peculiarly adapted, in the present age of extended knowledge and enlightened inquiry, for being " the testimony of Jesus;" and they cannot justly be viewed as of inferior importance or authority to any miracles whatever.

Though the founder of a new religion, or the messenger of a divine revelation, and his immediate followers, who had to promulgate his doctrine, would give clear and unequivocal proof, by working miracles, that their commission was from on high: yet,

---

* Hume's Essays, vol. ii. p. 137. This statement of Hume's, combined with the manifest truth of prophecy, shows how all his theory against the truth of miracles may easily be overthrown by an admission of his own. Prophecy being true, and uniformly true, and all prophecies being real miracles, miracles are *not* contrary to universal, or even in a restricted sense, to uniform experience. They " are rendered probable by so many analogies," (Ib. p. 134,) that on sufficient testimony they become proveable, even upon Hume's own principles, especially when the inspiration of those very Scriptures, which record the disputed miracles, is verified by other miracles, the truth of which is established and experienced. And thus the boldest dogmas of scepticism may not only be braved but reversed; and *it is more wonderful that the testimony*, sealed in blood and rendered credible by miracles equally great, *should be false, than that the miracles should be true.*

the relation between any miraculous event, wrought
in after-ages, and a religion previously established,
might not be so apparent. Or, even if it were, yet
any single and transient act of superhuman power,
being confined to a particular region, and cognizable
only by a limited number, the testimony of these
witnesses would be regarded only as secondary evidence, and could not, at least in a Christian land,
be substantiated by proof so complete as that which
was sealed by the blood of martyrs. And even if
perpetual manifestations of miraculous power (however much men in apparent vindication of their unbelief may unreasonably ask such proof,) were submitted to the inspection and experience of each individual in every age, they would only seem to distort
the order and frame of nature, and by thus disturb-
ing the regularity and uniformity of her operations,
would, from their very frequency, cease to be regarded as supernatural ; and influenced by the
same sceptical thoughts, those who now demand a
sign would then be the first to discredit it. And
true to reason and to nature it is, that those who
will not believe Moses and the prophets would not
be persuaded though one rose from the dead. For
the prophecies bear a direct reference to religion that
is easily comprehended, and that cannot be misapplied. They have a natural and obvious meaning
that may be known and read of all men. " Thus
saith the Lord " is their prefix ; this is the fact is
their proof. Instead of being weakened by the greatness of their number, the more they are multiplied,
or the more frequently that facts formerly unknown, or events yet future, spring up in their verification, their evidence is redoubled, and they are ever
permanent and existing witnesses that the word is of
God. And farther, the testimony which, in every
passing age, confirms their truth cannot be cavilled at :

it is not "diluted by transmission through many ages;"
it is borne, not to events in themselves miraculous, but
to natural facts, whether historical or geographical,
which have been proved by conclusive evidence, and
which in numerous instances still subsist to stand the
test of any inquiry. And even many of the facts,
(such as the whole history of the expatriated Jews,)
are witnessed by all, and need no testimony whatever
to declare them. And the records of the prophecies,
preserved throughout every age by the enemies of
Christianity, are in every hand. If, then, no evidence less exceptionable, more conclusive, or more
clearly miraculous could be given, the disciples of
Hume, in resigning an "academic" for a Christian
faith, have only to apply aright the words of their
master—"a wise man proportions his belief to the
evidence;"* and they may thus find—what he in
vain thought that he had discovered—an "everlasting check" against "delusion."†

It was the boast of Bolingbroke, in summing up
his "Philosophical" labours, that "he had pushed
inquiry as far as the true means of inquiry are open,
that is, as far as phenomena could guide him."
Christian philosophy asks no more. It lays open the
"means of inquiry," and presents, in the fulfilment
of many prophecies, "phenomena" more wonderful
than external nature ever exhibited, and demands
only integrity of purpose, and that "inquiry be pushed unto the uttermost," that candour and reason may
thus guide the impartial inquirer, by the light of
positive evidence and miraculous proof, to the conviction and acknowledgment of the inspiration of the
Scriptures.

The argument drawn by Volney from "The Ruin
of Empires," is completely controverted by facts

* Hume's Essay on Miracles, vol. ii. p. 117. † Ib. p. 116.

stated by himself, which, instead of militating against religion, directly establish the truth of prophecy ;—and the unsubstantial fabric which he raised needs no other hand but his own to lay it in the dust.

But ridicule alone has often supplanted reason, and has been held as a test of the truth, and directed especially against the prophecies. And may not an evidence of their inspiration be found even in this last retreat of infidelity! The ruins of the moral world are as obvious in the sight of Omniscience as the ruins of the natural—of cities or of kingdoms: and his word can fortel the one as well as the other. And if those who scoff at religion can perceive no evidence from any historical facts, or any external objects, they might look within, and they would find engraven on their own hearts, in characters sufficiently legible, a confirmation of the prophecies. And if they substitute railing for reason, and think to mar religion with their mockery, to all others they stand convicted, the living witnesses of the truth. "There shall come in the last days, scoffers, walking after their own lusts, and saying, where is the promise of his coming? for, since the fathers fell asleep, ALL THINGS CONTINUE AS THEY WERE FROM THE BEGINNING OF THE CREATION. For this they wilfully are ignorant of that, by the Word of God, the heavens were of old, and the earth standing out of the water and in the water, whereby the world that then was perished." "There shall be mockers in the last time."*

---

* 2 Pet. iii. 3.   Jude 18.

The Christian religion has thus to rank among its enemies many *false teachers* who were to arise, and who, as characterised in Scripture, *speak evil of the things that they understand not—who despise government—who are presumptuous and self-willed, who speak great swelling words of vanity to allure others, promising them liberty while they themselves are the children of corruption, and foaming out their*

But if unbelievers lay just claim to wisdom, and make a fair appeal to reason, then rather than place their security in abstract speculations, and tamper thus

shame. 2 Peter, chap. i. verses 1, 10, 12, 18.—Blasphemy, obscenity, and unmeaning abuse, are the weapons of their warfare: they seek to debase religion into a conformity with their gross and grovelling imaginations, speaking of things that they know not, they utter great swelling words of vanity, as if by a mere glance of their jaundiced mental vision, they could compass at once the whole of religious truth. But their arguments are as weak as their principles are base. And so manifestly does reason disclaim them, that for subverting their false assumptions, it is only necessary, in general, to make the contradiction as flat as the assertion is positive. As an example, it may be remarked, that in a list of aphorisms which lately issued from the London mart of infidelity, the most specious of the whole was thus expressed—"All other religions are false, and, therefore, the Christian religion is false also," or as the *argument* may be more logically stated—all other religions are false, and, therefore, the Christian religion is true. Yet who can look but with sorrow for the fate, as well as disgust and derision at the efforts of such pitiful cavillers, carping at the truth of the Christian religion—like unto foul and small fry (the less dignified the more befitting is the simile) nibbling at some weeds that have been cast by human hands upon a rock, and pressing with all their little strength to move it.

But there is another, and a different class of unbelievers,— to whom the words in the text no less strikingly apply; for they may be brought to confute the subtlest arguments of the ingenious sceptic, as well as to condemn the profane mockery of the most senseless railer. The great argument of infidelity, urged so strenuously in these *last days*, against the credibility of miracles, from the inviolability of the laws of nature, could not be more plainly or forcibly stated than in the words of the apostle, declaring what that argument, the result of modern science, would be. If it had not been urged, a part of Christian evidence, derived from the fulfilment of this prediction, would still have been wanting, and we should still have had to wait for the last argument of infidelity, from whence to draw a new illustration of the truth. But the apostle not only states, he also confutes what scoffers in the last days

with the immortal hopes of their fellow-men, rather than trust in ridicule as the test of religious truth, and call an assumed and yet unpaid license to blasphemy

would say, and not from scriptural authority, unavailing with them, but on philosophical principles, or from facts of which they are *willingly* ignorant,—viz. the creation of the world, and its having been overflowed by water, which show that all things are not as they were at the *beginning* of the creation. Hume, Bentham, and La Place, must yet veil their heads, in the academy as well as in the temple, before the humble fishermen of Galilee. And their reasonings need only to be rightly applied, that they may as strongly advocate the undoubted evidence which miracles give, that the doctrine is of God, as the facts attested by Gibbon and Volney demonstrate that the prophecies of Scripture were given by inspiration of God.—But such a subject can only be touched on in a concluding note; and abundant is the *evidence of prophecy*, seeing that it here needs only to be thus noticed. The transference of the leading argument of infidelity,—which a text and a fact may suffice to transfer,—into an additional and fundamental evidence of the truth, merits a more full consideration: and this new method of dealing with the deist is here referred to, that it may be free to every Christian's use; for it rests not on human invention, but is drawn from the infallible word of the living God—the same Scriptures which, to all who search them, are ever full of treasures, and in which are to be found the words of eternal life.

In these times of inquiry and discovery, it is pleasing to observe how the progress of science becomes ultimately subservient to the cause of truth. Philosophy begins to confess its great error, and to offer some expiation to religion. And in the short space since the publication of the sixth edition of this treatise, new testimony may now be subjoined to the preceding note, not less important towards the illustration of the evidences of Christianity, than the plates of Petra. *The recent origin of man* is a fact now universally admitted by geologists; and in a late number of the Edinburgh Review (No. 104, p. 396,) it is said, in reference to that fact alone, that "it seems to us to BE FATAL TO THE THEORY which we have presumed to call a *misconception* of the uniformity of causation, as signifying an *unalterable* sequence of causes and effects"—or in other words, that it is a demonstration

by the name of liberty—does it not behove them to look first to the positive evidence and miraculous proof of revelation, to detect its fallacy or own its power, and to quit their frail entrenchments, if, indeed, they find that the standard of Christian faith may, in despite of all their efforts, be fixed upon the

that all things have NOT *continued as they were from the beginning of the creation.* " Certain strata have been identified," continues the Reviewer, " with the period of man's first appearance. We cannot do better than quote from Dr. Pritchard's excellent book, *Researches into the Physical History of Mankind,* his comment and application of this fact. ' It is well known that all the strata of which our continents are composed were once a part of the ocean's bed. *There is no land in existence that was not formed beneath* THE SURFACE OF THE SEA, or that has NOT RISEN FROM BENEATH THE WATER. Mankind had a beginning, since we can now look back to the period when the surface on which they lived began to exist. We have only to go back, in imagination, to that age, to represent to ourselves that there existed nothing on this globe but unformed elements, and that in the next period there had begun to breathe, and move, in a particular spot, a human creature, and we shall already have admitted, perhaps, the most astonishing miracle recorded in the whole compass of the sacred writings,' " &c. Thus, in a better and more philosophic spirit, resting on a *fact,* of which the structure of the earth bears witness, and not on an unwarrantable and false assumption, men, without reference to the prediction, have at last discovered the very argument urged by the apostle in refutation of the sceptical saying of scoffers in the last days. *The heavens were of old, and the earth standing out of the water and in the waters.* The earth at first was without form and void. And since the *beginning* of the creation man himself was created. An *unalterable* experience has *not* therefore to be set up against the testimony of the Christian miracles; for there is experience of the truth of, " perhaps, the most astonishing miracle recorded in the whole compass of the sacred writings." The argument of the scoffers, and its manifest confutation, are alike confirmations of the truth of prophecy, itself, too, a miracle.

proudest towers of infidelity? Let them, in the words of the prophet, bring forth their witnesses, that they may be justified, or let them hear, and say, it is truth.

But, in conclusion, it may in reason be asked, if there be not something repugnant to the principles of Christianity in the mind of that man who will not hear Moses and the prophets, and who is slow of heart to believe all that they have spoken, though they afforded the means of detection in every prediction which they uttered, if their prophecies had been false—though they appealed to a vast variety of events which distant ages would bring into existence—though history has answered, and ocular demonstration has confirmed that appeal, our enemies themselves being witnesses—and although there *never was* any other truth that could be tried by such a test? Might he not be convinced of a doctrine less moral, or not quite according to godliness, by evidence less miraculous? Is there no reason to fear that the light of evidence, though sufficient to dispel the cloud upon the understanding, is yet unable to penetrate " the veil upon the heart?" Scepticism, at best, is not a subject for boasting. It is easy to exclude the noon-tide light by closing the eyes; and it is easy to resist the clearest truth by hardening the heart against it. And while, on the other hand, there are minds, (and Newton's was among the number) which are differently affected by the Evidence of Prophecy, and which cannot be callous, when touched by the concentrated rays of such light from heaven, whence can this great dissimilarity of sentiment arise from the same identical and abundant proof? And into what else *can* the want of conviction be resolved than into the scriptural solution of the difficulty—an evil heart of unbelief? " They will not come unto the light because the light would make them free."

But while the unbeliever rejects the means of conviction, and rests his hope on the assumed possibility that his tenets may be true—the positive evidence of Christianity convinces the unprejudiced inquirer, or rational and sincere believer, that it is impossible that his faith can be false. And when he searches out of the book of the Lord, and finds that none of them do fail, he looks on every accomplished prediction, even though it be the effect of the wrath of man, as a witness of God—he knows in whom he believes—he sees the rise and fall of earthly potentates, and the convulsions of kingdoms, testifying of HIM who ruleth among the nations, and accrediting his word—he experiences the conviction that the most delightful of all truth, the hope which perisheth not, is confirmed by the strongest of all testimony, that heaven itself hath ratified the peace which it hath proclaimed—he rests assured that prophecy came not of old time by the will of man, but that holy men of old spake as they were moved by the Holy Ghost—and, although he knows not the mode of the operations of the Spirit, he sees the demonstration of his power. And " taking heed thus unto the sure word of prophecy until the day dawn and the day-star arise in his heart," the true believer learns, from the things that are past, the certainty of the things that are to come hereafter —he rests not satisfied with a mere name that he liveth, while yet he might be dead—but, having obtained that " precious faith," the germ of immortality, which springeth up into eternal life, he experiences the power of the world to come, and unites the practice with the profession of religion—he copies the *zeal* of those who spend their strength for that which is in vain, and their labour for that which profiteth not, but he directs it to the attainment of an incorruptible inheritance, for he knows that his labour shall not be in vain while he yields obedience to that Word which is the Charter of his Salvation, and which so unequivocally bears the seal and superscription of the King of kings.

APPENDIX.

No. I.

CURSORY REMARKS ON SOME OF THE PROPHECIES OF DANIEL.

THE preceding pages are so far from exhausting the subject, or presenting a complete view of the evidence of prophecy, that they only occupy, for the greater part, a space which writers on prophecy have very sparingly touched. Prophecies fulfilled are the miracles of every age of the church. And while new evidence of the inspiration of the Scriptures can so abundantly be educed from geographical facts, discovered in the nineteenth century of the Christian era, there are other predictions, of far more momentous import, which have only partially met their completion, and which the future fate of the world has yet more fully to unseal. Much has been written on the more obscure prophecies, which have already been fulfilled. And different writers have speculated freely on the *mode* in which the predicted events, according to their interpretation, are to be brought to pass. But " the times and the seasons the Father hath in his own power." And, without entering into any minute exposition or detail, the following remarks may tend, in some measure, to show how the obscurity of the symbolical prophecies, which refer to events already past, is, in some instances at least, greatly over-rated—how the objections of infidels may be obviated, and their very arguments be still farther adduced in testimony of the truth of revelation, and how, notwithstanding the obscurity in which these prophecies are involved, it may be manifestly discerned in them, that He who ruleth among the nations has revealed his word to mortals, and that each vision depicted there is the glance of omniscience through the history of man.

The question respecting the more obscure prophecies which the Christian has to argue with the unbeliever is not—whether the same events might not have been foretold in a more distinct and definite manner, (for the predictions themselves are declared to be sealed, or to remain obscure, till the time of the end, or the period of their completion; and as they refer to the political state of the world, or to the successive governments that were to arise, there are obvious reasons for this purposed obscurity, which apply not to the numerous literal predictions.)—But the question *is*, whether, such as they are, and viewed in connexion with other prophecies, they bear not a closer and less convertible similitude to the events of which they were avowedly predictive, than human sagacity could have discerned or invented.

Although the divine mind be perfect in wisdom, yet that wisdom is unsearchable, and the mode of communicating any super-human knowledge must not only be regulated by the nature of the ultimate design of the special revelation, but be adapted also to the perception, capacities, and habits of thought of the human recipients. In the symbolical predictions of Daniel both these ends are perfectly attained. The first, as so expressed, required that the prophecy should be sealed for many days, which was therefore conveyed in a figurative manner. And the symbols themselves are such as were adopted in the practice, and familiar to the understanding of men, and when viewed in conjunction with the explanation given by the prophet, they are, after the event, abundantly significant. It is obvious from history, as well as from ancient coins, that different kingdoms were signified or marked by different emblematical representations. And, notwithstanding the diffusion of knowledge, the same practice is continued to the present day. Instead, therefore, of their being singular or unintelligible, the very method of representing kingdoms is used in these prophetic similitudes, which was then, and still is, common in the world, and which arose perhaps at first from necessity, and was sanctioned afterwards by use.

Not only is the emblematical representation given, but the significancy of the emblems is also explained. And in relation to the same events, in the cases about to be noticed, two different images or figures are represented to view. An accordance in each particular being requisite to a just historical interpretation of the prophecy, there is thus no possibility of any strained accommodation of the events to the prediction; and that interpretation, which is just in every particular, must be strictly and exclusively applicable. And such interpretation having been given, instead of their being now chargeable with impenetrable obscurity, it is not perhaps in the power of human language to give a more unequivocal and less ambiguous symbolical representation, which designedly was to be understood only after the event—of the rise of successive governments, than is given in the book of Daniel, by two different figures, accompanied by an explanation of each.

While the truth of the predictions of Daniel may be investigated in the present day, the undoubted certainty of his inspiration was accredited at the time in a manner at once easy to be understood, and impossible to be controverted, and altogether unparalleled in the annals of heathen oracles.

Nebuchadnezzar, the king of Babylon, at that time the most potent monarch in the world, had, in his conquests over the surrounding nations, subjected the Jews to his authority; and, among other tokens of obeisance which he demanded of the king of Judah, he required that certain princes of the children of Israel, high in character and skilful in wisdom, should be sent from Jerusalem, in order to be placed in his household, and to be numbered among the magicians and astrologers whom he was wont to consult, and who formed one of the appendages of his splendid court. Daniel was one of them. He and his friends of the house of Judah were soon " preferred far beyond all the wise men that were in all the realm." But in the court of a despot the highest subject is a slave. And it soon happened that their lives were in the greatest peril, from which no human prudence could have rescued them. It was the business of every courtier to minister to the will and pleasure of the king, otherwise their lives were in danger of being forfeited at once. And a cause of mental disquietude soon arose in the breast of the king, which his magicians were commanded to remove. His mind had been disturbed by dreams, " his spirit was troubled, and his sleep brake from him ;" and he whose will would brook no control called his wise men, and commanded them to make known the dream and the interpretation thereof. This was a test which all their pretensions could not abide, and a difficulty which all their artifice could not elude. They asked the king " to make known to them the dream, and they would show him the interpretation." In the latter respect they might easily have practised on the credulity of the monarch, and put his mind at ease. " But the dream had gone from him ;" if recalled to his recollection he would at once recognise it ; and those who pretended in other matters to be astrologers, and magicians, and sorcerers, and who could not then deceive him, were commanded to tell the dream itself, and then he should know that they " could also shew him the interpreta- tion." Compliance with a demand so unreasonable was impossible for man ; the attempt was utterly hopeless ; and " they answered the king and said, there is not a man upon the earth that can show the king's matter ; therefore there is no king, lord, nor ruler that asketh such things at any magician, or astrologer, or Chaldean. And it is a rare thing that the king requireth ; and there is none other that can show it before the king except the gods, whose dwelling is not with flesh." These words were true ; though they may have been inconsistent with the pretensions of the magicians when they were not so severely tried. But when the passions are inflamed, the spirit troubled or pride wounded, reason and truth are alike disregarded; and however unjustifiable or barbarous the deed, none could gainsay it: and the king being angry and very furious, and having previously told them that *there was but one decree for them,* commanded to destroy all the wise men of Babylon. All the art of man was baffled; " lying and corrupt words" could be of no avail; something beyond deception, and that could not be accused of it, was necessary here, and wholly unattainable by mortal. A fit occasion, combined as it afterwards proved to be with the revelation of the future fate of the world, was presented for the display of more than human wisdom. He alone, who knoweth the thoughts and intents of the heart, and who is a discerner of the spirit, could communicate to the mind of man that knowledge which the king required. And the God of Abraham, of Isaac, and of Jacob, who had chosen the children of Israel for his peculiar people, that all the families of the earth might finally be blessed in the seed of Abraham, heard the prayers of Daniel, and of the other captive princes of Judah, when innocently condemned to die; and he who turneth the hearts of men as the rivers of water, and who holds in his hands the thoughts of kings as well as of their subjects, was pleased to reveal the secret unto Daniel in a night vision. And it was to God that he expressed his gratitude, and ascribed all the praise.—" Then Daniel blessed the God of heaven. Blessed be the name of God for ever and ever, for wisdom and might are his. And he changeth the times and the seasons. He removeth kings and setteth up kings: he giveth wisdom to the wise, and knowledge to them that know understanding. He revealeth the deep and secret things. He knoweth what is in the darkness, and the light dwelleth with him. I thank thee and praise thee, O thou God of my fathers, who hast given me wisdom and might, and hast made known unto me now what we desired of thee, for thou hast made known unto us the king's matter." And as Daniel thus offered up his praise and gratitude in secret prayer unto God, so he boasted not of himself before the king, nor attributed the knowledge of the secret to his own wisdom, but gave all the glory unto God, declaring that there is a God in heaven that revealeth secrets, and maketh known WHAT SHALL BE IN THE LATTER DAYS. (Dan. chap. ii.)

Daniel told unto the king his dream—the vision of his head upon his bed—and the thoughts that had come into his mind, and that (till Daniel recalled them) had passed from his own remembrance.

It is impossible to conceive a more discriminating test of superhuman knowledge, or any means by which a stronger impression could have been made upon the mind of the king of the most positive conviction that Daniel was indeed the Prophet of God, and that as he had told him the dream, he had shown also the true interpretation thereof. And as the revealing of the dream afforded this indubitable proof to Nebuchadnezzar, so the dream itself, and its interpretation, and the exact completion of this prediction of events then future, gives to us in the present day proof as indubitable—that Daniel did make known the dream to Nebuchadnezzar—that the dream is certain and the interpretation thereof sure.

It is as easy for an impartial inquirer in the present day as it was for Nebuchadnezzar to judge of the truth of the words of Daniel. Every word of the Prophet would bring back to the mind of the king his own former thoughts, and every part of the prophecy still gives as striking demonstration that Daniel did indeed reveal what would come to pass thereafter, and what would be in the latter days. And although it was as utterly impossible for Nebuchadnezzar to know of those future events which Daniel foretold, as it was for the magicians to restore to him his own lost thoughts, yet nothing is now easier than to discern and to apply to each and every part of the prediction its successive and corresponding event. And it was not merely to satisfy the disquietude of Nebuchadnezzar's mind—it was not merely that the life of Daniel and of his fellows might be spared—that a condemned captive became thus an inspired prophet, but that the word of God might be ratified by supernatural evidence—that Christians in

every age might know in whom they have believed—
that the providence of God might finally be manifested
over all, and that if the gospel be hid, it may be hid
only to them that are lost, who seeing, see not, and
who hearing, will not understand.

The only requisite commentary on the predictions is
a simple and succinct recapitulation of the events which
they avowedly prefigured. The interpretation, which
is alike prophetic with the symbolical image, declares,
that a kingdom inferior to the Babylonian was immedi-
ately to succeed it—that another kingdom of brass was
then to arise, which was to bear rule over all the earth—
that the fourth kingdom was to be strong as iron, to
break in pieces and subdue all things, or all other king-
doms. The Persian empire was established on the sub-
version of the Babylonian,—the power or duration of
which it did not attain. The Macedo-Grecian empire
under Alexander the Great, succeeded to the Persian.
It is called a kingdom of brass, a metal more justly emblematical of the Grecian than any other—as they were
distinguished by their coats of brass, and denominated
the brass-clothed Greeks.* This empire is described
as having ruled over all the earth. It not only surpassed
in the extent of its conquests and dominion, the Babylonian and the Persian, but was literally called an universal empire ; and its founder is still known to fame,
as one of the greatest of conquerors who ever lived.
(These empires are more particularly described by
Daniel in his subsequent prophecies.) The next empire which extended its power over these countries was
the Roman. *It was strong as iron : forasmuch as iron*
breaketh in pieces, and subdueth all, and as iron that
breaketh all these shall it break in pieces and bruise. Iron
was its appropriate emblem. It was an iron crown
which its emperors wore (proverbially the iron crown
of Italy ;)—and an iron yoke to which it subjected
many nations : *It bruised all the residue of the former*
kingdoms, and brake them in pieces. It is impossible,
on a retrospect of this history, to give any representa-

* Homeri Il. B. 47.

tion, in so few words, more justly descriptive of the
Persian, Grecian and Roman empires. But the Roman empire itself was broken down—divided into different kingdoms—some of them powerful, and others
comparatively weak. The sovereigns of these different
kingdoms have been perpetually contracting matrimo-
nial alliances with each other—but, notwithstanding
this seeming bond of union, they have not united or
adhered together. The knowledge of these historical
truths, familiar to every reader, alone suffices for the
elucidation of the prophecy. *And whereas thou sawest
the feet and toes part of potter's clay and part of iron;
the kingdom shall be divided; but there shall be in it of
the strength of the iron, forasmuch as thou sawest the iron
mixed with miry clay. And as the toes of the feet were
part of iron and part of clay, so the kingdom shall be
partly strong and partly broken. And whereas thou
sawest iron mixed with miry clay, they shall mingle themselves with the seed of men: but they shall not cleave one
to another, even as iron is not mixed with clay.*

To Nebuchadnezzar, who aspired only after human
power and glory, the various empires that were in their
order to succeed his own, and tyrannize over the world,
were represented by a splendid image. But in the prophetic vision of the "Man of God" they appeared in
other colours, and assumed a very different form. And
under the appropriate symbol of wild beasts, varying in
fierceness and cruelty, and distinguished by monstrous
peculiarities, the successive empires of Babylon, Persia,
Macedon or Greece, and Rome—the future promoters
of idolatry and oppressors of man—were aptly characterised.

In the vision of the prophet, not only the number of
the kingdoms and the order of succession are the same,
and also the different characteristic features accordant
with those of the preceding symbolical representation,
but, to the brief outline given in the former, several
additional circumstances are annexed, and (in a manner
totally at variance with any wild and extravagant
fancies arising from mere pretended foreknowledge) the
nearer that the vision approaches to "the latter times"

it becomes the more copious and the more minutely defined.

The first kingdom, viz. the Babylonian, then existing, was represented by a lion that had eagle's wings. But although then worthy of such emblems, the wings wherewith it was lifted up were to be plucked. " It was to be humbled and subdued, and made to know its human state,*—a man's heart (instead of a lion's) was given it.—The second kingdom was the Persian ; it was noted by historians for its brutal cruelty,—and is prefigured by a bear. *This beast raised itself upon one side*, the Persians being under the Medes at the fall of Babylon, but presently rising up above them. *And it had three ribs in the mouth of it between the teeth of it*, signifying the kingdoms of Sardis, Babylon, and Egypt, which were conquered by it, but did not belong to its proper body."† The third beast represents the kingdom that was to succeed the Persian, which was the empire of the Greeks, first established over the east by Alexander the Great. It consisted of various nations, far more diversified in their manners and customs than were the Babylonians, Medes and Persians, and was thus spotted like a *leopard*. The rapidity of its rise and conquests is aptly denoted by its four wings, while the four heads are significative of the exact number of kingdoms into which it was divided. The fourth empire was the Roman. It was dreadful and terrible, and strong exceedingly, and diverse from all kingdoms. Such was the Roman empire, and such are the very words of the prophecy concerning the " fourth kingdom." The beast was terrible ; it had great *iron* teeth, it devoured and brake in pieces, and stamped the residue with the feet of it.—The Roman empire was larger, stronger, and more terrible, and of greater duration than any of the former ; it was diverse from all kingdoms that were before it ; and, on its fall, it was subdivided into a greater number of distinct kingdoms. Machiavel (for whose creed the church of Rome and

* Sir Isaac Newton's *Observations on the Prophecies of Daniel*, p. 29.
† Ibid.

infidelity can alone contend) who wotted not of the consequences of the historical fact, specifies by name the ten kingdoms into which the Roman empire was divided. Some of these kingdoms at length fell, and new ones arose. But, as Sir Isaac Newton remarks, they are still called the *ten kings* from their first number. And like the ten toes of the image, the fourth beast had *ten horns*, which the prophet interprets kingdoms, (v. 7, 24.) After these another power, diverse from the first, (v. 24.) and little at its commencement, was to arise, which was to subdue three kings. *In this horn were eyes like the eyes of a man, and a mouth speaking very great things, whose look was more stout than his fellows.* He was to *speak great words against* ("by the side of," or on an assumed equality with) *the Most High, to wear out the saints of the Most High: and to think to change times and laws, and they were to be given into his hands* for a long but yet limited period. The church of Rome rose to power, diverse from that of any other, after the dismemberment of the Roman empire. The exarchate of Ravenna, the kingdom of the Lombards, and the state of Rome, were subjected to its temporal as well as spiritual authority,* and plucked up before it. *In this horn were eyes like the eyes of a man.* "By its eyes it was a seer, Επισκοπος, a bishop in the literal sense of the word; and this church claims the universal bishopric. With his mouth *he spake very great things;* gave laws to kings and nations as an oracle, pretends to infallibility, and that his dictates are binding on the whole world."† His look was more stout than his fellows; the Pope, as head of the church, has not only ever claimed supremacy over every other bishop, but kings have often prostrated themselves before him and done the office of menials. And how closely does the character of *wearing out the saints of the Most High* befit the church of Rome? However much its character may now in reality or in appearance be altered, the time is

---

* Sir Isaac Newton's *Observations on the Prophecies of Daniel*, p. 73. Bishop Newton's *Dissert.* xiv.
† Sir Isaac Newton on *Daniel*, p. 75.

not distant, when every *auto da fe* (*act of* Romish *faith*) brought the recusants of idolatry—the worshippers of the Most High—to the stake, and by every refinement in cruelty did it try to wear them out. *And he shall think to change times and laws ;* " appointing fasts and feasts, canonizing saints, granting pardons and indulgences for sins, instituting new modes of worship, imposing new articles of faith, enjoining new rules of practice, and reversing at pleasure the laws both of God and men."*

The prophetic interpretation of another vision of Daniel now presents such a retrospective view of the history of the east, that scarcely the slightest comment is requisite to show its perfect adaptation to the events. *At the time of the end shall be the vision. I will make thee know what shall be in the last end of the indignation, for at the time appointed the end shall be. The ram which thou sawest having two horns are the kings of Media and Persia. And the rough goat is the king of Grecia ; and the great horn that is between his eyes is the first king* (Alexander the Great.) *Now, that being broken, whereas four stood up for it, four kingdoms shall stand up out of the nation, but not in his power* (which none of them ever attained.)—*And in the latter time of their kingdom,* (at a distance of time, but prevailing over the same territory,) *when the transgressors are come to the full,* (Isa. xxiv. 5, 6,) *a king of fierce countenance* (Mahomet, who proffered only submission or the sword,) *and understanding dark sentences* (wherewith the Koran pre-eminently abounds,) *shall stand up. And his power shall be mighty, but not by his own power,* (he possessed no hereditary dominion, and arose from nothing.) *And he shall destroy wonderfully, and shall prosper and practise, and shall destroy the mighty and the holy people, or the people of the holy ones* (the Christians.) *And through his policy shall he cause craft to prosper in his hand,* (by a faith accommodated to the passions of men.) *And he shall magnify himself in his heart.*

* Bishop Newton on *Daniel*, p. 75.

("There is no God but one, and Mahomet is his prophet.") *And by peace shall he destroy many.* Such
is the intrinsic despotism and withering influence of
Mahometan government, that under their sway countries naturally the most fertile, and long exuberant in
population and produce, have been depopulated and
destroyed to a greater degree by *peace* than any other
countries have been by war. *He shall stand up against
the prince of princes, magnifying himself even to the
prince of the host,* (calling himself a greater prophet
than Christ.) *It waxed exceeding great toward the
south, and toward the east, and toward the pleasant land,*
(Palestine) the very direction and progress, according
to Gibbon, of the greatest and most permanent of the
Mahometan conquests. *It cast down of the host and
of the stars to the ground* (Christian churches) *and
stamped upon them, and the place of the sanctuary* (Jerusalem) *was cut down. The vision was for many days.*
Many days have passed, and all is accomplished but
the last end of the "desolation, which has given the
sanctuary to be trodden under foot."

Looking back then upon those successive empires
which are the best known, and have been the most in-
fluential on the fate of the world, and comparing the
bare predictions and the prominent events, is there not
visible a chain of prophecy, without a link distorted or
broken, stretched by no human hand over the history of
man from the days of Nebuchadnezzar to the present
hour, and on which the future fate of the world hangs
suspended still? And without diverging to other matters, may not the primary question be here reverted to,
whether such as they are, these predictions bear not a
closer and less convertible similitude to the events of
which they were avowedly predictive, than human sagacity could have discovered or invented? And may
not a case be here put, which would try the reasoning
powers of reckless mockers, and bring this question to
the proof?

Were a despot now troubled at the thought, a thought
which no tyrant could brook, that the Bible is the word
of God, and that he who is higher than the highest re-

3

garded him; and were he to possess the power, and to
congregate around him all the illuminati—the magicians and astrologers—of modern times, and to demand
of them the cause why the image of Nebuchadnezzar
and the visions of Daniel bear so striking a resemblance
to those future kingdoms, and to the latter times of
which they were avowedly symbolical; and how, by
natural causes and human wisdom alone, the whole history of the Jews to the present hour was written, at the
very least, two thousand years ago; and how all the
countries, and all the people, and all the cities of whose
destiny they spoke, should accredit, to every jot and to
a very tittle, the words of the seers of Israel, and present in their history and fate, an exact counterpart of a
professedly prophetic delineation; and were they farther to be debarred from ridicule, and bound to reason,
and told that " they dared not prepare lying and corrupt words to speak before him," and that " there was
but one decree for them," if they did not make good
their professed claim to such wisdom, show the *sure interpretation* of the matter, resolve all his doubts, and
restore quietude to his troubled thoughts, such as words
of truth like Daniel's gave to the mind of Nebuchadnezzar; then, verily, much do we fear, would the lives
of the *philosophes* and *savans* of Europe be in no less
jeopardy than were those of their prototypes the wise
men and the soothsayers of Babylon.   And their poor
faith having no treasures in store to repay the life-blood
of a single mortal; no *hope*, though otherwise forfeited,
sufficient to bribe one solitary martyr to the block; to
what fitter terms than these (if their wisdom on such a
trial should fail them) could their blanched and quiver-
ing lips, long used to mockery before, give utterance
at last,—" There is not a man upon earth that can show
the king's matter; therefore there is no king, lord, nor
ruler that asketh such things at any magician, or astrologer, or Chaldean.   And it is a rare thing that the king
requireth; and there is none other that can shew it before the king, except the gods, whose dwelling is not
with flesh."*

* Daniel ii. 10, 11.

s

The frequent perversion of the "truth as it is in Je-sus," and the substitution in its stead of the "com-mandments of men;" the party animosities, and reli-gious wars and persecutions, so contrary to the spirit of the gospel, which have so long prevailed : the gross impostures, absurd superstitions, and impious rites which have often been forced into unnatural alliance with Christianity, and grafted by human hands into the heavenly stock; the domineering spirit of an unholy priesthood; the partial diffusion of the religion of Je-sus during many ages; and the delusions of a mani-fest impostor triumphing over the Christian religion even in the regions which gave it birth—have all prov-ed stumbling-blocks in the way of many, or a rock of offence on which they have made shipwreck of faith and of a good conscience. Yet all these are but the various combatings of the impure passions, and the worldly-mindedness of man against a holy and spiritual faith—the workings of a *predicted* "mystery of iniqui-ty :" and not only does the purity of the gospel itself remain unaffected by them all, but its truth, as the in-spired word of God, is the more fully established. Even here " God has not left himself without a wit-ness;" and " we do well to give heed to the sure word of prophecy, which shineth as a light in a dark place."

But the church of Christ, though long militant " against spiritual wickedness in high places," shall, ac-cording to the Scriptures, become even on earth finally triumphant.   And it is not merely from the analogy of the truth of the past that the certainty of the events yet future may be confided in ; for there is not wanting, in the actual state of the world, subsisting evidence of the germinating fulfilment of prophecy.   The rapid diffu-sion of knowledge; the numerous inventions and disco-veries in physical science ; and the immense accession they have given to the power of man ; the facilities of communication and frequencies of intercourse that now prevail throughout the world ; the nature of recent wars —contests for principles rather than for property ; the abandonment in different states and kingdoms of the principles and the practice of unrestricted and unmitigated despotism, and the establishment of constitutional governments in its stead; the ready expression and powerful efficacy of public opinion, sobered down as it is to the desire of substantial rather than theoretic liberty, and of its expansion throughout the world, and awed by the remembrance of all the exhibited horrors of anarchy and atheism; the manifold philanthropic and religious associations, so diversified in their objects, and active in their operation for alleviating the miseries, enlightening the ignorance, and ameliorating the moral condition of our species; and though last not least of all, the unexampled and astonishing dissemination of the Scriptures, and the avidity with which they are sought after in many a land; all these unite in giving the same promise to mortal hope which the words of Scripture impart to religious faith, that the " appointed time," whatever convulsions may yet intervene, is approximating, when despotism and superstition shall come to an end, and when brutal power, or governments fitly symbolized by wild beasts, shall cease to trample on the liberties of man. The powers of darkness are already shaken. He whose " look was more stout than his fellows" has been greatly humbled. His dominion has in part been *taken away*, and it will *be consumed and destroyed until the end.*

No. II.

PROPHECIES CONCERNING THE FINAL RESTORATION OF THE JEWS AND THEIR RETURN TO THE LAND OF JUDEA.

" THE Lord thy God will turn thy captivity, and will have compassion upon thee, and will return and gather thee from all the nations, whither the Lord thy God

hath scattered thee. If any of thine be driven out unto the outmost parts of heaven, from thence will the
Lord thy God gather thee, and from thence will he
fetch thee. And the Lord thy God will bring thee unto the land which thy fathers possessed, and thou shalt
possess it; and he will do thee good, and multiply thee
above thy fathers." (Deut. xxx. 3, 4, 5.) " And it shall
come to pass that the Lord shall set his hand again the
second time, to recover the remnant of his people,
which shall be left, from Assyria, and from Egypt, and
from Pathros, and from Cush, and from Elam, and from
Shinar, and from Hamath, and from the Islands of the
sea. And he shall set up an ensign for the nations, and
shall assemble the *outcasts* of Israel, and gather together the *dispersed* of Judah from the four corners of
the earth." (Isaiah xi. 11, 12, &c.) " Who are these
that fly as a cloud, and as the doves to their windows?
Surely the isles shall wait for me, and the ships of Tarshish first, to bring thy sons from far, their silver and
their gold with them, unto the name of the Lord thy
God, and to the Holy One of Israel, because he hath
glorified thee. And the sons of strangers shall build
up thy walls, and their kings shall minister unto thee,
for in my wrath I smote thee, but in my favour have I
had mercy on thee." (Isa. lx. 9, 10, &c.) " And they
shall build the old wastes, they shall raise up the former
desolations, they shall repair the waste cities, the desolations of many generations." (Isa. lxi. 4, &c.) " Thus
saith the Lord, if heaven above can be measured, and
the foundations of the earth searched out beneath, I will
also cast off all the seed of Israel, for all that they have
done, saith the Lord. Behold the days come, saith
the Lord, that the city shall be built to the Lord, from
the tower of Hananeel unto the gate of the corner; and
the measuring line shall go over against it; and it shall
not be plucked up nor thrown down any more for ever."
(Jer. xxxi. 37, &c.) " But ye, O mountains of Israel,
shall shoot forth your branches and yield your fruit to
my people of Israel; and I will multiply men upon you,
all the house of Israel, even all of it; and the cities
shall be inhabited, and the wastes shall be builded, &c.

For I will take you (O house of Israel,) from among the heathen, and gather you out of all countries, and will bring you into your own land." Ezek. xxxvi. 8. 10—24. "Thus saith the Lord God, behold, I will take the children of Israel from among the heathen, whither they be gone, and will gather them on every side, and bring them into their own land." (Ibid. xxxvii. 21, &c.) "Turn ye to the stronghold, ye prisoners of hope; even to-day do I declare that I will render double unto thee: when I have bent Judah for me, filled the bow with Ephraim, and raised up thy sons, O Zion, against thy sons, O Greece, and made thee as a sword of a mighty man," &c. (Zech. ix. 12, &c.) "Behold the days come, saith the Lord, that the ploughman shall overtake the reaper, and the treader of grapes him that soweth seed; and the mountains shall drop sweet wine, and all the hills shall melt.—And I will bring again the captivity of my people of Israel, and they shall build the waste cities and inhabit them; and they shall plant vineyards and drink the wine thereof; they shall also make gardens, and eat the fruit of them. And I will plant them upon their own land, and they shall be no more pulled up out of their land which I have given them, saith the Lord thy God." (Amos ix. 13, 14, 15.) "I will surely assemble, O Jacob, all of thee. I will surely gather the remnant of Israel; I will put them together as the sheep of Bozrah, as the flock in the midst of their fold; they shall make great noise by reason of the multitude of men." (Micah ii. 12.)

These prophecies, exclusive of many others, need no comment. They declare, as clearly as language can, that the Jews shall return to Judea, and be at last permanently re-established in the land of their fathers. The uniform experience of the literal truth of every prediction respecting their past history may suffice to give assurance of the certainty of their predicted restoration. And, amidst many signs that *the times of the Gentiles* are drawing towards their *fulfilment*, many concurring circumstances seem also to be *preparing* the way of the children of Israel. Scattered as they have been for

so many ages through the world, and maintaining still
their distinctive character, their whole history forbids
the thought that they will ever mingle among the nations, or cease to be, what they have ever been, a peculiar people. But while their history as a nation,
gave, for the space of many generations, unequivocal
attestations of an overruling providence, sustaining the
theocracy of the commonwealth of Israel; and while,
during a period of still greater duration, they have been
" a people scattered and peeled;" yet after the lapse of
so many ages, they are still reserved for illustrating the
truth, the mercy, and the glory of the God of Israel ;
at eventide it shall be light. They now begin, centuries
of persecution and spoliation having passed away, to
participate, in cases too numerous to be specified, of
benefits arising from the altered spirit of the times. And
possessed, as in an unexampled degree they are, of
silver and gold, and of large portions of the public funds
of various kingdoms, they may be said, even now, in
some manner, to *inherit the riches of the Gentiles.* And
commanding, as in a great measure they do, the rate of
exchange throughout Europe, they are entitled, from
the present influence of money on the security of governments, and on the art and results of war, to high political consideration ; and the time may not thus be remote, when they shall be *raised up as an ensign among
the nations.* Not naturalized to the isles of the Gentiles,
either by law or affection, or bound to any soil by the
possession of fixed property, which would be of no
easy transference ; but ever looking with undiminished
love to the *land of their fathers,* even after an expatria-
tion uninterrupted for nearly eighteen centuries, they
are ready—whenever the time shall be fulfilled—to *fly*
thither *like a cloud, and like doves to their windows.*
But to what degree, and in what manner the present
convulsions of the Turkish empire, combined with the
peculiar, and in many instances, novel condition of the
Jews, throughout Europe and America, shall be the
means of facilitating their eventual restoration to their
own land (which is ravaged by Arabs, and yields but
a scanty revenue to the Turks) no mortal can deter-

mine. It is enough for Christians to know, that two thousand of years, through nearly which period it has been dormant, can neither render extinct the title nor prescribe the heaven-chartered right of the seed of Abraham to the final and everlasting possession of the land of Canaan; that God *will remember the land and gather together* unto it his ancient people; and that his word concerning Zion, which he hath neither *forgotten* not *forsaken*, is, *I have graven thee upon the palms of my hands, thy walls are continually before me. Thy children shall make haste: thy destroyers and they that made thee waste shall go forth of thee,* &c.—(Isa. xlix. 16, 17, &c.) " And that through all the changes which have happened in the kingdoms of the earth from the days of *Moses* to the *present time,* which is more than three thousand two hundred years, nothing should have happened to prevent the POSSIBILITY of the *accomplishment* of these prophecies, but, on the contrary, that state of the *Jewish* and *Christian nations* at this day should be such as renders them easily *capable,* not only of a *figurative,* but even of a *literal completion* in every particular, if the will of God be so; this is a *miracle,* which hath nothing *parallel* to it in the phenomena of nature."

No. III.

ABSTRACT OF PROPHECIES RELATIVE TO THE GREAT APOSTACY.

CLEARLY revealed as is the will of God in Scripture, and perfectly calculated as is the gospel to effect the happiness of man, and faithful unto the death as many of the primitive Christians were,—it is no less manifest that an apostacy, or falling away from the faith, was

foretold. And who can read the Scriptures with an unbiassed mind, and look to the history of the Christian
Church, and doubt for a moment that there has been
an apostacy, or falling away from the truth and simplicity of the faith as it is in Jesus? Or who, in a like
unbiassed manner, can read the prophecies respecting
that apostacy, and cherish even a momentary doubt of
their application?

It would be foreign to the object of this treatise, and
it would require a volume rather than a concluding
page, to enter at large upon such a subject. But the
simple comparison of a few prominent predictions and
undeniable facts, which scarcely need any illustration,
may tend to show that much evidence of the inspiration of Scripture may be drawn from the obscure prophecies, and that their obscurity in a great measure
vanishes, on the most succinct combination of predictions and of facts.

The coincidence, not in meaning only, but in words,
which subsists between the following predictions, strikingly denotes their reference to, or connexion with the
same subject. And when viewed as a portraiture of
events now passed (or still in progress,) the apparent
obscurity arising from the adoption of symbols, or figurative representations, may be at once removed by
merely bearing in mind that in Scripture itself the term
beast is explained as denoting a king, kingdom, or reign-
ing power; and that, in the phraseology of the Old
Testament, idolatry, or the worship of false gods or
images, in any form, is uniformly represented as whore-
dom or fornication. Without straining either a word of
sacred writ, or a fact in history, it is left to every unprejudiced reader to determine on whose FOREHEAD it
is that the marks of apostacy and names of blasphemy
are so conspicuously written, that they legitimately
form a part of the testimony of Jesus. Rev. xvii.

The "*forbidding to marry,* and commanding to *ab-
stain from meats* which God hath created to be received with thanksgiving of them which believe and know
the truth," 1 Tim. iv. 3, are mentioned literally as prominent marks of the apostacy. And the celibacy of the

clergy, both regular and secular, and the multiplicity of fasts, appointed and observed by the church of Rome, are in complete and manifest accordance with the prediction. The former is expressly contrary to the sanction and authority of Scripture, which saith—" a bishop must be blameless, the husband of one wife;"—and the reason assigned for the latter, as taught in *the first Catechism or abridgment of Christian doctrine,** " that by fasting we may satisfy God for our sins," is a monstrous perversion of all Christian doctrine, and shows with how great a *falling away from the faith* the observance of such " commandments of the church" of Rome is accompanied.

Giving heed to doctrines of devils—literally of, or concerning, *demons*—a term often applied by Greek writers to those who were canonized or deified after their death, or who were accounted agents or mediators between gods and men, 1 Tim. iv. 3. The same word was used by the Athenians, (Acts xvii. 18.) when they accused Paul of being a setter up of strange gods or demons— because he preached unto them Jesus who had been raised from the dead.—*But in his estate,* (or in the stead of God) shall he honour *the God of forces,* or, as rendered in the margin, *Gods protectors,* divine guardians, or tutelary saints, Dan. xi. 38. The corruption of the pure worship of God, the introduction of demonolatry into the Christian Church, and the trusting to other intercessors than the one only Mediator, seem here evidently referred to. It is not needful to ask what church, as well as the Grecian, has *given heed to doctrines* concerning departed mortals, such as were believed on by heathens; or who have canonized dead men, worshipped them in *the stead of God,* believe on them as *strong protectors,* address them as intercessors, worship at their shrines, *regard their glory,* and *honour them with gold, silver, and precious stones, and pleasant things.* Dan. xi. 38.

Giving heed to seducing spirits, speaking lies in hypocrisy, 1 Tim. iv. 1, 2. *Whose coming is after the power*

---

* Published for the use of the London District, and printed by R. Keating, Brown & Co. London, Printers to the R. R. the Vicars Apostolic, 1812, p. 33.

of Satan with all power and signs and lying wonders, and with all deceivableness of unrighteousness, 2 Thess. xi. 9, 10. *By thy sorceries were all nations deceived,* Rev. xviii. 23. The power of working miracles is held by the church of Rome as a mark of the true church: but the assumption of that power is truly a mark of the great apostacy. And what else are wilful impositions, lying legends, and pretended miracles, the liquefying of the blood of St. Januarius, for example, still practised, thrice every year, in a church in Naples, but the *deceivableness of unrighteousness?* Or what creed is more common in Rome, to which the Pope and the Cardinals have given their sanction, than the working of miracles by the images of saints?

Speaking of the selfsame apostacy, it is said by the Apostle Paul, " the day of Christ shall not come except there come a *falling away* first, and that man of sin be revealed, the son of perdition, who opposeth and exalteth himself above all that is called God, or that is worshipped, so that he, as God, sitteth in the TEMPLE OF GOD, showing himself that he is God," 2 Thess. ii. 3, 4. These words, descriptive of *the man of sin,* are linked to the description of *the little horn in Daniel,* (p. 315) not only by a similarity of character, but by an identity of fate. *And he shall speak great words against the Most High.* Dan. vii. 25. Rev. xiii. 5, 6. It admits of no question who it is that has *exalted himself* most highly in *the Church,* that has assumed the claim of infallibility, and of titles which pertain to God alone, and to whom " adoration" is paid, when he is enthroned, in the most magnificent temple on earth, as the head of the Church.

The more closely that the connexion is traced between the prophecies of St. Paul, Daniel, and St. John, they become the more copious, discriminative, and defined. The beast having seven heads and ten horns,* which was subject to the authority of the great whore,† (or idolatrous church) is evidently connected, in its character, duration, and fate,‡ with the little horn of

---

* Rev. xiii. 1 ; xvii. 7.   † Rev. vii. 15.
‡ Dan. vii. 20, 21, 25, 26.   Rev. xiii. 5, 7, 10; xvii. 14.

Daniel's fourth kingdom, or the Roman. The locality, or seat of this dominion, *diverse* from the former kingdoms, could scarcely be more circumstantially defined. *The seven heads are seven mountains on which the woman sitteth,* (Rev. xvii. 9.) Rome was proverbially the *city on seven hills: and there are seven kings, five are fallen and one is,* (v. 10.) Five forms of government had before that time fallen, and another then existed. *And the ten horns which thou sawest are ten kings, which have received no kingdoms as yet.* The Roman empire, then entire, was, about the time of the establishment of popery, divided into ten kingdoms, corresponding with the ten horns of the fourth beast, or the toes of the great image, (pp. 313, 315.) *The woman which thou sawest is that great city, which* REIGNETH *over the kings of the earth.* The great city which then reigned over the kings of the earth was Rome. It is all but named. And under a symbol the very name was hid. The beast had *a name, a number, and a mark,* (Rev. xiii. 18; xv. 2.) *and his number is six hundred threescore and six.* (Among the Hebrews and Greeks all the letters were numerals, or equivalent to figures, which were not in use among them.) Three different designations being given, *three* corresponsive words, instead of one, as has been generally sought, seem to be required. The beast was first described by Daniel; and in Hebrew characters, *Romiith,** Roman, agreeing with *beast* or kingdom, contains the precise number, or that of his *name;* while *Lateinos,†* the *number* of his name, " which is the *number of a man;*" and *apostates,‡* the *mark,* the brand of

* ר R = 200	† Λ L = 30	‡ Α A = 1
ו o = 6	α a = 1	π p = 80
מ m = 40	τ t = 300	ο o = 70
י i = 10	ε e = 5	ς st = 6
י i = 10	ι i = 10	α a = 1
ת th = 400	ν n = 50	τ t = 300
———	ο o = 70	ν e = 8
666	ς s = 200	ς s = 200
	———	———
	666	666

the *apostacy*, both fatally contain the same prophetic number.

There are other characteristics which need no comment. " Come hither; I will show unto thee the judgment of the great whore *that sitteth upon many waters: with whom the kings of the earth have committed fornication, and the inhabitants of the earth have been made drunk with the wine of her fornication. The waters which thou sawest where the whore sitteth are peoples, and multitudes, and nations, and tongues,* Rev. xvii. 2, 15. *They shall be given into his hand,* Dan. vii. 25. *And power was given him over all kindreds, and tongues, and nations. And all that dwell upon the earth shall worship him, whose names are not written in the book of life,*" Rev. xiii. 7, 8. The *catholic* means the universal church. *The same horn made war with the saints, and prevailed against them. He shall wear out the saints of the Most High,* Dan. vii. 21, 25. *It was given unto him to make war with the saints, and to overcome them,* Rev. xiii. 7. *And I saw the woman drunken with the blood of the saints, and with the blood of the martyrs of Jesus,* Rev. xvii. 6.

She was arrayed in purple and scarlet colour, Rev. xvii. 4. the official clothing of the pope and of the cardinals, *and decked with gold and precious stones and pearls,* as also they are, and wherewith the decking of their churches, altars, and images did abound.

We ask not how all the subtilty of Jesuitism, or all the deceivableness of unrighteousness can rescue popery from the grasp of so many prophecies encircling it on every side; it is the purpose of these remarks, as connected with the evidence of prophecy, to show that even the long-continued and wide-spread apostacy from the Christian faith, which has often given a seeming sanction to infidelity, is itself a proof of the inspiration of Scripture; and that the war which has long been waged against those *who kept the commandments of God, and had the testimony of Jesus,* only serves the more to confirm the truth of that testimony.

No. IV.

THE kingdoms represented by the second and third beasts, or the bear and leopard, are again described by Daniel, in his last prophecy written in the third year of Cyrus over Babylon—the year in which he conquered Persia. For this prophecy is a commentary upon the vision of the ram and he-goat.

"Behold," saith he, "there shall stand up yet three kings in Persia, and the fourth (*Xerxes*) shall be far richer than they all ; and, by his strength, through his riches, he shall stir up all against the realm of Grecia. And a mighty king (*Alexander the Great*) shall stand up, that shall rule with great dominion, and do according to his will. And when he shall stand up, his kingdom shall be broken, and shall be divided towards the four winds of heaven, and not to his posterity, (but after their deaths,) nor according to his dominion which ruled : for his kingdom shall be plucked up, even for others besides those."* Alexander the Great, having conquered all the Persian empire, and some parts of India, died at Babylon, a month before the summer solstice, in the year of Nabonassar 425 ; and his captains gave the monarchy to his bastard brother, Philip Aridæus, a man disturbed in his understanding ; and made Perdiccas administrator of the kingdom. Perdiccas, with their consent, made Meleager commander of the army—Seleucus, master of the horse—Craterus, treasurer of the kingdom—Antipater, governor of Macedon and Greece—Ptolemy, governor of Egypt—An-

* Dan. xi. 2, 3, 4.

tigonus, governor of Pamphylia, Lycia, Lycaonia, and
Phrygia Major—Lysimachus, governor of Thrace—
and other captains, governors of other provinces; as
many as had been so before in the days of Alexander
the Great. The Babylonians began now to count by
a new era, which they called the era of Philip, using
the year of Nabonassar, and reckoning the 425th era
of Nabonassar to be the first year of Philip. Roxana,
the wife of Alexander, being left big with child, and,
about three or four months after, brought to bed of a
son—they called him Alexander—saluted him king,
and joined him with Philip, whom they had before
placed in the throne. Philip reigned three years under
the administratorship of Perdiccas—two years more
under the administratorship of Antipater,—and above
a year more under that of Polysperchon :—in all six
years and four months ; and then was slain, with his
queen Eurydice, in September, by the command of
Olympias, the mother of Alexander the Great.

The Greeks being disgusted at the cruelties of Olympias, revolted to Cassander, the son and successor of
Antipater. Cassander, affecting the dominion of Greece,
slew Olympias; and soon after shut up the young king
Alexander, with his mother Roxana, in the castle of
Amphipolis, under the charge of Glaucias, *an. Nabonass.*
432. The next year Ptolemy, Cassander, and Lysimachus, by means of Seleucus, formed a league against
Antigonus ; and, after certain wars, made peace with
him, *an. Nabonass.* 438—upon these conditions ;—that
Cassander should command the forces of Europe till
Alexander, the son of Roxana, came to age ; and that
Lysimachus should govern Thrace ; Ptolemy, Egypt
and Lybia : and Antigonus all Asia. Seleucus had possessed himself of Mesopotamia, Babylonia, Susiana, and
Media the year before. About three years after Alexander's death, he was made governor of Babylon by
Antipater ; then was expelled by Antigonus ; but now
he recovered, and enlarged his government over a great
part of the east, which gave occasion to a new era,
called *aera Seleucidarum.* Not long after the peace
made with Antigonus,—Diodorus saith, the same

Olympic year,—Cassander, seeing that Alexander, the son of Roxana, grew up, and that it was discoursed throughout Macedonia, that it was fit he should be set at liberty, and take upon him the government of his father's kingdom, commanded Glaucias, the governor of the castle, to kill Roxana and the young king Alexander her son, and conceal their deaths. Then Polysperchon set up Hercules, the son of Alexander the Great, by Barsyne, to be king; and soon after, at the solicitation of Cassander, caused him to be slain. Soon after that, upon a great victory at sea, got by Demetrius, the son of Antigonus, over Ptolemy, Antigonus took upon himself the title of king, and gave the same title to his son. This was *an. Nabonass.* 441. After his example, Seleucus, Cassander, Lysimachus, and Ptolemy took upon themselves the title and dignity of kings, having abstained from this honour while there remained any of Alexander's race to inherit the crowns. Thus the monarchy of the Greeks, for want of an heir, was broken into several kingdoms; four of which, seated to the four winds of heaven, were very eminent. For Ptolemy reigned over Egypt, Lybia, and Ethiopia—Antigonus over Syria and the Lesser Asia—Lysimachus over Thrace—and Cassander over Macedon, Greece, and Epirus, as above.

Seleucus at this time reigned over the nations which were beyond the Euphrates, and belonged to the bodies of the two first beasts; but after six years he conquered Antigonus, and thereby became possessed of one of the four kingdoms. For Cassander being afraid of the power of Antigonus, combined with Lysimachus, Ptolemy, and Seleucus against him;—and while Lysimachus invaded the parts of Asia next to the Hellespont, Ptolemy subdued Phœnicia and Cœlosyria, the sea-coasts of Asia.

Seleucus came down with a powerful army to Cappadocia, and, joining the confederate forces, fought Antigonus in Phrygia, and slew him, and seized his kingdom, *an. Nabonass.* 447. After which Seleucus built Antioch, Seleucia, Laodicea, Apamea, Berrhœa, Edessa, and other cities in Syria and Asia: and in them granted the Jews equal privileges with the Greeks.

Demetrius, the son of Antigonus, retained but a small part of his father's dominions, and at length lost Cyprus to Ptolemy; but afterwards killing Alexander, the son and successor of Cassander, king of Macedon, he seized his kingdom, *an. Nabonass.* 454. Some time after, preparing a very great army to recover his father's dominions in Asia—Seleucus, Ptolemy, Lysimachus, and Pyrrhus, king of Epirus, combined against him; and Pyrrhus, invading Macedon, corrupted the army of Demetrius, put him to flight, seized his kingdom, and shared it with Lysimachus. After seven months, Lysimachus beating Pyrrhus, took Macedon from him, and held it five years and a half, uniting the kingdoms of Macedon and Thrace. Lysimachus, in his wars with Antigonus and Demetrius, had taken from them Caria, Lydia, and Phrygia; and had a treasury in Pergamus, a castle on the top of a conical hill in Phrygia, by the river Caicus, the custody of which he had committed to one Philatærus, who was at first faithful to him, but in the last year of his reign revolted. For Lysimachus having, at the instigation of his wife Arsinoe, slain first his own son Agathocles, and then several that lamented him—the wife of Agathocles fled with her children and brothers, and some others of their friends, and solicited Seleucus to make war upon Lysimachus; whereupon Philatærus also, who grieved at the death of Agathocles, and was accused thereof by Arsinoe, took up arms and sided with Seleucus. On this occasion Seleucus and Lysimachus met and fought in Phrygia; and Lysimachus being slain in the battle, lost his kingdom to Seleucas, *an. Nabonass.* 465. Thus, the empire of the Greeks, which at first broke into four kingdoms, became now reduced into two notable ones, henceforward called by Daniel the kings of the south and north. For Ptolemy now reigned over Egypt, Lybia, Ethiopia, Arabia, Phœnicia, Cœlosyria and Cyprus; and Seleucus, having united three of the four kingdoms, had a dominion scarcely inferior to that of the Persian Empire, conquered by Alexander the Great.

All which is thus represented by Daniel."* *"And the king of the south* (Ptolemy,) *shall be strong: and one of his princes* (Seleucus, one of Alexander's princes,) *shall be strong above him and have dominion: his dominion shall be a great dominion."*

After Seleucus had reigned seven months over Macedon, Greece, Thrace, Asia, Syria, Babylon, Media, and all the east as far as India—Ptolemy Ceraunus, the younger brother of Ptolemy Philadelphus, king of Egypt, slew him treacherously, and seized his dominions in Europe; while Antiochus Soter, the son of Seleucus, succeeded his father in Asia, Syria, and most of the east; and, after nineteen or twenty years, was succeeded by his son Antiochus Theos, who having a lasting war with Ptolemy Philadelphus, at length composed the same by marrying Berenice, the daughter of Philadelphus; but after a reign of fifteen years, his first wife Laodice poisoned him, and set her son Seleucus Callinicus upon the throne. Callinicus, in the beginning of his reign, by the impulse of his mother Laodice, besieged Berenice, in Daphne, near Antioch, and slew her with her young son and many of her women. Hereupon Ptolemy Euergetes, the son and successor of Philadelphus, made war upon Callinicus; took from him Phœnicia, Syria, Cilicia, Mesopotamia, Babylonia, Susiana, and some other regions; and carried back into Egypt 40,000 talents of silver, and 2500 images of the gods, amongst which were the gods of Egypt, carried away by Cambyses. Antiochus Hierax at first assisted his brother Callinicus, but afterwards contended with him for Asia. In the mean time, Eumenes, governor of Pergamus, beat Antiochus, and took from them both all Asia, westward of Mount Taurus. This was in the fifth year of Callinicus, who, after an inglorious reign of twenty years, was succeeded by his son Seleucus Ceraunus; and Euergetes, after four years more, *an. Nabonass.* 527, was succeeded by his son Ptolemy Philopater. All which is thus signified by Daniel:†—" And in the end of years, they (the kings of the south and

* Chap. xi. 5.   † Chap. xi. 6, 7, 8.

north) shall join themselves together; for the king's daughter of the south *(Berenice)* shall come to the king of the north to make an agreement, but she shall not retain the power of the arm; neither shall she stand, nor her seed, but she shall be delivered up, and he *(Callinicus)* that brought her, and he whom she brought forth, and they that strengthened her in *(those)* times, *(or defended her in the siege of Daphne.)* But out of a branch of her roots shall one stand up in his seat *(her brother Euergetes,)* who shall come with an army, and shall enter into the fortress *(or fenced cities)* of the king of the north, and act against them and prevail; and shall carry captives into Egypt their gods with their princes, and precious vessels of silver and gold; and he shall continue some years after the king of the north."

Seleucus Ceraunus, inheriting the remains of his father's kingdom, and thinking to recover the rest, raised a great army against the Governor of Pergamus, now king thereof, but died in the third year of his reign. His brother and successor, Antiochus Magnus, carrying on the war, took from the king of Pergamus almost all the Lesser Asia, recovering also the provinces of Media, Persia, and Babylonia, from the governors who had revolted; and, in the fifth year of his reign, invading Cœlosyria, he with little opposition possessed himself of a good part thereof; and, the next year, returning to invade the rest of Cœlosyria and Phœnicia, beat the army of Ptolemy Philopater near Berytus; he then invaded Palestine and the neighbouring parts of Arabia, and the third year returned with an army of 78,000; but Ptolemy, coming out of Egypt with an army of 75,000, fought and routed him at Raphia, near Gaza, between Palestine and Egypt, and recovered all Phœnicia and Cœlosyria; *an. Nabonass.* 532. Being puffed up with this victory, and living in all manner of luxury, the Egyptians revolted, and, in the broils, 60,000 Egyptian Jews were slain. All which is thus described by Daniel;—" But his sons *(Seleucus Ceraunus and Antiochus Magnus, the sons of Callinicus,)* shall be stirred up, and shall gather a great army, and he *(Antiochus Magnus)* shall come effectually and overflow, and pass through and return, and *(again the next year)* be stirred up *(marching even)* to his fortress *(the frontier towns of Egypt ;)* and the king of the south shall be moved with choler, and come forth *(the third year,)* and fight with him, even the king of the north ; and he *(the king of the north)* shall lead forth a great multitude, but the multitude shall be given into his hand. And the multitude being taken away, his heart shall be lifted up, and he shall cast down many ten thousands ; but he shall not be strengthened by it; for the king of the north shall return," &c.*

About twelve years after the battle between Philopater and Antiochus, Philopater died, and left his kingdom to his young son, Ptolemy Epiphanes, a child of five years old. Thereupon Antiochus Magnus confederated with Philip king of Macedon, that they should each invade the dominions of Epiphanes which lay next to them. Hence arose a various war between Antiochus and Epiphanes, each of them seizing Phœnicia and Cœlosyria by turn ; whereby those countries were much afflicted by both parties. First Antiochus seized them ; then one Scopas, being sent with the army of Egypt, recovered them from Antiochus the next year, *an. Nabonass.* 550. Antiochus fought and routed Scopas near the fountains of Jordan, besieged him in Sidon, took the city, and recovered Syria and Phœnicia from Egypt, the Jews coming to him voluntarily. But, about three years after, preparing for a war against the Romans, he came to Raphia, on the borders of Egypt, made peace with Epiphanes, and gave him his daughter Cleopatra. Next Autumn he passed the Hellespont, to invade the cities of Greece under the Roman protection ; but was beaten by the Romans the summer following, and forced to return back with his army into Asia. Before the end of the year the fleet of Antiochus was beaten by the fleet of the Romans near Phocœa ; and, at the same time, Epiphanes and Cleopatra sent an embassy to Rome to congratulate the Romans on their success against their father Antiochus, and to exhort them to

---

* Ver. 10, &c.

prosecute the war against him into Asia. The Romans beat Antiochus again at sea near Ephesus, passed their army over the Hellespont, and obtained a great victory over him by land; took from him all Asia westward Mount Taurus; gave it to the king of Pergamus, who assisted them in the war; and imposed a large tribute upon Antiochus. Thus the king of Pergamus, by the power of the Romans, recovered what Antiochus had taken from him; and Antiochus retiring into the remainder of his kingdom, was slain two years after by the Persians, as he was robbing the temple of Jupiter Belus in Elymais to raise money for the Romans. All which is thus described by Daniel: " For the king of the north *(Antiochus)* shall return and shall set forth a multitude greater than the former; and shall certainly come after certain years, with a great army and with much riches. And in those times there shall many stand up against the king of the south *(particularly the Macedonians ;)* also the robbers of thy people *(the Samaritans, &c.)* shall exalt themselves to establish the vision, but they shall fall. So the king of the north shall come and cast up a mount, and take the most fenced cities; and the arms of the south shall not withstand, neither his chosen people, neither shall there be any strength to withstand. But he that cometh against him shall do according to his own will, and none shall stand before him; and he shall stand in the glorious land, which shall fail in his hand. He shall also set his face to go with the strength *(or army)* of all his kingdom, and make an agreement with him, *(at Raphia,)* and he shall give him the daughter of women, corrupting her, but she shall not stand on his side, neither be for him. After this he shall turn his face unto the isles, and shall take many; but a prince for his own behalf *(the Romans)* shall cause the reproach offered by him to cease; without his own reproach he shall cause it to turn upon him. Then he shall turn his face towards the fort of his own land, but he shall stumble and fall, and not be found."*

* Ver. 13—19.

Seleucus Philopater succeeded his father Antiochus, *an. Nabonass*, 561, and reigned twelve years, but did nothing memorable, being sluggish, and intent on raising money for the Romans, to whom he was tributary. He was slain by Heliodorus whom he had sent to rob the temple of Jerusalem. Daniel thus describes his reign :—" Then shall stand up in his estate a raiser of taxes in the glory of the kingdom, but within few days he shall be destroyed, neither in anger nor in battle."*

A little before the death of Philopater, his son Demetrius was sent hostage to Rome, in the place of Antiochus Epiphanes, the brother of Philopater; and Antiochus was at Athens, in his way home from Rome when Philopater died ; whereupon Heliodorus, the treasurer of the kingdom, stept into the throne. But Antiochus so managed his affairs that the Romans kept Demetrius at Rome, and their ally the king of Pergamus expelled Heliodorus, and placed Antiochus on the throne, while Demetrius, the right heir, remained an hostage at Rome. Antiochus, being thus made king by the friendship of the king of Pergamus, reigned powerfully over Syria and the neighbouring nations; but carried himself much below his dignity, stealing privately out of his palace, rambling up and down the city in disguise with one or two of his companions, conversing and drinking with people of the lowest rank, foreigners and strangers ; frequenting the meeting of dissolute persons to feast and revel ; clothing himself like the Roman candidates and officers, acting their parts like a mimic ; and, in public festivals, jesting and dancing with servants and light people : exposing himself by all manner of ridiculous gestures. This conduct made some take him for a madman, and call him Antiochus Επιμένης. In the first year of his reign he deposed Onias the High Priest, and sold the high priesthood to Jason the younger brother of Onias ; for Jason had promised to give him 440 talents of silver for that office, and 150 more for a license to erect a place of exercise for the training up of youth in the fashions of

* Ver. 20.

the heathen; which license was granted by the king,
and put into execution by Jason.   Then the king sending one Apollonius into Egypt, to the coronation of
Ptolemy Philometer, the young son of Philometer and
Cleopatra, and knowing Philometer not to be well affected to his affairs in Phœnicia, provided for his own
safety in those parts; and for that end came to Joppa
and Jerusalem, where he was honourably received; from
thence he went in like manner with his little army to the
cities of Phœnicia to establish himself against Egypt, by
courting the people and distributing extraordinary fa-
vours amongst them.   All which is thus described by
Daniel:—" And in his *(Philometer's)* estate shall stand
up a vile person, to whom they *(the Syrians who set up*
Heliodorus) shall not give the honour of the kingdom.
Yet he shall come in peaceably and obtain the kingdom
by flatteries; *(made principally to the king of Pergamus)*
and the arms *(which in favour of Heliodorus oppose*
him) shall be overflowed with a flood from before him
and be broken; yea, also, *(Onias the High Priest)* the
prince of the covenant.   And after the league made with
him *(the king of Egypt, by sending Apollonius to his co-*
ronation) he shall work deceitfully *(against the king of*
Egypt,) for he shall come up and become strong *(in*
Phœnicia) with a small people.   And he shall enter
into the quiet and plentiful cities of the province *(of*
Phœnicia), and *(to ingratiate himself with the Jews of*
Phœnicia and Egypt, and with their friends) he shall do
that which his fathers have not done, nor his fathers'
fathers: he shall scatter among them the prey and
spoil, and the riches *(exacted from other places;)* and
shall forecast his devices against the strongholds *(of*
Egypt) even for a time.*

These things were done in the first years of his reign,
an. Nabonass. 573; and thenceforward he forecast his
devices against the strongholds of Egypt, until the
sixth year.   For three years after, that is, the fourth
year of his reign, Menelaus bought the high priesthood
from Jason, but not having the price, was sent for by

* Ver. 21, 24.

the king; and the king, before he could hear the cause, went into Cilicia to appease a sedition there, and left Andronicus, his deputy, at Antioch. In the mean time, the brother of Menelaus, to make up the money, conveyed several vessels out of the Temple, selling some of them at Tyre, and sending others to Andronicus. When Menelaus was reproved for this by Onias, he caused Onias to be slain by Andronicus; for which fact, the king, at his return from Cilicia, caused Andronicus to be put to death.

Then Antiochus prepared his second expedition against Egypt; which he performed in the sixth year of his reign, *an. Nabonass.* 578; for, upon the death of Cleopatra, the governor of her son, the young king of Egypt, claimed Phœnicia and Cœlosyria from him, as her dowry; and to recover the countries, raised a great army. Antiochus considering that his father had not quitted the possession of those countries, denied they were her dowry; and, with another great army, met and fought the Egyptians on the borders of Egypt, between Pelusium and the mountain Casius. He there beat them, and might have destroyed their whole army, but that he rode up and down, commanding the soldiers not to kill them, but to take them alive; by which humanity he gained Pelusium, and soon after all Egypt —entering it with a vast multitude of foot and chariots, elephants, and horsemen, and a great navy. Then, seizing the cities of Egypt, as a friend he marched to Memphis, laid the whole blame of the war upon Eulœus, the king's governor, entered into outward friendship with the young king, and took upon him to order the affairs of the kingdom. While Antiochus was thus employed, a report being spread in Phœnicia that he was dead, Jason, to recover the high-priesthood, assaulted Jerusalem with above a thousand men, and took the city. Hereupon the king, thinking Judea had revolted, came out of Egypt in a furious manner, retook the city, slew forty thousand of the people, made as many prisoners, and sold them to make money; went into the Temple, spoiled it of its treasures, ornaments, utensils, and vessels of gold and silver, amounting to 1800 talents, and carried away all to Antioch. This was done in the year Nabonassar 578, and is thus described by Daniel;—" And he shall stir up his powers and his courage against the king of the south, with a great army; and the king of the south shall be stirred up to battle with a very great and mighty army; but he shall not stand; for they, *(even Antiochus and his friends,)* shall forecast devices against him; *(as is represented above:)* yea, they that feed of the portion of his meat shall betray and destroy him, and his army shall be overthrown, and many shall fall down slain. And both these kings' hearts shall be to do mischief; and they, *being now friends,* shall speak lies at one table, *against the Jews and against the holy covenant,* but it shall not prosper; for yet the end, *in which the setting up of the abomination of the desolation is to prosper,* shall be at the time appointed. Then shall he return into his land with great riches, and his heart shall be against the holy covenant, and he shall act *against it by spoiling the temple, and return to his native land.*"*

The Egyptians of Alexandria, seeing Philometer first educated in luxury by the eunuch Eulœus, and now in the hands of Antiochus, gave the kingdom to Euergetes, the younger brother of Philometer; whereupon Antiochus pretended to restore Philometer, made war upon Euergetes, beat him at sea, and besieged him and his sister Cleopatra in Alexandria; while the besieged princes sent to Rome to implore the assistance of the senate. Antiochus, finding himself unable to take the city that year, returned from Syria, leaving Philometer at Memphis to govern Egypt in his absence. But Philometer made friendship with his brother that winter; and Antiochus returning next spring, *an. Nabonass.* 580, to besiege both the brothers in Alexandria, was met in the way by the Roman ambassadors, Popilius Læna, C. Decimus, and C. Hostilius. He offered them his hand to kiss; but Popilius, delivering to him the tables wherein the message of the senate was written, bade him read those first. When he had read

* Ver. 25—28.

them, he replied he would consider with his friends
what was fit to be done ; but Popilius drawing a circle
about him, bade him answer before he went out of it.
Antiochus, astonished at this blunt and unusual imper-
iousness, made answer he would do what the Romans
demanded ; and then Popilius gave the king his hand
to kiss, and he returned out of Egypt. The same year,
an. Nabonass. 580, his captains, by his orders, spoiled
and slaughtered the Jews, profaned the temple, set up
the worship of the heathen gods in all Judea, and began to persecute and make war upon those who would
not worship them ; which actions are thus described by
Daniel :—" At the time appointed he shall come again
towards the south, but the battle shall not be as the
former. For the ships of Shittim shall come, *with an
embassy from Rome against him.* Therefore he shall
be grieved and return, and have indignation against the
holy covenant. So shall he do ; he shall even return
and have intelligence with them that forsake the holy
covenant."*

In the same year that Antiochus, by the command
of the Romans, retired out of Egypt, and set up the
worship of the Greeks in Judea, the Romans conquered the kingdom of Macedon, the fundamental kingdom
of the empire of the Greeks, and reduced it into a Roman province, and thereby began to put an end to Daniel's third beast. This is thus expressed by Daniel :—
" *And after him arms,* that is, the Romans, *shall stand
up.*" As ממלך signifies *after the king,* Dan. xi. 8, so
ממנו may signify *after him.* Arms are everywhere, in
this prophecy of Daniel, put for the military power of
a kingdom ; and they stand up when they conquer or
grow powerful. Hitherto Daniel described the actions
of the kings of the north and south ; but upon the conquest of Macedon by the Romans, he left off describing
the actions of the Greeks, and began to describe those
of the Romans in Greece. They conquered Macedon,
Illyricum and Epirus, in the year of *Nabonassar* 580 ;
thirty-five years after, by the last will and testament of

* V. 29, 30.

T

Attalus, the last king of Pergamus, they inherited that rich and flourishing kingdom, that is, all Asia westward of Mount Taurus; sixty-nine years after, they conquered the kingdom of Syria, and reduced it to a Roman province; and thirty-four years after, they did the like to Egypt. By all these steps, the Roman arms stood up over the Greeks; and after ninety-five years more, by making war upon the Jews, *they polluted the sanctuary of strength, and took away the daily sacrifice, and then placed the abomination of desolation.** For this abomination was placed after the days of Christ, Matt. xxiv. 15. In the sixteenth year of the Emperor Adrian, A. C. 132, they placed this abomination, by building a temple to Jupiter Capitolinus, where the temple of God in Jerusalem had stood. Thereupon the Jews, under the conduct of Barchochab, rose up in arms against the Romans, and in the war had fifty cities demolished, nine hundred and eighty-five of their best towns destroyed, and five hundred and eighty thousand men slain by the sword; and in the end of the war, A. C. one hundred and thirty-seven, were banished Judea, upon the pain of death; and thenceforward the land remained desolate of its old inhabitants.

In the beginning of the Jewish war, in Nero's reign, the apostles fled out of Judea with their flocks,—some beyond Jordan to Pella and other places; some into Egypt, Syria, Mesopotamia, Asia Minor, and elsewhere. Peter and John came into Asia, and Peter went thence by Corinth to Rome, but John staying in Asia, was banished by the Romans into Patmos, as the head of a party of the Jews, whose nation was at war with the Romans. By this dispersion of the Christian Jews, the Christian religion, which was already propagated westward as far as Rome, spread fast in all the Roman empire, and suffered many persecutions under it, till the days of Constantine the Great and his sons. All which is thus described by Daniel :—" And such as do wickedly against the covenant, shall he, *who places the abomination*, cause to dissemble and worship *the heathen gods;*

* V. 31.

but the people among them who do know their God, shall be strong and act, and they that understand among the people shall instruct many; yet they shall fall by the sword, and by flame, and by captivity, and by spoil many days. Now when they shall fall, they shall be holpen with a little help, viz. *in the reign of Constantine the Great; and at that time, by reason of their prosperity,* many shall *come over to them from among the heathen,* and cleave to them with dissimulation. But those of understanding there shall *still* fall to try God's people by them, and to purge *them from the dissemblers,* and to make them white even to the time of the end, because it is yet for a time appointed."*

Hitherto the Roman empire continued entire. But now, by the building of Constantinople, and endowing it with a senate, and other like privileges with Rome, and by the division of the Roman empire into the two empires of the Greek and Latin, headed by those two cities, a new scene of things commences, in which " a king, *the empire of the Greeks,* doth according to his will, and, *by setting his own laws above the laws of God,* exalts and magnifies himself above every God, and speaks marvellous things against the God of gods, and shall prosper till the indignation be accomplished. Neither shall he regard the God of his fathers, nor the *lawful* desire of women *in matrimony,* nor any god, but shall magnify himself above all. And in his seat he shall magnify MAHUZZIMS, *that is strong guardians, the souls of the dead;* even with a God whom his fathers knew not shall he honour them, *in their temples,* with gold and silver, and with precious stones and valuable things."† All which relates to the overspreading of the Greek empire with monks and nuns, who placed holiness in abstinence from marriage, and the invocation of saints, and veneration of their relics, and such like superstitions, which these men introduced in the fourth and fifth centuries. " And at the end the king of the south *(or the empire of the Saracens,)* shall push at him; and the king of the north, *(or empire of the*

---

* V. 32, 35.   † V. 36, 39.

Turks,) shall come against him like a whirlwind, with chariots and with horsemen, and with many ships; and he shall enter into the countries *of the Greeks,* and shall overflow and pass over. He shall enter also into the glorious land, and many countries shall be overthrown; but these shall escape out of his hands, even Edom and Moab, and the chief of the children of Ammon: *(that is, those to whom the caravans pay tribute.)* He shall stretch forth his hands also upon the countries, and the land of Egypt shall not escape; but he shall have power over the treasures of gold and silver, and over all the precious things of Egypt; and the Lybians and Ethiopians shall be at his steps."* All these nations compose the empire of the Turks, and therefore this empire is here to be understood by the king of the north. They compose also the body of the he-goat; and therefore the goat still reigns in his last horn, but not by his own power.

* V. 40, 43.

FINIS.

Lately Published,

By the same Author, in 2 vols. 12mo. fourth edition,
10s. 6d.

THE SIGNS OF THE TIMES,

As denoted by the Fulfilment of Historical Predictions, traced down from the Babylonish Captivity to the present time.

WITH MAPS.